THE DEVELOPMENT OF BRITISH IMMIGRATION LAW

The Development of
BRITISH IMMIGRATION LAW

VAUGHAN BEVAN

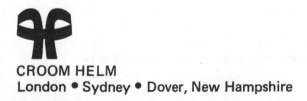

CROOM HELM
London • Sydney • Dover, New Hampshire

© 1986 Vaughan Bevan
Croom Helm Ltd, Provident House, Burrell Row,
Beckenham, Kent BR3 1AT
Croom Helm Australia Pty Ltd, Suite 4, 6th Floor,
64-76 Kippax Street, Surry Hills, NSW 2010, Australia

British Library Cataloguing in Publication Data

Bevan, Vaughan
    The development of British immigration law.
    1. Emigration and immigration law – Great Britain
    I. Title
    344.102'82   KD4134

    ISBN 0-7099-0663-3

Croom Helm, 51 Washington Street, Dover,
New Hampshire 03820, USA

Library of Congress Cataloging in Publication Data
applied for

Printed and bound in Great Britain by Mackays of Chatham Ltd, Kent

CONTENTS

PREFACE   vii

TABLE OF CASES   ix

Chapter 1   INTRODUCTION AND THEMES   1

Chapter 2   HISTORY   49

Chapter 3   CITIZENSHIP   104

Chapter 4   ENTRY CLEARANCE   164

Chapter 5   PRIMARY IMMIGRANTS   191

Chapter 6   SECONDARY IMMIGRANTS   242

Chapter 7   TEMPORARY IMMIGRANTS   276

Chapter 8   REMOVAL OF IMMIGRANTS

             Part I   Deportation   303
             Part II   Other Methods of Removal and
                       Appeals   345

Chapter 9   CONCLUSIONS   376

BIBLIOGRAPHY   389

INDEX   414

PREFACE

These strangers have engrossed a great part of the trade
to themselves and invite over their own countrymen and
employ them in their several trades when as the natives
are enforced for want of employment in their trades to
turn tankard bearers, porters, and to use other mean and
servile employments for a miserable subsistence or to live
idly or do worse, which cannot but be of very sad
consequence in short time.

These strangers take great houses, and divide them
into several habitations and take inmates and so pester
all places where they come to the great danger of
infection and noisome diseases which is found to be too
true by too often experience.[1]

For there is no entering the courts of St. James's and
Whitehall, the palaces of our hereditary kings, for the
great noise and croaking of the Frog-Landers.[2]

Times have not changed. Immigrants throughout the world are as
unwelcome today as they have ever been. In the United Kingdom
the last two decades have witnessed the pulling up of the
drawbridge against them by regular and unyielding degrees. The
principal 'invaders' to be repelled have been entrants from
the New Commonwealth. The legal mechanisms employed in this
process are described in this book. Reference to a broader
historical plane will illustrate, however, that the symptoms
of complaints against the immigrant and those mechanisms have
remained essentially the same for centuries.

Whilst the variety of laws and practices used against the
immigrant has usually been of universal application, history
has singled out the Jew, internationally, and the black, in
the West and the Old Commonwealth, as the most prolonged
targets. The U.K.'s treatment of the former had already paved
the way for its reaction to the latter and it is a mistake to
view the recent preoccupation of law and practice with

coloured entrants in isolation from the historical context. Moreover, account should be taken of the international context. Host societies have frequently welcomed immigrants for mercenary or altruistic motives but sooner or later the unmistakable and inevitable signs of xenophobia have appeared. In the aftermath of the abolition of slavery in the nineteenth century, British Colonies were eager to replace their labour and concerted attempts were made in the West Indies and Australasia to attract Indian and Chinese workers respectively. Yet these efforts were soon followed by resentment from the native population and by restrictive legislation designed to protect local labour. The U.K.'s record in immigration is thus far from unique. On the contrary, it is mirrored throughout the world and in many respects compares favourably with the experience of other countries.

This book is intended to draw out the main threads of immigration debate as it has seen expression in the law. For this purpose a wide variety of sources have been called upon and further guidance to the more inquisitive reader is supplied in the bibliography. In a wide subject and given the confines of space, some areas have had to forego detailed examination, principally the mechanics of the immigration appeals' system and the procedures for the variation of an immigrant's leave to remain, for which the reader is guided to practitioners' textbooks.

The author wishes to express his deep gratitude to Professor H.K. Bevan of the University of Hull for offering so many valuable comments upon the draft manuscript; to Sir Roy Marshall of the University of Hull for reading the draft and for his encouragement; to Mrs. Jean Hopewell for her fortitude and tireless effort in translating the manuscript into legible form: and to the publishers for their patient understanding.

----
1   Petition of the London Craftsmen against aliens, 1654.

2   Speech of Sir John Knight, against the Naturalisation Bill 1693 which would have assisted French Huguenots, Parliamentary History vol. 5, col. 856.

TABLE OF CASES

Abdul Malik v Secretary of State for the Home Department
    [1982] Imm. A.R. 183   181

Abdulaziz, Balkandali and Cabales v U.K. (1985) (15/1983/
    71/107-109)   43, 46, 226, 269, 385

Abdullah, E.C.O. Lahore v, [1973] Imm. A.R. 57   375

Addo, ex parte, R v Secretary of State, Times, 18 April 1985
    368

Afoakwah v Secretary of State for the Home Department
    [1970-72] Imm. A.R. 17   302

Agdeshman v Hunt (1917) 86 L.J.K.B. 1334   98

Agee v Lord Advocate (1977) S.L.T. (Notes) 54   333

Ahart, ex parte, R v Immigration Appeal Tribunal [1981] Imm.
    A.R. 76   296

Ahluwalia, ex parte, R v Immigration Appeal Tribunal [1979-80]
    Imm. A.R. 1   331

Ahmet v Secretary of State for the Home Department [1973] Imm.
    A.R. 1   239, 265

Ahmet Mehmet v Secretary of State for the Home Department
    [1977] Imm. A.R. 68   343

Ahmud Khan, ex parte, R v Immigration Appeal Tribunal [1982]
    Imm. A.R. 134   334

Ahsan, ex parte, R v Governor of Brixton Prison [1969] 2 Q.B.
    222   18, 364, 366

Ajaib Singh, ex parte, R v Immigration Appeal Tribunal [1978] Imm. A.R. 59   177

Akhtar, ex parte, R v Secretary of State for the Home Department [1981] 1 Q.B. 46   156

Aksoy, ex parte, R v Immigration Appeal Tribunal, Times, 29 October 1984   268

Alam, E.C.O. Lahore v, [1973] Imm. A.R. 79   270

Alam Bi v Immigration Appeal Tribunal [1979-80] Imm. A.R. 146   186

Alexander v Immigration Appeal Tribunal [1982] 2 All E.R. 766   40, 44, 300

Ali (D.M.) v Secretary of State for the Home Department [1973] Imm. A.R. 19 and 33   238, 340

Ali (M.M.H.) v Secretary of State for the Home Department [1978] Imm. A.R. 126   238

Ally, Secretary of State v, [1970-72] Imm. A.R. 258   297

Altaf v Visa Officer [1979-80] Imm. A.R. 141   182, 183

Al-Tuwaidji v Chief Immigration Officer [1974] Imm. A.R. 34   189

Ambach v Norwick 441 U.S. 68 (1979)   145

Amekrane v U.K. 16 Y.B.E.C.H.R. 356 (1973)   217

Amer v Secretary of State for the Home Department [1979-80] Imm. A.R. 87   301

Amin, ex parte, R v Entry Clearance Officer, Bombay [1983] 2 A.C. 818   41, 43, 44, 200, 225, 226, 300

Amirbeaggi, ex parte, R v Immigration Appeal Tribunal, Times, 25 May 1982   375

Amusu, E.C.O. Lagos v, [1974] Imm. A.R. 16   300

Anand v Secretary of State for the Home Department [1978] Imm. A.R. 36   307, 334, 335

Anderson, ex parte, R v Secretary of State [1984] Q.B. 778   341

Andronicou v Chief Immigration Officer [1974] Imm. A.R. 87
302

Anisminic v Foreign Compensation Commission [1969] 2 A.C. 147
160

Anseereeganoo, Secretary of State for the Home Department
[1981] Imm. A.R. 30   268

Anthony v Seger (1789) 161 E.R. 457   147

Aptheker v Secretary of State 378 U.S. 500 (1964)   161

Arbon v Anderson [1943] K.B. 252   40

Arif v Merryweather [1970] Crim. L.R. 221   44

Armat Ali, E.C.O. Dhaka v, [1981] Imm. A.R. 51   225

Armstrong, ex parte, R v Immigration Appeal Tribunal [1977]
Imm. A.R. 80   374

Aroyim v Rusk 387 U.S. 253 (1967)   157

Arshad v Immigration Officer [1977] Imm. A.R. 19   271

Arslan v Minister for Immigration (1984) 55 A.L.R. 361   330

Ashby v Minister of Immigration [1981] N.Z.L.R. 222   41, 43

Ashraf, Visa Officer, Cairo [1979-80] Imm. A.R. 45   375

Ashrafi v Immigration Appeal Tribunal [1981] Imm. A.R. 34
374

Asif Mahmood Khan, ex parte, R v Secretary of State for the
Home Department [1985] 1 All E.R. 40   43, 44, 270, 330

Asser v Peermohamed [1984] 46 O.R. (2d) 664   266

Associated Provincial Picture Houses v Wednesbury Corporation
[1948] 1 K.B. 223   159, 330, 348

Atibo v Immigration Officer [1978] Imm. A.R. 93   206

Atkinson v U.S. Government [1971] A.C. 197   371

Attorney General for Canada v Cain [1906] A.C. 542   38, 42

Attorney General of Hong Kong v Ng Yuen Shiu [1983] 2 A.C.
629   42, 44, 330

Attorney General v De Keyser's Royal Hotel [1920] A.C. 508
329

Attorney General v Sands (1669) 21 E.R. 720   146

Awa, ex parte, R v Secretary of State for the Home Department,
Times, 12 March 1983   183, 368

Ayettey v Secretary of State for the Home Department [1970-72]
Imm. A.R. 261   300

Azam, ex parte, R v Governor of Pentonville Prison [1974] A.C.
18   42, 365

Azhar Karim Khan v Secretary of State for the Home Department
[1982] Imm. A.R. 176   225

Backhouse v Lambeth L.B.C., Times, 14 October 1972   159

Bagas v E.C.O., Bombay [1978] Imm. A.R. 85   273

Bakhtaur Singh, ex parte, R v Immigration Appeal Tribunal,
Times 12 March 1984, and 15 December 1984   332

Baldacchino v Secretary of State for the Home Department
[1970-72] Imm. A.R. 14   302

Barbaro v Minister for Immigration and Ethnic Affairs 44
A.L.R. 690 (1982), 46 A.L.R. 123   330, 337

Bashir v Secretary of State for the Home Department [1978]
Imm. A.R. 150   334

Bashir, Visa Officer v, [1978] Imm. A.R. 77   274

Bastiampillai, ex parte, R v Immigration Appeal Tribunal
[1983] 2 All E.R. 844   186, 274, 375

Begum (Farida) v Immigration Officer [1978] Imm. A.R. 107
365

Begum (Inayat) v Visa Officer, Islamabad [1978] Imm. A.R. 174
263

Begum (Nazir) v Entry Clearance Officer, Islamabad [1976] Imm.
A.R. 31   263

Bernard v Entry Clearance Officer, Kingston [1976] Imm. A.R. 7
272, 273

Bhagat v Secretary of State for the Home Department [1970-72]
    Imm. A.R. 189   300

Bhagat Singh v Entry Clearance Officer, New Delhi [1978] Imm.
    A.R. 134   302

Bhajan Singh, ex parte, R v Secretary of State for the Home
    Department [1976] Q.B. 198   43

Bhambra, E.C.O. New Delhi [1973] Imm. A.R. 14   299

Bhatia, ex parte, R v Immigration Appeal Tribunal, Times, 12
    April 1985   250

Bhurosah, ex parte, R v Secretary of State for the Home
    Department [1968] 1 Q.B. 266   101, 160

Blackburn v A.G. [1971] 1 W.L.R. .1037   162

Blackie's House of Beef Inc. v Castillo 659 F. 2d 1211 (1981)
    365

Blackwell College of Business v Att. G. 454 Fed. (2d) 928
    (1971)   300

Bohon-Mitchell v Council of Legal Education [1978] I.R.L.R.
    525   300

Bouzagou, ex parte, R v Governor of Ashford Remand Centre,
    Times, 4 July 1983   224

Bovell v Entry Clearance Officer, Georgetown [1973] Imm. A.R.
    37   256

Bowie v Liverpool Royal Infirmary [1930] A.C. 580   264

Brahmbhatt, ex parte, R v Secretary of State for the Home
    Department, Times, 17 October 1983   154

Brizmohun, Secretary of State v, [1970-72] Imm. A.R. 122
    295

Brown v Entry Clearance Officer, Kingston [1976] Imm. A.R. 119
    181, 272

Brownell v Tom We Shung 352 U.S. 180 (1956)   369

Burk v Brown (1742) 26 E.R. 640   146

Butt v Secretary of State for the Home Department [1979-80]
    Imm. A.R. 82   334

C v Entry Clearance Officer, Hong Kong [1976] Imm. A.R. 165
   298

Caballero v Secretary of State for the Home Department [1974]
   Imm. A.R. 13   295

Cabel v Chavez-Salido (1982) 454 U.S. 432   386

Calvin's case (1608) 77 E.R. 377   92, 108, 146, 386

Campbell, Secretary of State for the Home Department [1970-72]
   Imm. A.R. 115   272

Castioni, Re [1891] 1 Q.B. 149   371

Capello v Minister for Immigration (1980) 49 F.L.R. 40   330

Chae Chan Ping v U.S. 130 U.S. 581 (1888)   38

Chajutin v Whitehead [1938] 1 All E.R. 159   366

Chanda v Immigration Officer [1981] Imm. A.R. 88   180

Chandler v D.P.P. [1964] A.C. 763   162

Channo Bi, Visa Officer v, [1978] Imm. A.R. 182   263

Chaudhary v Chavdhary [1985] 2 W.L.R. 350   264

Chavda v Entry Clearance Officer, Bombay [1978] Imm. A.R. 40
   273

Cheng, ex parte, R v Governor of Pentonville Prison [1973]
   A.C. 931   371

Chiew, ex parte, R v Immigration Appeal Tribunal [1981] Imm.
   A.R. 102   297, 300

China Navigation Co. v A.G. [1932] 2 K.B. 197   146, 160

Chopra v Secretary of State for the Home Department [1981]
   Imm. A.R. 70   225

Choudhary, ex parte, R v Secretary of State for the Home
   Department [1978] 1 W.L.R. 1177   42, 365

Chow Tom v Secretary of State for the Home Department [1975]
   Imm. A.R. 137   295

Chulvi v Secretary of State for the Home Department [1976]
   Imm. A.R. 133   295

Ciresi v Ahmad [1983] 1 W.W.R. 710   266

Clarke, ex parte, R v West London Supplementary Benefits
    Appeal Tribunal [1975] 1 W.L.R. 1396   263

Class-Peter v Secretary of State for the Home Department
    [1981] Imm. A.R. 154   263, 268

Claveria v Immigration Officer [1978] Imm. A.R. 176   365

Clipsham v Secretary of State for the Home Department
    [1970-72] Imm. A.R. 35   296

Constantinides v Secretary of State for the Home Department
    [1974] Imm. A.R. 30   265

Coomasaru, ex parte, R v Immigration Appeal Tribunal [1983] 1
    W.L.R. 14   43, 224   ·

Cooper v Wandsworth Board of Works (1863) 14 C.B. (N.S.) 180
    341

Costa v Secretary of State for the Home Department [1974] Imm.
    A.R. 69   225

Council of Civil Service Unions v Minister for Civil Service
    [1984] 3 All E.R. 935   162

Crew, ex parte, R v Secretary of State for the Home Department
    [1982] Imm. A.R. 94   270

Croning, Secretary of State v, [1970-72] Imm. A.R. 51   340

Csenyi v Secretary of State for the Home Department [1975]
    Imm. A.R. 92   338

Cuffy v Entry Clearance Officer, Georgetown [1976] Imm. A.R.
    66   272

Daganayasi v Minister of Immigration [1980] 2 N.Z.L.R. 130
    41

Darshan Singh Sohal, ex parte, R v Immigration Appeal Tribunal
    [1981] Imm. A.R. 20   332

Daubigny v Davallon (1794) 145 E.R. 936   92, 146

De Conway's case (1834) 12 E.R. 522   153

De Geer v Stone (1882) 22 Ch. 243   148, 151, 386

Deniz v Minister for Immigration (1984) 51 A.L.R. 645   375

Dennis v U.S. 341 U.S. 494 (1950)   145

Derrick v Secretary of State for the Home Department [1970-72]
    Imm. A.R. 109   340

Dervish v Secretary of State for the Home Department [1970-72]
    Imm. A.R. 48   342

De Wall's case (1848) 13 E.R. 666   153

Dias v Secretary of State for the Home Department [1976] Imm.
    A.R. 126   297

Din v E.C.O. Karachi [1978] Imm. A.R. 56   302

D.P.P. v Bhagwan [1972] A.C. 60   42, 94, 364

Dowhopoluk v Martin 23 D.L.R. (3d) 42 (1971)   153, 154

Drake v Minister for Immigration and Ethnic Affairs 24 A.L.R.
    577 (1979)   42

Dred Scott v Sandford 19 How 393 (1857)   145

Driver, ex parte, R v Plymouth Justices [1985] 2 All E.R. 681
    334, 372

Du Hourmelin v Sheldon (1839) 41 E.R. 203   146

Dumont, Secretary of State for the Home Department [1970-72]
    Imm. A.R. 119   265

Duroure v Jones (1791) 100 E.R. 1031   152, 386

Ealing L.B.C. v Race Relations Board [1972] A.C. 342   20

East African Asians case, 13 Y.B.E.C.H.R. 928 (1970), (1981) 3
    E.H.R.R. 76   81, 197, 275

Ekiu v U.S. 142 U.S. 651 (1891)   45, 366

Elk v Wilkins 112 U.S. 94 (1884)   40, 145

Ellerton, ex parte, R v Hampshire C.C., Times, 27 February
    1984   183, 367

Emmanuel v Secretary of State for the Home Department
    [1970-72] Imm. A.R. 69   272

Entick v Carrington (1765) 19 State Tr. 1029   365

Enwia, ex parte, R v Immigration Appeal Tribunal [1984] 1
    W.L.R. 117   238, 338

Evgeniou, Secretary of State v, [1978] Imm. A.R. 89   297

Fatima, ex parte, R v Secretary of State for the Home
    Department [1984] 3 W.L.R. 659   264

Felton v Callis [1969] 1 Q.B. 200   329

Fernandes, ex parte, R v Governor of Pentonville Prison [1971]
    1 W.L.R. 989   371

Fernandes v Secretary of State for the Home Department [1981]
    Imm. A.R. 1   43, 331, 342

Fernandez v Fernandez [1983] 4 W.W.R. 755   266

Foley v Connelie 435 U.S. 291 (1978)   145

Fong Yue Ting v U.S. 149 U.S. 698 (1892)   38, 329

Fourdrin v Gowdey (1834) 40 E.R. 146   147

Fox-Taylor, ex parte, R v Blundeston Prison Board of Visitors
    [1982] 1 All E.R. 646   341

Freyberger, ex parte (1917) 116 L.T. 237   156

Gastelum-Quinones v Kennedy 374 U.S. 469 (1963)   41

Georges and Minister for Immigration and Ethnic Affairs 22
    A.L.R. 667 (1978)   42, 337

Gerami, ex parte, R v Immigration Appeal Tribunal [1981]
    Imm.A.R. 187   301

Gheithy v Entry Clearance Officer, Dar-es-Salaam [1981] Imm.
    A.R. 113   275

Ghosh v Entry Clearance Officer, Calcutta [1976] Imm. A.R. 60
    299

Giambi, ex parte, R v Governor of Holloway Prison [1982] 1
    W.L.R. 535   339

Glean, Secretary of State v, [1970-72] Imm. A.R. 84   300

Goffar v Entry Clearance Officer, Dacca [1975] Imm. A.R. 142
   299

Goordin, ex parte, R v Secretary of State for the Home
   Department [1981] Imm. A.R. 24   365

Gout v Zimmerman (1847) 5 N.C. 440   153

Govinden, ex parte, R v Secretary of State, Times, 12 July
   1985   374

Gowa v A.G., Times, 31 July 1985   44

Grant, Secretary of State v, [1974] Imm. A.R. 64   296

Grant v Borg [1982] 1 W.L.R. 638   44, 332, 364

Greene v Secretary of State for Home Affairs [1942] A.C.
   284   99

Grenade, E.C.O. Port Louis v, [1978] Imm. A.R. 143   274

Gschwind v Huntington [1918] 2 K.B. 420   156

Gunatilake v Entry Clearance Officer, Colombo [1975] Imm. A.R.
   23   296

Gunnell, ex parte, R v Secretary of State (1983) L.Soc. Gaz.
   3238   42

Gupta v Secretary of State for the Home Department [1979-80]
   Imm. A.R. 52   343

H, Re (1982) 12 Fam. Law 172   270, 271

H, Re [1982] 3 W.L.R. 501   266

Haig v Agee 453 U.S. 280 (1981)   38, 161, 333

Haji v Secretary of State for the Home Department [1978] Imm.
   A.R. 26   297

Haj-Ismail v Minister for Immigration and Ethnic Affairs 40
   A.L.R. 341 (1982)   42, 330

Hamilton v Entry Clearance Officer, Kingston [1974] Imm. A.R.
   43   302

Hanks, E.C.O. Colombo v, [1976] Imm. A.R. 74   302

Hardial Singh, ex parte, R v Governor of Durham Prison [1984]
    1 W.L.R. 704   44, 321, 342, 369

Harisiades v Shaughnessy 342 U.S. 580 (1952)   38

Hasan v E.C.O. Bombay [1976] Imm. A.R. 28   274

Hashim v Entry Clearance Officer, Dacca [1974] Imm. A.R. 75
    224

Hashim v Secretary of State for the Home Department [1982]
    Imm. A.R. 113   302

Hassan, ex parte, R v Governor of Risley Remand Centre [1976]
    1 W.L.R. 971   19

Healy, ex parte, R v Governor of Pentonville Prison, Times, 11
    May 1984   234

Healy, ex parte, R v Guildford Justices [1983] 1 W.L.R. 108
    333

Hector v Secretary of State for the Home Department [1970-72]
    Imm. A.R. 41   265

Hipperson v Electoral Registration Officer, Times, 2 May 1985
    225

Hirani v H [1983] 4 F.L.R. 232   269

H.K., Re [1967] 2 Q.B. 617   185, 187

Holmes, E.C.O. Kingston [1975] Imm. A.R. 20   272

Home Office v Commission for Racial Equality [1982] Q.B. 385
    103, 159

Hosenball, ex parte, R v Secretary of State for Home Affairs
    [1977] 1 W.L.R. 766   40, 237, 274, 296, 310, 341, 372

Howard v Secretary of State for the Home Department [1970-72]
    Imm. A.R. 93   272

Hubbard, ex parte, R v Immigration Appeal Tribunal, Times, 16
    July 1985   375

Huda v E.C.O. Dacca [1976] Imm. A.R. 109   375

Hussain (Ashiq), ex parte, R v Chief Immigration Officer
    [1970] 1 W.L.R. 9   187, 299

Hussain, ex parte, R v Immigration Adjudicator, Times, 23 June 1982   367

Hussain, ex parte, R v Secretary of State for the Home Department [1978] 1 W.L.R. 700   42, 365

Hussain v Hussain [1983] Fam. 26   244

Idrish, ex parte, R v Immigration Appeal Tribunal, Times, 14 July 1984   266

Immigration and Naturalisation Service v Chadha 103 S. Ct. 2764 (1983)   38

Inland Revenue Commissioners v Bullock [1976] 1 W.L.R. 1178   264

Inland Revenue Commissioners v Duchess of Portland [1982] Ch. 314   264

Iqbal Haque v Entry Clearance Officer, Dacca [1974] Imm. A.R. 51   184, 270

Islam v Entry Clearance Officer, Dacca [1974] Imm. A.R. 83   299

Jan v Secretary of State for the Home Department (1983) New L.J. 744   274

Jayakody, ex parte, R v Secretary of State for the Home Department [1982] 1 W.L.R. 405   367

Jennings, ex parte, R v Governor of Holloway Prison [1983] 1 A.C. 624   371

Jephson v Riera (1835) 12 E.R. 598   148

Johnson, re, Roberts v A.G. [1903] 1 Ch. 821   148

Jones, Secretary of State v, [1978] Imm. A.R. 161   297

Jordan v Secretary of State for the Home Department [1970-72] Imm. A.R. 201   331

Joseph, ex parte, R v Immigration Appeal Tribunal [1977] Imm. A.R. 70   297

Joshi, E.C.O. Bombay v, [1975] Imm. A.R. 1   225

Joyce v D.P.P. [1946] A.C. 347   146, 156

Joyles, ex parte, R v Immigration Tribunal [1972] 1 W.L.R.
1390   40

Juma v Secretary of State for the Home Department [1974] Imm.
A.R. 96   300

Kassam, ex parte, R v Immigration Appeal Tribunal [1980] 1
W.L.R. 1037   226, 300

Kaur v E.C.O. New Delhi [1979-80] Imm. A.R. 76   276

Kelzani v Secretary of State for the Home Department [1978]
Imm. A.R. 193   344

Kember [1980] 1 W.L.R. 1110   234

Kent v Dulles 357 U.S. 116 (1958)   161

Khan (Asif Mahmood), ex parte, R v Secretary of State for the
Home Department [1985] 1 All E.R. 40   43, 44, 270

Khan (I.B.) ex parte, R v Secretary of State for the Home
Department [1977] 1 W.L.R. 1466   353

Khan (Mangoo), ex parte, R v Secretary of State for the Home
Department [1980] 1 W.L.R. 569   367

Khan (Shezada), ex parte, R v Immigration Appeal Tribunal
[1975] Imm. A.R. 26   299

Khanom v Entry Clearance Officer, Dacca [1979-80] Imm. A.R.
182   263

Kharrazi, ex parte, R v Chief Immigration Officer [1980] 1
W.L.R. 1396   287, 289, 298, 300

Khatoon Ali, ex parte, R v Immigration Appeal Tribunal
[1979-80] Imm. A.R. 195   41, 224

Khawaja, ex parte, R v Secretary of State for the Home
Department [1984] A.C. 74   41, 43, 46, 121, 133, 150,
169, 186, 187, 237, 342, 350ff

Khazrai v Immigration Officer [1981] Imm. A.R. 9   188

Kioa v Minister for Immigration 53 A.L.R. 658, 55 A.L.R. 624
(1984)   43, 330, 374

Kirkwood, ex parte, R v Secretary of State [1984] 2 All E.R.
390   43, 331, 342

Kleindienst v U.S. 408 U.S. 753 (1972)   341

Knauff v Shaughnessy 338 U.S. 537 (1950)   366

Kotecha, ex parte, R v Immigration Appeal Tribunal [1983] 1
    W.L.R. 487   186, 375

Kotronis, ex parte, R v Governor of Brixton Prison [1971] A.C.
    250   371

Kpoma v Secretary of State for the Home Department [1973] Imm.
    A.R. 25   299

Kroohs v Secretary of State for the Home Department [1978]
    Imm. A.R. 75   340

Kuldip Singh v Secretary of State for the Home Department
    [1970-72] Imm. A.R. 211   265

Kumar, E.C.O. New Delhi v, [1978] Imm. A.R. 185   302

Kwabena, ex parte, R v Secretary of State, Times, 28 May 1985
    368

Lai, E.C.O. Hong Kong v, [1974] Imm. A.R. 98   302

Lakdawalla, Secretary of State v, [1970-72] Imm. A.R. 26 161,
    162

Laker Airways v Department of Trade [1977] 1 Q.B. 643   162

Langridge v Secretary of State for the Home Department
    [1970-72] Imm. A.R. 38   189

Lapinid, ex parte, R v Immigration Officer [1984] 1 W.L.R.
    1269   352

Latiff v Secretary of State for the Home Department [1970-72]
    Imm. A.R. 76   295

Lavender v Minister of Housing [1970] 1 W.L.R. 1231   295

Lazarov v Secretary of State of Canada 39 D.L.R. (3d) 738
    (1973)   154

Lesa v A.G. [1982] N.Z.L.R. 165   148, 158

Levave v Immigration Department [1979] 2 N.Z.L.R. 74   158

Levy v Entry Clearance Officer, Kingston [1978] Imm. A.R. 119
    275

Liberto v Immigration Officer [1975] Imm. A.R. 61   189

Liversidge v Anderson [1942] A.C. 206   42, 99

London v Plasencia (1982) 459 U.S. 21   374

M^cdonald's case (1746-7) 18 State Tr. 860   146

M^cgillivary v Secretary of State for the Home Department
     [1970-72] Imm. A.R. 63   272

Mackeson, ex parte, R v Bow Street Magistrates (1982) 75 Cr.
     App. R. 24   333, 372

M^cveigh, O'Neill and Evans v U.K. (1983) 5 E.H.R.R. 71   224

Madhwa v City Council of Nairobi [1968] E.A. 406   225

Mahmoudi v Secretary of State for the Home Department [1981]
     Imm. A.R. 130   299

Mahmud Khan, ex parte, R v Immigration Appeal Tribunal [1983]
     Q.B. 790   268, 269

Malek, Visa Officer v, [1979-80] Imm. A.R. 111   187, 302

Malik v Secretary of State for the Home Department [1970-72]
     Imm. A.R. 37   270

Malik (Mohd), see Mohd Malik

Malungahu v Department of Labour [1981] 1 N.Z.L.R. 668   364

Mandla v Dowell Lee [1983] 2 A.C. 548   44

Manek, I.A.T. v, [1978] Imm. A.R. 131   273

Manmohan Singh v Entry Clearance Officer, New Delhi [1975]
     Imm. A.R. 118   302

Manuel, ex parte, R v Secretary of State for the Home
     Department, Times, 21 March 1984   368

Margueritte, ex parte, R v Secretary of State for the Home
     Department [1983] Q.B. 180   152

Markwald, ex parte, R v Francis [1918] 1 K.B. 617   148

Markwald v A.G. [1920] 1 Ch. 348   148

Martin, E.C.O. Kingston [1978] Imm. A.R. 100   272

Mayer v Minister for Immigration 55 A.L.R. 587 (1984)   43

Mealy, ex parte, R v Board of Visitors of Gartree Prison, ·
    Times, 14 November 1981   341

Mehmet, ex parte, R v Immigration Appeal Tribunal [1978] Imm.
    A.R. 46   331

Mehmet, ex parte, R v Immigration Appeal Tribunal [1977] Imm.
    A.R. 56   375

Meunier, Re [1894] 2 Q.B. 415   371

Miah (Aftab), Secretary of State v, [1970-72] Imm. A.R. 185
    270

Miah, ex parte, R v Secretary of State for the Home
    Department, Times, 19 July 1983   183, 367, 368

Middlesex case (1804) 2 Peck. 118   147

Minister for Immigration v Gaillard (1983) 49 A.L.R. 277   41

Mitchell v Secretary of State for the Home Department [1981]
    Imm. A.R. 140   334

Mo Szu Ti, ex parte, R v Immigration Appeal Tribunal [1982]
    Imm. A.R. 65   299

Mohamed v Knott [1969] 1 Q.B. 1   263

Mohamed Arif, re [1968] Ch. 643   19, 271

Mohammad, Visa Officer, Karachi v, [1978] Imm. A.R. 168   375

Mohan Singh v Entry Clearance Officer, New Delhi [1973] Imm.
    A.R. 9   189

Mohd Malik v Secretary of State for the Home Department [1981]
    Imm. A.R. 134   269, 334

Momin Ali, ex parte, R v Secretary of State for the Home
    Department [1984] 1 W.L.R. 663   183, 367

Mouncer v Mouncer [1972] 1 W.L.R. 321   334

Moussa, Secretary of State v, [1976] Imm. A.R. 78   295

Mukhopadhyay [1975] Imm. A.R. 42   275

Munasinghe v Secretary of State for the Home Department [1975]
    Imm. A.R. 79   295, 296

Muruganandarajah, ex parte, R v Immigration Appeal Tribunal,
    Times, 23 July 1984   238, 340, 375

Musgrove v Chun Teeong Toy [1891] A.C. 272   38, 42, 162

Musisi, ex parte, R v Immigration Appeal Tribunal, Times, 8
    June 1985   238

Mustafa v Secretary of State for the Home Department [1979-80]
    Imm. A.R. 32   340, 342

Mustafa, ex parte, R v Secretary of State for the Home
    Department, Times, 22 February 1984   364, 365

Mustun v Secretary of State for the Home Department [1970-72]
    Imm. A.R. 97   187, 302

Nadarajan, E.C.O. Madras v, [1976] Imm. A.R. 144   273

Naumovska v Minister for Immigration and Ethnic Affairs 41
    A.L.R. 635 (1982)   366, 368

Nawaz v Lord Advocate (1983) S.L.T. 653   366

Needham v Entry Clearance Officer, Kingston [1973] Imm. A.R.
    75   272

Newmarch v Newmarch [1978] Fam. 79   265

Nicolaides v Secretary of State for the Home Department [1978]
    Imm. A.R. 67   295

Nielsen, Re [1984] A.C. 606   372

Nisa v Secretary of State for the Home Department [1979-80]
    Imm. A.R. 20   273

Nourai v Secretary of State for the Home Department [1978]
    Imm. A.R. 200   302

Obeyesekere v Secretary of State for the Home Department
    [1976] Imm. A.R. 16   302

O'Connor v Secretary of State for the Home Department [1977]
    Imm. A.R. 29   343

O'Reilly v Mackman [1983] 2 A.C. 237   44

Osama v Immigration Officer [1978] Imm. A.R. 8   188, 225, 269

Owusu v Secretary of State for the Home Department [1976] Imm. A.R. 101   299

Ozter v Secretary of State for the Home Department [1978] Imm. A.R. 137   334, 335

Palacio, ex parte, R v Immigration Appeal Tribunal [1979-80] Imm. A.R. 178   188, 189

Papayianni v U.K. [1974] Imm. A.R. 7   266, 267

Parekh v Secretary of State for the Home Department [1976] Imm. A.R. 84   297

Parsons v Burk [1971] N.Z.L.R. 244   161

Parvez v Immigration Officer [1979-80] Imm. A.R. 84   189, 265

Patel, Secretary of State for the Home Department [1970-72] Imm. A.R. 227   273

Patel, Secretary of State for the Home Department [1979-80] Imm. A.R. 106   225

Patel (A.D.), Secretary of State v, [1975] Imm. A.R. 95   375

Patel (M.R.) v Entry Clearance Officer, Bombay [1978] Imm. A.R. 154   302

Patel (V.) v Immigration Appeal Tribunal [1983] Imm. A.R. 76   299, 300

Pearson v Immigration Appeal Tribunal [1978] Imm. A.R. 212   41, 280, 295

Peart, E.C.O. Kingston v, [1979-80] Imm. A.R. 41   225

Peikazadi, ex parte, R v Immigration Appeal Tribunal [1979-80] Imm. A.R. 191   297

Perera v Immigration Officer [1979-80] Imm. A.R. 58   187

Perrini v Perrini [1979] Fam. 84   264

Perween Khan, ex parte, R v Immigration Appeals Adjudicator [1972] 1 W.L.R. 1058   299

Peterkin, R v, ex parte, Soni [1970-72] Imm. A.R. 253   375

Phansopkar, ex parte, R v Secretary of State for the Home
    Department [1976] Q.B. 606   43, 185

Phillips v Entry Clearance Officer, Kingston [1973] Imm. A.R.
    47   273

Pillai v Mudanayake [1953] A.C. 514   145

Pinnock (D.V.M.) v Entry Clearance Officer, Kingston [1974]
    Imm. A.R. 22   271

Pinnock (M.E.) v Entry Clearance Officer, Kingston [1977] Imm.
    A.R. 4   272

Pochi v Minister for Immigration and Ethnic Affairs 43 A.L.R.
    261 (1983)   329

Prajapati, ex parte, R v Immigration Appeal Tribunal [1981]
    Imm. A.R. 199   181

Prata v Minister of Manpower and Immigration (1975) 52 D.L.R.
    (3d) 383   341

Pritpal Singh v Secretary of State for the Home Department
    [1970-72] Imm. A.R. 154   297

Puri v Secretary of State for the Home Department [1970-72]
    Imm. A.R. 21   300

Pusey, Secretary of State for the Home Department v, [1970-72]
    Imm. A.R. 240   272

Puttick v A.G. [1980] Fam. 1   266

Quazi v Quazi [1980] A.C. 744   264

Quereshi v Immigration Officer [1977] Imm. A.R. 113   299

R v Antypas (1973) 57 Cr. App. R. 207   336

R v Assa Singh [1963] Crim. L.R. 297   336

R v Ayu [1958] 1 W.L.R. 1264   372

R v Baidoo [1971] Crim. L.R. 293   337

R v Bangoo [1976] Crim. L.R. 746   343

R v Brailsford [1905] 2 K.B. 730   160

R v Caird (1970) 54 Cr. App. R. 499   337

R v Castelli [1976] Crim. L.R. 387   336

R v Clarke [1985] 2 All E.R. 777   44, 365

R v De Mierre (1771) 98 E.R. 463   147

R v Denison, ex p. Nagale (1916) 85 L.J.K.B. 1744   98

R v Docherty [1963] Crim. L.R. 106   337

R v Edgehill [1963] 1 All E.R. 181   336

R v Flaherty [1958] Crim. L.R. 556   372

R v Friedman (1914) 10 Cr. App. Rep. 72   42, 337

R v Gilbert (1921) 16 Cr. App. R. 34   337

R v Hartley [1978] 2 N.Z.L.R. 199   333

R v Hodges (1967) 51 Cr. App. R. 361   372

R v Kleiss (1910) 4 Cr. App. Rep. 101   42

R v Knockaloe Camp Commandant, ex p. Forman (1918) 87 L.J.K.B.
    43   98

R v Labbe [1966] Crim. L.R. 56   336

R v Lynch [1903] 1 K.B. 444   156

R v M^ccarten [1958] 1 W.L.R. 933   372

R v Milk Marketing Board, ex p. Austin, Times, 21 March 1983
    183

R v Mulroy [1963] Crim. L.R. 431   336

R v Nazari [1980] 1 W.L.R. 1366   188, 308, 321, 336, 337

R v Nembhard [1963] Crim. L.R. 447   336

R v Prager [1972] 1 W.L.R. 260   40

R v Quong wing (1913) 12 D.L.R. 656   12

R v Romano [1963] Crim. L.R. 638   343

R v Serry (1980) 2 Cr. App. R. (S) 336   321, 337

R v Symons (1814) 2 Stra. Madras Rep. 93   329

R v Thoseby and Krawszyk (1979) Cr. App. R. (S) 280   337

R v Tillman [1965] Crim. L.R. 615   336

R v Tshuma (1981) 3 Cr. App. R. (S) 97   337

R v Uddin [1971] Crim. L.R. 663   337

R v Veater [1981] 1 W.L.R. 567   372

R v Voisin (1918) 13 Cr. App. Rep. 89   40

R v Walters [1978] Crim. L.R. 175   337

R v Waltham Forest L.B.C. ex p. Vale, Times, 25 February 1985   149, 225

R v Williams [1982] 1 W.L.R. 1398   372

R v Yont [1967] Crim. L.R. 546   336

R v Zausmer (1911) 7 Cr. App. Rep. 41   42

Racal Communications [1981] A.C. 374   160

Race Relations Board v Charter [1973] A.C. 868   43

Race Relations Board v Dockers' Labour Club and Institute Ltd. [1976] A.C. 285   43

Rafiq v Secretary of State for the Home Department [1970-72] Imm. A.R. 167   270

Rahmani, ex parte, R v Immigration Appeal Adjudicator, Times, 14 January 1985   44

Ram v E.C.O. New Delhi [1978] Imm. A.R. 123   274

Ram, ex parte, R v Secretary of State for the Home Department [1979] 1 W.L.R. 148   367

Ramjane v Chief Immigration Officer [1973] Imm. A.R. 84   296, 302

Ramnial, ex parte, R v Secretary of State for the Home Department (1983) Law Soc. Gaz. 30   334, 342

Rashid v E.C.O. Dacca [1976] Imm. A.R. 12   300

Rashid, ex parte, R v Immigration Appeal Tribunal [1978] Imm. A.R. 71   375

Ravat v Entry Certificate Officer, Bombay [1974] Imm. A.R. 79 272

Raymond v Honey [1983] A.C. 1   40

Reed v Clark, Times, 12 April 1985   225

Rehman v Secretary of State for the Home Department [1978] Imm. A.R. 80   343

Rice v Connolly [1966] 2 Q.B. 414   366

S, Re (1980) 11 Fam. Law 55   271

Sacha, E.C.O. Bombay v, [1973] Imm. A.R. 5   275

Sadhu Singh v Entry Clearance Officer, New Delhi [1973] Imm. A.R. 67   266

Sadiq, Immigration Officer v, [1978] Imm. A.R. 115   302

Sae-Heng v Visa Officer, Bangkok [1979-80] Imm. A.R. 69   299

Safadi v Minister for Immigration and Ethnic Affairs 38 A.L.R. 399 (1981)   330

St. Germain, ex parte, R v Board of Visitors of Hull Prison [1979] Q.B. 425   40, 341

Salamat Bibi, ex parte, R v Chief Immigration Officer [1976] 1 W.L.R. 979   43

Salemi v Minister for Immigration and Ethnic Affairs 14 A.L.R. 1 (1977)   330

Sandal, ex parte, R v Immigration Appeal Tribunal [1981] Imm. A.R. 95   269

Santis, Bugdaycay, ex parte, R v Secretary of State, Times, 11 July 1985   375

Santos v Santos [1972] Fam. 247   335

Sanusi, Secretary of State v, [1975] Imm. A.R. 114   342

Sarwar, Secretary of State v, [1978] Imm. A.R. 190   295

Sawyer v Kropp (1916) 85 L.J.K.B. 1446   156

Scheele v Immigration Officer [1976] Imm. A.R. 1   188

Schmidt v Secretary of State for the Home Department [1969] 2
    Ch. 149   44

Schmitz (1971) 31 D.L.R. (3d) 117   267

Schneiderman v U.S. 320 U.S. 118 (1943)   157

Schtraks, ex parte, R v Governor of Brixton Prison [1964] A.C.
    556   371

Scot v Schwartz (1739) 92 E.R. 1265   92

Scott v Sandford 19 How (U.S.) 393 (1857)   40

Secretary of State v Udoh [1970-72] Imm. A.R. 89   342

Sezdirmezoglu v Minister for Immigration and Ethnic Affairs
    51 A.L.R. 561 (1984)   41

Sezdirmezoglu (No.2) 51 A.L.R. 575 (1984)   43

Shah (Nilish), ex parte, R v Barnet L.B.C. [1983] 2 A.C. 309
    43, 149, 225, 265, 327

Shah v Secretary of State for the Home Department [1970-72]
    Imm. A.R. 56   225

Shaikh, ex parte, R v Immigration Appeal Tribunal [1981] 1
    W.L.R. 1107   299, 301

Shamonda, E.C.O. Lagos, [1975] Imm. A.R. 16   302

Sharp v De St. Sauveur (1871) 41 L.J. Ch. 576   146

Shaughnessy v Mezei 345 U.S. 206 (1953) v Pedreiro 349 U.S. 48
    (1955)   369, 385

Shaughnessy v U.S. 73 S. Ct. 625 (1953)   366

Sheikh v Secretary of State for the Home Department [1970-72]
    Imm. A.R. 143   225

Shidiack (1911) S.A. Rep. 25

Shukar, Visa Officer v, [1981] Imm. A.R. 58   274

Sibal, E.C.O. New Delhi [1973] Imm. A.R. 50   274

Sidique, Secretary of State v, [1976] Imm. A.R. 69   301

Simon v Phillips (1916) 85 L.J.K.B. 656   98

Simsek v Minister for Immigration and Ethnic Affairs 40 A.L.R. 61 (1982)   214

Sindhu, Visa Officer [1978] Imm. A.R. 147   275

Singh (Gurdev) v R [1973] 1 W.L.R. 1444   331

Singh (H) v Immigration Appeal Tribunal [1978] Imm. A.R. 140   375

Sloley v Entry Certificate Officer, Kingston [1973] Imm. A.R. 54   271, 272

Sobanjo, E.C.O. Lagos v, [1978] Imm. A.R. 22   302

Soblen, ex parte, R v Governor of Brixton Prison [1963] 2 Q.B. 243   310, 341, 372

Somerzaul, Secretary of State for the Home Department v, [1970-72] Imm. A.R. 101   273

Stawczykowska, Secretary of State v, [1970-72] Imm. A.R. 220   297

Stewart v Entry Clearance Officer, Kingston [1978] Imm. A.R. 32   273

Stillwaggon, Secretary of State v, [1975] Imm. A.R. 132 295, 296

Stoeck v Public Trustee [1921] 2 Ch. 67   146

Suardana v Minister for Immigration (1980) 49 F.L.R. 8   338

Sudhakaran v Entry Clearance Officer, Madras [1976] Imm. A.R. 3   189

Sugarman v Dougall 413 U.S. 634 (1973)   145, 386

Tabag v Minister for Immigration and Ethnic Affairs 45 A.L.R. 705 (1983)   337

Tagle v Minister for Immigration (1983) 48 A.L.R. 566   330

Taj Bibi, Visa Officer v, [1981] Imm. A.R. 62   274

Taneja v Entry Clearance Officer, Chicago [1977] Imm. A.R. 9 224

Tarrant, ex parte, R v Secretary of State [1985] Q.B. 251
341

Thaker, Secretary of State v, [1976] Imm. A.R. 114   301, 375

Thakerar, E.C.O. Bombay v, [1974] Imm. A.R. 60   375

Thakrar, ex parte, R v Secretary of State for the Home
Department [1974] Q.B. 684   43, 101, 226, 227

Thompson, E.C.O. Kingston [1981] Imm. A.R. 148   272

Thornby v Fleetwood (1720) 93 E.R. 545   146

Torok v Torok [1973] 1 W.L.R. 1066   264

Tosir Khan v Entry Clearance Officer, Dacca [1974] Imm. A.R.
55   224

Turner v Williams 194 U.S. 279 (1903)   38, 329

Two Citizens of Chile, Secretary of State for the Home
Department [1977] Imm. A.R. 36   239

Ullah, ex parte, R v Immigration Appeal Tribunal [1982] Imm.
A.R. 124   269, 312

Unlugenc v Minister for Immigration and Ethnic Affairs (1983)
43 A.L.R. 569   269

U.S. v Laub 385 U.S. 475 (1967)   161

U.S. Government v McCaffery [1984] 1 W.L.R. 867   372

Valentine's Settlement, Re [1965] Ch. 831   270

Vecht v Tay (1917) 116 L.T. 446   156

Venicoff, ex parte, R v Leman Street Police Station Inspector
[1920] 3 K.B. 72   331, 332, 341, 372

Vervaeke v Smith [1983] 1 A.C. 145   266, 270

Vethamony, Secretary of State v, [1981] Imm. A.R. 144   295

Virdee, Secretary of State v, [1970-72] Imm. A.R. 215   299

Waheed Akhtar, Visa Officer [1981] Imm. A.R. 109   271

Watson v Nikolaisen [1955] 2 Q.B. 286   150

Wedad v Secretary of State for the Home Department [1979-80] Imm. A.R. 27   300

Weerasuriya, ex parte, R v Immigration Appeal Tribunal [1983] 1 All E.R. 195   186, 375

Weinberger v Inglis [1919] A.C. 606   147

Wheatley v Waltham Forest L.B.C. [1979] 2 All E.R. 289   150

Williams v Home Office (No.2) [1981] 1 All E.R. 1211   41, 185

Williams v Secretary of State for the Home Department [1970-72] Imm. A.R. 207   272

Williams v Smith (1982) S.L.T. 163   337

Winans v A.G. [1904] A.C. 287   264

Wirdestedt, ex parte, R v Immigration Appeal Tribunal, Times, 12 December 1984   42

Wong Yang Sung v M^cgrath 339 U.S. 33 (1950)   41

X v Sweden 4 E.H.R.R. 408   267

Yau Yak Wah v Home Office [1982] Imm. A.R. 16   334, 335

Yuksel, Secretary of State v, [1976] Imm. A.R. 91   331, 342, 373

Zahra v Visa Officer, Islamabad [1979-80] Imm. A.R. 48   265

Zaman v E.C.O. Lahore [1973] Imm. A.R. 71   274

Zamir, ex parte, R v Secretary of State for the Home Department [1980] A.C. 930   19, 27, 40, 61, 115, 133, 176, 237, 342, 347ff

Zandfani, ex parte, R v Immigration Appeal Tribunal, Times, 21 December 1984   297

Zezza, ex parte, R v Governor of Pentonville Prison [1983] 1 A.C. 46   371

Cases involving the E.E.C.

Adoui and Cornuaille v Belgium [1982] E.C.R. 1665   209, 235

Alaimo v Prefet du Rhone [1975] E.C.R. 109   233

Amarjit Singh Sandhu, ex parte, R v Secretary of State for the
    Home Department [1982] 2 C.M.L.R. 553, and on appeal,
    [1983] 3 C.M.L.R. 131   208, 213

Ayub, ex parte, R v Secretary of State for the Home Department
    [1983] 3 C.M.L.R. 140   229, 230

Bonsignore v Stadt Koln [1975] E.C.R. 297   234

Broekmeulen v Huisarts Registratie Commissie [1981] E.C.R.
    2311   232

Budlong and Kember, Re [1980] 2 C.M.L.R. 125   233, 234

Casagrande v Landeshauptstadt Munchen [1974] E.C.R. 773   232

Choquet [1978] E.C.R. 2293   232

Commission v Belgium [1980] E.C.R. 3881, [1982] 3 C.M.L.R. 539
    212

Commission v French Republic [1974] E.C.R. 359   231

Cristini v S.N.C.F. [1975] E.C.R. 1085   231

Dannenberg, ex parte, R v Secretary of State for the Home
    Department [1984] 2 W.L.R. 855   235

Diatta v Land Berlin, Times, 12 March 1985   233

Dona v Mantero [1976] E.C.R. 1333   229, 231, 233

F v Belgium [1975] E.C.R. 679   232

Forcheri v Belgium [1984] 1 C.M.L.R. 334   231, 232

Giangregorio v Secretary of State for the Home Department
    [1983] 3 C.M.L.R. 472   229, 231

Giovanni v Secretary of State for the Home Department [1977]
    Imm. A.R. 85   229

Gravier v Ville de Liege, Times, 12 March 1985   207, 231,
    300

Grewal v Secretary of State for the Home Department [1979-80]
    Imm. A.R. 119   233

Hayes v Secretary of State for the Home Department [1981] Imm.
    A.R. 123   234

Hessische Knappschaft v Singer [1965] E.C.R. 1191   232

Hoeckx v Scrivner, Times, 11 April 1985   231

Kenny v Insurance Officer [1978] E.C.R. 1489   231

Knoors v Secretary of State for Economic Affairs [1979] E.C.R.
    399   228

Levin v Staatssecretaris van Justitie [1982] E.C.R. 1035
    205, 229

Macmahon v Department of Education and Science [1982] 3
    C.M.L.R. 91   207

Mansukani v Secretary of State for the Home Department [1981]
    Imm. A.R. 184   236

Marsman v Rosskamp [1972] E.C.R. 1243   231

Michel S v Fonds National [1973] E.C.R. 457   232

Ministère Public v Auer [1979] E.C.R. 437   228

Monteil v Secretary of State for the Home Department [1984] 1
    C.M.L.R. 264   234, 235, 339

Morson v State of Netherlands [1982] E.C.R. 3723   229

Niemann v Bundesversicherungsanstalt [1974] E.C.R. 571   228

Nijssen v Immigration Officer [1978] Imm. A.R. 226   229, 235

Pecastaing v Belgium [1980] E.C.R. 691   235

R v Bouchereau [1977] E.C.R. 1999   234

R v I.L.E.A., ex parte, Hinde [1985] 1 C.M.L.R. 716   232

R v Kraus [1982] Crim. L.R. 468   234

R v Pieck [1980] E.C.R. 2171   229, 230, 234

R v Saunders [1979] E.C.R. 1129   234, 372

R v Secchi [1975] 1 C.M.L.R. 383   229

Reina v Landeskreditbank Baden-Wurttemberg [1982] E.C.R. 33
    231

Royer [1976] E.C.R. 497   211, 229, 233, 234, 235

xxxvi

Rutili v Minister for the Interior [1975] E.C.R. 1219   234, 235

Sagulo, Brenca and Bakhouche [1977] E.C.R. 1495   230

Santillo, ex parte, R v Secretary of State for the Home Department [1980] E.C.R. 1585, on reference back, [1981] Q.B. 778   211, 338, 339

Seco v E.V.I. [1982] E.C.R. 223   232

Sotgiu v Deutsche Bundespost [1974] E.C.R. 153   232

Van Duyn v Home Office [1974] E.C.R. 1337   209

Watson and Belmann [1976] E.C.R. 1185   230, 234

Webb [1981] E.C.R. 3305   232

Wurttembergische Milchverwertung v Ugliola [1969] E.C.R. 363   231

1 INTRODUCTION AND THEMES

> One of the rights possessed by the supreme power in every
> State is the right to refuse to permit an alien to enter
> that State, to annex what conditions it pleases to the
> permission to enter it, and to expel or deport from the
> State, at pleasure, even a friendly alien, especially if
> it considers his presence in the State opposed to its
> peace, order, and good government, or to its social or
> material interests.[1]

In the light of this statement it is frequently inaccurate and
impracticable to speak of an immigrant's "rights". Why and how
that should be so are some of the themes of this book.

Lord Atkinson's statement is based on a State's
"sovereignty" or, in modern parlance, nationalism. In no other
area, not even defence, does the term sovereignty have such an
absolute meaning in practice. Various consequences flow from
sovereignty. Firstly, international law has made little
headway. From the Greek city state to a twentieth century
democracy, political groupings have reserved to themselves the
sole right to determine who may enter and who may obtain
citizenship. Customary international law can only mirror that
practice. The few forays of international treaty law have in
the main ventured only so far as to cater for the treatment of
certain groups once admitted to a country,[2] whilst leaving the
terms of their initial admission to the province of the host
country.[3] As the Supreme Court of the U.S. observed in 1888,
"That the Government of the United States, through the action
of the legislative department can exclude aliens from its
territory is a proposition which we do not think open to
controversy. Jurisdiction over its own territory to that
extent is an incident of every independent nation. It is a
part of its independence. If it could not exclude aliens it
would be to that extent subject to the control of another
power".[4] Second, the impotence of international law highlights
the lack of substantive rights which an immigrant can claim.

He may seek the privilege of entry. Beyond that a State may
concede rights to him, but even then the rights tend to be of
a procedural rather than substantive nature, for example, a
right of appeal before exclusion or natural justice before
deportation. Even States with written constitutions and Bills
of Rights generally offer little help. In the U.S., for
example, the constitution has frequently been thrown out of
the window in the face of immigration disputes.[5] Third, the
omnicompetence of each State can breed amongst the native
population a feeling of superiority and a greater outlet for
xenophobia and economic self-interest than would be possible
if some external checks were available. This in turn can lead
to the abuse, sometimes violent, of immigrant communities and
the dubbing of them as scapegoats for economic, social,
political and religious difficulties. When these emotions are
translated into policies which discriminate against the
immigrant, racism results. Fourth, the immigrant usually has
no ready legal defence to raise against such internal attacks.
Governments tend to be unsympathetic. Occasional defences
depend on humanitarian concession (e.g. the adoption of a
system of appeals against administrative decisions by the
Immigration Appeals Act 1969) or enlightened, and usually
short-lived, liberalism (e.g. that which resisted immigration
control in the U.K. until 1905 or stalled the adoption of a
literacy test in the U.S. until 1917).[6] Fifth, in the narrower
legal context, sovereignty has meant that a State can select
unhindered the most effective tools of control, namely,

   (i) discretion, usually entrusted to a Minister and then
       delegated by him to his officials,
  (ii) secrecy, e.g. unpublished instructions to junior
       officials,
 (iii) very broad and elastic terminology e.g. deportation as
       'conducive to the public good', denial of citizenship
       because of crimes of 'moral turpitude',
  (iv) denial of adequate procedural redress e.g. the appeal
       from overseas,
   (v) informal mechanisms of control e.g. the administrative
       manipulation of queues of applicants waiting for
       permission to enter.

Sixth, the impact of sovereignty is frequently seen in the
fundamental issue of 'who belongs to the State so as to fit
him for citizenship?'. For example, in the U.K. citizenship
was not open to Jews until 1826 and in the U.S. only to 'free
white aliens' in 1790, whilst native red Indians could not
qualify as U.S. citizens until 1924. Similarly the process of
acquiring, and frequently the granting of, citizenship are
solely at the sovereign's discretion and any procedural
safeguards are concessions.
       Seventh, and most importantly, the belief in sovereignty

naturally leads to a desire to defend it. This includes the special provisions normally adopted to defend the very security of the State e.g. in the discretionary denial of entry or citizenship to 'subversive' applicants. It also underlies the perennial roots of opposition by the native population to immigration viz. the feared decline in the State's values, be they economic, cultural, racial, political or religious.

The U.S. is a good example of the pervasive effect of sovereignty in the fields of immigration and citizenship. In a country where the assertion of constitutional rights is both commonplace and frequently effective, these fields are sparingly represented. It was not until 1952 that naturalisation was open to all, the blatantly discriminatory 'national origins quota' survived until 1965 and the Constitution has frequently been cast aside in deference to the Executive's prerogative over matters of foreign affairs, of which immigration is one.[7]

A. THE RIGHTS AT STAKE

To the student of human rights, immigration and nationality offer a fertile ground for study because they raise such a wide range of issues of civil liberties. Any of the following rights may be involved:

(1) to life, notably the treatment of potential refugees. Those fleeing by boat from countries in south east Asia are a recent example

(2) to move

(3) to a home and protection, acquired through citizenship

(4) to natural justice or due process, for example, in the entry clearance or visa systems, the conditions of detention for alleged illegal immigrants, and, in deportation

(5) to speak, for example, through the use of deportation, on 'conducive to the public good' grounds, against political activists

(6) to non-discrimination on the grounds of race, national origins, nationality (e.g. the preferential status given to E.E.C. entrants), sex (e.g. in relation to the admission of spouses), and age (e.g. the criteria for the admission of aged dependants)

(7) to marry, for example the admission of fiances

(8) to family life, for example the unification of family members

(9) to work, for example, the sharp contrast between E.E.C. and non-E.E.C. citizens

(10) to liberty and thereby to the freedom from arbitrary and inhumane detention

(11) to full political and civil status, usually as

incidents of citizenship, such as the opportunities
for voting and landownership

(12) to privacy, for example, in relation to the entry
clearance procedure and the collection of personal
data

(13) to be treated humanely by accountable officials
governed by the rule of law.

B. THE ADVANTAGES OF IMMIGRATION[8]

(1) New blood
This is inextricably linked with the economic impetus (below)
which immigrants can give to a host society; but it is worthy
of separate identification. It has historically benefited
societies which are either confident in themselves and eager
for additional inspiration, such as the middle period of the
Victorian era, or "new" themselves and thus keen to acquire
new ideas and invigoration. The latter can be seen most
clearly in the offspring of the British Empire - the policies
of the U.S., Australia and Canada. In recent times, this
advantage of immigration has all but disappeared beneath the
blanket of nationalism and economic self-interest. However, it
still emerges in the preference given to scientists, artists
and similarly qualified immigrants. For, economic benefits
aside, such people are still welcomed or tolerated because of
their supposed originality.

(2) Economic advantage
Economic motives represent the major attraction for
immigration, as they do the major justification for its
control. Until this century, these motives were in the main
overtly constructive in the U.K. setting - the attraction of
foreign labour to invigorate the country's economy. As a
Select Committee observed in 1843,

> It has often been laid down by economical writers, that it
> is desirable for every people to encourage the settlement
> of foreigners among them, since by such means they will be
> practically instructed in what it most concerns them to
> know, and enabled to avail themselves of whatever foreign
> sagacity, ingenuity, or experience may have produced in
> art and science which is most perfect.[9]

At the same time, and in the twentieth century particularly,
imported labour has been used to fulfil more mundane purposes
- for jobs which are unpopular with the native population even
in times of high unemployment, for example, the encouragement
of immigrants to work in cotton mills or local transport or to
man ships or in Australia the use of Chinese coolies (Kanaka
Labour) to farm plantations in tropical conditions or in the

Caribbean and U.S. the importation of slaves to serve similar functions.

Even when control is instituted against general labour, the skilled and gifted are frequently favoured. Thus, in recent times, doctors have been excepted from the full application of the entry clearance system; in the mid-1930s the skilled Jewish refugees stood a higher chance of untroubled entry; and the professional and artistic refugees have today a considerably stronger possibility of securing asylum.

(3) Charity

Political and humanitarian propaganda can be gained by the host society being seen to assist the displaced and refugees.

This motive is inevitably linked with the foreign policy of the host society. For, in the process of granting refuge, the values of the host society can be paraded and the 'weaknesses' of the foreign State directly or indirectly exposed. At the same time, the ready bestowal of asylum can reinforce the host society's belief in its own values. Elements of this appeared, at least at the formal level, in the reception into the United Kingdom of Ugandan Asians in 1972 and Vietnamese refugees in 1979. But the heyday of this aspect was the mid-Victorian era when the press, in particular, revelled in boasting of Britain's virtues to Continental Governments who were seen as unduly alarmed at internal dissension and at Britain's reception of their political opponents. This posture reaffirmed the Victorian values of individual freedom. It can be seen too in the efforts of the British Government, in the aftermath of the abolition of slavery and in the context of a multiracial Empire, to suppress the attempts by Australia and New Zealand in the 1890s to discriminate against Asiatic and Chinese immigrants.

Humanitarian concern also underlies the reception of dependants of primary immigrants. Thus, the U.K. has repeatedly affirmed the pledge to allow their entry; the U.S., Australian and Canadian systems give similar priority, in their points' system, to such groups.

This aspect of immigration does not necessarily mean that the indigenous population <u>likes</u> the immigrants. Indeed, the ready reception of refugees has frequently coincided with mercenary motives. Thus, the Protestant refugees of the 1580s and 1680s came here when English society was not overpopulated and the Monarchy was willing to encourage economic regeneration. Again, the fickleness of welcome is apparent when refugees become too numerous (e.g. the Jews of the 1890s and the Poles of 1979 were tolerated but not in 1905 and 1982, respectively) or successful (e.g. the protestations of trade guilds against foreigners in the seventeenth century and the

British Medical Association in 1938 against the influx of Jewish doctors).

C. MOTIVES OF THE IMMIGRANT

These are reflected in the above-mentioned advantages of immigration. In previous centuries the spirit of adventure also played a major role. It is still a real motive and not one to be derided, if given a chance for expression. But today the opportunities of primary immigration are so restricted that it is only secondary immigration - the unification of families - which accounts for the sizeable share of immigration.

D. CAUSES OF HOSTILITY TO IMMIGRATION

(1) Economic fear
This lies at the root of most opposition to immigration (as will be shown in chapter 2). Foreigners can be tolerated, if not welcomed, when they bring new skills to the native economy or are willing to perform the least popular jobs. However, as soon as the immigrants begin to squeeze the economic livelihood of the indigenous population, the petitions for control on their entry begin and are invariably acceded to ultimately by host Governments, either because of such petitions or because, when the general economy becomes depressed, immigrants are a natural scapegoat (even though the causes of the depression may be much more fundamental and internationally based).

To students of economics this statement may appear too obvious but it cannot be underestimated. To the student of immigration law, it is essential to grasp, since from this fear stems the origin of control and many of the ancillary fulminations against immigration. These then underlie so many of the laws and practices, for example, the work permit scheme, the determination to detect illegal entrants, the controls on students, husbands and fiances, and the careful examination of male children in the entry clearance system.

As one commentator has observed,

> Apart from the pressure of vested interests, manufacturers and artisans alike, the basic motives for protection in the Middle Ages and the succeeding centuries down to the present day have always been the fear of unemployment, coupled with the desire to foster infant industries.[10]

For example, in 1852 Parliament laid down the conditions for the transportation of emigrants such that only one could be shipped "for every fifteen superficial feet of the passenger deck".[11] In response to Colonial demands for imported labour the Act was amended in 1855 to allow the shipment of "Natives

of Asia or Africa" at the rate of one for every twelve feet.[12]
Yet as soon as Chinese immigrants outlived their economic
usefulness, Australia and New Zealand passed laws to prohibit
or restrict their further immigration.[13]

The law has been used in several ways to express local
economic fear. The most obvious are quotas on the number of
entrants and a work permit scheme which seeks to relate
particular applicants to specific jobs. Before that stage is
reached, the law has been used indirectly, by, for example,

(a) imposing higher taxes on immigrant-made goods,
(b) requiring immigrants to procure expensive licences to
    trade, e.g. a double fee for alien miners in
    California and New South Wales in the nineteenth
    century, aimed at the Chinese immigrants,
(c) requiring employees to pay foreign labour at the same,
    and not cheaper, rates as local workers,
(d) excluding aliens from working in certain sensitive
    areas, and confining certain types of employment to
    citizenship.

Recent events in other countries have illustrated the
perennial nature of economic opposition to immigrants. Thus,
the colonial history of France led to entry preferences for
its former dependencies and many, notably North Africans, took
advantage. In times of economic recession and unemployment,
the native backlash began and was illustrated by the electoral
success of the right wing in 1983, with foreign labour taking
the blame for economic difficulties.[14] Although there are many
resident Italian and Spanish workers, the backlash was
primarily directed towards the readily visible components of
immigrant labour - North Africans. Nervous official reaction
appeared through repatriation grants and attempts to control
illegal entry, as witnessed by the exclusion of black British
entrants at Channel ports in August 1983. In Germany, economic
success rather than colonial ties attracted foreign labour.
Indeed, the Government encouraged it, under the euphemistic
title of guestworkers (gasterbeiters), to help to man the
economic growth and to fill the unpleasant jobs. Yet, as
economic fortunes changed, that labour was singled out for
blame by imposing restrictions on entry and offering financial
inducements to immigrants (mainly Turks) to leave the
country.[15] Legislation was debated in the U.S. in 1983 and 1984
to make the employment of illegal entrants unlawful (Mexicans
being the target)[16] and in Australia lower quotas for entrants
and a clampdown on illegal entrants were announced in
September 1982 and May 1983.[17]

(2) Social conditions
These objections centre upon the pressures on housing, public
health, health services, state benefit payments, education and

morality. They can be loosely classified as direct and indirect. As to direct, these include, for example, fears of

(a) the introduction of disease. Tuberculosis has been a recent feature of anti-immigrant literature in the U.K. Medical tests are among the first forms of immigration control to be employed.

(b) Delays in housing opportunities or entitlement which, it is claimed, have been exacerbated by immigrant families who are content to live in overcrowded private accommodation or who are also queueing for publicly provided accommodation. Thus overcrowding in some cities was the principal preoccupation of the Royal Commission on Aliens[18] in 1903 and motive behind the Aliens Act 1905.

(c) Moral decline which immigrants are likely to bring. For example, West Indians and Africans have been associated in some eyes with promiscuity[19] and Jews with usury and both will therefore lead to the demise of native vigour and independence.

The main indirect objections are,

(i) cultural decline. Anti-immigration opinion has feared the dilution and ultimate destruction of the host society's values. This was, for example, a central motive of the 'national origins quotas' in the U.S. in 1917 and 1924 which gave preference to immigrants of North European stock,[20] and of the 'all White' immigration policies of Australia, Canada and New Zealand. It has featured as a theme of U.K. opposition to immigration, partly because of the apparent unwillingness of the ethnic communities to forego their own cultures and embrace that of the native population.

The law has been readily used to safeguard culture in the field of citizenship. Countries have required applicants for naturalisation to satisfy various tests such as language, 'good character' or "a knowledge and understanding of the fundamentals of the history, and of the principles and form of the government, of the United States".[21]

(ii) State benefits. The immigrant's reliance on Poor Relief and, more recently, on the fuller panoply of social welfare has naturally produced indignation in the native population, since it implies that 'hard-pressed citizens are forced to subsidise destitute and mercenary foreigners'. This indignation has repeatedly seen expression in the law, e.g. as a feature of the Aliens Act 1905 - the power to remove aliens who, within 12 months of entry, relied upon

8

public funds; as a theme of the tougher Immigration Rules of 1980; and recently as the imposition of charges for use of the National Health Service by some overseas visitors.

(iii) The pressure upon educational resources, which can result in overcrowded and therefore inferior conditions for home students. Thus, overseas students should not be subsidised by the host State.

(3) Public order

Immigrants have for long been associated with crime, either as part of their economic activities (witness the allegations in the eighteenth century that alien goldsmiths practised forgery or in the nineteenth that Jews resorted to fraudulent usury) or directly such as their recently alleged predisposition to 'mugging'. In earlier centuries, the argument was put more subtly - that successful immigrants produced unemployment amongst native workers who in turn fell into criminal pursuits. Public order in the wider sense may also be affected by the violent opposition which may be vented upon immigrants. For example, disturbances in Notting Hill, Nottingham and other places in the late 1950s spurred Parliament into hastier discussion of controls on Commonwealth immigrants.

As with poor health, a criminal record is one of the first criteria to be singled out for immigration control. It is also a common strand of deportation powers.

(4) National security

Fears for national security in the periods before, during and after wartime have acted as timely catalysts for immigration control.They were the justification for legislation during the Napoleonic wars - the precedent for modern controls. The assassination of President McKinley in 1901 prompted a statute of 1903 in the U.S. directed against, inter alia, anarchists.[22] The anti-German feeling in the U.S., which led to the Espionage Act 1917 and Sedition Act 1918, tipped the scales in favour of a long debated and awaited literacy test for immigrants. It is not just the advent of war which galvanises Governments into tighter controls but also its uneasy aftermath. For example, in the U.K. the opportunity was taken in 1919 to prolong the Aliens Restriction Act 1914 and in the U.S. the Cold War of the early 1950s saw repeated efforts to check potential security threats.

Since historically it is based on the concept of allegiance, citizenship is also used in defence of the State. The very grant of citizenship is usually discretionary and subject to an overriding element of State security, either in general terms such as the 'good character' requirement in the U.K. or the detailed list of disabilities in the U.S.[23] Similarly, 'allegiance' has led to many States prohibiting dual nationality for their citizens. Even when citizenship has

9

been obtained, 'sensitive' employment or political positions may be reserved to the native-born. Article 48(4) of the E.E.C. Treaty provides a perfect illustration of this caution. In spite of the very generous freedom of movement given to E.E.C. workers and their families, art. 48(4) permits the Member State to draw the line at "employment in the public service".

(5) Religion
Internationally, religion maintains its importance for immigration principally because it can determine whether refugees will be admitted. In the U.K. this factor is chiefly of historical importance. In the thirteenth century the fears of the resident clergy about the religious practices of the Jews played a part in their victimisation and ultimate expulsion in 1290. In the sixteenth century the vacillating religious persuasions of the Monarchy (Henry 8, Mary and Elizabeth) dictated whether Papists or Protestants were acceptable as refugees. In the late nineteenth century, the Jews' religious practices again featured as part of the native fear for the decline in traditional moral values, whilst for the same reason, it took until 1826 to abolish the 'Oath and Sacrament' conditions for naturalisation. More recently religion has played a subsidiary role and in terms of race relations rather than immigration control. For example, the Sikhs have been a focal point for racist attacks.

(6) Strangeness
Although this factor is linked to others, it deserves a brief but separate mention because it is frequently the very strangeness of aliens which precedes the other complaints against them and which then invariably reinforces those complaints. Visible signs of difference, such as colour, eating habits, and mode of dress or speech, can paint for native eyes a picture of 'suspicious foreigners', unwilling to conform to the standards of the indigenous population. This picture is then confirmed when aliens are seen living together, apart from 'normal' society. It commonly appears in what can be called the 'but argument' which typically runs thus, 'I am not against blacks, they work hard and some of them seem quite nice, but they are different from us' or more bluntly, 'I am not against them, but I wouldn't let my daughter marry one'. Strangeness can then quickly lead to the stereotyping of immigrants, with the real or imaginary sins of a few being visited on all. Thus, all Jews can be seen as avaricious and parasitic, and each applicant from the Indian subcontinent is prone to falsify his family history in order to gain entry.

(7) Racial purity and superiority
These factors assumed particular prominence at the turn of the

century in the guise of social Darwinism and thereafter in
eugenics. In the 1880s, for example, nativism in the U.S. was
largely kept at bay since the bulk of immigration came from
Northern Europe but later, as East Europeans and Mediterranean
peoples made the journey, their distinct characteristics added
a new dimension to immigration politics viz. that the national
racial stock was in danger of being diluted and even overrun.
The theory of evolution fitted the bill nicely in the U.S.,
U.K. and Old Commonwealth. Darwinism however was merely a
topical coathanger on which to base feelings of racial purity
and superiority which had existed for centuries. They had, for
example, featured in the dramatic repeal of the 'Jew Bill'
(which had permitted Jews to apply for naturalisation) in 1753
and in the U.K.'s early reaction to negroes.[24] The concomitant
to racial purity is racial superiority. This was undoubtedly
encouraged by imperialism, which taught that uncivilised
nations, subdued by conquest and fit only for slavery in many
cases, had no claim to, or prospect of, equality with the
conquering race. From the many examples, one can look to the
Times in 1866 which observed that Negroes are "careless,
credulous, and dependent; easily excited, easily duped, easily
frightened".[25] The lesson was not lost on the emerging
Commonwealth countries of Australia, Canada and New Zealand
which valued their North European ancestry and set their faces
against coloured and oriental immigration. For example, to
quote an Australian politician, "the Chinaman knows nothing
about Caucasian civilisation or the laws of a country like
this. In fact, a Chinaman is a mere dumb animal and never
could be anything else. It would be less objectionable to
drive a flock of sheep to the poll than to allow Chinamen to
vote. The sheep at all events would be harmless".[26]

Arguments centred on racial superiority have spurred the
rise of anti-immigration groups[27] and provided them with an
opportunity to appeal to nationalism and with an excuse for
particularly crude propaganda. Only relatively recently has
the law in the U.K. sought to curb the more virulent
expression with the offence of incitement to racial hatred.[28]
But, apart from its many inherent weaknesses,[29] the offence
does not catch such opinion if it is couched in more
restrained or academic language. It would not, for example,
have caught the following defence of the Commonwealth
Immigrants Act 1962 -that it was necessary lest "the swarming
millions of the world would eventually overrun her [Britain]
and set the seal of their explosive birthrates and resultant
poverty upon her".[30]

Racial purity is frequently defended in terms of the
necessary homogeneity of the host society. It has been a
central plank of recent U.K. policy that coloured immigration
has to be restricted to assist internal racial harmony. It
also lay behind, and is mirrored by, the 'all white' policies
of Australia, Canada, New Zealand and the U.S. For example,

the Australian position was thus explained in 1949; "It is true that a measure of discrimination on racial grounds is exercised in the administration of our immigration policy. That is inevitable in a policy which is based on the concept that the homogenous character of the population, which settled and developed the country, shall be maintained."[31] This form of opposition to immigration contains an ironic contradiction. On the one hand, immigrants are seen as efficient and therefore economically successful or as a threat to the native stock by their vigour; on the other hand, they are seen as spongers off the State or as so inferior in quality as to jeopardise the native racial stock.

Laws have been used in various ways to enshrine or preserve racial purity. Statutes may be neutral in tone, as in the U.K. recently, but passed in circumstances where their effect is bound to be felt harder by particular groups of applicants (e.g. the Commonwealth Immigrants Acts 1962 and 1968). A statute may be openly discriminatory, forbidding the immigration of certain races or restricting them to very small annual quotas e.g. the 'Asia-Pacific Triangle' under the Immigration and Nationality Act 1952[32] which, by the simple use of lines of longitude and latitude, excluded unwanted immigrants into the U.S., or the Chinese Immigration Act 1927 which prevented the entry into Canada of many categories of Chinese. Citizenship has been a rich source of direct discrimination e.g. the confinement of naturalisation to adherents of the State's Established religion;[33] the denial of citizenship to Negroes[34] and to Red Indians[35] born in the U.S.

More common have been acts of indirect discrimination. Taxes and licences can be used for this purpose. Thus the Customs Act 1832 required a ship's captain to enter a bond guaranteeing to reimburse any parish for any relief paid out to 'Native Africans' whom the captain had landed in the U.K. Language and literacy tests on admission can serve the same purpose and have the operational advantage of flexibility. Natal chose this method in 1897 by requiring each immigrant to write out an application for entry in English and it was soon copied by New Zealand in 1899 and Australia in 1901. After lengthy controversy a literacy test for immigrants was adopted by the United States in 1917. The law has frequently been used with a protective motive to defend the native population from unnecessary contact with the alien influences. Thus in R v Quong Wing,[36] a Canadian court upheld as intra vires a Saskatchewan statute prohibiting white women from, inter alia, working in, or frequenting any restaurant, laundry or place of amusement owned or managed by Chinese, Japanese or other Orientals. White women and their morality had to be protected.

E. LEGAL CHARACTERISTICS OF U.K.'s IMMIGRATION CONTROL

Many of these characteristics are not peculiar to the U.K. For example, executive discretion is a common factor of immigration control throughout the world. However, there are some aspects which take their shape from the U.K.'s legal system. Most of these stem from the lack of a written constitution and a Bill of Rights.

(1) The separation of citizenship laws and immigration laws
Before 1948 the relationship between the two laws was relatively straightforward. British subjects, including anyone born in the Empire, were free from immigration control whereas aliens could be restricted on their entry and even in their internal movement. However, by preserving the right of all Commonwealth citizens to enter the U.K., the British Nationality Act 1948 stored up difficulties which became prominent when increasing numbers of New Commonwealth citizens chose to exercise that right in the 1950s and 1960s. Immigration legislation between 1962 and 1971 was therefore concerned with providing a series of piecemeal derogations from the rights of citizenship. The British Nationality Act 1981 is designed to impose some order by defining citizenship afresh and correlating it with immigration control. However, it will take many years before the complex legacy of earlier Commonwealth concessions is shaken off. Moreover, the reform is incomplete since the rights accruing from citizenship are not set out by the 1981 Act and, consequently, nor are those of non-citizens.
    The separation of the immigration and citizenship laws not only leads to complexity but also illustrates the U.K.'s unwillingness to go to the drawing-board and to plan its immigration and citizenship policies comprehensively.

(2) Nature of the primary legislation
The British Nationality Act 1981 leaves little to chance. Its provisions are complicated, bordering on obfuscation, with surprisingly little scope for secondary legislation. On the other hand, the Immigration Act is very much a skeleton with the body left to the Rules. As one would expect from a country which has refused to adopt a modern Bill of Rights, both Acts are largely bereft of statements of principle. Practically, this means that:

    (a) rights are usually residual in nature, submerged beneath qualifications, and
    (b) laymen are faced with a daunting task of comprehension. The Nationality Act, for example, is for the legal connoisseur not the general public.

(3) Nature of the secondary 'legislation'
The Immigration Rules enjoy a peculiar legal status. They must be placed before Parliament and can be vetoed within forty days, as happened in December 1982.[37] In operation they have an

ambiguous role. On the immigration appellate system (the Immigration Appeals Tribunal (I.A.T.) and the adjudicator) they are binding - s.19(1), Immigration Act 1971. Yet before the courts they are mere guidelines. As Lord Denning M.R. observed, "They are not rules of law. They are rules of practice laid down for the guidance of immigration officers and tribunals ... they are not rules in the nature of delegated legislation so as to amount to strict rules of law".[38] This means that the Rules "are not to be construed with all the strictness applicable to the construction of a statute or a statutory instrument. They must be construed sensibly according to the natural meaning of the language which is employed. The rules give guidance to the various officers concerned and contain statements of general policy regarding the operation of the relevant immigration legislation".[39]

One consequence of this hybrid nature of the Rules[40] is that it gives the Government a double chance of success. If it loses before the I.A.T. on a point of construction, it can appeal to the courts and argue that the Rules are, after all, only 'rules of practice'.[41] A further consequence is that the traditional legal principle of ultra vires can be hard to apply in the face of amorphous rules. But even if a court is prepared to construe the Rules strictly, their flexible content frequently offers a defence to the Secretary of State e.g. the qualification of 'normally' litters the Rules

(4) Subsidiary 'rules'
The tradition of secrecy in Government and the shadow of the Official Secrets Act 1911 mean that much of the administration of immigration control can be achieved by internal circulars, instructions and guidance to Government agencies, such as Home Office and Foreign Office officials, the police and officials of other interested departments (e.g. the Inland Revenue, Department of Employment and Department of Health and Social Security) - for example, the former employment of virginity and x-ray tests in entry clearance procedure which was based on unpublicised internal instructions to immigration officers, or the internal administrative guidance governing the interrogation of foreign husbands and fiances seeking to enter the U.K.[42]

A particularly good example of this (and the following characteristic) has been the deployment, since 1968, of entry vouchers for United Kingdom citizens based in East Africa. Because the scheme is non-statutory,[43] it can be run as the Government sees fit and thus in accordance with whatever criteria and guidance it issues to immigration officers. In the light of Amin, the possibility of judicial review could only arise in the most exceptional circumstances involving, for example, clearly demonstrated bad faith on the part of an immigration officer. In truth administrative law offers slender redress against such opaque 'rules'.

(5) Discretion
Discretion appears throughout immigration law and practice and citizenship. It is essential, but needs to be checked. The guidelines governing the use of deportation powers is an all too rare example of an attempt to structure discretionary decision-making. The link which judicial eyes have made between immigration and foreign affairs has helped to stall the control of discretion. It is only relatively recently (the 1970s) that immigration has become more legalistic and this change has coincided with the late development of British public law. Unfortunately for the entrant, the traditions of discretion and judicial timidity, aided by the absence of a Bill of Rights, are too well established to be easily disturbed by such developments.[44]

(6) Secrecy
Secrecy is the most formidable enemy of human rights and is a natural consequence of broad discretion. One can compare the way in which the discretionary power of the Home Office enables prison administration to be regulated without public discussion.[45] Immigration has an extra dimension in that it is traditionally associated with foreign affairs and they are in turn the traditional preserve of the executive arm of Government. When this factor is added to the U.K.'s preoccupation with secrecy in administration, it is not surprising that citizenship and immigration are littered with instances of secrecy. The provision of vouchers for U.K. passport holders (UKPHs) in 1968 is again a simple example. The scheme was instituted after discussion with other Commonwealth Governments, but full details of its administration were not revealed and the annual quota of vouchers for those awaiting in India remained secret until 1981. The assessment of an applicant's good character for the purposes of citizenship is another example of jealously guarded secrecy. The use of virginity and x-ray tests to vet entrants was discreetly introduced.[46] The compilation by immigration officers of a Suspect Index[47] of questionable entrants and the stamping of passports with secret codes[48] are further examples of the many measures introduced without public discussion. The fact that the entry clearance procedures operate overseas places a further limitation on accountability.

(7) Division of responsibility
The Immigration Department in the Home Office occupies the central role,[49] but it must work closely with other departments - with the Foreign Office in relation to the provision and deployment of entry clearance officers and to the policy on refugees, with the Department of Employment in the delegation of the work permit scheme, with the Police Department in the Home Office for the registration of aliens and detection of unlawful entrants, and with the Department of

Health and Social Security for detecting the unlawful use of public funds by immigrants. This fragmentation of responsibility, when allied to the above-mentioned characteristics, presents formidable difficulties to the independent scrutiny of Government action.

(8) Adversarial tradition

The tradition of adversarial resolution of legal disputes in U.K. law has unfortunate consequences for immigration and nationality. It induces the Home Office to 'close ranks' to protect colleagues (e.g. the entry clearance officer overseas) and fosters the drawbridge mentality which sets its face against the admission of immigrants. Under this system the onus lies on the entrant to establish each component of his claim and there is no obligation on the civil servant, who may, for example, have learned information favourable to the immigrant from other Government Departments, to divulge it. It can be contrasted with the values underlying an inquisitorial system which seek to establish the truth rather than 'play the adversarial game'.[50]

(9) Judicial Review

Immigration is a subject linked with foreign policy. In that sense it falls within a sphere where the courts are very slow to intervene.[51]

The constitutional and legal protection which aliens have managed to secure have tended to arise in the procedures for expulsion rather than at the entry stage. The latter is seen more as a privilege and a matter for the host State's discretion for which natural justice has inevitably a minor role. For example, the U.S. Constitution has made some headway in the former but not the latter.[52] The Immigration Appeal Board in Canada made similarly significant progress (given the difficulties of the broad legislation) before 1976 in deportation matters and the 1976 Act concentrates appellate supervision in the removal sector.[53] In the U.K. the Immigration Appeals Act 1969 (even when amended and implemented by the Immigration Act 1971) was the most significant advance which the rule of law and natural justice have made in U.K. immigration practice, and the executive power of removal was, ultimately, the scene for the strongest assertion of judicial review to date.[54] In Australia, given the history of extremely broad executive discretion, it has been the removal powers against which judicial review has had the most (though limited) success.[55]

Until the mid-1960s the U.K. courts played little supervisory role in immigration matters. The importance of determining an applicant's status as subject or alien (principally because of the former's ability to own and inherit land) meant that by far their greater involvement lay in the field of citizenship. A regular flow of jurisprudence resulted.[56] As to immigration, for long periods there were no barriers to entry and thus appeals to the law were not needed. When Parliament began to erect them, the alien was confronted with the proposition that he did not have "a legal right, enforceable by action, to enter British territory".[57] Similarly, the Crown's undisputed right to pass whatever laws it deemed appropriate for the expulsion of aliens[58] confined the courts to a mechanical role in the machinery of deportation - the power to order (1793-1816) or recommend removal (1905).[59] This inherent weakness was exacerbated by wartime legislation partly because it gave the courts little room for manoeuvre and partly because their tradition of deference was so well established as to exclude defiant judicial review.[60] The aggregation of discretionary powers in the hands of the Secretary of State was a further disincentive to judicial review.[61]

Against this background and without the support of a Bill of Rights or a sophisticated system of administrative law, it is hardly surprising that the judicial review of immigration legislation and practice since 1962 has been limited. It began reasonably well with the Commonwealth Immigrants Acts of 1962 and 1968 offering the opportunity to interpret 'lawyer's law' and some decisions favourable to the individual.[62] The turning point came with the Immigration Act 1971, not simply because it closed loopholes in the earlier law but also because the political climate of opposition to, and fears of, large-scale immigration infected the judiciary. Indeed, the judiciary in some respects led the way in tightening immigration controls.

   (a) The ensuing trend was set by the House of Lords in Azam v Secretary of State.[63] There Azam and two others had entered the country illegally in breach of s.4 of the Commonwealth Immigrants Act 1962. As the law then stood, he was liable to prosecution for up to 6 months after entry. He survived that period undetected and in effect claimed that he was no longer in breach of the law, he must therefore be here lawfully and the recent Immigration Act 1971 could not deny him the right to stay. The majority of the House of Lords disagreed. Azam had entered illegally and remained an illegal entrant, even though he could not be prosecuted under the earlier law. Since his illegal status persevered, the removal provisions of the 1971 Act could apply. Lord Wilberforce fell back on a standard ploy: if Azam's argument was correct, Parliament could easily have said so in the 1971 Act. As to his contention that the decision would cause upheaval to people who had been in the U.K. for some time and who now faced removal, His Lordship used another ploy which has frequently been used in such circumstances - the Home Secretary still had a discretion to allow such people to stay and he would doubtless take account of human factors. This reliance on the administration's rectitude is a useful mechanism for courts and the Immigration appellate authorities to appear to soften the blow of their decisions.

Lord Salmon would have none of this, duly dissented and expressed an alternative statutory interpretation. After 6 months, Azam's unlawful act fell away, a common law right to stay arose and that was not affected by the subsequent statute. According to him the 1971 Act was just as capable of his interpretation as that of the majority and, since the Act affected the rights of the individual, his more restrictive interpretation should be applied so as to conform to civil liberties.

The decision in Azam meant the retroactive application of the 1971 Act. This aroused the dismay of many M.P.s who claimed that they had not intended that, and the decision was instrumental in provoking an amnesty for illegal entrants in 1974.[64] It revealed a failure on the court's part to use traditional interpretative techniques to save civil liberties and, above all, set the style of judicial attitude to immigration cases thereafter. Lord Salmon's judgment on the other hand illustrated what could be done if the will was there.

(b) The use of habeas corpus is a good illustration of the judiciary's mood towards immigration in the 1970s. The cases of Ahsan and Hassan can be compared. In the former,[65] Pakistani, but British, subjects were detained for unlawful entry but the Crown could not prove that they had been caught within 24 hours of their entry, as the 1962 statute prescribed. It was held by the majority that the return to a writ of habeas corpus had to go further than recite the statutory power of detention. It had to establish the condition precedent to detention (capture within 24 hours of landing). The fact that British subjects were involved was a crucial determining factor for the court in imposing the additional onus on the Crown. As Blain J. observed, the 1962 Act constituted "a statutory fetter on the freedom of the subject, a fetter necessary for reasons which concern Parliament but which do not concern this court. The consequences may go to the very liberty of the subject ... Parliament must not be supposed to have put upon the subject the burden of proving freedom from liability to detention in prison of a citizen who has done nothing unlawful, unless that burden is expressed in the clearest and most unequivocal terms".[66]

Seven years later in Hassan,[67] however, (by which time Pakistan had left the Commonwealth) the court took a very different view. The order for detention of the Pakistani was valid on its face[68] and that was a sufficient response to the writ of habeas corpus, for "the onus is upon the applicant to show a prima facie case that his detention is illegal".[69] Ahsan was distinguishable since it involved a British subject.

(c) In a series of cases[70] in the mid-1970s the courts reaffirmed the weakness of habeas corpus and strengthened the Executive's powers of removal under the 1971 Act against illegal entrants. The process culminated in the controversial decision of Zamir.[71] It is clear that this judicial development exceeded the expectations of the Home Office[72] but significantly the Home Secretary gratefully accepted the boon and did not exercise his discretion so as to confine the removal powers to their originally intended scope.[73]

(d) A further small but neat illustration of the courts' deference to the policy of immigration control can be seen in the context of wardship. In Arif[74] the applicant sought to use wardship to counter the 1962 Act. It was held to be a misconceived application. Lord Denning made clear the sentiments of the Court of Appeal - "Parliament laid down [in 1962] a full and complete code to govern the entry or removal of immigrants from the Commonwealth and has entrusted the administration of it to the immigration officers. So much so that the courts ought not to interfere with their decisions save in the most exceptional circumstances."[75] This narrow interpretation of wardship can be contrasted with the broader scope given to it in other areas, even in the face of a statutory code.[76] The same judge left no doubt as to his sympathies six years later when offering this advice to an unsuccessful United Kingdom Passport Holder from Uganda, "He ought to consider this. His father and mother are in India. His wife and two children are in India. It might be better for him to join them in that great country, where there may be more scope for him than here. This country is not large enough to take in all those whom we would gladly accept".[77]

(e) The firm stance of the judiciary is further illustrated by the closely linked topic of race relations. Although the first two Race Relations Acts (1965 and 1968) were clearly deficient in their scope and terms, it is also clear that the courts did not exert themselves to remedy the defects. In two cases the House of Lords reversed the Court of Appeal and concluded that s.2 of the Race Relations Act 1968 did not outlaw discrimination in clubs.[78] The Dockers' Labour Club and Institute case raised the possibility that 4,000 working men's clubs, with a membership approaching $3^1/_2$ million, could discriminate on the basis of colour. Whilst the statutory phrase in dispute was admittedly unclear, it was, as Lord Morris demonstrated in the Charter case, and the Court of Appeal in both, capable of a literal and benevolent interpretation. The same difference in approach can be seen in Ealing L.B.C. v Race Relations Board[79] where the House of Lords chose a restrictive interpretation of 'national origins' under the 1968 Act, held that it did not include nationality and that therefore discrimination on the grounds of nationality was not covered by the Act. Support was again found in an old chestnut of statutory interpretation - if Parliament had intended to cover discrimination on the basis of nationality, it could easily have said so. To the dissenter, Lord Kilbrandon, the arguments were finely balanced but since the Act was a piece of social reform, it should be interpreted in that light so that nationality was included.

(f) The technicality of the Rules in the 1970s coincided with a growth in administrative law[80] and in concern for the civil liberties of immigrants. Appeals to the court increased but frequently turned on technical argument.[81] There were occasional successes for the immigrant,[82] but the trend was in the main against them. The lack of a Bill of Rights and an Administrative Court to bolster the courts is only a partial exculpation of their record. For even they presuppose a judiciary's willingness to exert itself in favour of civil liberties. The refusal to make fuller use of the European Convention on Human Rights is an illustration of the unwillingness.[83] The courts are reluctant to employ the Convention even as a guide to statutory interpretation.[84]

(g) At first sight the 1980s have brought a change of attitude in favour of the individual. In a remarkably swift volte-face, Zamir was unanimously reversed with references to the need "for a robust exercise of the judicial function in safeguarding the citizen's rights"[85] and "the jealous care our law traditionally devotes to the protection of the liberty of those who are subject to its jurisdiction".[86] The refinements which had surrounded 'ordinary residence' were removed[87] with immediate, but not long-term,[88] benefits to overseas students. The term 'ethnic' in the Race Relations Act 1976 was "construed relatively widely"[89] so as to embrace Sikhs and reverse a disturbing Court of Appeal decision that the wearing of turbans could be prohibited at a school. The Immigration Rules were "construed sensibly according to the natural meaning of the language which is employed"[90] so as to reverse the Court of Appeal and hold that an immigration officer had an overriding discretion to admit a prospective student who did not yet satisfy the strict criteria for entry. In the footsteps of Khawaja came a decision of the Divisional Court breathing further life into the writ of habeas corpus by requiring the Secretary of State to consider the deportation of persons held in detention, with urgency and expedition.[91] In the same year the Privy Council used the relatively novel principle of "legitimate expectation" to quash a removal order, made against an illegal entrant into Hong Kong, on the ground that the wide removal powers had been qualified by a Government undertaking to consider each case on its merits and thus entitled a prospective deportee to the bare essentials of natural justice.[92] In 1984 the Court of Appeal ruled that by voluntarily announcing his policy on the admission of children for adoption purposes, the Secretary of State had raised a 'reasonable expectation' that he would observe that policy. When he failed to do so, his decision could be overturned.[93] In 1985 the House of Lords interpreted s.26 of the 1971 Act narrowly and thereby avoided an increased role for the police in the investigation of immigration offences.[94] Most of these decisions[95] have not been based on novel common law developments (the tools to find in favour of the immigrant have always been available) but on judicial willingness. That willingness can be linked in part to the repercussions of the Scarman Report[96] in 1982 and the avowed official concern for ethnic minorities and public disorder. It may also be connected with the realisation that the bulk of coloured immigration is over, that the numbers of entrants are steadily declining and that the 'hold them back lest we be swamped' attitude of the 1970s is no longer so urgent.

(h) However, administrative law is still at a primitive stage of development and the occasional victory for the immigrant and judicial review can appear·Pyrrhic when viewed against the background of the last two decades.[97] Moreover, it would be premature to herald the recent magnanimity of the House of Lords as a permanent change of attitude. For the tradition of firmness towards immigration control is so well established and, as the House showed in 1983,[98] it is still quite prepared to support the Executive when the merits are balanced. Indeed, it is suggested that Amin was a perfect vehicle for the House to express further enlightened approach, especially since the matter for resolution (the administration of vouchers to U.K. Passport Holders) was uncluttered by precedents.

F. THEMES OF U.K. POLICY

(1) Lack of planning
In part this is due to the fact that the U.K. has not enjoyed the luxury of starting anew as a nation, unlike Commonwealth countries which have been able at an early stage of development to identify the type of immigrants they wanted. Of course this advantage can be abused. For in deciding (a) who is needed most and (b) who will fit into the host society best, States have tended to adopt racist policies e.g. the 'all white' approach in Australia, Canada, New Zealand and South Africa and the 'national origins quota' in the U.S. However, the advantage does at least enable a coherent policy to be formulated, one which can, if the will exists, then include provision for the reception and integration of mixed races. By contrast, the U.K.'s response to immigration has tended to be reactive rather than pro-active; ad hoc measures to cope with immediate problems. The unrestricted entry of Commonwealth citizens by virtue of the British Nationality Act 1948 is an excellent example of an unplanned open-door policy without sufficient thought being given to its long-term consequences. Thus, when the first batches of coloured entrants arrived after 1945, they were directed to employment exchanges and no further arrangements were made to deal with them. As the Minister of Labour pointed out, "If they suffer any inconvenience, the blame will be on those who sent them and not on those who receive them".99 When those long-term consequences emerged they were inevitably dealt with in a blunt and piecemeal fashion. Thus, in 1962 the Commonwealth Immigrants Act was passed amidst fears about the number of entrants and their effect on economic and social conditions. Yet, the research and public debate which precede similarly important measures were absent. Emotion and assertion governed instead. One can contrast the Royal Commission which preceded the Aliens Act 1905, or the Green Paper and Parliamentary Committee which preceded the reformulation of Canadian policy in 1976. The lesson is further illustrated by the Report of the Overseas Students Trust100 in 1982 into the options for a policy towards overseas students in higher education. Detailed research into the facts and comparative materials was conducted and a series of options was presented. It is unfortunate that a wide-ranging inquiry by Governments into all aspects of immigration law has been missing in the past two decades.

Again, though Governments have recently and repeatedly stated their belief in racial harmony, their supporting actions have not been fully committed. Reception centres for entrants, advisory and retraining services, and educational facilities have been slender.[101] The Government's role as a contractor has not been utilised properly to enforce the economic integration of immigrants.[102] One can compare here the much more positive commitment recently adopted in the U.S. to enforce equal opportunity programmes for Government contractors.[103] U.K. Governments have in brief adopted a lukewarm policy to the assimilation of immigrants. 'Once admitted, leave them to make their own way' has been the underlying approach rather than a concerted effort to translate platitudes into action.[104]

Thus the lack of a fundamental and wide-ranging overhaul of policy has been a signal characteristic of recent U.K. law.

(2) The Commonwealth
The law has been directly concerned in reflecting the U.K.'s changing views towards the Commonwealth. In 1948 it reaffirmed the practice of centuries by allowing entry as of right to Commonwealth citizens. Since 1962 it has been directed towards diluting the legal, political and sentimental obligations in various stages, culminating in the British Nationality Act 1981.

(3) Importance of the E.E.C.
The uncompromising legislative provisions for freedom of movement in the E.E.C. and the bold stance of the Court of Justice in their support contrast starkly with the lot of non-E.E.C., aspiring immigrants. Above all, in the E.E.C. field, the law is concerned with rights, not privileges, of entry. Apart from highlighting the disabilities attaching to non-E.E.C. entrants, the benevolent provisions of E.E.C. law illustrate perfectly the many national barriers which have to be dismantled before freedom of movement can be made effective. Thus, article 48 of the Treaty, which proclaims the principle of freedom of movement, cannot achieve its purpose without the support of much detailed secondary legislation, article 7 (which prohibits discrimination between nationals of Member States) and the considerable legislation under article 51 (which guarantees to E.E.C. nationals a variety of State financial benefits wherever they happen to be in the Community).

(4) International Law

It is an accepted maxim of international law that every sovereign nation has the power, as inherent in sovereignty, and essential to self-preservation, to forbid the entrance of foreigners within its dominions, or to

23

admit them only in such cases and upon such conditions as it may see fit to prescribe.[105]

This maxim retains its vitality and is certain to continue to do so. There are two possible limitations which must be carefully distinguished but neither of which represents a serious challenge to the maxim. Firstly, international law obligations, usually voluntarily initiated, may qualify the sovereign power. The voluntary nature of this obligation points to treaties. The Treaty of Rome is the best example of a surrender of sovereignty over immigration, but there have been earlier examples. Special treatment for diplomatic representatives boasts the longest tradition. Extradition since the late nineteenth century is well accepted and expanding in times of international terrorism. The grant of citizenship can involve in international law the acceptance of responsibilities,[106] as the U.K. discovered in 1972 in relation to expelled Ugandan Asians (UKPHs) and, to a much lesser extent, in relation to Kenyan Asians in 1968 and which it may yet discover in relation to Hong Kong. Other examples of international obligations include the embarrassment caused to the U.S. Federal Government in the late nineteenth century by States which sought to discriminate against Chinese immigrants in defiance of a treaty (the Burlingaume Treaty) signed between the U.S. and China;[107] the 'Gentleman's agreement' between the U.S. and Japan in 1907 ending Japanese immigration into the U.S.;[108] the embarrassment caused to the U.K. by Australian States whose discrimination against Chinese immigrants was incompatible with the U.K.'s treaty obligations to China.[109] More recent examples include the U.N. Coventions on the Status of Refugees (1951) and on the Reduction of Statelessness (1961) (which are reflectéd in the U.K. Rules and the Nationality Act 1981). However, the voluntary nature of treaty obligations means that international law has limited success in the area of immigration, as is emphasised by the facts that the U.K., though a signatory, has not ratified the Fourth Protocol to the European Convention of Human Rights (dealing with freedom of movement) and has deposited fatal reservations to the U.N. Covenant on Civil and Political Rights 1966 in respect of immigration and nationality.

The second, and separable, potential limitation on sovereignty comes occasionally through international pressure e.g. the U.K.'s agreement to accept a proportion of refugees, as in 1979 in relation to Vietnam, and, after E.E.C. pressure, to amend the British Nationality Act 1981 so as to entitle Gibraltarians and employees at Community institutions to qualify for the full benefit of British Citizenship.

(5) Bipartisan Policy
One of the strongest features of recent U.K. policy has been its bipartisan nature. Ever since the Labour Party produced

its White Paper in 1965 which endorsed the need for firm immigration control, there has been little difference in substance between Government and Opposition. Ritual denunciations by the latter against the former have of course been frequent but, when the roles have been reversed, there is little to choose between their records. Labour Governments are due some credit for enacting race relations legislation (though in a piecemeal fashion). On the other hand they are, it is suggested, more reprehensible because of their patent hypocrisy in having, formally at least, embraced the immigrant's case whilst in Opposition, yet ignored and frequently weakened it when in Government. This bipartisan policy has meant that

(a) the immigrant's quest for justice has been effectively denied throughout the period when requests for immigration have been heaviest and
(b) sections of the ethnic communities have become deeply cynical, not merely about the Executive, but also about the law.

(6) Concern for Civil Liberties

There have been many instances of this theme tempering the excesses of immigration control. For example, the liberal opinion of the Victorian era delayed control over aliens until 1905; belief in the ideals of the New World stalled the adoption of a literacy test in the U.S. until 1917 and national origins quotas until 1921; and attachment to the Commonwealth ideal lasted in the U.K. until 1962. More recently, the package of measures dealing with entrants to Australia also included the abolition of an English language test (which previously counted for 6 out of the 60 points required for entry); the updated Canadian legislation of 1976 emphasised the policy of racial equality; the infamous national origins quotas in the U.S. were abolished in 1965 in an atmosphere of civil rights' awareness; the proposed legislation in the U.S. in 1984 to control the employment of illegal immigrants was tempered by an amnesty for those who had entered before 1981; and the 1983 changes in the U.K. Rules were prompted in part by potential condemnation of previous practice under the European Convention on Human Rights.

Sensitivity to issues of civil liberties has produced other consequences. Firstly, Governments have sought to soften the blow of controls by issuing declarations and even policies in favour of race relations. Second, they have chosen indirect and therefore less overt methods of immigration control e.g. the administrative manipulation of visa systems. Third, being aware of the difficulty in walking the tight rope of control and race relations, they have often left backbench opinion to force change rather than 'lead from the front'. Fourth, the language of immigration debate has altered. The more extreme outbursts are of course still uttered by racist groups as they have been for centuries, but pangs of conscience have played a part in hiding forceful feelings - witness the lengths to which individuals may go in order to conceal their true feelings on immigration.

Increasing concern for civil liberties has certainly forced some countries to handle immigration issues sensitively. However, it is equally true that States have preserved for themselves all the powers necessary to control immigration severely, that they remain very willing to use them and that concessions to libertarian pressures are usually matched or exceeded by legislative measures for control.

(7) Immigration and Race Relations

Immigration control stems ultimately from the fears perceived by the host community about immigrants. This can be translated into the official imposition of civic, economic, legal and political disabilities placed on those immigrants who are admitted. Their potential economic effect and their strange habits and culture usually lead to other unofficial discrimination and hostility against them, for example, the mounting opposition and legal disabilities against Jews in the thirteenth century which reached a crescendo in 1290 with their expulsion. Signs of native opposition can thus be used negatively by a Government as a convenient coathanger to justify immigration control, for example, the Home Office's fear of creating a 'Jewish problem' (public disorder and violence against them) was a factor in carefully regulating the influx of Jews in the mid-1930s.[110] Since the 1960s internal racial harmony has been used positively by Governments to justify restriction, the argument being that immigration control is necessary for good race relations. Governments have thus harnessed the growing concern for good relations to the cause of tightening controls. The two subjects cannot be divorced since they form the same plank of official policy.

Concern for race relations has also been used as a sweetener to immigration control - the 1962 Act was matched by the establishment of the Commonwealth Immigrants Advisory Council in 1962 and the National Committee for Commonwealth Immigrants in 1964. The volte-face by the Labour Government in favour of tough controls in 1965 was counterbalanced by the first Race Relations Act, the Commonwealth Immigrants Act 1968 by the second and the 1971 Act and its continuation under a Labour Government by the third in 1976.[111] This use of race relations has, however, been superficial rather than realistic and comprehensive. This is illustrated by the continuing high levels of racial discrimination and disadvantage and the unwillingness of Governments to commit sustained effort and expenditure to their alleviation, not least in the Government's role as a major employer.[112]

26

In truth, the immigration/race relations policy can be a neat camouflage for defending institutional racism. It sounds plausible and humanitarian and avoids charges of racial superiority or economic self-interest.

As to the adverse effect of immigration control on race relations this is very rarely and only recently acknowledged officially. Thus, one of the reasons for relaxing the tough restrictions on returning residents in 1982 was the adverse effect which their implementation had on community relations[113] and similarly the exemption from the Data Protection Act 1984 for immigration information was dropped because it was "outweighed by the advantages for good race relations".[114] More fundamentally, the effect breeds amongst ethnic communities anger and resentment which are hardly beneficial to racial harmony, e.g. the considerable delays in uniting families because of the entry clearance procedure, or the judgment and consequences of the Zamir[115] decision.[116] On the native population, it confirms their suspicion of immigrants. Thus careful control is needed so as to prevent immigrants from taking jobs, houses etc. A tough policy of control is hardly likely to induce the population to treat entrants equally, especially since the conditioning of centuries has to be overcome, a conditioning which portrays immigrants as ultimately unwelcome. In its evidence to the Select Committee on Immigration and Race Relations in 1977, the Joint Council For The Welfare of Immigrants commented "What vitiates the assumption that a restrictive immigration policy allays racial hostility is the psychological effect, on both white and black, of the restrictive measures and of what is said to justify them". The effect of restrictive measures "has been to educate the white population thoroughly to believe that the presence of black people is an evil, in itself, and one so menacing as to override all other considerations".[117]

In short, the weaknesses of a policy which says 'immigration control is needed for good race relations' are that the former is pursued too rigorously and the latter half-heartedly.

(8) Assimilation or diversity

A host State must decide whether it wants immigrants to be identified with the native population or whether it is prepared to tolerate cultural diversity. The former is unattractively paternalistic and unattainable in the short-term, unless entrants are carefully selected because of their similar race and culture.[118] The latter exposes the immigrant - he is a readily visible scapegoat to which some, at least, of society's ills can be ascribed[119] - and it reinforces the belief of the native population that the immigrant is 'different' and unwilling to integrate. Thus, by 1976 according to one point of view some "inner-city centres ... have been changed out of all recognition ... [R]eality is

27

that immigrants in some areas are preserving their alien customs, religions and other practices which are very strange. The English language is sometimes furiously resisted. How is it possible to contemplate integration under these circumstances?".[120] In the U.K. diversity has been the officially preferred policy. As the Home Secretary remarked in 1966,

> I define integration not as a flattening process of assimilation but as equal opportunity, accompanied by cultural diversity, in an atmosphere of mutual tolerance. This is the goal.[121]

This noble policy must, however, contend with the 'scapegoat' phenomenon directed towards immigrants. This necessitates determined official efforts to eradicate discrimination and frequent and firm affirmations by the Government in support of immigrants. The affirmations have been muted compared to the vigour with which immigration control has been advocated.

(9) The Language of Immigration
It is not only the arguments about immigration which have persisted but also the language employed to sustain them. The principal metaphor is aquatic and references abound to floods, torrents, rivers, streams, pools, flows, trickles, dams, barriers and floodgates. Given the passions which immigration arouses, it is not surprising that the history of debate is rich in invective. This still thrives in the publications of the racist groups (e.g. the National Front's youth magazine 'Bulldog') and more commonly in graffiti. However, the sensitivity to race relations and sanction of the criminal law, in the shape of the offence of incitement to racial hatred, have meant that argument today tends to be couched more frequently in more guarded tones. For example, the suggestion by Mr. Enoch Powell[122] that a Department of immigration and repatriation (with the emphasis on the latter and with the subtle argument that new Commonwealth entrants have acquired from the U.K. skills which would be beneficial to their ancestral countries) be set up or by a Monday Club[123] pamphlet that financial inducements be offered to produce 50,000 repatriations per year, are only thinly veiled versions of the 'kick them out' policy. At official level the recent tones have been much more guarded with references being made to the 'pressure', 'public concern' and the like aroused by the subject. For example, in a statement of Government policy in 1982, a Home Office Minister produced the following understatement:

> What we have always said is that there has been a certain amount of tension and apprehension which can lead to friction because people have this sense of pressure from

immigrants coming into this country. I think that by achieving a reduction in immigrant numbers we have, in fact, helped to relieve this sense of pressure and I think that is for the good of race relations.[124]

It is commendable that speakers feel constrained to tread carefully when speaking of immigration control, but underlying such statements are the unmistakeable messages of unwelcome to immigrants and of appeasement to the native population. Rather like sex in earlier times, blunt references to immigration control are frequently taboo and are replaced by euphemisms and innuendo.

Another characteristic of immigration debate is to argue by extremes. Thus, a response to a call for the liberal treatment of immigrants is either automatically prefaced by the 'overriding need for firm immigration control', or concluded by the warning that capitulation to the call will 'open the floodgates'. For example, the Home Office emotively warns that "to fail to take action against people who have deliberately abused the law would not be fair to those who have observed it".[125] Yet no one suggests inaction; rather the issue concerns the extent of that action. Similarly, a ruling by the European Court of Human Rights[126] in favour of fiances and husbands of settled immigrants is greeted by the headline, 'A Bride's Charter', and arouses fears 'that thousands of foreign men will now flood into the country'.[127]

The media, like politicians, see little popularity in espousing the cause of immigrants, preferring to concentrate on the negative side of immigration and pandering to public antipathy. One Minister was prompted to remark, "I think it is a very good thing for race relations that immigration should not be making headlines in this country; it helps everybody, particularly those people who are coming to this country".[128] This statement is superficially attractive, for tension in race relations' terms would doubtless be eased if immigration difficulties were to be ignored by the media. They would not, however, disappear. So, more important is the way in which the immigrant is portrayed by the press and by the speeches of politicians which it reports. More moderate exposition is required, for example, placing the level of immigration in the context of emigration from the U.K. and eschewing references to 'floods' and similar metaphors. Politicians should take a central role by providing copy to the press which concentrates on the positive side of immigration.

G. POLICY OPTIONS

(1) No restriction
For most of the U.K.'s history since 1066 this has been the preferred policy. It ended for aliens in 1905 and for Commonwealth citizens in 1962. An open-door policy does not

mean that aliens are unrestricted in what they can do once admitted or that they are free from the possibility of expulsion. Thus, the grant of citizenship may be denied to them or carefully regulated; their economic activities may be circumscribed e.g. by the payment of extra taxes, the denial of trading licences, an obligation to train local workers in their business; legal, civic and political rights may be withheld.

(2) Qualitative control

Once control has been inaugurated in the U.K. this method has been the most popular; and the criteria used are universal. The first to be excluded are normally the spies, the destitute, the ill and criminals (e.g. Aliens Act 1905). In times of political unrest, troublemakers are an obvious target (e.g. the aliens legislation from 1793 to 1814 directed against France). In economic recession, the economically superfluous are readily barred (e.g. the abolition of Category C voucher holders (mainly unskilled) in 1965 but not the skilled and professional - see also the current r.33 which sets out a list of professions which do not need a work permit). Once primary immigration is regulated, humanitarian concession normally requires the admission of dependants with preference being given to them over other applicants (e.g. the points' system in Canada and Australia and the preference quotas in the U.S.). Since, however, the numbers inevitably exceed the heads of household already admitted, a State which is concerned with the annual figures for immigration will turn its attention to this area. Thus, controversy will surround the definition of dependants (e.g. aged parents, uncles and aunts) and their age limits (e.g. for children), and steps will be taken to prevent primary immigrants from entering under cover of dependency (e.g. husbands, fiances and male children).

An alternative method is to ally the above criteria to race, by excluding immigrants on a straight ethnic basis. Blatant examples appear in the Old Commonwealth and the U.S. In these countries considerable steps were taken, for example, to exclude Chinese and Japanese immigration. Thus, in 1882, four years before the dedication of the Statue of Liberty, the Chinese Exclusion Act[129] was passed in the U.S. following pressure from the individual States. The same result had almost been achieved by the States of Australia by the end of the 1880s. In 1907 a Gentleman's Agreement was reached between the U.S. and Japan to exclude Japanese immigrants.[130] In the U.S. 87% of immigrants who landed in 1882 came from northern Europe. By 1907 however 80% came from southern Europe. Strenuous efforts were then made to reverse this change and preserve the 'Anglo-Saxon stock'. Thus, in 1917[131] undesirable Asian immigrants were excluded by the simple expedient of outlawing immigration for those persons born within specified, geographical areas (the Asia-Pacific Triangle, in effect most of the Far East). As to the rest, in 1921[132] each group of entrants was confined to 3% of their representation in the 1910 Census and in 1924[133] this policy was further promoted in favour of North European settlers by cutting the proportion to 2% and the baseline to the Census of 1890 (which favoured the North Europeans much more). Compared to the 'all white' policies of Australia, Canada and New Zealand and the national origins quotas in the U.S., the U.K.'s policy of excluding coloured immigrants has been much less blatantly expounded. Acts and Rules have been neutrally worded, with a universal application in theory. It has, instead, been the practical effect which has matched the more overtly prejudicial laws of other countries. The prime example is the concept of patriality under the 1971 Act (s.2), the definition of which inevitably favoured potential entrants from the Old Commonwealth. This policy has been continued under the British Nationality Act 1981. British Dependent Territories Citizenship and British Overseas Citizenship have been given mainly to those in the New Commonwealth yet the statuses do not entitle the holder to enter the U.K. Other indirect methods of qualitative control have included a wide range of criteria, such as literacy tests, to sift out the more assimilable immigrants as in the U.S. and Australia.

(3) Quantitative control
This method can be direct or indirect. As to the former, the proscription can take the form of a simple quota on certain kinds of entrants.[134] In the U.K. examples are the annual issue of work permits, the quotas allowed to United Kingdom Passport Holders (UKPHs) and any international arrangements for the reception of refugees. Such direct methods are unusual unless linked to (2), above, (e.g. quotas according to the qualitative criterion of nationality or quotas of dependants subject to a ceiling for each country). More commonly the methods employed are indirect such as

(a) taxes on entry e.g. the U.S. in 1882 and Australia throughout the 1870s and 1880s;
(b) limitations on the number of immigrants which a ship could carry e.g. the Aliens Act 1905 (limited to 20), the Chinese Immigrants Restriction Act 1881 (New Zealand);
(c) administrative measures calculated to ease the rate of admission e.g.[135] the deployment of immigration officials to process applications for entry, changes in the mode and standard of proof required of prospective entrants, and pressures on the sponsor of incoming dependants in the host country. The U.K.'s entry clearance system offers a ready illustration.

In the U.K. method (2) has been traditionally employed but, in the face of pressure of numbers, it has been regularly used alongside (3).

(4) A complete bar

Apart, obviously, from the prohibition of specific classes (e.g. the insane or destitute), in the U.K. this method has been used infrequently on a general level. Historical examples are the banishment of Jews from 1290 until the mid-seventeenth century and the exclusion of religious refugees in the sixteenth century. However, modern practice has come close to such a policy in indirect ways, for example, the admission of aged dependants for settlement or even visits is often extremely limited. Thus, the number of successful applicants from the Indian sub-continent "has been virtually nil".[136]

(5) Visas

The use of a preliminary hurdle for immigrants to surmount while in their country of origin is a feature of current international migration control.[137] The aspiring immigrant must normally apply to the diplomatic representatives of the country of destination to secure preliminary approval for entry. Consequently

(a) any approval for entry is strictly preliminary and can be overturned on arrival; ·
(b) approval is usually based on wide discretionary powers; and
(c) a successful challenge to the exercise of that power is extremely difficult since it depends on what procedures for appeal have been conceded by the host country. In the U.K. system the procedures are illusory, as members of the House of Lords observed in 1983.[138]

H. STATISTICS

The recording of the number of entrants is the first and least step which a country can take in regulating immigration. The collection of such data can then fulfil various purposes. Firstly, and obviously, it informs the host country of the scale of its immigration. Second, it can then assist the country's assessment of its future capacity to absorb immigrants. If, third, the collection of details is allied to a power to exclude certain types of entrant, undesirable categories can then be weeded out. Basic statistics are thus essential to a sensible and coherent policy of immigration. Yet the U.K. offers a particularly poor record in this respect.

The statutory provisions for record collection of 1836[139] quickly fell into disuse and this meant that until 1905 the only reliable, but limited, indicator of immigration were the Censuses. The more sophisticated Act of 1905 still contained many deficiencies (e.g. the exception for cabin passengers). It has only been since 1914 that the recording of aliens' entry has been adequately supplied (e.g. by registration with the police, the issue of work permits). The treatment of Commonwealth citizens followed the same course. They remained free from calculation and control until 1962 and thereafter the collection of data has developed in a piecemeal fashion. The frequent modifications over the past twenty years in the way in which the data have been collected and presented have made long-term comparisons inaccurate. There have been two primary sources

   (a) Home Office statistics which are published quarterly and annually. They are designed to record immigrants not visitors and give an accurate reflection of those non-British citizens entering for settlement and for other specific purposes such as study or employment. They exclude British citizens and those who have entered via the Common Travel Area.
   (b) The Office of Population and Censuses and Surveys (published quarterly and annually) which commenced in 1961 and is run by the Department of Trade and Industry. It collects data on "immigration and emigration which is needed for demographic purposes and as an input for economic and social studies".[140] The data consist of interviews with a random sample of passengers. From them limited projections of future immigration are possible.

There are secondary sources for work permits (Department of Employment) and students (Department of Education and Science).
   Both primary sources are irreconcilable,[141] partly because of the different definitions employed and partly because of the different methods employed to collect the information. Both systems, but particularly that of the Home Office, have met with considerable criticism. The most devastating came from the Select Committee (1978) which observed generally, "There are no reliable figures about immigrants now resident in the United Kingdom: no reliable statistics which can be described as indicators of immigration: and, even under immigration control, no official estimates published of the numbers that may be expected to apply to be, and will be, admitted in the future, in any particular category, or overall".[142]
   One of the most serious omissions from current statistics is the lack of reliable data on emigration from the U.K. They used to be collected but, when Sir Claus Moser produced two reports highlighting their inaccuracy,[143] the Home Office

concluded that implementation of his recommendations would be too expensive and terminated the collection of embarkation statistics in 1977. The implication for immigration debate of this omission is obvious. Debate is one-sided when only the numbers of entrants are publicised. The counterbalancing effect of emigration is either ignored or understated.

As regards figures on entry, the traditional lack of systematic and accurate information has had a powerful impact on debate and, indirectly, on Government policy. Thus, a feature of debate since 1960 has been a preoccupation with the 'numbers game', and the absence of precise data and sound forecasts has enabled opponents of immigration to make merry with alarmist predictions; for example, about the size of the coloured population at the turn of this century. They can give greater credibility to statements such as the following:

> Immigration has completely altered the face of certain parts of this country. It has, as we know, created foreign enclaves in our midst. It has brought into this country alien people who live alongside us, whose religion, customs and habits are quite different from ours. In this way it has fundamentally altered the character of this country.[144]

In turn, imprecise or unavailable statistics have meant that frequently Governments, had they wished to, have been unable to counter rumour with hard facts. On the contrary, Governments have tended to be swayed by rumour. For example, the tightening of controls on the admission of husbands and fiances in 1977 was clearly prompted by the fear of a 'flood' of such entrants. Yet, when pressed, the Government was unable to quantify the fear. Before the 1979 general election the leader of the Opposition, in outlining its policy, referred to fears that "this country might be rather swamped by people with a different culture"[145] and the subsequent Conservative Party Manifesto made similar use of the public's fears of the size of coloured immigration in order to justify restrictive proposals. Yet throughout the debate at that time exaggeration rather than sober calculation of figures prevailed. Similar uncertainty has surrounded other aspects of statistics. The cancellation of the 1976 Census and the omission, after fierce public controversy, of a question on ethnic origin from the 1981 Census mean that not even an accurate picture of the size of the immigrant population in the U.K. is available. Even as regards students, the Foreign Affairs Committee recently commented, "We were surprised to discover the inadequacy of the official statistics on the numbers of overseas students as a whole ... Students are confused with trainees; students on short courses are confused with students on a full academic year's course; even the stock of students is confused with the flow of students through the system".[146]

The absence of precise data has been a major barrier to the public awareness of the realities of immigration and to the possibility of any relaxation in the rigours of control.

I. CURRENT POSITION

1. In 1982 and 1983 the total number of passengers given leave to enter the U.K. remained roughly the same, about $11^1/_2$ million, and in 1984 rose to $12^1/_2$ million. Of these over 5 million were E.E.C. nationals.[147]
2. Those accepted for settlement (either on arrival or the removal of time limits) in 1984 were 50,950 the lowest figure since 1973. As the following Table shows, there has been a steady fall in this category since 1976:

Total Acceptances for settlement (thousands of persons)

1972	92.2	1978	72.3
1973	55.2	1979	69.7
1974	68.9	1980	69.8
1975	82.4	1981	59.1
1976	80.7	1982	53.9
1977	69.3	1983	53.5

3. Of the 50,950 in 1984,

   (a) 26,720 were Commonwealth citizens
   (b) 24,230 were foreign nationals (including Pakistan)

4. As regards (a), they included:

3,590	Australia
4,180	Bangladesh
5,140	India
2,460	New Zealand
2,690	British Overseas Citizens

   As regards (b), they included:

1,670	Iran
5,510	Pakistan
3,750	U.S.
1,600	stateless/refugees

5. Expressed in terms of likely colour, 15% of the 50,950 in 1984 came from the Old Commonwealth, 38% from the New Commonwealth and 11% from Pakistan.
6. Most significantly, those accepted in 1984 for settlement on arrival (22,970) were the lowest figure since 1962.

   The West Indians were the first coloured immigrants of significant number to enter the U.K. after 1945. The vast majority had arrived by the beginning of the 1960s. Their immigration has for long been negligible.[148] Entrants from the Asian sub-continent then predominated. The admission of their dependants has been steadily falling, after reaching a peak in 1975/6 for India and in 1977 for Pakistan. A further indication of this trend is the decline in applications for entry clearance in the Indian sub-continent which dropped by over 10,000 from 1978 to 1984.[149] The exception is Bangladesh whose primary immigrants tended to reach the U.K. after those from India and Pakistan. Applications from their dependants are still therefore holding steady.[150] Overall, if 1976 is used as the base year, entrants from the New Commonwealth and Pakistan have fallen by nearly two thirds for settlement on arrival and by a third for settlement on removal of time limits.

7. Elsewhere, entrants from the Old Commonwealth and foreign nationals have either remained constant or risen relatively slightly.[151] Work permit holders have numbered around 18,000 since 1977, with only 17% coming from the Commonwealth; residence permits issued to E.E.C. nationals have remained within the 6-8,000 bracket since 1975. The controversial category of entry for marriage has fluctuated in response to changes in the Rules. In 1984, 3,710 husbands and fiances entered compared to 4,300 fiancees. What has concerned public and official opinion, of course, is the large percentage of New Commonwealth and Pakistan applicants (2,040 out of the 3,710 men and 5,580 out of the 8,010 total for husbands, fiances and fiancees). For those in the Asian sub-continent marriage remains the best opportunity for primary immigration.[152] Yet in terms of overall immigration the numbers remain disproportionately small compared to the public outcry which they have generated.

8. Entry for marriage is one illustration of how the annual statistics can only be properly read in the light of changes in the Rules, since changes can affect the right or rate of entry; e.g. the decisions to admit husbands and fiances in 1974, to control them in 1977, to tighten control in 1980 and to relax control in 1983;[153] the tightening control over relatives in 1980. Similar effects on statistics can be readily and more insidiously achieved by changes in administration e.g. deployment of entry clearance officers (e.c.os.), changes in the entry clearance (e.c.) procedure,[154] efforts to detect illegal entrants.[155]

9. Since 1968 primary immigration from the New Commonwealth and Pakistan has been clearly under control. UKPHs are the only sizeable outstanding obligation. That from the E.E.C. has fallen since 1973 and is likely to remain low for as long as economic conditions are uninviting. The Old Commonwealth offers a potentially enormous entry of former patrials who have the right to enter though the number who do has so far remained fairly constant and low.[156] As to secondary immigration only the latecomers from Bangladesh are out of step with the pattern of steady decline and

they too will decrease soon. In the absence of a register of dependants yet to enter the U.K., it is not possible to estimate reliably the scope of secondary immigration. Proposals to compile such a register have to date foundered and it is now too late in the day for the cost of such an exercise to be justified. The preoccupation with it in the late 1970s however is illustrative of the hold which "the numbers game" has on public opinion and the desperate search for further controls in an area which is already overpoliced. What is clear is that the scale of secondary immigration is steadily decreasing. It will never end, partly because the Rules permit limited forms of entry e.g. for marriage, and partly because the U.K. will not close its doors to all unforeseen migration. The frequent use by politicians of the slogan 'end to immigration' or references to its 'finite nature' are thus misguided, not simply because they are factually wrong but also because they tend to reinforce in the public eye the overwhelming importance of statistics. When those statistics are in turn unavailable, the fear tends to grow.

----

1   Lord Atkinson in A.G. for Canada v Cain [1906] AC 542, at p.546.

2   E.g. the Conventions on the Status of Refugees (1951) and of Stateless Persons (1954), the Convention on the Elimination of Racial Discrimination (1966).

3   The E.E.C. Treaty is a notable exception, see ch. 5.

4   Per Mr. Justice Field in Chae Chan Ping v U.S. 130 U.S. 581.

5   E.g. Fong Yue Ting v U.S. 149 U.S. 698 (1892); Turner v Williams 194 U.S. 279 (1903); Harisiades v Shaughnessy 342 U.S. 580 (1952).

6   39 Stat. 874.

7   From the many examples, consider Fong Yue Ting v U.S. 149 U.S. 698, Haig v Agee 453 U.S. 280; cf. Immigration and Naturalisation Service v Chadha 103 S. Ct. 2764 (1983).

8   So as to avoid any duplication, chiefly with chapter 2, footnote references are in the main avoided for the examples used in this chapter.

9   Select Committee on the Laws Affecting Aliens, 1843, P.P. vol. v, p.iv.

10   Lipson, The Economic History of England, vol. II, p. xc.

11   Passengers Act, 15 and 16 Vict. c.44.

12   16 and 17 Vict. c.84.

13   E.g. Chinese Immigration Restriction Act 1888 (Victoria) and see the facts of Musgrove v Chun Teeong Toy [1891] A.C. 272.

14   E.g. the Front National's 12% electoral vote in a by-election at Morbihan on 11 December 1983. Cf. the success of right wing political parties in elections to the European Parliament in 1984 (10 from France's Front National, 5 from the Italian Socialist Movement and one from the Greek Epen party).

15   Times, 4 July 1983, for an account of the measures, e.g. a payment of DM 10,500 and a partial refund of pension contributions to each unemployed foreign worker prepared to depart.

38

16 Immigration Reform and Control Bill. For background, see Guardian, 24 July 1982, Economist, 6 June 1981, p.46.

17 And see Times, 8 January 1983. Cf. Nigeria's expulsion of Ghanaian labour in 1983 and 1985.

18 Cmnd. 1741.

19 For a powerful account of such beliefs, see Walvin, Black and White, (1973).

20 Cf. the comments of Senator Alan Simpson, sponsor of the Immigration Reform and Control Bill 1983, "if language and cultural separatism rise above a certain level, the unity and political stability of the nation will, in time, be seriously eroded".

21 S.312 Immigration and Nationality Act 1952. Note the shift in Australia's policy in June 1985 to encourage more British settlers by according greater value to English language ability. The change follows a decline in British emigration and a rise in East Asian emigration.

22 32 Stat. 1213.

23 E.g. membership of, or affiliation to, the Communist Party - Immigration and Nationality Act 1952, s.313.

24 See the account of Elizabethan attitudes to 'Blackamoors' in Walvin, Black and White, (1973).

25 10 April 1866.

26 John Woods M.P. for the State of Victoria in a debate on voting rights, 10 November 1881 Victorian Parliamentary Debates, p.699. For a rich source of material see Price, The Great White Walls are Built. Cf. the excellent illustration of racial superiority in the despatch of the Prime Minister of Victoria to the U.K. Government, Times, 2 June 1888, p.5.

27 E.g. the British Brothers League in the U.K. at the turn of the century, in the U.S. the Know Nothing Party in the 1850s and Klu Klux Klan in the 1920s, in Australia the Anti-Chinese and Asiatic League of the Commonwealth at the end of the nineteenth century and in New Zealand the White Race League in 1905.

28 S.6 Race Relations Act 1965; see now s.70 Race Relations Act 1976; cf. New Zealand, Race Relations Act 1971, s.25.

29 See Bindman (1982) NLJ 299. For proposals to strengthen the offence, see Review of Public Order Law, Cmnd. 9510, paras. 6.5-6.9 (1985).

30 Longmore, Immigration Limited: Britain's Case, Mankind Monographs IV, 1962. See too, Bertram, West Indian Immigration, Eugenics Society, 1958 (a diatribe against the mixing of races and in favour of 'quality' control on the entry of aliens).

31 Minister for Immigration, Australian Tradition in Immigration, (1949), p.5. See further London, Non-White Immigration and the 'White Australia' Policy, (1970); cf. the increased agitation in Australia in 1984 over the rise in the level of Asian immigration and the fall in migrants from Northern Europe.

32 The limitation dated from 1917.

33 7 Jam 1 c.2 (1609).

34 Scott v Sandford 19 How (U.S.) 393 (1857); reversed in 1868 by the passage of the Fourteenth Amendment to the Constitution.

35 Elk v Wilkins 112 U.S. 94 (1884); reversed in 1924 by Act of Congress (43 Stat. 253). Cf in New Zealand the decision by the Minister of Internal Affairs in 1908 not to naturalise any more Chinese, which meant that for 44 years no Chinese were naturalised, see Fong, Chinese Immigration in New Zealand, p.36ff.

36 (1913) 12 D.L.R. 656.

37 H.C. Debs. 15 December, col. 355; see Joyles [1972] 1 WLR 1390.

38 Hosenball [1977] 1 WLR 766, at 780-1, and see also Geoffrey Lane L.J. at 785-6.

39 Per Lord Roskill in Alexander [1982] 2 All ER 766, at p.770.

40 Or "para-statutory framework", Lord Wilberforce in Zamir [1980] A.C. 930, at 948. Cf. the status of the Prison Rules (1964, S.I. 1964/388) and Standing Orders (e.g. Arbon v Anderson [1943] K.B. 252, St. Germain [1979] Q.B. 425, Raymond v Honey [1983] A.C.1) and the Judges' Rules (Home Office Circular 89/1978, Appendices A and B), see R v Prager [1972] 1 WLR 260, R v Voisin (1918) 13 Cr.App.R. 89.

41 Cf. Pearson [1978] Imm. A.R. 212 (Court of Appeal).
Whereas, if the immigrant asks the court for a flexible
interpretation, he is often met by the view that the rules
must be strictly obeyed e.g. Khatoon Ali [1979-80] Imm. A.R.
195.

42 See Guardian, 21 March 1984 and paras. 5.9. 10-15 of the
C.R.E. Report into Immigration control Procedures (1985).

43 See the analysis of the majority in the House of Lords in
Amin [1983] 2 A.C. 818, and further ch. 5.

44 Cf. the position in Australia where judicial review and
natural justice have made little headway, e.g. Minister for
Immigration v Gaillard 49 A.L.R. 277 (1983), which ruled that
s.7 of the Migration Act 1958 means what it says - "the
Minister may, in his absolute discretion, cancel ...." - and
that natural justice, even in its most limited form, has no
role to play. See also Sezdirmezoglu 51 A.L.R. 561 (1984).

45 Obvious examples include the use of drugs or secure units
to control troublesome prisoners, see the facts of Williams v
Home Office (No.2) [1981] 1 All E.R. 1211.

46 Until given wide publicity in 1979 (Guardian, 1 and 9
February 1979) and withdrawn - H.C. Debs. 9 February, col.
312, 21 March, col. 672 (virginity tests), 22 February, col.
2075 (x-rays for pregnant women prohibited).

47 'Box 500', as revealed by the Guardian 24 October 1979.

48 See the account by Grant (1979) L.A.G. 155.

49 For a description of the various divisions in the Home
Office, see the Report on the Work of the Immigration and
Nationality Department (1984, Home Office), at p.9.

50 Contrast Daganayasi v Minister of Immigration [1980] 2
N.Z.L.R. 130 (natural justice obliged the Minister to disclose
a medical referee's report to the entrant so that she could
deal with its findings).

51 Cook J. in Ashby v Minister of Immigration [1981] N.Z.L.R.
222, at p.226.

52 E.g. Wong Yang Sung v McGrath 339 U.S. 33.(1950); Gastelum
-Quinones v Kennedy 374 U.S. 469 (1963).

53 Immigration Act 1976, c.52, Part IV.

54 In Khawaja [1984] A.C. 74.

55 E.g. Re Georges 22 A.L.R. 667, Drake 24 A.L.R. 577, Haj-Ismail 40 A.L.R. 341; in similar vein, cf. A.G. of Hong Kong v Ng Yuen Shiu [1983] 2 A.C. 629.

56 See chapter 3.

57 Musgrove v Chun Teeong Toy [1891] A.C. 272, at p.282; cf. the position of prisoners e.g. the privilege, not right, of parole -Gunnell (1983) L.S.Gaz. 3238.

58 A.G. for Canada v Cain [1906] A.C. 542.

59 There are a few reported cases giving guidance on relevant factors to be considered e.g. R v Kleiss (1910) 4 Cr. App. Rep. 101, Zausmer (1911) 7 Cr. App. Rep. 41, Friedman (1914) 10 Cr. App. Rep. 72.

60 For an excellent example, see Liversidge v Anderson [1942] A.C. 206.

61 For a recent example of a decision which shuts the door to the review of discretion, see Wirdestedt, Times, 12 December 1984.

62 See Bhagwan [1972] A.C. 60, and Ahsan and Phansopkar, infra.

63 [1974] A.C. 18.

64 H.C. Debs. 11 April 1974, col. 637. Extended until the end of 1978 - H.C. Debs. 29 November 1977, col. 125.

65 [1969] 2 Q.B. 222.

66 At p.241.

67 [1976] 1 W.L.R. 971.

68 By the simple statement, "I detain this man by virtue of an order under paragraph 16 of Schedule 2 to the Act of 1971", at p.979.

69 Ibid.

70 Principally, Hussain [1978] 1 W.L.R. 700, Choudhary [1978] 1 W.L.R. 1177. For a discussion of administrative law in immigration see Harlow and Rawlings, Law and Administration, chs. 16 and 17.

71 [1980] A.C. 930; for a fuller discussion, see chapter 8.

72 H.C. Debs. 29 November 1977, col. 125.

73 H.C. Debs. 20 July 1978, col. 306.

74 Mohamed Arif [1968] Ch. 643.

75 At p.661.

76 Cf. Re D [1977] Fam. 158, Re H [1978] Fam. 65, Re C.B. [1981] 1 All E.R. 16, Re J. [1984] 1 All E.R. 29.

77 Thakrar [1974] Q.B. 684, at p.707.

78 Race Relations Board v Charter [1973] A.C. 868; Race Relations Board v Dockers' Labour Club and Institute Ltd [1976] A.C. 285.

79 [1972] A.C. 342.

80 The development is perfectly illustrated by the decision in Asif Mahmood Khan, [1985] 1 All E.R. 40.

81 Not simply by the immigrant; see the subtlety of the Home Office's case in Coomasaru [1983] 1 W.L.R. 14.

82 E.g. Phansopkar [1976] Q.B. 606.

83 Salamat Bibi [1976] 1 W.L.R. 979; cf. Bhajan Singh [1976] Q.B. 198; Amin [1983] 2 A.C. 818. See also Fernandes [1981] Imm. A.R. 1, Kirkwood [1984] 2 All E.R. 390. Cf. the reasoning in Ashby v Minister of Immigration [1981] 1 N.Z.L.R. 222 in relation to the U.N. Convention for the Elimination of Racial Discrimination; and in Australia, see Sezdirmezoglu (No.2) (1984) 51 A.L.R. 575, Kioa v Minister for Immigration (1984) 53 A.L.R. 658, 55 A.L.R. 624 and Mayer v Minister for Immigration (1984) 55 A.L.R. 587.

84 For an illustration of the benefit which the Convention can bring, see Abdulaziz, Balkandali and Cabales v U.K., press 29 May 1985.

85 Per Lord Bridge in Khawaja [1984] A.C. 74 at p.122.

86 Per Lord Scarman at p.111.

87 Shah [1983] 2 A.C. 309.

88 For Parliament reversed the effects of the decision - Education (Fees and Awards) Regulations, S.I. 1983/973.

89 Per Lord Fraser in Mandla v Dowell Lee [1983] 2 A.C. 548, at p.563; for the Court of Appeal, see [1983] Q.B.1.

90 Per Lord Roskill in Alexander [1982] 2 All E.R. 766, at p.770. See also Grant v Borg [1982] 2 All E.R. 257 in which the House held in favour of the immigrant by ruling that an offence under s.24(1)(b)(i) of the 1971 Act was not a continuing one; see the attempt to reverse the effects of the decision - Immigration Offences (Amendment) Bill 1984. Cf. Arif v Merryweather [1970] Crim.L.Rev. 221.

91 Hardial Singh, [1984] 1 All E.R. 983.

92 A-G of Hong Kong v Ng Yuen Shiu [1983] 2 A.C. 629.

93 Asif Mahmood Khan, [1985] 1 All E.R. 40

94 R v Clarke, Times, 21 June 1985.

95 Except for Ng and Khan, supra, which were based on the concept of 'legitimate expectation', which originated in Schmidt v Secretary of State [1969] 2 Ch 149 and was endorsed in O'Reilly v Mackman [1983] 2 A.C. 237.

96 The Brixton Disorders 10-12 April 1981, cmnd. 8427.

97 For relatively minor victories for the immigrant, see for example, Rahmani, Times, 14 January 1985, Gowa v A.G., Times, 27 December 1984.

98 Amin [1983] 2 A.C. 818.

99 H.C. Debs. 8 June 1948, col. 1852.

100 See ch. 7.

101 The Polish Resettlement Act 1947 and the Ugandan Resettlement Board of 1972 were notable exceptions.

102 Cf. the Government's insignificant efforts to ensure racial equality in the civil service e.g. the revelation before the Home Affairs Committee in 1981 that the sole example of formal training had been a seminar in the Civil Service College in 1977, H.C. 424-1, para. 45 (1980-81).

103 Through the use of non-discrimination clauses and machinery to enforce them - Committee on Government Contract Compliance (1951), subsequently the Office of Federal Contract Compliance (1965), and see Exec. Order 11478 (1969).

104 Witness further the delay over the implementation of the

Commission for Racial Equality's Code of Practice for employers which was drafted in 1981 but did not take effect until April 1984.

[105] Per Mr. Justice Gray in Ekiu v U.S. 142 U.S. 651 (1891), at p.654.

[106] E.g. U.N. Declaration of Human Rights (1948) art. 13(2): see Oppenheim, vol. I, Para. 294; Weis, p.45-49.

[107] See Price, The Great White Walls are Built.

[108] U.S. Executive Order No. 589.

[109] See Willard, History of the White Australian Policy to 1920.

[110] See sources cited by Sherman, The Island Refuge.

[111] Significantly, however, the statutory prohibition on racial discrimination does not extend to the procedures for immigration control.

[112] From the extensive literature, note the Report of the Home Affairs Committee on Racial Disadvantage, H.C. 424 (1980-81).

[113] C.R.E. Report on Immigration Control Procedures (1985), paras. 5.16. 1-8.

[114] H.O. Report on the Work of the Immigration and Nationality Department (1984), ch. 11, para. 20.

[115] [1980] A.C. 930.

[116] Cf. the favourable and expedited treatment accorded to a South African athlete's application for citizenship (Miss Zola Budd) in April 1984 and the resentment which its haste provoked amongst coloured applicants.

[117] H.C. 201, Evidence, vii.

[118] E.g. language tests or the national origins quotas formerly used in the U.S. to favour North European immigrants.

[119] Note the recent opposition in France to North African workers, in Germany to Turkish guestworkers and in Nigeria to imported Ghanaian labour.

[120] Mr. Nicholas Winterton M.P., Times, 20 November 1976.

[121] See Patterson, Immigration and Race Relations in Britain,

p.113.

[122] Times, 10 May 1982. See further Guardian, 12 July 1980 and Times, 9 November 1981, 6 October 1982.

[123] Immigration, Repatriation and the Commission for Racial Equality, Proctor and Pinniger (1981).

[124] Mr. Timothy Raison M.P., interview with the Guardian, 10 May 1982.

[125] Report on the Work of the Immigration and Nationality Department (1984), p.5 during a statement of policy.

[126] Abdulaziz, Balkandali and Cabales v U.K., press 29 May 1985.

[127] Daily Mail, 29 May 1985.

[128] Mr. Timothy Raison M.P. in Evidence to H.A.C. (1982), Q.364.

[129] 22 Stat. 58.

[130] 37 Stat. 1504.

[131] 39 Stat. 874.

[132] 42 Stat. 5.

[133] 43 Stat. 153.

[134] E.g. s.7, Immigration Act 1976 (Canada) whereby the Government annually sets an 'appropriate' figure for immigration.

[135] See the 1924 Johnson-Reed Act in the U.S., supra, and the development of entry clearance in the U.K. since 1962.

[136] Home Office Minister in evidence to the Home Affairs Committee (1981-82) H.C. 90-II Q 451 and see further Q 448 and Appendix 11, para. 19 (New Delhi).

[137] Contrast the Migration Amendment Act 1979 (Australia) which required a visa in addition to an entry permit; see also the Immigration Bill 1983 (New Zealand). For the dramatic effect which a visa requirement can have, see the case of Sri Lanka in 1985 (H.C. Debs. 3 June 1985, col. 52).

[138] Khawaja [1984] A.C. 74.

[139] 6 and 7, Will IV, c.11.

[140] OPCS, Occasional Paper 15 (1979), p.1.

[141] Appendix 2, Select Committee on Race Relations and Immigration (1978) H.C. 303.

[142] Report, para. 41. For the detailed criticisms see paras. 42-49, and the Second Moser Report - Report on the general significance of statistics of admissions and embarkations, Sir Claus Moser.

[143] Ibid, and Report on errors relating to embarkations of Commonwealth citizens from Heathrow, January 1973-July 1974, the First Moser Report.

[144] Mr. John Stokes M.P., H.C. Debates, 4 March 1976, col. 1643 (a debate on the Race Relations Bill). Such sentiments are scattered throughout recent discussion, see, for example, those cited in Garrard, The English and Immigration; Foot, Immigration and Race in British Politics.

[145] Granada Television interview, for the transcript, see Times, 31 January 1978.

[146] Third Report, Foreign Affairs Committee, H.C. 553 (1979-80), para. 12.

[147] These and the following statistics are taken from Home Office: Control of Immigration Statistics, 1984 cmnd. 9544 and earlier issues (for a full list, see Bibliography) and the Home Office: Statistical Bulletins (published quarterly).

[148] E.g. in 1982, 190 were accepted for settlement on arrival from Commonwealth Caribbean countries.

[149] Cmnd. 9544, Table 6

[150] 8,830 in 1984. Of all Bangladeshis accepted for settlement in 1984, 94% were women and children.

[151] Noticeable increases between 1979 and 1981 were largely due to the admission of stateless persons and refugees, principally Poles and Vietnamese. In 1983 and 1984 the number of Old Commonwealth immigrants accepted for settlement increased from 5,160 (1982) to 7,440 (1984).

[152] Apart from the admission of stateless persons and refugees who have accounted for sharp increases between 1979 and 1981.

[153] E.g. applications in the Indian Sub-Continent rose from 1,230 in 1982 to 3,300 in 1983.

154 Cf. UKPHs, on the one hand the increase in the annual quota of vouchers in the early 1970s, on the other the refusal to accelerate the entry of those remaining in India.

155 Thus the number dealt with under a tough policy in 1980 were 1,500, as compared to 960 in 1979.

156 Though political uncertainty in South Africa and Zimbabwe may produce a steady source, as may Hong Kong. Most citizens of the latter have no right of entry into the U.K. but, since they hold British passports, the U.K. may find it difficult to shirk responsibility in the face of international pressure if a settlement with China is not reached or breaks down. Many citizens of the former are able to trace an ancestral connection with the U.K. so as to obtain full British Citizenship e.g. the case of Miss Zola Budd, the athlete, in April 1984. Figures for settlement from the Old Commonwealth in recent years are - 7,440 (1984), 5,800 (1983), 5,160 (1982), 5,380 (1981), 6,880 (1980).

2 HISTORY

> Of course, our own safety and the safeguards for our people and for our nation must be the first consideration, and where it is a choice between our own safety and the safety of our people and the infliction of hardship upon an alien, then that hardship becomes necessary and ceases to be unjust.[1]

Most legal books include an historical introduction to set the scene and for some it is a necessarily pedestrian and questionably relevant burden. For this work, it is essential because in studying the current law and practice of immigration it is remarkable how many of the issues have been encountered before and dealt with in the same way as today. The historical section describes in outline the main features. It refers to some of the parallels which can be drawn with current experience, but there are many more which appear in the later chapters on the current law. It will be seen that the Immigration Act 1971 and its Rules, against which many have fulminated, are no worse, and are in some respects better, than the many measures and attitudes which the U.K. has adopted in this field for centuries.

Amongst the historical themes to emerge, the following can be briefly noted:

   (i)   the primary motive for encouraging immigration into the U.K. in the 1950s - economic - was the same as that which operated 700 years ago and in the intervening centuries;

 (ii) the same arguments in favour of control of immigration have similarly continued e.g. unemployment, health dangers, overcrowding, State security and loss of cultural and national identity;

(iii) uninhibited sovereignty of each State has determined, with rare exceptions, immigration policy;

 (iv) consequently the legal classification of entry as a

privilege has led to the aggrandisement of discretionary power in the hands of the Executive and to timidity from the judiciary in challenging its exercise.

The history of U.K. immigration law falls broadly into four phases.

A. FROM THE CONQUEST TO THE END OF THE EIGHTEENTH CENTURY

This long period is marked firstly by the use of foreign labour to promote the native industries but subject to control whenever it became too successful, and secondly by the occasional influx of refugees.

(1) The Early Period
Immigration, usually as a part or consequence of conquest, had taken place frequently before 1066 in the shape of, for example, the Angles, Danes, Romans and Saxons. The feature of the Norman invasion was that it heralded permanence and stability. It should not be forgotten that for over 900 years England (and for lesser periods the rest of the United Kingdom) has remained free from invasion and has not had to face the attendant problems of displaced native populations or involuntary miscegenation of races. This factor has proved significant in moulding a certain aloofness amongst the native population and a belief in its sovereign right to determine its own economic, cultural and social self-interests. Moreover, from the earliest times, the simple fact of the U.K's geographical separation from Europe has made it relatively easy to regulate the flow of immigration.

(a) The Jews
The invasion of 1066 brought in its wake industrial and commercial immigration. Jews, in particular, were encouraged by the Crown to enter and to assist in the fiscal running of the Kingdom.[2] The money which they raised was taxed to fill the Royal coffers.[3] They did not enjoy the legal rights of citizenship and lived in separate quarters (Jewries). However, as the King's chattels, they enjoyed Royal protection, had special laws governing mortgages and bonds and their affairs were administered by a separate division of the Exchequer Court. Succeeding Monarchs gave their protection to Jews.[4] However, the latter's increasing wealth, secured in part by the acquisition of land from loan defaulters, and rumours of their "superstitious" practices and unconventional lifestyle led to increasing hostility towards them from the local population. Indeed, after the Barons' war, statutes began to confine the Jews. They were not entitled to own real property, to employ Christian servants, to build new synagogues, to act as physicians, to eat with Christians or to walk the streets

50

without wearing the Jewish mark of two white or coloured tablets of wool.[5] This coincided with the increased avarice of the Crown. Jewish wealth was taxed with increased ferocity until Edward I responded to public opinion demanding that they renounce usury, by expropriating their property and expelling them from the Kingdom in 1290.[6]

The saga of the Jews highlights many of the themes of succeeding immigration. First, it illustrates the predominance of the Royal Prerogative -Jews were introduced and protected by Royal patronage and ultimately departed by the Crown's fiat. Second, as with many immigrants, Jews were specifically imported to fulfil an economic function but when they became too successful in popular eyes, or unproductive in official terms, they were victimised and expelled. Third, that process germinated the seeds of what have become time-honoured objections to immigrants, viz., their economic effect on the native population, their cultural, religious and social differences, their effect upon crime, and their racial inferiority. All these facets gelled together in the thirteenth century to produce legislative, social and violent reaction against the Jews of such intensity that it was not until the time of Cromwell that they were discreetly permitted to re-enter.[7] Fourth, it is a salutary reminder against complacency in viewing the history of the U.K's immigration policy.

(b) Other Aliens
In addition to the Jews, other foreigners were officially encouraged to enter in order to boost and modernise the economy by imparting their technical skills and, of course, to increase the Crown's revenue. Magna Carta had provided that all merchants shall have safe and secure exit from England and entry to England, with the right to tarry there and to move about, for buying and selling.[8] The Carta Mercatoria of 1303[9] was a declaration of faith in the economic usefulness of aliens, allowing them to enter, trade and live freely in return for the payment of customs duties.

Aliens entered under Royal privilege and protection and an idea of their numbers appears from records such as the Domesday Book, archives of merchant gilds and parish registers.[10] Edward III took a particular interest in imported labour and pushed hard for an open door policy. For example, to modernise the cloth industry, a 1337 statute granted skilled weavers safe conduct and franchises to pursue their crafts[11] and large numbers of foreigners, mainly Flemish (because of unrest in Flanders), settled throughout England.[12] Once admitted, foreigners and infant industries were often cocooned from further foreign competition by protective legislation against imports.[13] By that same statute of 1337 the import of foreign cloth and the export of English cloth were forbidden. As a carrot to alien workers, the Crown was able to offer a form of citizenship, with its attendant legal and trading rights, through the executive grant of letters of denization.[14]

(2) The Fifteenth Century

In the 15th century in particular, resentment against foreign workers grew, as it had against the Jews, but was confined to the economic ramifications rather than associated with racial and religious slurs. Quite simply the aliens had been too successful and at the expense of native workers, who either lagged behind the former's skills or had not learned from them. As the preamble to a statute of Richard III complained, strangers would "not take upon them any laborious Occupations, as going to Plough and Cart, and other like business ... and will in no wise suffer nor take any of the King's Subjects to work with them" with the result that subjects "for lack of Occupation, fall into idleness, and be Thieves, Beggars, Vagabonds, and People of vicious Living ...".[15] The Middle Ages saw a running battle between the emerging middle class of native merchants and the pride of local boroughs on the one side and the country's need for resources[16] and aliens' skills and tax-producing wealth on the other, with each vying for the ear of the Crown. Typical of these was the struggle between the Merchant Adventurers and the Hanseatic League, the Hansards having been granted trading privileges which lasted until the mid-sixteenth century.[17]

Native resentment to the economic success of aliens displayed itself in three ways, which were to be repeated in succeeding centuries. First, restrictions were imposed on the economic activities of foreigners inside the U.K. Principal of these was the hosting of aliens whereby aliens were required to lodge with native merchants and to conduct their business under the supervision of the latter.[18] In the reign of Richard III, aliens were not allowed to engage in handicrafts unknown to local workmen and could only work as servants of the King's subjects.[19] Under Henry VI, they could not sell their goods to other alien merchants and local towns were allowed to police the provision.[20] Repeated measures were passed to stop the export of gold and silver, thus forcing aliens to spend their money in England.[21]

Second, as local industries prospered, protectionist measures were passed to keep out foreign goods and to restrict foreign trade to native merchants and, in the shape of Navigation Acts, to English ships.[22]

Third, resentment against aliens and the inability of the Crown to curb their wealth frequently reached such a pitch that aliens were physically attacked and some driven out. Riots in London in 1456 and 1457 drove Italians out of the city; the May Day of 1517 saw further riots by the young unemployed reminiscent of so many which have followed.[23]

(3) The Sixteenth Century

This threefold pattern was repeated in the 16th century, but with a new element - the plight of religious refugees. This century of vacillating political and religious allegiances meant that the admission of aliens depended more than ever on the holders of the Crown. Thus, the religious antics of Henry VIII favoured Catholics in the earlier years of his reign but later offered a sanctuary to Protestants from the uncomfortable retaliation of European Catholic Governments.[24] On the accession of Mary, alien Protestants were <u>personae non gratae</u> and French non-denizens were expelled,[25] whereas under Elizabeth I they were allowed to return. The latter's reign saw a particular influx of Dutch in and around 1567, who fled at the approach of a vengeful Duke D'Alva, and of French after the St. Bartholomew Day's massacre of Protestants in Paris in 1572. Here, and a century later with the Huguenots, can be seen the start of that 'tradition of compassion' for refugees which has lasted, however variably and thinly, until the present day.

Many of the refugees were destitute on arrival, and unemployment and pauperism followed. They tended to remain aloof from the native population by settling in their own religious communities. These settlements were obtained by grant of the Crown, often with an alien designated as responsible for their good order.[26] These concentrations of aliens added to the mistrust and hostility of the local population. The preamble to one of the controlling statutes echoed the complaints of earlier centuries when it spoke of the "sundry deceits and falsehoods practised by" the strangers; the charge that "they have not only conveyed and hid all their unlawful, untrue, subtil, and deceitful wares, which they untruly, subtilly, unsubstantially, and deceitfully have made ... and utter to our Subjects at excessive and unreasonable Prices"; the unemployment of native craftsmen who "be constrained to live in Idleness" and thus "fall to Theft, Murder and other great Offences".[27] Restrictions included a ban on aliens working in certain industries[28] or certain districts[29] and withdrawal of the full rights of denization.[30] The above-mentioned Act of Richard III remained on the statute book and, like many Immigration Acts to follow, served as a model. It was revived and modified.[31] Under the Henry VIII versions, aliens were forbidden, <u>inter alia</u>, to take alien apprentices[32] or keep more than two alien servants, and the wardens and bailiffs of towns had the power to search for and supervise aliens.

Two features of the 16th century particularly worthy of note were firstly, the use of the Royal powers. Henry VIII used them widely to grant the immensely important status of denizen (a form of second class citizenship but with legal and trading rights) and even delegated the power to the Lord Chancellor and the Master of the Rolls.[33] For example, with the war against France in 1544, aliens were offered the choice of deportation or denization and 1,862, the largest number of the century, opted for the latter.[34] Yet, in the 1558 war against France, Mary was able to revoke the denizations of 1544 by Royal Proclamation.[35] Under Elizabeth I, who, like Edward III, had a keen eye for the economic inventiveness of aliens, Royal powers were frequently used to grant patents,[36] licences and denization to aliens for the exploitation of new industries or as a reward for such efforts. A broad range of industries, including glassmaking, drainage, printing and the revival of the linen and woollen trades benefited. The flexible use of Royal powers enabled the Crown not only to dictate its wishes to the reluctant local populace but also to assure the aliens of safe passage and protection[37] and thus reasonable prospects of financial success. Second, once that success threatened the livelihood of natives, petitions to the Crown began but they were economic rather than cultural complaints. Even the references to aliens committing economic crimes were overshadowed by those complaints of natives resorting to idleness and violent crime.

In spite of Elizabeth I's favourable regard for the economic ingenuity of aliens and her disposition to allow them to settle, legislative steps were taken to protect and entrench native workers, not so much by the express imposition of disabilities on aliens but more by the grant of trading privileges to her subjects. Thus, the Navigation Acts which had begun in 1381 still protected English merchants and ships in the expanding overseas trade. Moreover, monopolistic rights were given by Royal Charter to those companies which were established and allowed to exploit imperial trade. Best known was the East-India company (1600), but there were many others such as the Levant Company (1581), African Company (1588) and Russian Company (1566). Moreover, whilst official patronage of foreign, economic skills could be countenanced, the religious, and hence public order, implications of immigration were a different matter. Thus, in 1585 Jesuits and seminary priests who were alleged to have induced "sedition, rebellion and open hostility" amongst the local population were ordered to leave the Realm.[38]

(4) Seventeenth and Eighteenth Centuries

In these centuries the same see-saw of encouragement and discouragement of aliens continued, but the factor of nationality assumed a greater role and the arguments against aliens became even more recognisable to those of today.

Aliens were still admitted and, particularly after the Restoration, were even encouraged. For example, the importation of "vast quantities of linen cloth" at the expense of native workmen prompted an Act of 1663 to encourage the local manufacture of linen cloth and tapestry. Aliens were encouraged to settle and make the products here. The attraction of naturalisation after three years' residence was offered so that they could enjoy "all privileges whatsoever as the natural-born subjects".39 Under Cromwell, Jews were allowed to return for the first time since 1290. Most importantly, the persecution of Protestants in France resulted in 1685 in the revocation of the Edict of Nantes (which had allowed Protestants their religious freedom in 1598). Large numbers of Huguenots fled to England and via England to North America. They were officially welcomed. In 1681 Charles II declared that he held himself "obliged, in honour and conscience, to comfort and support all such distressed Protestants, who, by reason of the rigours and severities, which were used towards them upon the account of their religion, should be forced to quit their native country".40 Royal protection was reaffirmed in 1689 by William and Mary. The official welcome arose partly because at that time England was felt to be underpopulated (mainly through emigration to the Colonies) and partly because the Huguenots brought their skills and ingenuity to the aid of the economy.41

Complaints of the indigenous population naturally countered this latest wave of alien immigration and they were again mainly economic grievances. For goldsmiths, "aliens and strangers do take away a great part of the living and maintenance of the free goldsmiths ... who are thereby exceedingly impoverished ... they make and sell many deceitful jewels, pearls and counterfeit stones ...".42 Clock makers complained that their art was brought into disrepute by the aliens' shoddy goods and that the aliens were touting for business and undercutting native prices.43 The more insidious, non-economic arguments against aliens were added, foreshadowing those of the late nineteenth century. Thus, to London craftsmen, "These strangers take great houses, and divide them into several habitations and take inmates and so pester all places where they come to the great danger of infection and noisome diseases which is found to be too true by too often experience".44

However the climate of opinion, at least at official level, excluded the real possibility of these complaints being translated into immigration control. Instead, the issue of citizenship, in particular naturalisation, became the focal point for arguments about aliens and dominated the immigration debate until 1793, when immigration control proper took over.

The role of citizenship
By 160845 the law on citizenship was, briefly, that

(1) all persons born within the Crown's Dominions were subjects of the Crown,
(2) children born to such subjects outside the Dominions acquired the same status,
(3) everyone else was an alien.

As for aliens, "now the word alien is a legal term and amounts
to as much as many words; an alien must be an alien ne. It
implies being born out of the liegeance of the King, and
within the liegeance of some other state".[46] They could be, and
were, subjected to a range of civic, economic and legal
disabilities. For example, certain trades could be denied to
them, they did not enjoy parity before the courts or in the
ownership of property and they could be forced to pay higher
customs' duties. Conversely, subjects could be expressly
favoured, principally by the grant of monopolistic trading
rights. Of these the Navigation Acts were particularly potent.
For example, by a statute of 1660,[47] trade between England and
the colonies had to be carried by English-owned or manned
ships "for the increase of shipping and encouragement of the
navigation of this nation". No alien could carry on trade as
merchant or factor in the plantations. To avoid an alien
importing prohibited goods indirectly via France, for example,
the goods had to be brought direct from the place of
manufacture. Non-English ships had to pay double aliens
customs.[48]

An alien could change his legal status to that of fully
naturalised subject[49] by Act of Parliament or to the more
circumscribed status of denizen[50] by the issue of Royal letters
of patent. Denization was granted on request or on the Crown's
initiative. It was used frequently by the Crown to encourage
the settlement of specific, economically useful aliens. During
the seventeenth century the importance of aliens to the
economy was reflected in the several attempts made at
increasing their opportunities for naturalisation. Both
existing methods were, it was argued, too cumbersome. Bills to
simplify the procedure (by the simple taking of the Oath and
Sacrament) were keenly debated in 1667, 1672, 1680 and 1693.[51]

Most of the arguments were by now well-worn. On the one
hand, aliens brought new blood, ideas and skills to regenerate
the nation. On the other hand, the principal objection
remained the feared economic success of those aliens who would
be naturalised. Such newly created subjects would soon 'take
over'. "Shall an English Parliament let in strangers to
under-sell our country, which they may easily do, whilst they
live in garrets, pay no taxes, and are bound to no duty?"[52]
Moreover, the concept of allegiance which lay at the root of
citizenship, raised the spectre of the undermining of the
State's security if so many aliens were to be allowed to enjoy
full civic status.

Finally, in 1708, Parliament agreed that "the increase of
people is a means of advancing the wealth and strength of a
nation", and passed an Act revolutionising naturalisation by
prescribing simply the taking of the Oath and Sacrament.[53]
However, the change proved to be too drastic and by 1711
Parliament was convinced that "divers mischiefs and
inconveniences" had ensued "to the discouragement of the

natural-born subjects and to the detriment of the trade and wealth thereof" and thus repealed the Act of 1708.[54] It appeared that too many destitute aliens had entered the country from the Palatinate and had turned public opinion against them.

Attempts continued during the eighteenth century both to reinstate the 1708 procedure and to make naturalisation available to a wider class of applicants, for, under an Act of 1609, the "grace and favour" of naturalisation was only available to "such as are of the religion now established in this Realm".[55] Applicants for naturalisation had thus to take the sacrament, the Oath of Supremacy and the oath of allegiance. America led the way to reform. In 1740 the Crown agreed[56] that Protestants and others could be naturalised after 7 years' settlement in America and after taking the Oath. Quakers and Jews were allowed to omit parts of the Oath. In 1747 the Act was extended[57] so that those who refused to take the Oath could instead make a Declaration of Fidelity. In fact America showed how readily the Crown was willing to alter the laws of naturalisation if its interests dictated it. Men were needed on the King's side in America and naturalisation was a useful inducement. Again, as a simple example, under an Act of 1749 to help the fishery industry,[58] foreign Protestants serving 3 years on an English ship who took the Oath were deemed to be naturalised subjects. If they departed the King's Dominions for more than a year, the benefit was forfeited.

Specific, mercenary manipulation of naturalisation laws could be tolerated, even advocated, but that society was not ready for more general relaxation was strikingly evidenced by the 'Jew Bill' of 1753 which for Jews removed the requirement of taking the Sacrament. It did not, however, prescribe a general form of naturalisation and thus the expensive process of a Private Act of Parliament was still needed. Yet this modest measure provoked such hostility that it was repealed a year later. Out of the woodwork came the usual commercial objections - that Jews would become too successful economically and at the expense of native traders. These were supplemented by protestations of the Church's supremacy and by a fierce sense of national pride. The invention of printing since the last Jewish turmoil in the thirteenth century meant that propaganda flourished and much of it has survived.[59] The themes are familiar. For example,

> if those of true English blood have not now the power to prevent opening this sluice for letting the torrent in upon us, can we hope that they will have power enough to shut it up after the torrent is broken in, and the Jews are become possessed not only of all the wealth, but of many, perhaps most, of the land-estates in the Kingdom?[60]

The aquatic reference is a standard formula and if one

substitutes blacks for "Jews" and jobs for "land-estates", we have a twentieth century theme. The Jews offered an opportunity to add crude racial twists to the traditional themes. Thus a contemporary ballad ran,

> But, Lord, how surprised when they heard of the News,
> That we were to be servants to circumcis'd Jews,
> To be Negroes and Slaves instead of The Blues,
>   which nobody can deny.[61]

The xenophobia is illuminating, especially the reference to Negroes. It illustrates how deep-seated native prejudices are. Admittedly, a century later public opinion was so much in favour of refugees that Palmerston's Government was defeated when it tried to control aliens.[62] But two centuries later the same economic, racial and cultural themes have been repeated and reflected in current immigration laws and debate.

Liberalisation of naturalisation did not take place until the nineteenth century. In 1826 the religious test was abolished[63] and in 1844 the procedure was replaced,[64] along the lines of the ill-fated Act of 1708 (an Oath, payment of a fee and issue of a certificate).

B.   1793-1836 NAPOLEONIC LEGISLATION

In the meantime, towards the end of the eighteenth century, immigration control replaced naturalisation as the contentious issue. However, the pretext was national security not economic or racial motives. With emigration under way to the colonies and the Industrial Revolution's thirst for labour, control was not needed on the traditional economic grounds, and the numbers of immigrants were not a cause for concern. Instead, the pending conflict with France brought fears of political and military subversion.

The main elements of today's immigration laws were fashioned in the aftermath of the French Revolution and during the Napoleonic Wars. Thus, the first statute of 1793[65] was passed to prevent "much danger" that "may arise to the publick Tranquillity from the Resort and Residence of Aliens", notably revolutionary troublemakers from France. Masters of ships had to declare to customs officers the number and details of aliens on board (s.1). This device became a stock in trade response to the need for control and was copied soon afterwards in the United States[66] and later in the emerging Commonwealth countries.[67] Aliens themselves were placed under a corresponding duty to declare their personal details (name, rank, occupation, place of prior six months' residence) and to obtain from the customs' officer a certificate recording those details (s.4). Failure to do so or the making of a false declaration invited prosecution and the mandatory expulsion of the alien for whatever period the court thought fit (s.3).[68]

Copies of Certificates and Declarations were forwarded by the Customs officers to the Secretary of State, and thus began the system of central record-keeping. As to qualitative control, the Crown was empowered by Proclamation or Order in Council

(a) to prohibit the landing of aliens "of any description" if it was felt "necessary for the safety and tranquillity of the kingdom", or
(b) to permit landing only at designated ports (s.7).

The former is the precursor of today's "conducive to public good" power of exclusion and removal[69] whilst the latter is represented by the system of authorised ports of entry.[70] The primary sanction for disobedience was placed on the carrier, a convenient and administratively simple expedient which is now common place in international travel. In 1793, any master wilfully neglecting to obey a Proclamation was fined £50 for each unauthorised alien and his ship could be seized and forfeited.

In the atmosphere of turbulent relations with France at the turn of the century, the Act went much further by providing a system of internal control, which served as a model for control during wartime in the U.K. in the twentieth century.[71] Thus, aliens required passports to travel from the port of entry to their destination; the Crown could order those arriving after 1792 to reside in certain districts; on arrival at the intended residence passports had to be produced to the local magistrate; the production of passports could be demanded at any time; and travel between districts required new passports.[72] As a further check, housekeepers could be required to furnish details of aliens residing with them. Exemption was granted to seamen, diplomats and children under the age of 14. Although merchants required a passport, it was, in line with the spirit of Magna Carta, couched in general terms and entitled the holder to travel freely within the realm.

Three methods of removal of aliens were prescribed:

(1) The Crown could order "any alien" to depart the realm. If he refused, he could be arrested, detained, sentenced by a court to one month's imprisonment and removed thereafter (ss.15, 16).
(2) If the Secretary of State apprehended that the alien would not obey an order to depart, he could be detained at once and removed "in such a manner as shall be suitable to his or her rank and situation" (s.17).
(3) For those aliens already committed to gaol, the Secretary of State could deport if he deemed it "necessary for the public safety" (s.29).

At first sight and in comparison with the dearth of structured control which had preceded it, the 1793 Act appears Draconian. On the other hand,

    (a) it was passed in the context of unease over events in France,

    (b) _bona fide_ merchants were excluded from its operation,

and

    (c) it contained some legalism, with frequent references to the need for judicial endorsement of control. Penalties had to be confirmed by Justices and financial, but not, significantly, other penalties, could be appealed to Quarter Sessions.[73] In the expedited form of removal an alien who sought to excuse his behaviour could appeal to the Privy Council. Of course, the opportunity for judicial redress by no means guaranteed that it would be obtained, but the references to it indicate the importance attached to the rule of law. Such importance did not generally appear in subsequent emergency legislation.

The Act's real importance lay in the fact that so many of the features of modern control appeared within it e.g. entry via designated ports, licences to enter, a central system of record keeping including reports of hoteliers, control on internal movement by passports and an unfettered and expeditious power of removal.

Since the Act was aimed at potential troublemakers from France, it did not prevent the grant of asylum to entrants. By 1798, it was felt by Parliament that "Refuge and Asylum which ... have been granted to persons flying from the oppression and tyranny exercised in France ... may ... be abused by persons coming to this Kingdom for purposes dangerous to the interests and safety thereof".[74] Thus, the 1793 Act, which had been renewed annually, was refined and replaced by a tougher model, with the following principal provisions:

    (i) Control was extended to merchants and retrospectively to those aliens who had entered the country before 1792.

    (ii) Aliens had not simply to register upon arrival but had to obtain a Royal Licence before being allowed to reside. Such Licences could be open-ended or tied to residence in a particular place or subject to a time limit or "such restrictions or conditions, as His Majesty shall seem fit". To obtain one, the alien had to supply fuller details than under the 1793 Act about, for example, his parents, previous residence and reasons for leaving his country of origin. With remarkable similarity to the position reached judicially in 1979 in <u>Zamir</u>,[75] he could be punished by imprisonment and transportation if he obtained a Licence "without disclosing" to the issuing official his "true name and description" (s.19). He could be similarly punished for failure to procure, or observe the conditions of, a Licence, by, for example, moving outside the specified place of residence. This in effect required all aliens to present themselves for examination at ports of entry - a requirement which was crucially overlooked in the Commonwealth Immigrants Act 1962.[76] Those appointed by the Crown to issue licences, the early immigration officers, could refuse a Licence as they thought fit (s.4). Two consequences could follow - the alien could be brought before a Justice of the Peace and committed to gaol pending removal or he could be given time to establish a claim to a Licence by being released, in effect, on bail.

(iii) Any magistrate or mayor, the forerunner of the police, was still entitled to demand that any alien produce his Licence and to check for compliance with it (s.15).

(iv) An alien suspected of being "a dangerous person" could be detained, interrogated and then either released, or detained "for such time ... as His Majesty shall think fit" or removed (s.16).

(v) To leave the realm a passport was required, the main sanction being an automatic fine of £500 on the master of the vessel.

(vi) Interestingly, if, in proceedings under the Act, the defendant succeeded, treble costs (as opposed to double in 1793) were automatically awarded against the plaintiff (s.27).[77] This was a salutary sanction which, it is suggested, would not be entirely amiss in today's laws.

Although it was passed as emergency legislation, the barebones of the 1798 Act are very similar to the position which obtains today. Chief of these is the Licence which is the forerunner of the entry clearance. A second common strand is the large discretion given to the Crown,[78] for example, in exempting an individual or class of alien, in the attachment of conditions to a Licence and in the decision to remove an alien.

In 1802, the earlier Acts were replaced.[79] The milder climate between France and the U.K., as witnessed by the signing of an extradition treaty covering murder, forgery or fraudulent bankruptcy,[80] meant that much of the 1802 Act was concerned with registration requirements for aliens and the carrying ships. A standard counterfoil was prescribed for use at ports of entry. On completion, one half was given to the alien, the other was kept in a register and a copy was sent to the Secretary of State. Significantly, however, the column containing the customs officer's "remarks" about the alien did not appear on the alien's copy. Here is the forerunner of the immigration intelligence files. On the whole the Act was more relaxed - the licences to reside at designated places and passports to leave the country were omitted. On the other hand, expulsion by Royal Proclamation or Order in Council was again permitted, and no limitations or guidelines on its use were specified. Although an appeal was available to the Privy Council, the breadth of the removal power was such that the only grounds of appeal were those in which the alien claimed to fall within an exception - as a mariner, diplomat, domestic servant, child under 14 or if there was doubt as to his alien status.

A kind of temporal <u>habeas corpus</u> operated, since, if the removal of the alien was delayed and he remained in custody for two months, he could then apply to court for his release. The court could either release him or continue the detention. The need for such a time limit has not lost its force when the current practice of detaining alleged illegal entrants is considered.

The outbreak of hostilities with France led in 1803 to the repeal of the 1802 Act and a reversion to the harsher terms of the 1798 model,[81] with licences to enter, specified places of residence, the monitoring of internal movement, internment, removal by executive decree and passports to leave the realm. The limited rights of appeal against removal which had appeared in the 1793 version, were not included. In other words, the Act bore the hallmarks of emergency legislation seen subsequently in 1914 and 1939. These provisions lasted until 1814 when the more relaxed terms of the 1802 model were restored (including the penalty of treble costs on the plaintiff if he failed).[82] The see-saw continued in 1815 with the return of the tougher 1803 model.[83] It made provision, <u>inter alia</u>, for the appointment of an Inspector of aliens at ports to administer the system of entry licences and for the issue of warrants to search aliens' houses for arms. Again the Secretary of State was given wide powers of review. For example, all refusals of licences to reside were sent to him for approval; magistrates had the power to detain and examine aliens suspected of being dangerous and, if their suspicions were confirmed, they had to send their opinion to the Secretary. He then decided whether the alien was to be released or deported. Yet, in the following year the 1815 Act was not renewed but replaced by the more liberal 1802 model.[84] In 1826, control was considerably relaxed. The Act of 1816 was allowed to lapse and its provisions for removal and internal control were not repeated. In its place came a mechanism principally designed for the registration of aliens.[85] Firstly, it sought to achieve a census by requiring all resident aliens to submit details of their presence to the "Aliens Office in

Westminster" - the first statutory reference to a separate department of State responsible for aliens. Second, entrants and masters of vessels had to furnish declarations of details on arrival. A counterfoil certificate (again excluding the "Remarks" column) was given to the alien (s.4). The significant difference was that the alien had to surrender his passport at the port of entry. This was then sent, along with a copy of his declaration, to the Secretary of State. Further declarations as to residence had to be sent to the Secretary at six monthly intervals. On leaving, the alien signed a declaration of departure and in return he received his passport back. In theory, the scheme was a simple one to operate and, incidentally, recognised the increased State practice of issuing passports to citizens. The Act reflected not only the better relations with France and the passing of danger but also the pending period of Victorian liberalism, the confidence of which had no need for immigration control. Parliament was, however, concerned about the immigration of blacks. Thus, in 1832, a vessel's master had, in addition, to declare if he had taken on board any persons "being or appearing to be natives of Africa" and had to furnish a bond of £100 to reimburse any parish which had subsequently to support such a person.[86] In fact, the immigration of blacks, which had never been high, remained low throughout the nineteenth century.[87]

The operation of the 1826 Act proved to be cumbersome and in 1836 the process of winding down immigration control culminated in a greatly simplified legislative scheme which lasted until 1905.[88] Retention of passports by the Secretary of State was abolished, and the alien had no longer to send a certificate of entry or half-yearly declarations of residence to him. After three years' residence he was able to obtain a certificate from the Secretary exempting him from the Act - a sort of latter-day indefinite leave to stay. What remained was a simple procedure - a declaration of details by the alien and ship's captain on arrival, the production but not surrender of a passport and the issue of a certificate to the alien with a copy being transmitted to the Secretary. On departure the alien surrendered the certificate, thereby enabling the Government to maintain a constant survey of the alien population. Thus, the qualitative control which had operated with varying rigour from 1793 to 1826 was replaced by, in essence, an exercise in book-keeping and identification of aliens. The 1836 Act soon fell into disuse. It was revived in 1890 in the atmosphere of unease at Eastern European immigration, but its accuracy remained very doubtful.[89]

This flurry of legislative activity between 1793 and 1836 established with resounding clarity that "It is the undoubted right of every independent State to permit or to prohibit the residence of foreigners within its dominions as it shall see fit".[90] It will be noted that most of the essential features of modern control appeared in the Napoleonic legislation - the Secretary of State assumed broad, overall control; a system of entry clearance and the role of passports emerged; removal on suspicion of danger is not far removed from today's "conducive to public good" power; the duty to report to the police remains, as does the emphasis on the carrier's responsibilities; the central compilation of records and the surrender of passports during stay merely foreshadow today's computers and the matching up of departures against records of leave to stay. Conceived in times of emergency, these features have become the norms of general immigration control.

C.   1836-1905

Once the friction with France died down, the confidence and liberal sentiments of the Victorian age largely forestalled the imposition of controls of aliens. The century witnessed two major phases of immigration into Britain - the Irish in the 1830s and 1840s and the mainly Jewish refugees from Eastern Europe towards the end of the century. The 1836 Act in theory governed throughout, but in practice it quickly fell into disuse. As a Select Committee observed in 1843, "it is very generally disregarded by Foreigners and it is never enforced by the authorities".[91] Only a small fine (£2) for disobeying the requirements of registration was imposed and there was "no provision in the statute for recovering the penalties of disobedience; it is consequently only conformed to by such persons as are either ignorant of that defect, or are led to observe the law of the country from a sense of propriety".[92] Thus, of 794 aliens who landed at Hull in 1842, only one registered, whilst none of the 1,174 at Southampton did so. Britain became in fact a 'safe bet' for immigrants and, in particular, refugees. They were admitted freely and between 1823 and 1906 (the commencement of the Aliens Act 1905) no person was lawfully removed. This was partly due to the prevailing self-confidence of Victorian society and partly to the fact that aliens could be encouraged, or at least tolerated, because of the vitality which they could add to an already energetic population.

A hiccup occurred in 1848 due to the popularity of Britain for continental refugees. A Bill was introduced amidst unspecified[93] fears of internal insurrection which particularly undesirable aliens might foment. The Government claimed that it needed legislative means to "debar those persons from the power of abusing the hospitality they received, and endeavouring to excite throughout Her Majesty's dominions distrust of the Government of the United Kingdom - to provoke intimidation, or effect alterations in that Government".[94] In an atmosphere of political unrest on the Continent and in Ireland and the rumblings of the Chartist movement at home,[95] the Bill was passed comfortably. It allowed the Secretary of

State to remove aliens where he deemed it to be expedient "for the preservation of the peace and tranquillity of the realm".96 Before removal, the alien could appeal to the Privy Council and, like the procedure in security cases today, he was to be provided with a "general summary of the matters alleged against him" (s.3). The Act did not apply to aliens who had been resident in the country for three years before 1848, it lapsed after two years and no alien was removed under its provisions.97

One reason for the lack of official hostility to immigrants during most of the nineteenth century was the relatively small numbers. Emigration of British subjects to the Colonies (e.g. Canada, Australia) and the United States relieved the pressure of overpopulation, whilst, amongst the immigrants, many treated the U.K. as a port of call en route to North America.98 It is hard to believe that even the laissez-faire ethos of Victorian society would have withstood large-scale net immigration and the attendant economic and social problems. This meant that public opinion was not sufficiently agitated to call for control. On the contrary, confidence and belief in the English ideals of liberty were opposed to immigration control.99 This was perfectly illustrated in 1858. Following bomb explosions in Paris which were linked to refugees in Britain, an Alien Bill was prepared but not published. Instead a Conspiracy to Murder Bill was put forward to extend the crime of conspiracy to cover offences abroad. It was seen by many, however, to be in effect an Alien Bill so as to assuage the French Government. In a fit of indignation at such effrontery, the Bill and the Government were defeated.100 The most interesting points in this episode for the current discussion were:

(1) The fact that the fierce Parliamentary and public opinion was founded upon nationalism and the refusal to see the country appear to submit to foreign demands, rather than upon any particular love of refugees. "Most of them were unloved by most Englishmen, who made them feel very little welcome, but tolerated their presence in deference to what purported to be a great and selfless humanitarian principle: the doctrine of asylum."101

(2) The shattering effect of a Government defeat on a matter concerning refugees did much to stave off immigration control until 1905. For even when large numbers of refugees began to enter from East European Countries towards the end of the century, the sacrosanct and proud principle of asylum was deeply embedded in liberal values and stood firm.

Immigration in the Colonies
In fact the U.K. devoted more attention in this period to

observing, and in part seeking to curb, the efforts of its Colonies to deal with Asiatic immigration. This gave a further opportunity to the U.K. to express liberal values but also provided a range of legislative precedents for the U.K. when it too adopted statutory controls in 1905. The subsequent preoccupation of the U.K. with coloured immigration is mirrored by that of the Old Commonwealth with coloured and, more particularly, oriental entrants.

The abolition of slavery by the British Government led in various ways (e.g. withdrawal of investment capital) to a shortage of labour in Colonial plantations. At the same time, India experienced unemployment as a result of the U.K.'s efficient textile industry and Australia, Canada and South Africa needed cheap and resilient labour to exploit their natural resources (principally the mining industries). Attempts were therefore made to ship Asians and Chinese to fill Colonial needs. Lest slavery be introduced by the back door, there followed a tussle between the anti-slavery lobby and the Colonies for the ear of the U.K. Government.[102] In 1853 Parliament responded by relaxing the physical conditions for the shipment of Africans and Asians;[103] whereas in 1855 the Chinese Passengers Act sought to prevent abuses in the carriage of emigrants from ports in the Chinese seas.[104] The Governor of Hong Kong was empowered to pass and enforce conditions of shipment. Schedule A to the Act specified such matters as the physical space to be allotted for Chinese passengers, and the dietary and medical supplies to be supplied. The Act proved to be of very limited success.[105]

As the century proceeded, Pacific Colonies in particular devoted more of their efforts to deterring non-European immigration. Several methods were employed:

(i) A poll tax to be paid on entry by each immigrant e.g. Immigrants Restriction Act 1881 (New Zealand) -£10.[106]
(ii) Tonnage restrictions, limiting the number of immigrants to the ship's tonnage e.g. Chinese Immigration Restriction Act 1888 (Victoria) - one passenger for every 500 tons.[107]
(iii) The exclusion of undesirable categories of immigrant e.g. Immigrants Restriction Act 1899 (New Zealand) -criminals and the destitute.
(iv) Education and literacy tests e.g. Immigration Restriction Act 1901 (Australia) - the immigrant to satisfy a dictation test given in any language by the immigration officer.[108]
(v) Licences on economic activities e.g. Chinese Restriction and Regulations Act 1888 (New South Wales) - Ministerial authority needed for an immigrant to engage in mining.

The U.K. expressed concern at some of these measures and when,

66

in 1896, the Australian States attempted to extend their anti-Chinese legislation to cover Indians, the Bills were denied the Royal Assent on the grounds that they discriminated against a country within the Empire.[109] Resort was instead sought in the more indirect concept of literacy tests (adopted by Australia in 1901 and New Zealand in 1899) and opposition by the British Government waned as it became obvious that the U.K. would soon need to adopt statutory immigration control.

D.   1905 TO THE PRESENT

(1) Aliens Act 1905

(a) Background
The last twenty years of the nineteenth century witnessed a new and larger influx of refugees into the U.K. Most were Jews, expelled or fleeing from East European countries, notably Russia and Poland.[110] The effects of this immigration were similar to those which occurred in the thirteenth century. Jews tended to congregate in particular parts of the country. The East End of London became the most notorious but there were other notable settlements in, for example, Leeds and Manchester. Their economic activities again aroused the animosity of native workers, principally because of the notorious 'sweating system'. This was described as a system "under which sub-contractors undertake to do work in their own houses or small workshops, and employ others to do it, making a profit for themselves by the difference between the contract prices and the wages they pay their assistants".[111] Many small businesses sprang up and, in the words of a contemporary account,

> in the vast majority of cases, work is carried on under conditions in the highest degree filthy and unsanitary. In small rooms not more than 9 or 10 feet square ... six, eight, ten and even a dozen workers may be crowded. ... In these sweating dens nineteen twentieths of the toilers must be Jews, large numbers of whom are as yet unable to speak the language of the country they work in.[112]

Two Select Committees looked into the matter.[113] The House of Commons Select Committee generally sought to dispel the fears and reported that the dangers had been exaggerated. But it did feel that legislative control would probably be needed at some stage as overcrowding in the cities increased.

Attempts were made to legislate in 1894 (by the Marquis of Salisbury) and 1898 (by the Earl of Hardwicke), but the liberal elements in Parliament, greatly helped by the moderate Report of the Select Committee, managed to delay immigration control until 1905.

During this period, the opposition to aliens assumed a

well-worn guise - references were made to their effect on trade, unemployment, housing, and sanitary conditions, their strange habits, their impact on native values and culture, their crimes, and the sheer size of their numbers. In a statement which could easily be found today, one complainant observed, "you can scarcely find a street into which the alien has not penetrated".[114] Again, on Sundays in London "there are some streets you may go through and hardly know you are in England".[115] Opponents of immigration were, not for the last time, considerably assisted by the woeful lack of statistical evidence about aliens. This enabled fearmongering to be readily voiced, with no danger of refutation. The important changes in the content and style of the campaign were, firstly, the more skilfully orchestrated opposition to aliens, partly as a result of better means of communication and partly because of a Parliament more receptive to shades of public opinion and pressure. In particular, the British Brothers League,[116] the forerunner of the British Union of Fascists and the National Front, was founded in 1901 and sought to channel bitterness. Second, to the usual armoury of anti-alien propaganda was added the charge of racial inferiority based on Darwin's theory of evolution. To a society which had exerted much effort in subduing and exploiting the 'savages' in the Empire, such an argument had obvious attractions, especially when linked to a scientific theory. Its primitive assertion at the turn of the century has over the years been refined by pseudo-scientific analysis to produce the more subtle arguments of eugenics. But at root it remains the same - the dilution of the strength of native Anglo-Saxon stock by breeding with inferior races. Third, opponents were able to point to recent immigration legislation in other countries, notably the United States. The argument ran, "even the U.S. has had to halt indiscriminate immigration. All the more need is there for the U.K. to do so".

(b) Birth of the Aliens Act 1905

The Government responded to the pressure for reform by setting up a Royal Commission in 1901. It reported in 1903, with one dissenter,[117] and its proposals on immigration control were implemented in 1905. In a statement which bears true today, the Commission observed, "we have no accurate guide as to the number of alien immigrants in this country".[118] It had to rely on the census of 1901 which indicated 270,000 aliens resident in the U.K. out of a total population of 41.5 million (compared to 220,000 out of 37.7 million in 1891). What the Commission certainly did have were complaints about the way in which the aliens behaved.

From its voluminous evidence, the Royal Commission summarised those complaints as follows:

(1) that on their arrival they are (a) in an impoverished

and destitute condition, (b) deficient in cleanliness,
and practise insanitary habits, (c) and being subject
to no medical examination on embarkation or arrival,
are liable to introduce infectious diseases;

(2) that amongst them are criminals, anarchists,
prostitutes and persons of bad character ...;

(3) that many of these being and becoming paupers and
receiving poor law relief, a burden is thereby thrown
upon the local rates;

(4) that on their arrival in this country they congregate
as dwellers in certain districts ...;

(5) that this influx into limited localities has caused
the native dweller to be dispossessed of his house
accommodation ...;

(6) that ... the native tradesmen ... have suffered loss
in trade and, in many instances, have been superseded
by aliens;
[In particular by aliens working for lower wages.]

(9) in addition to these allegations it was complained of
Jewish immigrants (a) that they do not assimilate and
intermarry with the native race, and so remain a solid
and distinct colony; and (b) that their existence in
large numbers in certain areas gravely interferes with
the observance of the Christian Sunday.[119]

On such charges the Commission's findings were balanced. On
the one hand, it found the charges of illness and unclean-
liness unproved and could draw no firm conclusions on the
economic effects of aliens.[120] For example, the allegation of
"serious direct displacement of skilled English labour" had
not been proved.[121] On the other hand, it was concerned at the
apparent level of crime amongst aliens and, above all, it was
in relation to the thorny issue of overcrowding that the
Commission was most persuaded to head for control. It
recommended that the public health laws be enforced more
rigorously and that, as soon as a particular district reached
saturation point, it should be declared a prohibited area and
newly arrived aliens should be prevented from settling there.

The relative balance of the Commission's findings were
countered by its recommendation that a system of immigration
control be established at ports of entry, through a new
Immigration Department, to exclude undesirable aliens, who
were defined as "criminals, prostitutes, idiots, lunatics,
persons of notoriously bad character or likely to become a
charge upon public funds".[122] These proposals, of specific
classes of excludable aliens, were clearly influenced by the
laws of other countries. Indeed, the Commission's terms of
reference specifically included an examination of how other
jurisdictions had coped with immigration.[123] It collected
evidence[124] on laws in other countries and was clearly impressed
by those of Canada,[125] Natal and the United States which

prohibited specific classes of aliens. The Commission was then able to proceed smoothly to a neat balance whereby immigration should not be halted, but should be controlled to weed out the 'undesirables' (supra).

Of these comparative models the U.S. can be mentioned. From 1798 to 1875 no Federal laws were passed to deal with immigration. However, in the second half of the nineteenth century, opposition to aliens grew. The complaints were similar to those voiced in Britain - the destitute state of the aliens on arrival, their propensity to crime and disease, and the dilution which those from the Mediterranean countries would cause to the well-settled North European stock. The laws which were then passed were specifically directed against defined classes of alien - criminals and prostitutes in 1875,[126] lunatics and those liable to resort to public funds in 1882,[127] many of those brought in under employment contracts to work at cheaper wages than the indigenous population in 1885,[128] the diseased and immoral (including polygamists) in 1891[129] and beggars and anarchists in 1903.[130] Here then was a ready model for the first modern immigration Act in the U.K. - qualitative control of designated aliens. As will be seen, most of the excludable categories in U.S. law were encompassed in the U.K. legislation.

(c) The Act
In the face of continued public and Parliamentary pressure, the Government finally conceded legislation in 1905. That year (like 1962 for Commonwealth citizens) was the watershed for aliens' entry. The liberal tradition of most of the nineteenth century was finally breached and was never to return. It can be compared with the Immigration Act 1917 in the U.S. which, after years of controversy, imposed a literacy test on all aspiring immigrants. Bills to do so had been in the air since 1897 but had been consistently vetoed by the President.[131] Once the barrier, which had assumed the status of an affirmation in the American ideal, had been broken, tighter restrictions soon followed.[132]

Under the Aliens Act 1905, 'immigrant ships', those carrying more than 20 steerage passengers,[133] had to berth at ports where immigration officers were employed. The master of any ship had to submit and sign returns to the port officials, detailing the number and type of aliens on board.[134] The immigration officers boarded the ship. Transmigrants (those intending an onward journey to, for example, North America) were excluded from control as were 'cabin passengers', who were defined as those "entitled to use the cabin, state rooms, or saloons where the accommodation is superior to that in any other part of the ship devoted to carrying passengers".[135] This last provision emphasised the real thrust of the Act - the deterrence of the destitute - but also provided a simple means of evasion. All remaining aliens were then examined by an immigration officer and medical officer. They could be detained for this purpose.

The grounds for exclusion in s.1(3) were:

(1) Lack of means to support himself and any dependants. Under the broad discretion vested in him the Secretary of State interpreted this requirement to be £5 per applicant and £2 for each dependant. If the alien had that money, it was generally sufficient for entry.[136] Or

(2) Lack of ability to acquire sufficient means. This clearly favoured skilled migrants whose employment prospects would be more favourable, but the immigration officer was still obliged to consider the state of the labour market in the particular trade.[137] Or

(3) Lunacy. Or

(4) Disease or infirmity whereby the alien was likely 'to become a charge upon the rates or otherwise a detriment to the public'. These grounds placed considerable power in the hands of medical officers, a position which still obtains today, whilst the reference to public funds is a common thread of Napoleonic and contemporary control. Moreover, the 'detriment to the public' category is a catch-all, residual power analogous to the later 'conducive to the public good' power. Or

(5) Sentence abroad for an extraditable crime, save for political crimes. Or

(6) The existence of an expulsion order made previously under the Act.

The striking tendency of the earlier Napoleonic legislation, namely to vest broad powers in the Secretary of State, was copied; e.g. his judgment was final on the definition of 'immigrant ship' (s.8(2)), 'steerage passenger' (s.8(3)) and 'political' offence in the context of extradition (s.8(4)), and he had the power to vary many of the Act's criteria by regulation. On the other hand, the alien did have a right of appeal, within 24 hours, against refusal of entry, to an Immigration Board at the port of entry. Grounds for refusal and a notice of his right of appeal had to be given to him.

Expulsion orders could be made following:

(i) a conviction and court recommendation,

(ii) judicial certification that the alien had within 12 months of entry been in receipt of public funds[138] or appeared to lack adequate means or was living "under insanitary conditions due to overcrowding",

(iii) sentence abroad for an extraditable crime.

Expulsion was a two-stage procedure, as today, with the Secretary of State having complete discretion over whether to implement the prior judicial decision.

The Act had been forced on the Liberal Government, and the Home Secretary to a degree sought to soften its impact. Thus, in the early days of the Act's operation, he felt obliged to write to the Immigration Boards expressing concern at the rigid application of the Act and hoping that the benefit of the doubt would be given to those alleging persecution and who were thus seeking refugee status.[139] Instructions to similar effect were issued to immigration officers.[140] The press was allowed to attend the Boards, legal representation was conceded, an exception of hardship was permitted, especially for women and children, and shipping companies were allowed to set up receiving houses in some ports in 1909 to accommodate immigrants pending examination by immigration officers. Moreover, the Home Secretary exempted from examination those shipping companies which operated adequate security against the disembarkation of undesirable immigrants. The number of aliens examined on landing was in effect quite small compared to the large number of exceptions. These measures are a ready indication of the supervisory role of the Home Secretary and of how his discretion can be used positively to ameliorate immigration legislation.

This amelioration soon subsided however. In much of the public mind the die was already cast against the alien, whatever the Home Secretary believed. The famous Sidney Street siege cast aliens as a danger to the State and brought to the surface the traditional objections to immigration.[141] A further, neat illustration of this stereotyping of aliens is provided by the economic frustrations of the native population in South Wales, which were given vent in attacks on Jews, who were envied and criticised for their comparative wealth and were thus seen as a legitimate target.[142] A Private Member's Bill was prepared in 1911 to restrict immigration[143] and the Government responded with the Aliens (Prevention of Crime) Bill. But both failed through lack of Parliamentary time. The outbreak of war concentrated the minds of Parliament wonderfully. With talk of spies in the air and the Home Secretary able to report that 21 had been rounded up in the previous 24 hours, the Aliens Restriction Bill completed all its stages, including Royal Assent, within a day.[144]

(2) Aliens Acts and Orders 1914-1920

The Aliens Restriction Act 1914 essentially gave the Secretary of State a free hand to regulate aliens as he saw fit. Thus, he could pass regulations governing their entry, residence and deportation and, ultimately, "any other matters which appear necessary or expedient with a view to the safety of the realm".[145] Arrangements made under the Act were "designed to cause as little inconvenience as possible to alien friends,

while leaving effective control over dangerous enemy aliens".[146]
It was subsequently described by Lord Hailsham as "one of the
least liberal and one of the most arbitrary systems of
immigration law in the world".[147] The subsequent Aliens
Restriction Order 1914 followed closely the scheme of the
Napoleonic legislation, with designated ports, duties on the
carrier and a requirement that aliens live in designated
places.[148] The courts became involved in the interpretation of
the wartime legislation,[149] but only to concede to the
Government a free hand.[150] It was held that the 1914 Act did not
derogate from the Crown's prerogative which could be used to
intern enemy aliens and which could not be challenged by
habeas corpus.[151]

(3) The Inter-War Years
The Aliens Act 1919 stated that the provisions of the 1914 Act
could apply at any time and were not limited to wartime. This
simple but devastating change converted emergency legislation
into general law and confirmed the style of U.K. immigration,
viz, a skeletal statute supported by detailed rules drafted by
the Secretary of State. The opportunity was taken of
increasing internal restrictions on aliens. Thus, the
imprecise common law was strengthened by making it an offence
for an alien to cause sedition or disaffection amongst ·the
armed forces or civilian population, or to cause industrial
unrest in an industry in which he had not been bona fide
employed for two years. Aliens were barred from appointment to
the civil service and their employment on British ships was
curtailed.[152] The Aliens Order 1920 (as amended) established the
framework of, firstly, the control of aliens and subsequently
the general Rules which operate today. Importantly, it
provided for a system of work permits to be issued by the
Ministry of Labour. Alien employment was not only brought
under control but its regulation also shifted the emphasis to
the Commonwealth as the future source of the U.K.'s labour
requirements. Aliens had to land at approved ports and seek
leave of entry from an immigration officer. Refusal was
mandatory if, inter alia, the alien was unable to support
himself and his dependants or if he was of unsound mind or
medically unfit. Leave could be subjected to conditions at the
discretion of the officer. Many of the features of the
Napoleonic legislation were copied, but in more detail. Thus,
carriers had to supply returns of alien passengers and were
used as part of the process of control; aliens had to register
their particulars locally and again if they changed residence;
in return they received a registration certificate; the police
could demand to see such certificates or passports at any
time; hoteliers had to maintain records of alien guests;
aliens could not embark without permission. Deportation
provisions, very similar to today's, were spelt out. In other
words, a comprehensive code existed to deal with the entry,

residence and expulsion of aliens, which took its inspiration from the Napoleonic legislation and the scheme of which ultimately governed all entrants.

The liberality of the previous century was soon forgotten. The spirit of the Aliens' legislation rapidly infected official policy and attitudes. Thus, in 1924 the Home Secretary could say to his men in the field, "If, when considering the desirability or otherwise of an alien's presence in the U.K., doubt arises, benefit should be given to the country, not to the alien".[153] As far as aliens were concerned the liberal treatment had been overthrown in 1905 and was never to return.

In between the two World Wars, Commonwealth citizens remained free from controls. Yet economic depression and the continued emigration of Britons to the Old Commonwealth avoided the controversy of any large-scale immigration into the U.K. In the mid-1930s however the exodus of Jews from Europe presented very similar difficulties to those of the previous century. The differences were

(1) that the Aliens' Order provided a mechanism for regulating their entry and
(2) that the principle and tradition of asylum were not so sacrosanct but had to be measured against the economic and social effects of large-scale immigration.

Thus, it appears that the Home Office was well aware of creating a 'Jewish problem' (pressure on jobs and housing resulting in a native backlash) similar to that which had forced the Act of 1905. Considerable steps were taken to slow down the rate of entry. Entrants were certainly not welcomed officially. On the contrary, a fear of encouraging more applicants meant that the Government refused to offer financial assistance to entrants on arrival but left their reception to increasingly stretched, private organisations.[154] Understaffing at the Home Office delayed the processing of applications for entry. Considerable use was made of Departmental instructions to immigration officers and consular staff.[155] Visas were required in 1938, and applicants had to establish the means (or potential to obtain them) for their own maintenance. They were to be "discreetly questioned" to see whether they were using the pretext of a visit to conceal an intention to stay. If a visit was the expressed purpose, the passenger was required (with an air of unreality given the surrounding circumstances) to sign an undertaking that he would not overstay. Those who openly sought emigration had to show that they were suitable candidates, i.e., whether they were likely to be an asset to the U.K. On the other hand, influential applicants in the fields of science, medicine, law, and the arts were given priority.[156] The use of administrative instructions were subsequently to be a feature of the control of the new Commonwealth immigration. Their deployment in the 1930s was a useful model (e.g. the use of visas). Apart from being very effective, they have the particular advantage to the Government of avoiding public legislation and consequential debate.[157]

The scale of refugee emigration in the 1930s was admittedly too large for one country to accommodate. It was an international problem. On the other hand, the U.K. did not go far out of its way to assist when one remembers

(i) the size of the Commonwealth and the room which could have been found within it for refugees had the U.K. chosen to take a more sympathetic attitude to the entrants and a stronger line with its fellow nations and

(ii) that the total refugee immigration (from Austria, Czechoslovakia and Germany) to the U.K. from 1933 to October 1939 amounted to a modest 55,500.[158]

(4) 1945-1962

At the outbreak of the Second World War, immigration control against aliens was, of course, exercised more rigorously. For example, the Home Office took over from the Ministry of Labour the responsibility for issuing work permits. More important however, was the general emergency legislation[159] which was built on the precedents of 1793 and 1914, affected all persons and, <u>inter alia</u>, gave the Secretary of State broad[160] and unreviewable[161] powers of detention.

After World War II the shortage of labour in the U.K. led to three phases of immigration - Polish settlers, European Volunteer Workers and coloured immigrants. The first stemmed mainly from the Polish Second Corps who had fought with the Allies and did not wish to return to Poland. They are worthy of mention because of the programme of assistance which was devised to promote their integration. The Polish Resettlement Act 1947 established a corps to solve the problems of education, health, housing, and general welfare of the settlers. Overall, the official efforts made to alleviate these problems were considerable and stand in sharp contrast to the position of succeeding immigrants. It is to be regretted that similarly coordinated action was not taken to assist them. Thus, the second phase (entry of European Volunteer Workers) was treated in a much more mercenary fashion. They were admitted on a 12 months' basis, they could not change employment without the approval of the Ministry of Labour and in many industries collective agreements were reached between management and unions at the expense of EVWs (e.g. a quota was fixed for each industry, no recruitment of local labour was possible and they were subject to first dismissal in the event of redundancy).[162]

In 1948 when other Commonwealth countries were more

concerned to relate immigration control to their own citizenship, the U.K. decided to reaffirm the right of all Commonwealth citizens to enter the U.K. without restriction. It was, with hindsight, a sentimental and idealistic gesture which soon turned sour when too many Commonwealth citizens, predominantly coloured, decided to exercise that right, too many for the comfort of the native population. The British Nationality Act 1948 was the source of all subsequent debate and controversy in immigration and race relations. It led to piecemeal backtracking from the Act's philosophy. It was perhaps expecting too much of the U.K. Government to foresee these difficulties in 1948 especially since the U.K. was short of labour at the time, the Commonwealth had played a major part in the recent war and the U.K. still had visions of grandeur as head of an international organisation. As the Minister for Colonial Affairs remarked in 1954, "we still take pride in the fact that a man can say Civis Britannicus sum whatever his colour may be, and we take pride in the fact that he wants and can come to the Mother country".[163] A more powerful criticism is the lack of coherent decision making when the 'problem' of coloured immigration emerged. At that stage the realities and implications of the 1948 Act should have been fully explored by research, perhaps through a Royal Commission, and a comprehensive policy instituted. Instead, the U.K. chose to respond instinctively thereafter (in 1962, 1965 and 1968 for example) and with increasing rigour, and inevitably opened itself to criticisms, on the one hand that it had acted too late, and on the other that it had acted in an alarmist and racist fashion. The U.K.'s response was piecemeal both in immigration and race relations legislation. The comment of the Lord Chancellor in 1965 reflected this pervading theme of recent history, "Just as until 1962 we had no real national plan about immigration, so we had no national plan as to how those who were here were to be integrated or assimilated into the population".[164]

Immigrants from the Caribbean were amongst the first to take advantage of the right of entry.[165] The first large contingent (500) arrived in 1948 at Avonmouth on board the Empire Windrush but the annual total remained small (an estimated 1,000) until the effect of the Immigration and Nationality Act 1952 of the U.S.[166] was felt. Under that Act an annual entry quota of 2,000 was placed on persons with ethnic origins (not simply birth) in the "Asia-Pacific Triangle" (which covered virtually all Asian countries from India eastwards, but not Australia and New Zealand). Furthermore, a quota of 100 was placed on Jamaicans (who had previously averaged 1,000 entrants per year). Caribbean emigrants[167] thus looked to the U.K. Immigrants from Asia and the Far East followed in the 1950s, but it should not be overlooked that the Irish outnumbered the coloured entrants throughout the heyday of coloured immigration. Thus, according to the 1951

Census there were 472,000 Irish residents and 74,500 coloured residents in the U.K.; in 1961 the figures were 644,400 and 336,600 respectively.[168] The number of coloured Commonwealth citizens who entered the U.K. during the 1950s can only be estimated. More accurate figures only began with the Act of 1962. It would appear that 1956 was the first peak year with about 37,500 net arrivals; in 1960 they rose to 58,000, and in 1961 to 115,000.[169] At the beginning of the 1960s, the Asian entrants overtook those from the Caribbean in the annual rate of entry.[170] The possibility of legislative control was raised in Parliament in 1958 when a backbench M.P. asked whether it was time to end the open-door policy to the Commonwealth, in view of the number of entrants and the consequential pressure on jobs, housing and schools.[171] The Junior Minister refused to offer legislation but sought to assuage speakers by assuring them that the Government was aware of the problem and would 'keep an eye on it'. As the number of coloured entrants increased, so did the objections. Their effect on employment, housing, education, cultural and social life were listed, frequently in crude racist tones, in very much the same way as opposition had been voiced against the Jewish refugees at the turn of the century.[172] Fears were ·exacerbated by the disturbances at Notting Hill in 1958 and were fanned by forthright press comment.[173] Eventually, the Government's Party Conference in the autumn of 1961 was promised action and the first control on Commonwealth immigration was enacted the following summer so as to deal with the "troublesome phenomenon".[174]

(5) The Commonwealth Immigrants Act 1962
By the standards of immigration legislation, the Commonwealth Immigrants Act 1962 enjoyed a leisurely Parliamentary progress. It was advertised at the Conservative Party Conference in October 1961, passed its Second Reading in November, received its Royal Assent in April 1962 and came into force in July 1962. The background to, and passage of, the Bill included the following features.

(i) It was preceded by the time-honoured objections to immigration, viz, its effect on unemployment, housing (in particular the overcrowding of immigrants in particular areas), education and health services, its dilution of the 'national stock' and 'character' and its dangers to public health and order.

(ii) Just as the Aliens Act 1905 was the watershed of Victorian sentiments towards asylum, so the 1962 Act broke the barrier of sentiment and attachment to the Commonwealth. Once that barrier was cleared, there was no looking back. As with aliens, the future lay in a bipartisan policy of stricter control for the Commonwealth.

(iii) Thus, the Act served as a precedent for the subsequent Labour Government which was able in 1965 to say, in effect, that it was only widening the path cleared by its predecessor.

The Parliamentary debates revealed much of the hypocrisy and subtlety which have thereafter bedevilled immigration. Thus, in introducing the Second Reading the Home Secretary[175] was keen to praise immigrants patronisingly for "the courteous and efficient way in which so many of them serve us in our hospitals" etc. But he soon switched to more emotive language when describing how an economic recession would be made worse "if others continued to flock into this country". To the objection that too much discretion was being given to the Executive, he pointed to the Parliamentary accountability of the Secretary of State - a justification frequently repeated in later years. To the demand for a right of appeal against refusal of entry, he set the tone for the decade by replying, "Our experience of administering immigration up to date is that the freer we leave our immigration officers the better and more successful the administration, subject to the responsibility of the Secretary of State".

In the first 10 months of 1961 the Government estimated that the net figure of immigration from the West Indies and Asia was 113,000.[176] During the next 8 months the momentum increased, partly in an attempt to "beat the Bill". Thus, from January to June 1962, 94,900 entered. The Act required those who held Commonwealth passports and who wished to enter for employment to apply for a work voucher. These vouchers were then regulated by the Ministry of Labour. For the first time Commonwealth citizens could be deported (after a court recommendation). Though the Act was a "temporary provision" (the preamble) and the section on entry was due to expire at the end of 1963, permanent control was in fact firmly laid. Of the three categories of vouchers (A for employers in the U.K. who had a specific job for a Commonwealth citizen, B for skilled applicants and C for all others), A and B were given priority and in 1965 category C was abolished and an annual quota of 8,500 set for the others.[177] Since the Act did not prevent the entry of dependants of those who had been admitted, they took over as the major source of immigration.

The use of employment vouchers under the 1962 Act was seen by the Department of Employment not as "a manpower supply scheme specifically tailored to the needs of British industry" but as simply a straightforward limit on the number of entrants.[178] This staggeringly short-sighted admission illustrates perfectly the lack of planning in British immigration policy. The opportunity to shape that policy in a practical, relevant and useful fashion was ignored in preference to a reflexive and expedient response. There were exceptions - Barbados and Trinidad. Both entered a recruitment scheme with London Transport, under which they were notified of job vacancies in the U.K., advertised, recruited and then trained the applicants.[179]

The White Paper of 1965[180] heralded the start of bipartisan policy towards immigration, for within 3 years of its opposition to the 1962 Act, the Labour Party, suitably stung by the defeat of a Cabinet Minister at a race-charged election in Smethwick, not only embraced the principle of control over Commonwealth entrants but sought to refine and strengthen it.[181] The Home Secretary had already set the scene in Parliament by expressing concern at the evasion of the 1962 Act,[182] and Lord Mountbatten had been despatched to try to persuade the sending countries to apply a brake to their emigrants.[183] The White Paper was preoccupied with the need to prevent evasion by tightening up the scrutiny of applicants, and controlling the flow of entrants "to our small and overcrowded country".[184] This change of heart by the Labour Party cannot be underestimated in importance in the U.K.'s recent immigration history. It meant that thereafter

(a) Governments presented a united face in favour of strict immigration control and

(b) any fulminations against that control by the Labour Party when in Opposition could not be taken seriously.

The White Paper sought to achieve its aim by abolishing Category C vouchers, cutting the remainder from 20,800 to 8,500 per year and, in relation to Category A vouchers, limiting each Commonwealth country to 15% of the total. Entry clearance was encouraged for dependants, the concession previously given to children aged between 16 and 18 was withdrawn, documents were to be scrutinised more carefully on entry, students and visitors were subject to time limits on their stay (1 year and 6 months respectively) and medical tests were increased. This framework

(1) moved the control of Commonwealth citizens much closer to that already employed against aliens;

(2) set the scene for today's practice; and

(3) was achieved largely by non-statutory instructions to officials, a practice which has been the hallmark of subsequent law.

The White Paper sought to soften the blows for Commonwealth citizens by announcing steps to promote their integration into the U.K. A National Committee for Commonwealth Immigrants was to be formed to coordinate stronger measures for integration. Much was expected of voluntary effort rather than official expenditure, and the emphasis lay on steady progress in the belief that integration would somehow be achieved without highlighting the ethnic community too greatly. In fact the White Paper was an excellent example of the recent recipe for successful control of immigrants - tougher immigration control and liberal sentiments in support of racial harmony but not matched by tough and comprehensive action to achieve the latter. Indeed, the potentially more important step of 1965, the first Race Relations Act, was typical of the tentative progress towards equal opportunity. In supporting the Bill, the Home Secretary observed "It would be an ugly day in this country if we had to come back to Parliament to extend the scope of this legislation".[185] That day arrived within 3 years and again after 10 years. The 1965 Act lacked powers of enforcement and crucially omitted employment. The inadequacies of the legislation were soon highlighted by two influential reports (by the Political and Economic Planning Unit and the Street Report) which revealed the scale of racial dis-crimination and the potential role for the law. Model II of the Race Relations Act was passed in 1968 with a stricter approach, but that too lacked sufficient investigatory powers and necessitated Model III in 1976 (again after P.E.P. reports which revealed the continuing level of discrimination), which closely mirrored the more sophisticated provisions of the Sex Discrimination Act 1975. It is of course easy to criticise with hindsight, but it was not beyond contemporary learning for Parliament to have passed a much more effective Race Relations Act in 1965, and for the Government to have invested more than platitudes in pursuit of integration. The 1965 Act fulfilled a more limited purpose - to salve the conscience of a party which by 1965 had completed a somersault by not only accepting the need for immigration control but also by strengthening its scope.

(6) The Commonwealth Immigrants Act 1968
The Act of 1962 had not affected citizens of the United Kingdom and Colonies (U.K.C.s).[186] Many Asians in East Africa chose to take out this citizenship in preference to that of their adopted African residence, since they feared victimisation by the newly independent African countries. The reason for this victimisation was the perennial economic one - Asians had proved a successful middle class and stood in the way of the native blacks. The policies of discrimination against Asians, particularly in Kenya, prompted those who held United Kingdom passports to exercise their right of entry into the United Kingdom in the mid-1960s. By February 1968, an average 750 were leaving Kenya each day. As Sir Cyril Osborne wrote to the Daily Telegraph, "It will not be long before there will be more coloured than white people in Britain. English people will become strangers in their own land".[187] To halt this influx, the Government introduced the Commonwealth Immigrants Act 1968, passing through both Houses between Tuesday evening and Thursday morning.

The Act confined the right of entry to those U.K. citizens who had a close ancestral link with the U.K. The result was that many Asians who had claimed United Kingdom citizenship through registration at U.K. High Commissions were unable to establish such a link and were admitted by a quota system -initially set at 1,500 per year. The Government estimated that 200,000 East African Asians were hit by the Act.[188] Others contributed to the panic by estimating as many as 1 million. Was this Act a piece of blatant discrimination? An example of broken promises - since Asians were led to believe, by the 1962 Act and on the granting of independence to Kenya in 1963, that the option of United Kingdom citizenship carried with it the right to enter freely? Or was it an exclusion justifiable on the grounds of public policy and good race relations, since the United Kingdom could not absorb all these immigrants at once? The latter has considerable force given the desire to appease the considerable disquiet voiced by public opinion. As one Minister subsequently revealed,

> As progressives we were opposed to capital punishment, persecution of homosexuals and racial prejudice, whereas a large section of our working-class supporters regard such ideas as poison. What they hate most is our softness on colour. It nearly cost us the election of 1964 - particularly in the West Midlands - and it was widely felt that our improved majority in 1966 was due to our new tough line on immigration control. That is why as a Government we were panicked in the autumn of 1967 by top secret reports predicting a mass expulsion of Asians from East Africa and began to make contingency plans for legislation which we realized would have been declared unconstitutional in any country with a written constitution and a supreme court.[189]

Moreover, the 1968 Act was passed without any reference to the manpower needs of the U.K. and with an apparently arbitrary figure of annual quotas. The concern to appease public opinion cannot excuse the Draconian way in which the voucher scheme was administered, as the European Commission of Human Rights subsequently reported[190] and the Home Affairs Committee subsequently indicated.[191]

Apart from dealing with U.K.C.s, the Act slipped in a constraint on all Commonwealth children by limiting entry to those under 16 and whose parents were, or were about to be, settled in the U.K. (s.2).The aim was to prevent fathers from merely bringing their elderly sons for employment. The effect was dramatic. In the 3 months prior to the Act 1,032 male children entered to join a sole parent, 3 months after the Act 39 were admitted, in the next 3 months the figure fell to 14.[192] Tighter controls in the Rules on the admission of elderly, dependent parents meant that only 6 were admitted in the 8 months following the Act.[193]

The 1968 Act achieved the final break with unwelcome primary immigration from the Commonwealth. It served to cast the Labour Party as cynical and hypocritical, in spite of its attempt to appease by passing the second Race Relations Act. The culpability was exacerbated because, whereas the Tory Party had accepted control consistently since 1962, the Labour Party had performed a volte-face and was pushing for control as eagerly as any right wing Government. In 1969 the Home Secretary could be heard to emphasise strongly the bipartisan approach to strict control and to speak proudly of the Act's curtailment of floods of immigrants.[194]

The "chicken came home to roost", however, in 1972 with the expulsion of Asians from Uganda. The Conservative Government, which in opposition had denounced the plight of East African Asians under the 1968 Act but which had done little to remedy that plight once in office (save for the increase in vouchers to 3,000 per year), was faced with international pressure to accept the moral and ultimately legal[195] responsibilities for them. In spite of the inevitable fearmongering at the likely "floods of immigrants", the Government conceded responsibility and, to its credit, took the unusual and overdue step of creating an official mechanism to supervise the reception and dispersal of the Ugandan Asians.[196] The "credit" however is poorly deserved, since

(a) it is highly unlikely that the U.K. would have reacted thus had it not been for the international pressure and opinion which saw the U.K. as legally responsible for citizens carrying U.K. passports,

(b) U.K. Governments have exerted no rigorous efforts to recover the expropriated property of the Asians from the Ugandan Government, and

(c) they have displayed remarkable indifference to the admission of those United Kingdom Passport Holders (U.K.P.H.s) who have been waiting in other countries (principally, India). The 1972 incident was instead one of a Government's hand being unwillingly forced.

Following upon the second Race Relations Act in 1968 came an apparently more substantial "sweetener" to immigration control in the shape of the Immigration Appeals Act 1969,[197] which sought to establish a comprehensive structure of appeals against decisions of the Secretary of State. This marked a welcome return to a feature of the Napoleonic legislation (which had incorporated a judicial component into the process of control) and of the 1905 Act (which had set up immigration boards at the designated ports of entry). Thereafter, apart from court recommendations, removal of aliens had been unappealable. A partial remedy had been introduced in 1956 wher,eby an alien, who had been lawfully resident in the U.K. for two years and was to be deported, could make representations to the Chief Metropolitan Magistrate. Large gaps remained, however, especially over the initial refusal to allow entry. The establishment of a system of adjudicators and an Immigration Appeal Tribunal by the 1969 Act was marred, firstly, by its additional requirement that wives and children seeking entry had to obtain an entry clearance certificate (s.20) and second by the fact that the Act was crucially amended by a provision in the Immigration Act 1971 that those refused a visa to enter (entry clearance) could only appeal from overseas. The expansion of entry certificates was to have crucial consequences for secondary immigration in the following decade, consequences which were far more important than the other, well-intentioned provisions of the Act.

(7) The Immigration Act 1971

This Act was the culmination of legislative changes of the 1960s. It was "plainly intended to be a comprehensive code".[198] It is still the principal Act. Yet, its substantive importance was not significant. In reality the groundwork had already been laid in 1962 and 1968, and, since the Act preserved the statutory rights of dependants to enter as secondary immigrants, it was really concerned with the fine tuning of the existing law. This was achieved principally through the powers of expulsion (e.g. family deportations and administrative powers of removal) and by completion of the merging of the Rules on Commonwealth citizens and aliens. Thereafter, the Rules and administrative practice dominated immigration policy.

The greater importance of the Act lay in the controversy surrounding the concept of patriality and its scope. The way in which it was handled by the Government emphasised the racist intent and effect of the U.K.'s immigration policy. For the Government in November 1972 was defeated on the draft Immigration Rules for having failed to allow second generation "British" subjects free entry. This led to the reintroduction of an earlier proposal, the so-called "grandfather" clause, and the Rules were approved in February 1973.[199] Under this provision, a Commonwealth citizen who can show that one of his grandparents had been born in the U.K. is entitled to entry clearance and indefinite leave to stay. The concession obviously favoured white British emigres.[200] It can be, and is, defended on the grounds of ancestral links, culture and sentiment, but, coming as it did in a package of Rules which tightened controls for most other immigrants, it accentuated their harshness and presaged the official policy of more rigorous control for the rest of the decade. It cast doubts on the sentiments expressed by the Home Secretary in moving the Second Reading of the Bill, that "... it is enormously important to reassure the immigrants already here that they will suffer no loss of status under the Bill, that in this country there will be no first or second class citizens".201

(8) 1973-85

With the legislative framework firmly laid and operative in 1973, the rest of the decade was notable for the role of administrative practice in securing control and for the repetition of well-known arguments over immigration. The following are selected as features:-

(a) An increased determination to detect and deter illegal immigration; e.g. more detailed scrutiny of applications by entry clearance officers (e.c.os), restrictions on husbands and fiances in 1977 and, with the help of the courts, greater use of the administrative powers of removal for illegal entrants. Symptomatic of this approach was the all-party report of the Select Committee on Race Relations and Immigration (1978).202 This was the first and only major report on immigration of the decade and thus assumed particular significance. Its publication was greeted with considerable controversy not simply because of its recommendations but also because of its unanimity.203

The Report was preoccupied with the need to batten the hatches more securely against immigration. For example, the Committee's examination of the Department of Employment204 centred on the very small numbers of immigrants admitted to work in the hotel industry and as nurses. Yet the Committee launched into it as if it had discovered a scandal. For the entry of more distant relatives (e.g. parents) the figures were already low and the criteria tough, but the Committee was still worried about its open-ended nature and recommended that it be kept under review. This was typical of the Committee's efforts to search for any possible way of tightening control. Amongst its recommendations were the following:- a Government declaration of no more primary immigration beyond existing commitments, an annual quota for entrants from the Indian subcontinent, priority for wives and children, all future-born children must be admitted before they reach the age of 12, more resources made available to catch overstayers and illegal entrants, DHSS to tighten its identity checks and an inquiry into a system of internal control.

The Report was significant in three principal ways. Firstly, it was symptomatic of the drawbridge mentality which had taken over in the 1970s. Second, although the Government's Response to it was unenthusiastic,205 most of its recommendations have been subsequently implemented (by changes in the Rules in 1980 and 1983 and administrative means e.g. priority queues, DHSS identity cards). Third, it undervalued the importance of race relations. Thus, "the committee appears to have been swept along by the current fixation of politicians of all parties with the question of immigration, leaving the vastly more important long-term issue of racial integration within Britain to flounder in the wake".[206]

(b) 1978 was important not only for the Select Committee's Report but also for a public debate which aired the traditional themes of immigration and indicated the mood of the decade. It was heralded by a controversial acquittal under the incitement to racial hatred provisions.[207] Given the weaknesses of the law, as it then stood,[208] the controversy lay not so much in the fact of acquittal[209] as in the observations of the presiding judge,[210] who said "Of course, we cannot accommodate here unlimited numbers of immigrants coming into this country, but it is not something to be ashamed of ... Homes are scarce. It is said that immigrants will occupy homes which are needed by ordinary English folk in this country. Members of the jury, those are matters upon which people are entitled to hold and declare strong views expressed in moderate terms".[211]

The traditional and popular drawbridge approach to immigration, which underlies these sentiments, was pursued in the same month with a television interview in which the Leader of the Opposition remarked:

> People are really rather afraid that this country might be rather swamped by people with a different culture and you know, the British character has done so much for democracy, for law and done so much throughout the world that if there is any fear that it might be swamped people are going to react and be rather hostile to them coming in. So, if you want good race relations, you have got to allay people's fears on numbers.[212]

This passage contains well-worn themes of immigration control -

(1) the emotive connotations of 'swamping',
(2) the need to preserve the British character from dilution, and
(3) the most emphasised feature since 1962, the link with good race relations.

In the light of the political storm, which followed

these remarks,[213] the Opposition Leader, two weeks' later, clarified the position by announcing that the Conservative Party would honour the U.K.'s existing legal commitments to prospective entrants (U.K.P.H.s and dependants of those already settled) and that it would 'work towards' the ending of, rather than 'end' immigration.[214] In April further details were announced by the Shadow Home Secretary[215] of a "tough but fair" policy which included a register for dependants, a "flexible and variable" annual quota for their entry, a new Nationality Act, the admission of husbands, fiances and more distant relatives only in exceptional circumstances, greater vigilance in detecting illegal entrants and an inquiry into a system of internal control. In other words the Report of the Select Committee in the preceding month was generally endorsed. The measures were then incorporated within the Conservative Election Manifesto of 1979.

Apart from a Nationality Act in 1981 and tougher control on husbands and fiances in 1980 (modified in 1983), most of the substantial proposals have not been implemented. Instead, changes in the Rules in 1980 and 1983 concentrated on a 'fine tuning' of existing control. In terms of the reduction in the number of entrants, their effect has been marginal compared to the rhetoric of 1978. The reasons for this were obvious in 1978. For, once the commitment to U.K.P.H.s and dependants was reaffirmed, there could be no prospect of reducing the rate of entry to anything beyond a minor degree. The 'commitment' and 'reduction' were incompatible. Moreover, as a former Prime Minister pointed out at the time,[216] the 1971 Act and Rules had already given the Government all the powers it needed to deal with immigration effectively. Moreover, if the defence of the British character is the real issue, it is insufficient[217] to promise an end to immigration whilst ignoring the facts that in 1978 there was a coloured population and there will be at the turn of the century.

Instead the Conservative Party proposals in 1978 can be expressed as follows, 'there is little that a Government can realistically do to end immigration, but the public fear its consequences and politicians should therefore appease that opinion and make the appropriate noises'. Under this approach, if many people believe that immigration is a serious problem, that very belief becomes the problem and politicians can harness it to the attractive argument that good race relations are at stake. What it lacks is a credible and courageous moral leadership setting out the reality of immigration and seeking to allay the public's fears. The Labour Government of the day made much political capital out of the Opposition's pandering to restrictionist opinion, but such has been the bipartisan approach to immigration since 1965 that its protestations were disingenuous. Firstly, it had already tightened control by the restrictions on husbands and fiances in 1977.[218] Second, the controversial Report of the Select Committee in 1978 was unanimous. Third, part of the Government's attack on the Opposition was based on the premise that 'the law and practice were already very tough and that there was no need to go further'.[219] This line of attack was framed with one eye looking to electoral repercussions, viz., public fear of immigration is classless and there are few votes to win and many to lose by being seen to 'go soft' on the issue.[220] Indeed in July the Home Secretary refused to curb the increased removal of illegal immigrants which had resulted from the courts' interpretation of the 1971 Act (the Zamir line of cases).[221]

(c) The greater sophistication and manipulation of the entry clearance procedure as the prime method of control. One of its many advantages from the official point of view was that it shifted the daily administration of control overseas and out of the glare of publicity, which had preceded the 1962 and 1968 Acts, at U.K. ports of entry.

(d) In spite of repeated declarations in support of racial harmony and a third Race Relations Act in 1976, the official action in support of the aim remained woefully inadequate e.g. in the slender use of Government contracts to promote equal employment opportunity and the lack of financial efforts to reduce racial disadvantage. To ethnic communities this was all the more discouraging since immigration figures began to fall steadily in the second half of the decade and there should in theory have been greater scope for active promotion of racial harmony. The plea by the Chairman of the Commission for Racial Equality is as valid today as it was in 1978 - "May we please hear increasingly from Mrs. Thatcher and her colleagues (and from members of the present Government) about their positive policies for tackling racial disadvantage and discrimination ..."[222]

(e) A growing awareness of the civil liberties' implications of immigration. This in turn produced a greater resort to legalism by appeals to judicial review. Yet, by the time that the awareness and legalism began to show modest signs of success at the start of the 1980s, the tide of immigrants was steadily but consistently ebbing. The problem of

numbers was a declining one and the few successful
challenges to immigration policy came too late in the
day to help the bulk of modern immigration.

(f) An example of this late challenge arose in February
1985. The Commission for Racial Equality (CRE)
published its much awaited and leaked formal
Investigation into Immigration Control Procedures.
Prompted by the revelation in 1979 that a virginity
test had been employed on an Indian fiancee at
Heathrow Airport, the CRE decided that an investigation would assist in the elimination of racial
discrimination.[223] Its general conclusions were that
immigration control had been operated too strictly in
order to detect ineligible entrants and to the
detriment of race relations, and that a change in
emphasis was needed in favour of fairer treatment for
the eligible. The Report confirmed many fears - the
uncompromisingly suspicious attitude of the
immigration authorities towards passengers from
certain countries and the often unfair methods by
which those suspicions are expressed. It should be
noted here that the CRE Report was frequently
restrained, by its terms of reference, from voicing
more strident criticisms of its target. Nevertheless,
the Report is the most independent and extensive
survey yet conducted into immigration control into the
U.K. As to its effect, the most signal and unique was
its investigation into areas which have by long
tradition remained secret and sensitive to civil
servants. In this process the CRE enjoyed access to
those internal administrative instructions which guide
immigration officers and in fact quoted from them
extensively in the Report. This prompted the Home
Secretary to announce[224] that the instructions were
under review and that future versions might be
published. Indeed he promised more openness from his
Department about its work. More fundamentally the CRE
argued that a change of emphasis by the Home Office
towards a fairer treatment of immigrants 'could' bring
substantial benefits to race relations.[225] This is
doubtful for, it is submitted, the level of racial
discrimination has been so entrenched that a
relaxation of immigration procedures would come so
late as to improve race relations marginally, if at
all. From the viewpoint of the resident immigrant
population it would probably be seen as a cosmetic
operation, implemented, significantly, now that large
scale immigration has passed. To have effect such a
change in emphasis would have to be accompanied by a
concerted and wide ranging attack on racial

discrimination, an attack which no Government or Opposition has been prepared to mount.

The CRE Report stressed that the Home Office works on the 'pressure to emigrate' theory viz. that evasion of immigration control is most prevalent amongst entrants from countries where there is the greatest economic, political or social pressure to leave.[226] These are predominantly New Commonwealth and Third World countries. The CRE concluded[227] that there was insufficient statistical or other evidence to support the link between evasion of control and 'pressure to emigrate'. The fact that a large number of apprehended evaders come from poor countries is, it argued, due to biased methods of detection and the stereotyping of those nationalities as likely evaders. This conclusion is highly debatable; (1) the CRE does after all concede that the aforementioned pressures are the real motives for emigration.[228] Since the majority of primary immigrants in the 1950s and 1960s came from certain countries, it is to be expected that the greatest pressure of secondary immigration will arise in those countries and that, given the rigidity and strictness of the U.K.'s immigration law, the incentive to evade control will loom large. (2) If the Home Office can detect so many evaders by stereotyping, the temptation may be to increase rather than decrease the extent of stereotyping and the CRE's criticism may backfire. (3) In fairness to the Home Office, it is extremely difficult in the inherently uncertain field of law-breaking to envisage statistical evidence which could not be faulted.[229]

Whatever the statistics can or do not reveal, it is suggested that the CRE's general approach is correct on grounds of principle. Its conclusions support some of the themes in this book which call for a more open-minded approach to individual immigrants, for natural justice and, more generally, for a less hostile attitude to immigration and a positive commitment by Governments to improve race relations. Moreover, it should be noted that 35 million passengers arrived at U.K. ports in 1983. 12 million were subject to control yet only 14,665 were refused leave to enter.[230] Perhaps it is more accurate and prudent to acknowledge that the U.K.'s immigration procedures are a very effective deterrent against illegal entrants and that to relax the country's 'guard' slightly would hardly open a 'floodgate'. For, at the end of the day, the geography of the U.K. will always mean that, compared to the vast majority of countries, effective immigration control is a simple exercise.

----
1   Home Secretary, moving the Second Reading of the Aliens
Restriction Bill, H.C. Debs. 15 April 1919, col. 2746.

2   See generally, 'A History of the Jews in England', Roth;
'Expulsion of the Jews from England', Abrahams.

3   Their importance to the economy as revenue gatherers was
acknowledged under Henry III by an injunction against them
leaving the Kingdom without licence - Patent Rolls 1218, p.80.

4   Note the Charter of Liberties to the Jews of 1201, Charter
Roll 2 John, m.5.

5   See Statuta de Judaismo, 1218, 1222, 1253 and 1275.

6   Their role as lenders to the Crown was taken over
principally by the Lombards and Templars. It was reckoned that
15,060 Jews were expelled, Stow, Annals, at p.313.

7   The return was officially authorised by the Privy Council
in 1664.

8   9 Henry III, c.30, 25 Ed I c.30.

9   Charter Roll, 2 Ed. III, m.11, no.37; see also 9 Ed III,
c.1 (1335), renewed in 1351.

10   Note the important role which the feudal household played
in offering employment opportunities to aliens, see
Cunningham, Alien Immigrants to Britain, p.42-47.

11   11 Ed. III, c.5.

12   For an account of the woollen industry, see Lipson,
Economic History of England, vol. I, ch.9: but there were many
other industries which benefited from foreigners, such as
mining and clock making.

13   For the silk industry, see 3 Ed. III, c.3, 22 Ed. III,
c.3, 1 R III, c.10, 33 Henry VI, c.5, 19 Henry VII, c.2.

14   See further chapter 3. Another concession to aliens was
trial de medietate linguae, i.e. by a jury composed of equal
numbers of Englishmen and aliens (see 28 Ed III, c.13;
endorsed in 1429 by 8 Hy VI, c.29).

15   1 Rich. III, c.9.

16   E.g. alien merchants bringing fish and victuals could sell
them in spite of special grants and letters patent available

to native merchants and it was an offence to obstruct these aliens, see 6 R II, c.10 (endorsed by 1 Hy IV, c.17 and 14 Hy VI, c.6).

17   See the accounts by J. Wheeler, 'A Treatise of Commerce', 1601; H. Zimmern, 'The Hansa Towns', 1889. The privileges were lost in 1552.

18   Hosting began in the 12th century and was reintroduced or at least re-affirmed at regular intervals e.g. 9 Ed. III, c.2, 5 Hy IV, c.9.

19   1 R III, c.9.

20   18 Hy VI, c.4.

21   Lipson, Economic History of England, vol. 1, 531-3.

22   E.g. to combat the Gascon wine trade, 5 R II, c.3, 14 R II c.6. The first Navigation Act was passed in 1381.

23   See the account in Stow, Annals at p.848ff; and further the expulsion of Bretons in 1415 (3 Hy V, c.3) and the requirement that Irishmen resorting to the Realm should give sureties for their good behaviour (2 Hy VI, c.8).

24   For an account of those who threw in their lot with the Crown, see 'Letters of Denization and Acts of Naturalisation', W. Page, Huguenot Society (1893).

25   4-5 P and Mary c.6.

26   See the account by J.S. Burn, "History of the Foreign Refugees", (1846).

27   21 Hy VIII c.16 (1529).

28   E.g. pewter and tin, 25 HY VIII c.9, bookbinding 25 Hy VIII c.15.

29   E.g. alien weavers of worsted in Yarmouth and Linn so as to protect native weavers, 14 and 15 Hy VIII c.3.

30   E.g. 22 Hy VIII c.8, 32 Hy VIII c.16.

31   14-15 Hy VIII c.2, 21 Hy VIII c.16, 32 Hy VIII c.16.

32   Thus forcing them to employ native labour; cf. the current Immigration Rules which require self-employed immigrants to create local employment, H.C. 169, r.36 and see ch.7.

33 See Page, supra, p.xx.

34 Ibid, p.Lii.

35 By virtue of 4-5 P. and Mary c.6.

36 See Hulme, History of the Patent System, 12 L.Q.R. 141, at 145-150.

37 See, for example, the letter from the Queen to the Justices of Cumberland ordering them to ensure the safety of German miners, reproduced in Tudor Economic Documents, ed. Thirsk and Cooper p.249; and from the Privy Council to protect Dutch bag makers, ibid, p.319.

38 27 E I, c.2.

39 S.3 of 15 Car. II, c.15.

40 See House of Commons Journals, X, p.666.

41 For an account of their influence, see Smiles S, The Huguenots.

42 (1621) P.R., S.P. 14/127, no.12; quoted in Seventeenth Century Documents, ed. Thirsk and Cooper at p.716.

43 (1622), ibid. no.15; quoted ibid. at p.718.

44 (1654), P.R.O. S.P. 18/71 no.20.1, para. 8; quoted ibid at p.727.

45 The year of Calvin's case 77 E.R. 377, which clarified aspects of the law.

46 Daubigny v Davallon (1794) 145 E.R. 936, at 937-8.

47 12 Car. II, c.18.

48 Cases then arose to determine the nationality of the ship or its crew; for one concerning the cited statute, see Scot v Schawrtz (1739) 92 E.R. 1265.

49 He became a natural-born subject, save for some offices to which he was still barred (e.g. member of Parliament), see Blackstone, Commentaries, Book 1, Chapter 10, p.374.

50 The status was "a kind of middle state, between an alien and natural-born subject", ibid.

51 E.g. Journal of the House of Commons XI, 28-129, and at 61

for the petition of London merchants against the Naturalisation Bill.

52 Sir John Knight speaking against the 1693 Bill –
Parliamentary History, vol. 5, col. 854.

53 7 Ann, c.5.

54 10 Ann, c.5.

55 7 Jam. 1, c.2.

56 13 Geo. II, c.7.

57 20 Geo. II, c.44.

58 22 Geo. II, c.45.

59 For a list, see Magna Bibliotheca Anglo-Judaica: A
Bibliographical Guide to Anglo-Jewish History, (1937), Roth C.

60 (1753) Parliamentary History, XIV, col. 1381.

61 Quoted by Roth in A History of the Jews in England, at
p.219.

62 See p.81

63 6 Geo. IV, c.67.

64 7 & 8 Vic., c.66.

65 33 Geo. III c.4. The history of Executive discretion would
seem to argue against the need for legislation to achieve the
purpose; see the contrasting views of Craies, 6 L.Q.R. 27 and
Haycroft, 13 L.Q.R. 165.

66 In 1798 in the first Federal legislation on the subject, 1
Stat. 570.

67 E.g. Australia, Canada.

68 If the alien returned within that period, he was
transported for life.

69 See Rules 85 and 159, H.C. 169 (1982-83).

70 See Immigration Act 1971, Sched. 2, para. 26.

71 E.g. Defence of the Realm Act 1914. Cf. the internal
control on movement operated in South Africa, through the

Natives (Urban Areas) (Consolidation) Act 1945.

72 Cf. today's system of identity cards employed on the Continent and the call by the Select Committee (1978) to consider its introduction in the U.K.

73 E.g. s.39.

74 33 Geo. III, c.50.

75 [1980] A.C. 930 and see Ch 8.

76 See D.P.P. v Bhagwan [1972] A.C. 60.

77 But this provision was not repeated in the subsequent legislation until 1814.

78 The discretion was illustrated further in the same year by 38 Geo. III, c.77 whereby an Order in Council could vary the time limits in the principal Act.

79 42 Geo. III, c.92.

80 See s.21.

81 43 Geo. III, c.155.

82 54 Geo. III, c.155.

83 55 Geo. III, c.54.

84 56 Geo. III, c.86.

85 7 Geo. IV, c.54.

86 2 and 3 Will. IV, c.84, ss.4 and 5.

87 See further, Walvin, Black and White (1973).

88 6 and 7 Will. IV, c.11.

89 Royal Commission, infra, para. 46-54.

90 King's Advocate to the Earl of Aberdeen (1828) F.O. 83/2317, see British Digest of International Law, vol. 6, p.15.

91 House of Commons Select Committee on the Laws Affecting Aliens, 1843, P.P. vol.v., p.ix.

92 Ibid.

94

93 See the guarded statement of the Marquess of Lansdowne on introducing the Bill, vol.98 Hansard, col. 136-8 (11 April 1848); cf. the unspecified dangers mentioned in the Commons, ibid, col.560-2 (1 May 1848).

94 Marquess of Lansdowne, vol. 98 Hansard, col. 265 (13 April 1848).

95 A large demonstration had taken place a day before the Bill was announced. The mood can be gauged by 11 Vict. c.12, an Act for the better security of the Crown and Government of the U.K., which had passed through Parliament at the same time and which broadened the scope of, and tightened the penalties for, anti-Governmental activities.

96 11 Vict. c.20.

97 See the Returns at 1850 P.P. vol. xxxiii (p.227).

98 The U.K. Government assisted this to a limited extent in the early 1850s by the provision of public funds to pay for the fare across the Atlantic; see Porter, the Refugee Question in mid-Victorian Politics, (1979) at p.160 and the sources cited therein. The book is an excellent and lucid account of the position of refugees at this time.

99 This extended to the provision of public funds to help aliens; see Papers relating to Polish Refugees, 1850, P.P. vol. xxxiii (a grant of £10,000 being provided).

100 See the emotions expressed at the Second Reading, vol. 148 Hansard col. 1741-1847 (19 February 1858); Porter, supra, ch.6.

101 Porter, supra, p.124.

102 See Cumpston, Indians Overseas in British Territories 1834-1854.

103 16 and 17 Vict. c.84.

104 18 and 19 Vict. c.104.

105 See Campbell, Chinese Coolie Emigration, ch.3.

106 Increased to £100 in 1899. Cf. Chinese Immigrants Regulation Act 1877 (Queensland).

107 Cf. Chinese Immigrants Act 1888 (New Zealand) - 1 per 100 tons.

[108] See also Immigration Act 1906 (South Africa) and cf. the case of Shidiack (1911) S.A. Rep. 25; Immigration Restriction Act 1899 (New Zealand).

[109] See generally, Willard, History of the White Australia Policy to 1920.

[110] For a summary of the causes of this emigration, see Royal Commission on Alien Immigration, 1903, Evidence, cd. 1742 Q 1339.

[111] Report to the Board of Trade on the Sweating System at the East End of London, (1887) P.P. vol. LXXXIX.

[112] Ibid., at p.7. See a similar Report on the position in Leeds, P.P., 1887, vol. LXXXVI.

[113] House of Commons Select Committee on Immigration and Emigration, First Report, P.P., 1888, vol. XI, Second Report, P.P., 1889, vol. X. House of Lords Select Committee on the Sweating System, PP., 1888, vols. XX, XXI; 1889, vols. XIII, XVI; 1890, vol. XVII.

[114] Royal Commission, infra, Ev. Q 8558.

[115] Sir William Marriott during a debate on 'destitute aliens', vol. 8. Hansard, col. 1205 (11 February 1893). For an excellent account of the complaints against aliens, see Gainer, The Alien Invasion.

[116] Cf. the rise of the American equivalents - the Know-Nothing Party and the Klu Klux Klan; and in New Zealand the White Race League (1905).

[117] Royal Commission on Alien Immigration 1903, Cd. 1741 and Evidence, Cd. 1742, 1743.

[118] Report, para. 88.

[119] Para. 38.

[120] Para. 126-132.

[121] Para. 131.

[122] P.41. Cf. the dissent of Sir Kennelm Digby who pointed out, *inter alia*, that the mischiefs of immigration were not as great as had been claimed and that those which existed could be tackled by less elaborate machinery than that proposed by the majority.

123 The House of Commons Select Committee had earlier paid particular attention to possible lessons from the experience of the U.S. - P.P., 1888, vol. XI.

124 For the U.S., see the Commission, Ev. Q.16313.

125 The Acts of 1886 and 1902. For the precedents of Australia and New Zealand see earlier.

126 18 Stat. 477.

127 22 Stat. 214.

128 23 Stat. 332 and 24 Stat. 414.

129 26 Stat. 1084.

130 32 Stat. 1213. For an account of U.S. legislation in this period, see Garis, Immigration Restriction, (1927).

131 First by Cleveland in 1897 and subsequently by Presidents Taft and Wilson.

132 E.g. in 1918 to exclude anarchists, and in 1921 to impose quotas according to the national origins of the entrants (refined and reinforced in 1924).

133 S.8(2). Reduced to 12 by Order in Council in December 1905 but raised to 20 in March 1906 - Regulations made under the Aliens Act 1905, cd. 2879.

134 Cf. the obligation to reveal whether a ship had employed Lascars (those of Indian origin) as seamen before the ship could enter port - 4 Geo IV, c.80, s.27 (1823) and Merchant Shipping Act, 1894 s.125(4).

135 Cd. 2879, p.19.

136 Ibid, p.39.

137 Ibid., p.39.

138 Cf. the provisions which had operated to similar effect in the nineteenth century to remove Lascars who had left their ships and been convicted of vagrancy, 4 Geo IV, c.80, s.31 (1823) and Merchant Shipping Act 1894, s.185.

139 Cd. 2879, p.29; dated 9 March 1906.

140 Ibid, p.30.

[141] For a neat illustration of the association of aliens with crime, note the illuminating correspondence between the Secretary of State and His Honour Judge Rentoul (H.C. 63, 1909), following a speech of the latter in which he had expressed alarm at the prevalence of crime amongst aliens. His inaccuracies and scaremongering were pointed out by the reasoned replies of the Secretary. See further H.C. Debs. 8 February 1911, cols. 276-7, where the Home Secretary clearly refuted the alleged link between immigration and increased crime. In fact aliens had fallen from 2.2% of the prison population in 1904 to 1.2% in 1910.

[142] The attacks began in Tredegar and were directed against 'extortionate' Jewish landlords and shopkeepers, see Times, 23-25 August 1911, Jewish Chronicle, 25 August 1911.

[143] For Second Reading of this Aliens Bill, see H.C. Debs. 28 April 1911, col. 2106.

[144] See vol. 65 Hansard, 5 August 1914, col. 1986. It was introduced at 3.30 p.m. and received the Royal Assent at 7.0 p.m.

[145] S.1(1)(K). Only Sir William Byles voiced concern at the "very dangerous power" being given to the Home Secretary, Hansard, supra, col. 1990.

[146] Home Secretary (McKenna), Hansard, supra, col. 1986.

[147] Then Mr. Quintin Hogg, at H.C. Debs. 22 January 1969, col. 504.

[148] In addition, the Defence of the Realm Act 1914 imposed martial law. Its supplementary Order allowed detention (i.e. internment for "public safety or defence of the Realm" - regulation 14B). For an illuminating account of the treatment of aliens, see J.C. Bird, Control of Enemy Alien Civilians in Great Britain 1914-1918, Thesis, University of London, 1981. See further, Sir Edward Troup, The Home Office (1925).

[149] E.g. Simon v Phillips (1916) 85 L.J.K.B. 656; Agdeshman v Hunt (1917) 86 L.J.K.B. 1334.

[150] See R v Denison ex p. Nagale (1916) 85 L.J.K.B. 1744 (an order specifying an alien's place of residence was not subject to reasonableness, it had only to be honestly made).

[151] R v Knockaloe Camp Commandant (1918) 87 L.J.K.B. 43.

152 Quite Draconian restrictions were also placed on former enemy aliens, ss.9-11.

153 Sir William Joynson-Hicks on a visit to the Immigration Service, quoted by Roche, 'The Key in the Lock', at p.107.

154 See H.C. Debs. 23 May 1938, col. 834.

155 See Sherman, Island Refuge, p.90-91, and generally for a detailed account of the UK's policy at this time; see also Wasserstein, Britain and the Jews of Europe, 1939-1945, (1979).

156 See the Home Secretary's statement of policy, H.C. Debs. 22 March 1938, col. 991.

157 Ibid, for a refusal by the Home Secretary to reveal the full extent of his instructions to his officers.

158 Home Secretary, H.C. Debs. 12 October 1939, col. 538. For a debate on the plight of refugees, see H.C. Debs. 21 November, col. 1428, and, for the Government's position, col. 1463. Cf. the U.K.'s attitude to displaced persons after the War - see Bethell, Last Secret: Forcible Repatriation to Russia; Tolstoy, Victims of Yalta.

159 Emergency Powers (Defence) Acts 1939 and 1940 and Regulations made thereunder.

160 E.g. the notorious reg. 18B (Defence (General) Regulations 1939) which permitted detention of, inter alia, persons of hostile associations or prejudicial to public safety.

161 Liversidge v Anderson [1942] AC 206; Greene v Secretary of State [1942] AC 284.

162 See Hepple, Race, Jobs and the Law, at p.70-72. More generally, Tannahill, European Volunteer Workers in Britain.

163 H.C. Debs. 5 November 1954, col. 827, during an adjournment debate on the issue of immigration.

164 Lord Gardiner, at H.L. Debs. 10 March 1965, col. 166

165 The U.K. had experienced some coloured immigration from overseas armed forces serving in the U.K. during the War, see Guardian, 7 January 1984 for an account.

166 66 Stat. 163; 8 U.S.C. 1101. Often known, after its Congressional sponsors, as the McCarran-Walter Act.

[167] See generally, Peach, West Indian Migration to Britain.

[168] Censuses of 1951 and 1961, as interpreted by Rose, Colour and Citizenship, p.97 and App. III.4.

[169] Home Office Estimates.

[170] For an analysis of immigration between 1959 and 1962, see Leech, Race vol. VIII, No.4 (1966). For an account of the sending countries, see Rose, op cit, ch.5, and of the development in the 1950s, ch.6.

[171] H.C. Debs. 3 April 1958, col. 1415 ff; although possible action had been discussed earlier at Cabinet level in 1950 and 1955.

[172] See Foot P, Immigration and Race in British Politics (1965).

[173] Ibid.

[174] Macmillan H, At the end of the Day (1973) p.73.

[175] H.C. Debs. 16 November 1961, col. 687.

[176] Ibid, col. 804.

[177] White Paper, Cmnd. 2739, para. 14. By that time there were 300,000 applications outstanding for C vouchers, ibid., para. 6.

[178] Evidence to Select Committee (1969), Q 2101, 2146 and Summary of Evidence by Bottomley and Sinclair, para. 34.

[179] Ibid., p.497-500.

[180] Cmnd. 2739.

[181] In November 1963, the Labour Party had voted against renewal of the 1962 Act but its Election Manifesto of September 1964 noted that "Labour accepts that the number of immigrants entering the U.K. must be limited".

[182] H.C. Debs. 9 March 1965, col. 248; and H.L. Debs. 10 March 1965, col. 94 (an estimated 26,700 evaders, of whom 10,000 were from the new Commonwealth).

[183] H.C. Debs. 4 February 1965, col. 1284.

[184] Para. 12.

185 Sir Frank Soskice, H.C. Debs. 16 July 1965, col. 1056.

186 Provided their passports had been issued by the U.K. and not on behalf of it e.g. by a Governor - see Bhurosah [1968] 1 QB 266.

187 For a detailed account of the background to the Act see Steel, No Entry.

188 H.C. Debs. 27 February 1968, col. 1246.

189 Mr. Richard Crossman, Times, 6 October 1972. For the ambivalent, if not quietly hostile response of the T.U.C. to immigration, see Miles and Phizacklea, The T.U.C., Black Workers and New Commonwealth Immigration 1957-73, (1977).

190 13 Y.B. E.C.H.R. 928 (1970).

191 Report on Immigration from Indian Sub-Continent, H.C. 90-1, Part III (1981-82).

192 Home Secretary, H.C. Debs. 13 November 1969, col. 435.

193 Ibid., col. 438.

194 Ibid., col. 427 ff.

195 See further ch.5; cf. however the view of Lord Denning M.R. in Thakrar [1974] Q.B. 684.

196 The Ugandan Resettlement Board.

197 Modelled on proposals of the Wilson Committee, cmnd. 3387 (1967).

198 Per Orr L.J. in Thakrar [1974] Q.B. 684, at p.708.

199 See H.C. 79 (1973), r.27; now r.29, H.C. 169 (1983).

200 Between 1973 and 1976 only 184 from the Asian subcontinent qualified - Home Office, Control of Immigration Statistics.

201 H.C. Debs. 8 March 1971, col. 43.

202 H.C. 303-I (1977-78).

203 Though Labour members were soon seeking to play down this aspect, Mr. Syd Bidwell M.P., Guardian, 8 April 1978, Mr. Fred Willey M.P., Times, 20 June 1978.

204 Evidence, H.C. 303-II, Q 648 ff.

205 It rejected the proposals for a system of internal control, an annual quota and entry of children only under the age of 12 (which it regarded as "inhumane"); on the other hand, the Response did emphatically stress the Government's commitment to firm control and offered no hope to liberal opinion, see cmnd. 7287 (July 1978).

206 Western Mail, Leader, 22 March 1978.

207 Acquittal of John Kingsley Read on 6 January; see the weekend press for 7 and 8 January 1978.

208 Race Relations Act 1965, s.6: see Lester and Bindman, Race and Law, ch.10.

209 The accused at a public rally was alleged, inter alia, to have referred to the recent death of an Asian as 'One down and a million to go'.

210 Judge McKinnon who revealed that at school his nickname had been 'nigger', gave a summing-up which was favourable to the defence and, on acquittal, wished the accused well. See Times, Guardian, 7 January.

211 Guardian, ibid.

212 Mrs. Margaret Thatcher M.P., World in Action, (Granada Television) 30 January 1978. See Times 31 January, for a partial transcript and H.C. Debs, 31 January, col. 240.

213 Immigration was hardly out of the news in the next 3 months.

214 Speech to the Young Conservatives' Conference, 12 February 1978.

215 Speech to the Conservative Central Council, 7 April 1978. See Times, Guardian, Daily Telegraph 8 April, Observer 9 April.

216 Mr. Edward Heath M.P., Times, 14 February 1978.

217 Or "the cruellest folly or deception", in the words of Mr. Enoch Powell M.P. in a speech to the Coventry Management Club on 18 February 1978; for a transcript, see Observer, 19 February.

218 See ch.6. The basis of those restrictions remains today.

219 See the sentiments expressed at Question Time following

the Opposition Leader's T.V. interview, H.C. Debs. 31 January 1978, col. 240 ff.

220 See the illuminating letter of Mr. Syd Bidwell M.P. (a member of the Select Committee) - Guardian, 8 April 1978. Note also the letter from the Prime Minister to the Opposition Leader proposing a round-table conference so as to "evolve a common approach to immigration and race relations", text, Times 15 February 1978.

221 H.C. Debs. 20 July 1978, col. 306; cf. the Government's commitment to act firmly against illegal entrants in its Response to the Select Committee, Cmnd. 7287, paras. 27, 28.

222 Mr. David Lane, letter to the Times, 11 April 1978.

223 This prompted the Home Office, under its different immigration and nationality hat, to try to veto the investigation, see Home Office v Commission for Racial Equality [1982] Q.B. 385.

224 Times and Guardian, 13 April 1985. The Government's initial reaction to the Report can be seen at H.C. Debs., 23 May 1985, col. 1168, where the Report was debated.

225 Report, para. 11.6.9.

226 See Appendix 1 to the CRE Report for the Home Office's view.

227 For a summary of the CRE's view, see Report, paras. 2.5.1.ff.

228 Report, para. 2.5.4.

229 For the CRE's criticisms, see Report, paras. 6.16.1.ff.

230 See Home Office, 'A Report on the work of the Immigration and Nationality Department' (1984), ch.5.

3 CITIZENSHIP

The first and most obvious division of the people is into
aliens and natural-born subjects. Natural-born subjects
are such as are born within the dominions of the Crown of
England; that is, within the ligeance, or, as it is
generally called, the allegiance of the King; and aliens,
such as are born out of it.[1]

A. ROLE OF CITIZENSHIP

The shape of a State's immigration policy ultimately stems
from its view of citizenship. Only when the latter has been
determined can the former be defined and elucidated. Both are
essentially matters for the State's sovereign discretion.
Indeed, a State's right to decide its own composition is one
of the first hallmarks of sovereignty, not least because of
its implications for defence. For example, citizenship was an
ancillary cause of the American war of independence, for which
the emerging constitution made clear provision, viz., Congress
shall have the power to establish a uniform rule of naturalisation.[2] Moreover, the grant of citizenship is, and always
will be, an area jealously preserved to a State's sovereignty.
This is reflected in the lack of progress in international law
towards the codification of nationality laws and the
acceptance of legal obligations by States. Even in the more
cohesive atmosphere of the E.E.C., very limited progress has
been made - the adoption of a Passport Union has been
extremely slow and it does not trespass on the Member State's
right to define its own nationals.
    Consequently there are no rules as to how citizenship
shall be granted. For example, for States eager to acquire
citizens, the requirements may be objective and straightforward e.g. birth, residence. For others, historical
considerations may be important e.g. the Republic of Ireland
in relation to Northern Ireland, the U.K. in relation to the
Commonwealth. For most, adherence to the State's values via

language, culture or racial ties will be required. Whichever basis is chosen, the framing of nationality legislation is an opportunity for a State to define itself, as it pleases.

In this process States have always distinguished between those who belong, those who wish to belong and aliens. The first category covers both citizens and those forced to belong such as the conquered and slaves; the second encompasses naturalisation or frequently a middle or second class status. An early but still typical approach was that of Ancient Greece which divided persons into citizens, settlers and strangers. Several common motives have lain behind policies of citizenship -

B. MOTIVES FOR CONFERRING CITIZENSHIP

Many of these appear in the historical outline (below) and can be mentioned briefly here.

(1) For the defence of the State. This appears in the concept of 'allegiance'. Though to many it is unfashionable to speak of allegiance today, perhaps because of its feudal connotations of subservience, it has a long and influential history in English law and still describes an essential feature of citizenship, <u>viz</u>., the element of loyalty which ultimately calls upon the citizen to take up arms in defence of the State.[3] This motive can arise in several ways -

    (i) as a consequence of territorial sovereignty e.g. the grant of citizenship to all within the boundaries of the British Empire;

   (ii) as an inducement to potential allies e.g. the grant of <u>civitas</u> under the Roman Empire to neighbouring and sympathetic countries;

  (iii) as a reward for, or encouragement to, military service.

(2) For cultural and social identity. This overlaps with the interests of defence but extends further into the concept of nationhood. It seeks to attract those who are more readily assimilable into the adoptive country and who are therefore 'likely to become good citizens'. "A new scheme of citizenship should reflect the strength of the connection which various groups of people have with the U.K. ... [and the new category of British Citizens should cover] those who have close links with the U.K. ... and who can be expected to identify themselves with British society."[4]
The connecting factor may be;

    (i) religious e.g. the Act of 1609[5] which required the

applicant for naturalisation to take the Sacrament;

(ii) racial e.g. the laws of the U.S. which at first (1790) confined naturalisation to "free white persons" and then denied citizenship to Negroes until 1868,[6] to Red Indians until 1924,[7] the Chinese until 1943 and Filippinos and Asian Indians until 1946;

(iii) political e.g. denial of citizenship to those who advocate the overthrow of the Government, by means of a "good character" test or more specific prohibitions;[8]

(iv) cultural e.g. a knowledge of the country's history, language and political institutions before naturalisation is permitted.[9]

This purpose of homogeneity can be illustrated by the discrimination which is frequently practised against resident non-citizens (e.g. the legal right to hold land for their own benefit was denied to aliens until 1870 in the U.K., lest the nation be subject to undue foreign influence; denial to aliens of access to public office - art. 48(4) E.E.C. Treaty).[10]

(3) For economic purposes - both to encourage trade with foreigners and to preserve its benefits for the State's own nationals. As to the former, citizenship has been used as a carrot to alien settlers when new skills are needed; e.g. the second class status granted to settlers in Ancient Greece, or the naturalisation offered to European settlers in England in the sixteenth century so that they might modernise native industry. As to the latter, citizenship (of individuals and companies) is frequently the yardstick for allotting trading privileges; e.g. by licences, lower taxes and customs duties, the Navigation Acts in England which reserved the sole or most fruitful benefits of trade to native merchants being a prime example.

Motives (2) and (3) illustrate the vital importance of citizenship in framing a State's immigration policy. Not only does it draw the necessary distinction between citizens and others for the purpose of control at ports of entry, but it can also be used positively to increase or stem the flow of immigration by attaching different civil, political and economic rights according to citizenship status - with the citizen enjoying full legal status and the foreigner varying degrees of disability. The apogee of subtle distinctions was reached under Roman Law with a formidable classification of status. The basic distinction lay between cives (citizens), servi (slaves), latini (a half-way house between citizenship and alienage) and peregrini (aliens), but this was in turn subdivided into remarkably subtle classes, each with its own set of privileges and legal and social rights.[11]

C. CRITERIA FOR CONFERRING CITIZENSHIP

(1) The simplest criterion is that of birth within the State's boundaries - <u>ius soli</u>. It is arbitrary, encompassing, for example, the pregnant traveller whose child will acquire the local citizenship but may risk losing his parent's nationality if dual citizenship is forbidden by the parent's nationality law. On the other hand, it has the supreme advantage of simplicity.

(2) To cope with its citizens who travel abroad, States then permit citizenship by descent. Since this proceeds on the basis that the citizen wishes his children to retain links with his own country, he is usually required to display some interest in it. For some citizens, the interest is automatically assumed - diplomats, armed forces, transmission to the first generation. For others the conferring State may require positive action such as registration of the birth at its consular offices or a period of residence in its territory prior to confirmation of the citizenship.

(3) Elaborate criteria are usually prescribed for those foreigners who wish to become citizens. It is here that the conferring State can give the greatest scope to its nationalism since it has the opportunity of defining what type of person it deems worthy enough to be assimilated within its society.

D. THE EARLY HISTORY OF CITIZENSHIP

In England citizenship depended upon allegiance. This concept of allegiance stemmed from the feudal system of personal loyalty owed by the tenant to the Lord of the manor. It was applied on a national basis once the Monarchy had taken a firm hold over the country in the thirteenth century. It was closely linked to the territorial scope of the Lord's, and then the King's, power. It followed from this tie that all persons born within the King's rule automatically became his subjects,[12] even if the child was illegitimate[13] or if his parents were aliens.[14]

The concept of allegiance is crucial to an understanding of citizenship law. As will be seen, most of the difficulties in the law have stemmed from the concept. Thus, it gave rise to rights and obligations on the part of State and subject. "Because as the subject hath his protection from the King and his laws, so on the other side the subject is bound by his allegiance to be true and faithful to the King."[15] Herein lies the basis of diplomatic protection which may be claimed from the State by the subject.[16] The citizen's obligations were regarded by the law as immutable. "As the ligatures or strings do knit together the joints of all the parts of the body, so doth ligeance join together the sovereign and all his subjects ... ligeance and obedience of the subject to the sovereign is due by the law of nature; _ergo_ it cannot be altered."[17] Allegiance could only be divested with the approval of the Crown. Consequently treason could be committed regardless of the subject's wishes as to citizenship.[18] This perpetual aspect of allegiance was one of the subsidiary causes of the American war of independence. When British emigres became naturalised in America, potential troops to serve in the British army against France were lost. Thus, the Governor of the Colonies was instructed not to approve naturalisation Bills submitted to him,[19] and a proclamation was passed permitting press-gangs to search neutral vessels for British born seamen who had been naturalised in America.[20] The indelibility of allegiance induced the belief that, like a domicile of origin, a person must always have a nationality. Statelessness was consequently a late developed concept.[21] With the growth in international travel and commerce, this indelibility proved increasingly inconvenient, and was finally abolished by the Naturalisation Act 1870 - which enabled subjects to free themselves by making a declaration of alienage.

The earliest citizenship law could proceed logically from this simple concept of allegiance, for it readily identified those who did not belong to the State. "[N]ow the word alien is a legal term and amounts to as much as many words; an alien must be an alien ne. It implies being born out of the liegeance of the King, and within the liegeance of some other State."[22] But this consequence applied equally to children born abroad to subjects and soon proved inconvenient in military, commercial and testamentary terms. It was reversed in 1351 so that "all children inheritors, which from henceforth shall be born without the ligeance of the King, whose fathers and mothers at the time of their birth be and shall be at the faith and ligeance of the King of England, shall have and enjoy the same benefits and advantages" as natural-born subjects.[23] Consequent upon these terms, much of the ensuing jurisprudence revolved around testamentary law. Typical was Calvin's Case which finally resolved certain doubts over the meaning of the 1351 Statute.[24] There a child born in Scotland and therefore alien born, sought to bring an action for personalty and realty in England. After argument and consideration by virtually all the legal luminaries of the day it was held that persons born before the union of the Crown under James 1 were aliens but those born after it were subjects because they owed allegiance to the Monarch.

The motives for denying aliens the right to inheritance within England were spelt out as follows,

(1) lest the secrets of the realm be discovered,

108

(2) lest the revenues of the realm be enjoyed by strangers and

(3) to allow inheritance would tend towards the destruction of the realm, "for then strangers might fortify themselves in the heart of the realm, and be ready to set fire on the Commonwealth".[25]

Consequently the common law ruled that, though an alien could purchase land, he held the title for the Crown and not for his own use,[26] and could not succeed to property.[27]

The position at the end of the seventeenth century can thus be summarised:-

(a) All persons born within the Crown's Dominions were subjects of the Crown. The position was equivalent to that reached in Roman law in 212 A.D. under the Emperor Caracalla. It provided an inbuilt mechanism for extending citizenship as the Dominions expanded. It was this simple principle, based on allegiance and retained in 1948, which was the pretext for modern immigration laws.

(b) Children born to Crown subjects outside the Dominions acquired the same status.

(c) All non-subjects were aliens and could be subjected to a range of legal and economic disabilities.

(d) Aliens could change their status in two ways –

  (i) By obtaining naturalisation through an Act of Parliament. The person assumed the status of a natural-born subject, save for some offices which were denied to him.[28]

  (ii) By acquiring the more limited status[29] of a denizen through the grant of Royal letters of patent. The grant, which lay firmly within the Crown's prerogative,[30] could be made on request or on the Crown's initiative, e.g. to encourage the settlement of traders.

Both methods were expensive and subject to delay. Few could finance the expense of an Act and, in addition, the need to take the Oath and Sacrament effectively excluded Roman Catholics and Jews. The requirement of the Sacrament was eventually removed in 1826, and in 1844 the pioneering liberality behind an earlier, short-lived Act of 1708 (below) was restored, allowing a simple and modern-looking form of naturalisation.

E. THE USEFULNESS OF CITIZENSHIP

Historically, citizenship has been used by the State for three main purposes.

(1) The encouragement of immigration.
This has a dual purpose.

   (a) To promote trade. The grant of denization was
   frequently used by the Crown to encourage the
   settlement of skilled aliens, and often accompanied
   Royal licences to practise and exploit particular
   industries. Statutes offering naturalisation had the
   same purpose. For example, foreign Protestants working
   in the whale fishery industry for three years could be
   naturalised without the necessity of an Act of
   Parliament, but, to emphasise its mercenary economic
   motive, the benefit was lost if the subject left the
   King's Dominions for more than 12 months.[31] Foreign
   Protestants were encouraged on a large scale in 1708
   by the offer of a simpler form of naturalisation, so
   that they might be a "means of advancing the Wealth
   and Strength of a Nation".[32] The relaxation in the
   naturalisation laws in 1844 came after a Parliamentary
   Committee had concluded that foreigners were not being
   encouraged sufficiently to settle.[33]
   (b) To strengthen national defence. Thus, all aliens who
   served for two years on board English ships during
   wartime were automatically naturalised.[34]

(2) The protection of trade.
As with immigration laws, this has been a central motive of
citizenship. For infant industries or those in which the alien
had proved to be too successful, the citizen/alien distinction
was employed to debar the latter or place him under financial
disabilities. For example, in 1660 trade between England and
its colonies was confined to English owned ships so as to
increase the "shipping ... navigation of this nation";[35] no
alien could trade as merchant in the plantations; any saltfish
which he imported was subject to double aliens customs (unless
carried on an English ship). Under the Navigation Acts, the
foreign born could not own a British-registered ship. The
success of the 1708 Act (above) in attracting German settlers
to "the Detriment of Trade and Wealth" of the kingdom led to
its swift repeal in 1711.[36] Similarly, evidence that foreigners
were becoming naturalised solely to gain immunities and
indulgences in trade and not to reside in Britain led to an
Act of 1774 under which all subsequent Bills for naturalisation had to contain a clause whereby the alien could not
become entitled to full trading rights unless he had resided
in Britain or its Dominions for seven years after passage of
the Bill.[37]

(3) To express nationalism and protect nationhood.
The battlelines, familiar to immigration debate, between
liberals and restrictionists, were drawn during the attempts

110

in 1667, 1672, 1680 and 1693 to allow the naturalisation of foreign Protestants, and this motive of nationalism featured as part of the movement to reverse the Act of 1708 (above). The gist of the complaint was the dilution of racial stock and culture which might result if the 'doors to citizenship were thrown open'. Such arguments were successful in England but they were less pertinent for America since there the Monarchy wished to encourage adherents to its rule and actively promoted naturalisation. Thus, in 1740[38] Parliament not only permitted the naturalisation of foreign Protestants and others settled in America by the taking of the Oath but also allowed Quakers and Jews to benefit by allowing them to take it and to omit the offensive parts of the Oath. In 1747 in a more desperate attempt to encourage subjects, those who refused to take the Oath were permitted instead to make a Declaration of Fidelity.[39] In Britain, however, the expression of nationalism resurfaced in the furore over the Jew Bill of 1753. This permitted Jews to promote Bills for naturalisation without the requirement of taking the Sacrament.[40] It produced an outcry from the Church which foresaw the dilution of its influence, from commerce which feared the economic success which Jews would achieve if allowed all the privileges of naturalisation and more generally from those who were alarmed at the potential cultural damage and loss of nationhood. The Act was repealed in the following year.[41]

Expression of nationalism is seen in milder form in the reservation of sensitive jobs or privileges to 'genuine' citizens; for example, the right to vote,[42] offices of trust such as constable, churchwarden, or the civil service,[43] positions of financial power.[44]

Following a Parliamentary Committee which had urged wider access to citizenship,[45] the law was placed on a modern-looking basis in 1844.[46] All resident aliens who intended to settle could be naturalised by sending a Memorial of details to the Secretary of State, taking the Oath and paying the fees. But, as has remained the case, there was no appeal against refusal. As in immigration, the Secretary of State was entrusted with broad discretion. The liberal Victorian atmosphere went further in 1870 by abandoning the indelibility of alienage and by removing all remaining disabilities on aliens over personal and real property. On the other hand, foreign naturalisation or the marriage of a woman to an alien led automatically to the loss of British citizenship and a declaration of alienage was allowed for others.

Moreover, by interpretation of earlier statutes,[47] the common law in 1882[48] made it clear that citizenship could be transmitted by birth outside the Dominions to the second generation. In 1914 this was confined to the first generation, but such was the outcry, echoed in the controversy which surrounded patriality and the 'grandfather clause' under the current Act and Rules in 1971, that in 1922 a system of registration was instituted whereby the birth of a child overseas could be registered at a British consulate, followed by a declaration of citizenship when the child reached the age of majority. In this way, citizenship could be transmitted indefinitely.

Thus the stage was reached where citizenship could be acquired by any of three methods: birth, covering "Any person born within His Majesty's dominions and allegiance";[49] automatic entitlement through the registration of second and subsequent generations born overseas; and naturalisation of aliens at the discretion of the Secretary of State. The simplicity of ius soli stands in sharp contrast to the complexity of current law.[50]

F. BRITISH NATIONALITY ACTS 1948-1981

Since the Crown was regarded as indivisible, a subject could not claim to belong to a separate part of the Empire. To have taken another nationality would have denied allegiance to the Crown as the supreme ruler of the whole Empire.[51] This principle had of course to bow to the demands and, ultimately, independence of the Colonies and this was recognised at the Imperial Conference of 1926. Thereafter, the Dominions were to be separate, autonomous units, "equal in status, in no way subordinate one to another in any respect of their domestic or external affairs, though united by a common allegiance to the Crown, and freely associated as members of the British Commonwealth of Nations".[52] Dominions naturally wished to define their own citizens.[53] Canada led the way in 1946.[54] This prompted a Commonwealth Conference the following year at which it was agreed that, whilst each Dominion would be free to frame its own citizenship laws, all such citizens would be British subjects and recognised as such by the other Dominions. Crucially, however, each Dominion had the prerogative to decide what the status of British Subject entailed. For example, Australia was to recognise Indians as British subjects but was still free to devise an immigration policy to keep them out.

The U.K. responded to the Conference with the British Nationality Act 1948.[55] This created a citizenship of the United Kingdom and Colonies (UKC). It was obtained on traditional grounds, namely, (a) ius soli, (b) automatically for the first generation born overseas and by registration thereafter (registration within one year for automatic effect, thereafter permissive), or (c) marriage to a UKC husband. If the Act had stopped there, few of the subsequent immigration laws would have been necessary. In an atmosphere of post-war, imperial sentiment it went further, however, and by the following provisions reinforced the policy of the 1914 legislation[56].

(a) All Commonwealth citizens were British citizens regardless
    of whether they had any other nationality. All had the
    right of entry into the U.K.
(b) All citizens of the Commonwealth were entitled to register
    as UKCs after one year's ordinary residence in the U.K.
(c) Those Commonwealth citizens who resided in, but did not
    become citizens of, a particular country when it framed
    its nationality laws (e.g. on independence) were allowed
    to become UKCs. The principal beneficiaries were East
    African Asians who chose to exercise that option in the
    1960s.
(d) Because of the various British commitments to the
    Commonwealth, a complex series of citizenship categories
    resulted. Apart from UKCs, and the common terms of British
    subject and Commonwealth citizen, there were British
    Protected Persons (those linked to British Protectorates
    or trust territories),[57] Irish citizens born before 1949
    who elected to retain British status as well, and British
    Subjects without Citizenship (those born before 1949 who
    did not subsequently qualify as citizens of India and
    Pakistan).

The misguided idealism of the British Nationality Act can be
contrasted with the more selfish realism of the Old
Commonwealth. It came about in part because the U.K. had no
'immigration problem' at the time. On the contrary, it wished
to encourage foreign labour, whereas Canada, for example, had
come to grips with the need to define its citizens at the turn
of the century because of its decision to regulate unwelcome
immigration.[58] The Canadian Citizenship Act 1946 was the
culmination of an immigration process which sought to
distinguish between those who belonged to Canada and the rest.
Similarly, Australia in its Naturalisation Act 1903 excluded
'aboriginal natives of Asia, Africa and Pacific Islands', as
part of its 'all white' policy. Even when, in 1920, it was
forced to agree to the common citizenship of the Empire, it
fell back on immigration controls to exclude undesirables. In
New Zealand also, though all Commonwealth citizens had the
right to register as New Zealand citizens,[59] they could only do
so after residence of one year. In turn, residence needed an
entry permit and they were issued in line with the country's
all white policy (e.g. Immigration Restriction Act 1908).
   The British Nationality Act 1981 is ultimate recognition
of the immigration reality for which junior members of the
Commonwealth had catered, however distastefully, for many
years and with which the U.K. had ingloriously contended since
1962. Until 1981 the basic concepts of citizenship remained
unchanged.[60] Instead immigration laws were used, at first in
1962 to deny automatic entry to all Commonwealth citizens,
then in 1968 to limit the rights of entry of UKCs. Finally in
1971 the shorthand of 'patriality' was invented to summarise

this development of immigration control and as a substitute for reform of citizenship laws; patriality was used to describe those who were free from immigration control. The consequence was that a person could be a patrial but not necessarily a citizen of the U.K. In something of an understatement of the position, the Home Secretary told Parliament in 1977 that the "present law on nationality has for long been outmoded and difficult to follow".[61] The Green Paper of that year proposed two types of citizenship - British Citizenship (BC) and British Overseas Citizenship (BOC), the latter for those connected with dependencies and entailing no right of entry into the U.K. The Conservative Government produced a White Paper[62] and suggested a third category - British Dependent Territories Citizenship (BDTC).[63]

The British Nationality Bill was debated at a time of high tension in race relations. As the Home Secretary observed, "Citizenship is inevitably a sensitive matter about which people feel very strongly".[64] Indeed the debates contained the broad spectrum of arguments from benign but frequently ill-informed criticism to historical references to allegiance and nationhood and from condemnation as a racist measure to demands that restrictive immigration control be maintained. The Government acceded to some of the criticism and accepted many ameliorating amendments. The result is a statute of formidable complexity, certainly not one for the layman. It came into force on 1 January 1983.[65]

G. THE BRITISH NATIONALITY ACT 1981

Under U.K. law, the following categories of citizenship have to be considered:

> British Citizenship (BC), 'otherwise than by descent' or
>   'by descent'.
> British Dependent Territories Citizenship (BDTC).
> British Overseas Citizenship (BOC).
> British National (Overseas) (BN(O))
> British Subject.
> British Protected Person.
> Commonwealth Citizen.
> Citizens of Eire.
> E.E.C. nationals.

In introducing the Second Reading of the Bill,[66] the Home Secretary referred to the Labour Government's Green Paper wherever possible, and, although the Opposition forcefully opposed the Bill, it should not be overlooked that much of the groundwork, in terms of policy, had already been presented by that Paper.

One motive for reform was the need to clarify the law. That motive has palpably failed. The Act is the most complicated piece of legislation dealing with civil liberties. Even in the categories of citizenship, a bewildering variety have still to be considered (see above).

In spite of occasional Government protestations to the contrary, the Act has considerable implications for immigration. The main justification behind it, after all, was that the 1948 Act "no longer gives any clear indication of who has the right to enter the U.K. Citizenship and the right of abode, which ought to be related, have over the years parted company with each other".[67]

H. THE ACQUISITION OF BRITISH CITIZENSHIP

(1) Birth in the U.K.[68]

By this method a person qualifies for citizenship under any of the following conditions:-

(a) If one parent is a British Citizen (s.1(1)(a)).
(b) If one parent is settled in the U.K. (s.1(1)(b)).The definition of 'settled' is the same as that employed in the Immigration Rules, viz., ordinary residence without a time limit on stay (s.50(2)).[69] This will normally be indicated by a passport endorsement. The liberal decision of Shah[70] on the meaning of ordinary residence will not benefit many children, since their parents' residence for education or other temporary purposes will, of course, be subject to a time limit on stay.[71] The residence must in any event be lawful (s.50(5)) and not, for example, obtained by deception at the port of entry. The reversal of Zamir[72] has reduced the wide scope of entry by deception, but deception is still capable of a broad interpretation (see ch.8). On the other hand, the fact that only one parent needs to be settled means that a fiancee's or wife's unlawful entry will not prevent BC for the subsequently born child if the husband is lawfully resident.
(c) If the child is new-born and abandoned and (a) or (b) are presumed (s.1(2)).[73] This provision complies with the U.K.'s international obligations[74] but is a narrow concession:-

   (i) 'Abandoned' in criminal and family law means a child "left to its fate".[75]
   (ii) Citizenship is a presumption and will be rebutted if there is evidence to show that (a) or (b), above, were not satisfied.
   (iii) 'Newborn' is not defined and this is justified on the alarmist fear that parents might 'dump' their older children in the U.K. in the hope that they would acquire BC. A Junior Minister

suggested[76] that a court might well allow a one year old child to qualify and pointed to the Secretary of State's discretion to register other 'hard-luck' children as citizens. It is unfortunate that the benevolent use of executive discretion was so frequently relied upon during debate of the Bill to justify the inclusion of limitations, and here especially, since the number of abandoned children, of whatever age, are unlikely to be many. A broader concession would certainly not have been fatal to the Bill's overriding aims.

(d) If before the child reaches the age of 18, either parent satisfies (a) or (b) and the child is registered (s.1(3)).[77] Since primary immigration has for long been at a low level and since it is extremely difficult to switch from temporary to more permanent immigration status (e.g. from student to employee), there will be few parents who will graduate to (a) or (b). The principal beneficiaries of this provision will be the children of E.E.C. nationals who gain employment in the U.K., refugees and UKCs admitted under the voucher system.

(e) If the child has remained in the U.K. for 10 years after birth and is registered (s.1(4)). A maximum of 90 days' absence per annum is permitted, though the Secretary of State may extend the period if there are special circumstances. The applicant must be resident in the U.K. at the time of application but can apply at any time throughout his life. So, a child who spends the first 12 years in the U.K. and emigrates, can return later and register. The most frequent cases are likely to be the child who is abandoned or left in the U.K by his parents (e.g. for education) or whose parents have died before satisfying conditions (a) or (b). The applicant may face considerable difficulties and certainly inconvenience, in proving the fact of residence. His school records may only begin at age 5. Health records will be more useful, but much information may have disappeared along with the parents and the onus is clearly on the applicant to obtain it. Moreover, there is no right of appeal against a refusal of registration.

For most children, their parents will have become BCs or settled within the 10 years if they really wish to maintain contact with the U.K. and category (d) will apply. The present category will therefore be a very small one, in spite of the amount of controversy which forced the Government to accept it during the passage of the Bill. It is, however, an illustration of the considerable complexity which has followed from the abandonment of the simplicity of ius soli.

(f) If the child is legally adopted by a BC or a married couple, one of whom is a BC (s.1(5)).[78] It is of course possible for parents, under threat of departure, to leave their children with BC relatives or friends but the adoption must be by court order and not de facto.[79] Adopters of overseas children can take advantage of this provision but the immigration difficulties, in getting the child into the U.K., can be considerable if the Home Office is determined to prevent this potential evasion of control.[80]

It should be noted that compliance with any of the above conditions automatically confers citizenship. Identical provisions govern the status of British Dependent Territories Citizenship for those born within such Territories.

Under the new law, a child of parents who, for example, die soon after his birth without obtaining citizenship for him, must ask the Secretary of State to exercise his overriding discretion to register any minor as a BC (s.3(1)), or hope to be adopted by BCs (s.1(5)), or wait until the age of 10 and register (s.1(4)).

At face value, the argument in favour of abandoning the principle of ius soli is attractive. Why should the child born to a parent temporarily in the U.K. (e.g. as extended holidaymaker or student) automatically acquire British Citizenship? It can lead to the anomalous position that the parents can be legally deported but the child, as a citizen, cannot. This 'point of principle' was strongly pushed by the Government, but was accompanied by a fear based on "an increase in our potential immigration commitment"[81] which the indiscriminate application of the ius soli would produce; or, as the White Paper put it (para. 43), the creation of "a pool of considerable size". It was impossible to supply accurate figures but the Junior Minister roughly estimated that "between 3,000 and 6,500 children [were] born each year to parents who are neither citizens nor settled".[82] There are several objections to the fear:

(a) The rough estimates do not mean that all these children will ever exercise the right to citizenship by taking out a passport. On the contrary, the law of their parents' nationality might well prohibit dual nationality so that the children will not do so. Most who leave the U.K. with their parents will not return.

(b) As to the deportation point, "nearly always the parents take the children with them".[83] The problem only arises in "one or two cases".

(c) As to the 'point of principle', that has to be

balanced against the practicalities and it is abundantly clear that the abandonment of the simple <u>ius soli</u> has necessitated complex statutory provisions and administrative alternatives. Chief of these were the amendments subsequently made to the Immigration Rules to cover those children who were not born to BCs or settled parents but who travel abroad and seek re-entry.[84]

(d) Another, consequential practicality is the unease in terms of race relations which the abolition of <u>ius soli</u> sparked off during debate of the Bill and which will be caused to those coloured children who are born in the U.K. and do not gain citizenship and who may well face administrative difficulties when they seek to re-enter the U.K. or subsequently seek to prove their entitlement to registration as citizens or subsequently encounter State agencies which demand proof of civic status (e.g. for education purposes).

(e) Since the Government was unable to produce evidence of abuse of <u>ius soli</u> for immigration purposes, why change a principle which had lasted for 700 years? The answer, it is submitted, lay in the political capital which could be gained by being seen to be active in tightening immigration control, especially since the Government had little room for manoeuvre in other areas of control.[85] Significantly, during Committee, the 'point of principle' frequently gave way to discussion about the immigration consequences.

(2) Birth outside the U.K.

[It is essential in this context to distinguish between BC (as previously described in relation to Birth in the U.K. and referred to in this section as 'BC otherwise than by descent') and 'BC by descent'.[86] Only the former can automatically transmit status to children born abroad.]

(a) <u>First Generation born abroad</u>
Citizenship is acquired automatically under s.2 if,

   (i) either parent is a BC otherwise than by descent; or
  (ii) either parent is a BC and is employed by the Crown or in specially defined service;[87] or
 (iii) either parent is a BC and is employed by an E.E.C. institution.

In cases (ii) and (iii) the child becomes a BC <u>otherwise than by descent</u> (s.14(2)), whereas if he falls within (i) he becomes a BC <u>by descent</u>. In other words, in the normal case of (i) where BCs (otherwise than by descent) are abroad, their children automatically acquire BC by descent – the first generation. But, as will be seen, any grandchildren born abroad must use the registration procedures (below) if they wish to acquire BC - the second generation. For (ii) and (iii) children however, they can transmit citizenship to their foreign born offspring (the second generation) automatically as if they had been born in the U.K. At common law, only children born abroad to ambassadors were regarded as natural-born subjects[88] but statute extended the status to children of members of the armed services.[89] Under the 1981 Act, the concessions in (ii) and (iii) are narrow. Crown Service is a well-recognised term.[90] The original Bill did not mention the E.E.C., but it was added after pressure from E.E.C. civil servants and the European Commission and European Parliament. The scope of 'Community Institution' is not defined,[91] but it cannot cover the Council of Europe or the many other international bodies which are based in Europe (e.g. in Switzerland).[92] Moreover, the recruitment for the E.E.C. post must have taken place in a Member State.[93] Thus, a director of a British based company who is working in Singapore and who then joins the Commission in Brussels cannot benefit from the concession. The unsatisfactory answer to such a case and to those working in private, as opposed to Government, employment overseas must lie in the overriding discretion of the Secretary of State to register children as BCs. The 'E.E.C. concession' is tightly drawn and out of step with the spirit lying behind the principle of free movement in the Community.

The narrowness of these provisions is regrettable. For example, a natural-born BC is sent to work for ICI in the Far East and marries there. He dies after his children are born there. They are BC by descent and cannot pass citizenship to their foreign-born children unless registration is satisfied (below). If their father had worked for the British Embassy in Singapore, they could. It is hard to distinguish which employment is doing greater good for British interests.[94]

(b) Second Generation born abroad
Considerable doubt arose in the fourteenth century over the status of children born to subjects whilst abroad.[95] The famous statute de natis ultra mare in 1351 sought to clarify the position by permitting transmission of citizenship but its precise interpretation remained in doubt for over 500 years. Was it necessary for both parents or only one, and if so which one, to be an English subject? In 1882 the Chancery Division decided that it was sufficient that the father be a natural-born subject.[96] Transmission under early statutes was clearly limited to the first generation and transmission to the second generation born overseas was not permitted by common law. As the opportunities for travel extended, statutes extended it to the second generation in the eighteenth century.[97] In 1914 it was again limited to the first. Such was the outcry in favour of retaining ancestral links that the

second generation transmission was restored in 1922 but only on the basis of registration of the child at a British consulate.[98] The 1948 Act retained this scheme. The 1981 Act similarly allows transmission to the second generation but has made complex additions to the process of registration. Whereas the 1948 Act allowed registration for indefinite generations and imposed no residence requirement, the 1981 Act seeks to confine registration to those who have indicated by three years' residence in the U.K. a continued interest in the U.K. The way in which this is achieved is tortuous and makes the terms of s.1 (above) look straightforward in comparison:-

Children whose grandparents were BC in the sense of (1) above and whose parents were born abroad (and thus BC by descent) are entitled to be registered as citizens if either of the following sets of conditions is satisfied (s.3):

(a) (i) payment of the fee;
   (ii) a parent is a BC by descent (birth abroad);
 (iii) one of that parent's parents is or would have been a BC otherwise than by descent under the Act (e.g. born in the U.K.);
  (iv) a parent has spent 3 years in the U.K. prior to the child's birth (a maximum of 270 days spent abroad will not jeopardise the period).[99];
   (v) registration is made within 12 months of the child's birth.[100]

Since the 3 years' residence need not have immediately preceded the birth, it may not be a meaningful indicator of a desire to retain a link with the U.K. For example, X is born in the U.K., his son Y is born in Argentina. The family returns immediately to the U.K. for 3 years, and then emigrates to Argentina. Twenty years later Y's son Z is born in Argentina. Z can be registered as a BC. On registration the child becomes a BC by descent only.

A more meaningful indicator of attachment to the U.K. is, however, alternatively offered by the following set of conditions:

(b) (i) payment of the fee;
   (ii) a parent is a BC by descent;
 (iii) after birth, the family[101] spends 3 years in the U.K.;
  (iv) registration is made before the child reaches 18;
   (v) the parent(s) agree to the registration.

On this route to citizenship, the child's status pending completion of the residence is that of a potential citizen, which may mean difficulty if he travels abroad, e.g. on holiday. On the other hand, registration under (b) makes him a BC 'otherwise than by descent' and thus able to transmit citizenship automatically to his children born abroad. It will be seen that registration under (b) is a potentially indefinite procedure provided that the family keeps returning to the U.K. to show a 3 year commitment to the country. In the example above, Y could choose to return to the U.K., register Z after 3 years and Z would become a BC otherwise than by descent.

Arbitrary though the period of 3 years is, it is equally arbitrary to suggest others and, if citizenship is to connote a sense of belonging, it is a reasonable requirement and certainly not as 'arbitrary' as the previous law which specified merely an act of registration. A further improvement lies in the fact that either parent can satisfy the ancestral connection with the U.K.,[102] whereas under the 1948 Act transmission was confined to the male line.[103]

The essential difference between (a) and (b) is that only children registered under the latter acquire BC 'otherwise than by descent' (with the consequential ability to transmit citizenship automatically to children born abroad). This can place parents in some difficulty, for on birth of their child overseas they must decide whether to register him within 12 months under (a) (as a BC by descent) or to hold fire and decide to return to the U.K. for 3 years during the child's minority and register him under (b) (as a BC otherwise than by descent). If, for whatever reason, they fail to return, the child may become stateless. It would be fairer to allow registration under (a) to be converted into registration under (b) by proof of subsequent residence.

(3) Registration of the British-connected (s.4)

This is a miscellaneous category and is the legacy of Britain's Commonwealth connections. The requisite conditions are:

(a) Payment of the fee.
(b) The applicant must be a British Dependent Territories Citizen or British Overseas Citizen or British Subject or British Protected Person or British National (Overseas).[104]
(c) He must be lawfully resident in the U.K. for 5 years (with a maximum of 450 days allowed to be spent abroad during that period). The decision in Khawaja[105] has reduced the scope of unlawful entry but illegal entry is still a broad concept.
(d) He must have spent no more than 90 days abroad in the fifth year of the residence and in that year must not have been subject to a time limit on his stay (though other conditions e.g. as to employment, might have operated).

The successful applicant becomes a BC otherwise than by

121

descent but the obvious limitation to its use is the initial entry of the applicant into the U.K. under the immigration laws. This provision can be described as the Commonwealth preference section and is the successor to s.6 of the 1948 Act. Under that Act a Commonwealth citizen could be registered as a citizen of the U.K. and Colonies after one year's ordinary residence, which was a major benefit over the normal, longer residence required of aliens for naturalisation. At first the provision was of little importance, since U.K. citizens and Commonwealth citizens had the same rights of entry into the U.K. It was in 1962, when Parliament began to distinguish between the two for immigration purposes, that s.6 offered the practical advantage of gaining the right to stay. However, the immigration legislation extended the period of residence to 5 years before stay was guaranteed. Moreover, the applicant had, of course, to negotiate the difficulty of entry in the first place, and thus the preferential treatment of the Commonwealth preference was watered down. The current provisions maintain that course, and there is little difference between registration and naturalisation (see below). The most significant is the discretionary power of the Secretary of State to waive the preconditions for those engaged in Crown and related service. It was used, with lightning effect, in May 1985 to enable a Hong Kong Chinaman to become a BC and thus join a Sino-British liaison group responsible for the transfer of the territory's government in 1997. [106]

(4) Naturalisation

There are two methods[107] - the general procedure, or naturalisation through marriage (Schedule I). The respective conditions can be set out comparatively:

Naturalisation generally	Naturalisation through marriage
(a) of full age (18) and capacity	of full age (18) and capacity
(b) payment of the fee[108]	payment of the fee
(c) oath of allegiance	oath of allegiance
(d) 5 years,[109] lawful[110] residence[111]	3 years, lawful residence
(e) no current time limit on stay	no current time limit on stay
(f) good character	good character
(g) linguistic competence[112]	currently married to a BC.
(h) intention to make the U.K. his principal home or to work abroad in Crown or related service.	

The award of both types of naturalisation is discretionary, whereas that via marriage was an entitlement under s.6(2) of the 1948 Act. The position is thus restored to that of 1609, viz., that naturalisation has "been ever reputed matters of mere Grace and Favour".[113] This element of discretion is firmly endorsed by the special power which the Secretary of State has to waive most of the preconditions for naturalisation if "in the special circumstances of any particular case ... [he] thinks fit" (Sched. I, para. 2, 4). This includes the additional and welcome power to waive the language test because of the applicant's age or physical or mental condition. The test itself examines oral ability and does not, as many countries have specified, require a written sample.[114] Both the style of general naturalisation and its elements have remained essentially the same since 1844 and 1870 respectively.

As to naturalisation via marriage, sex discrimination has generally operated so as to enable the wife, but not the husband, of a citizen to gain nationality, "because the primary allegiance is expressed through the male, through his specialisation, and through his social function".[115] Strangely the effect of marriage was unclear at common law, though the balance of authorities would seem to suggest that, like other incidents of marriage, the husband's status prevailed.[116] The Nationality Act of 1844 clarified the position by enacting that an alien woman was naturalised on marriage to a British subject.[117] In 1870, with the abolition of the indelibility of allegiance, a general principle was adopted whereby a wife took the nationality of her husband, whatever it might be, but that, if she was born as a British subject and then married an alien, she could resume her British status after his death. In 1914 she could do so on dissolution of the marriage and, it was further enacted, she could retain her citizenship even if her husband changed his. The automatic acquisition of the husband's citizenship was strongly criticised, but a Parliamentary Committee[118] failed to agree on reform. Eventually, it was decided in 1933 to implement a Hague Convention[119] of 1930 which offered, inter alia, a British woman greater opportunities of retaining, or reverting to, her British status independently of her husband's decision.[120]

The Act of 1948 abolished the rule whereby the wife of a British subject automatically acquired his citizenship. Instead she could choose to register as a citizen. The 1981 Act places husbands and wives on the same footing, but at the same time tightens up the law by making the award of citizenship for either spouse discretionary and subject to residence and good character qualifications.[121] The changes fit in conveniently with the restrictive immigration Rules, under which entry for marriage faces considerable hurdles[122] and marriages undergo a probationary period before permanent stay is conceded. The principle of sex equality is thus compromised by the reality of immigration control. Moreover, the provisions are a cynical step to equality for they reduce the rights of wives and then apply them to all spouses.

Good character
This requirement is a legacy of letters of denization. Before issuing them the Home Secretary required a certificate of good conduct to be signed by a trustworthy person.[123] It has always been a matter for the Home Secretary's discretion. During debate of the 1981 Bill some indication was given of his approach.

> A person with a serious criminal record cannot be regarded as a person of good character. Equally, it is normal to refuse applicants with few or no convictions who are strongly suspected of being engaged in crime or are known associates of serious criminals. Sexual morality, however, is not normally taken into account, nor are, for instance, homosexual activities within the law. Scandalous sexual misbehaviour might, however, when combined with other personal characteristics, be a factor in a very few cases. Applicants are expected to meet their financial responsibilities. Financial irresponsibility, serious insolvency or bankruptcy invariably leads to refusal. But mere financial incompetence is not necessarily a bar, and neither is unemployment or receipt of social security benefits. Where a person is in debt but is making efforts to repay what he owes, it is usual to postpone a decision on his application for a year or two to give him time to put matters right. Commercial malpractices are taken seriously. They are usually calculated and sustained acts which reflect adversely on the applicant's general character.
>   Defects of temperament on their own are not normally held to bar an applicant on grounds of character. Heavy drinking, gambling or a disinclination to work are not in themselves sufficient to warrant refusal. There comes a point in a very few cases, however, where failings of this type become so pronounced, or notorious in the locality, that it would be unwise to grant naturalisation.[124]

Many may find these categories of sins and grounds for suspicion unnecessarily wide. The description highlights both the flexibility of the requirement and the dangers inherent in that flexibility. Consequently, an attempt was made to incorporate within the Bill a right of appeal against a decision to refuse citizenship because of bad character. The Home Secretary's arguments against it have, it is suggested, a relevance going beyond nationality and into immigration, for they illustrate the typical official attitude in these fields and the gamut of arguments which are rehearsed to resist change. Their numbers are more formidable than their merits.

(a) It was argued that a right of appeal is incompatible "with the general principles underlying naturalisation as it has always existed in our law".[125] However, to cite history begs the question of whether these principles are sound.

(b) A central principle is that "Naturalisation has always, in this as in many other countries, been within the gift of the State ... no one has a right to another country's citizenship".[126] The proposed amendment however did not purport to remove the State's 'gift' but merely structure its operation.

(c) "It would be extremely difficult to decide what justiciable criteria should be laid down."[127] It is submitted

   (i) that the State ought in principle to be able to specify what criteria it demands of potential citizens, and
   (ii) that, even if criteria cannot be rigidly specified, they can, as in deportation procedures, at least be listed as guidelines.[128]

(d) "It is simply not practicable to reconcile rights of appeal with the exercise of an absolute discretion." However, the discretion is not "absolute" at present. Judicial review is possible if it can be shown that the Minister has grossly abused his discretion. More importantly, as deportation shows, it is quite possible for discretion to coexist with appellate safeguards.

(e) The Minister's discretion would be fettered for future cases. This is no bad thing if an appellate authority has shown that he has previously exercised it improperly. In any event, no two cases are identical and he would therefore still retain flexibility in subsequent cases.

(f) "Control of who should be allowed to obtain our citizenship would be" lost. Governments do not like to lose power, of course, but a right of appeal would ensure that the power was exercised according to the spirit in which it was originally given by Parliament. As the Federal Court in Canada has observed, to decide the issue of citizenship on unrevealed and undisputed evidence is "shocking to one's sense of Justice".[129]

(g) Discretion allows the Minister to be flexible. In so far as discretion allows a Minister to change, in secret, the "way in which particular types of case should be considered", it is undemocratic and dangerous to civil liberties. In so far as it permits him to be lenient to the exceptional case, such an overriding discretion (to help the applicant) is certainly not incompatible with a right of appeal.[130]

(h) Refusals averaged "just under 10 per cent a year over the last five years".[131] Therefore there was no need for a right of appeal. Smallness of numbers does not, however, justify the perpetuation of unfairness. Moreover in 1980, that 10% amounted to no less than 1201.[132]

(i) In any event, the Government usually gives the reasons for its decision in cases of failure to satisfy the residence and language tests and does so for 'good character' cases whenever possible.[133] However, this is not an absolute rule. Moreover, the fact that reasons are, apparently, so frequently given already should encourage statutory acknowledgment of the practice and provision for an appeal against those reasons.

(j) It would be difficult to give reasons in security cases. The possibility of hearings in camera or at worst an exception for such cases is an answer to that argument.

(k) For good measure, the cost of administering an appellate system was mentioned. But this would depend upon the type of system selected. There are unlikely to be many cases and the attendant cost of running an appellate system is one which society should in principle be prepared to bear.

(l) If the task were given to the judiciary, it would be overburdened and in any case High Court judges are too eminent for the task. This is a matter of opinion. It is arguable that such eminence is particularly needed when such an important issue is at stake. Moreover,

(i) on the Home Secretary's admission, cases of refusal are few, and

(ii) the judicial task could always be given to more junior judges if the workload proved to be too heavy for High Court judges.

The important point is that a right of appeal be recognised in principle.

(m) Under the traditional system of accountability the Home Secretary is already answerable to Parliament, whilst his civil servants can be investigated by the Ombudsman. The weaknesses and unpredictable success of both methods are well known. Their proper role is to check on policy and administrative practice, and they are an inadequate substitute for a standard appeals procedure.

The interposition of a court in the process of naturalisation would only be a realistic safeguard if the legislation which it has to interpret is sufficiently specific. To give it the task of interpreting 'good character' is unlikely to achieve much.[134] In addition, the State should be able to set out the criteria for naturalisation with precision. The Home Secretary revealed, during passage of the Bill, some of the criteria employed and there is no reason, beyond Governmental stubbornness, why such guidance should not be set down in legislation.

(5) Gibraltar and the Falkland Islands (s.5)
Citizens of Gibraltar are entitled to register as British Citizens following a last-minute victory in the House of Lords during passage of the Bill.[135] It succeeded partly because of E.E.C. implications (lest there be discrimination against Gibraltarians contrary to Community obligations) and partly because of pressure from within Parliament. Such pressure was also exerted on behalf of other Dependencies, principally Hong Kong, but this was more easily resisted. Instead they were allotted a second division status which retains a link with the U.K. in name but not in substantive terms (see below). Events in 1982 added a new dimension and the British Nationality (Falkland Islands) Act 1983 was promptly passed to give Falkland Islanders the status of British Citizens. The steadfast refusal of the Government to extend citizenship to the islands in 1981 eventually[136] evaporated. The episode is an extreme example of the inherently political nature of citizenship laws. A crucial factor in this extension was the small number of people involved. It is hard to believe that a Government would so readily accede to a Private Member's Bill if Hong Kong had been the territory in question.
The concession to Gibraltar is however tempered by the fact that those who choose to register become BCs 'by descent', and not 'otherwise than by descent', with consequential limitations on their ability to transmit citizenship to their children born overseas (s.14(1)(d); and there is a similar limitation for certain cases in the Falkland Islands, see s.3, 1983 Act).

(6) Transitional Arrangements
The sensible aim of linking citizenship to rights of entry will take many years to become fully operational. In the meantime, the legacy of the Commonwealth and the complexity which it has created for citizenship laws will continue under the various transitional provisions. These in essence seek to ensure that all those who were or could have become patrials or UKCs under the former law retain that right provided that it is exercised within a stated period after 1st January 1983. Reference is thus necessary to the Immigration Act 1971 and

earlier legislation.[137] The following categories of persons are eligible.

    (a) Those who acquired BC on commencement of the British Nationality Act 1981 because of their prior U.K. citizenship, *viz*.,

        (i) All those UKCs with the right of abode (patrials) - s.11(1). This included those emigres, mainly in the white Commonwealth, who were patrials.

        (ii) Those who were UKCs under the British Nationality (No.2) Act 1964 (via their mother's citizenship) provided that they already had a right of abode because of residence or that their mothers had, or would have, become BCs under the 1981 Act - s.11(2).

        (iii) Those registered on birth at High Commissions in the Commonwealth because of ancestral connection with the U.K. through the male line.

    (b) Registration as a BC because of the father's close connection with the U.K. - s.9. A person born abroad within 5 years of commencement of the 1981 Act can be registered (within 12 months of birth) if

        (i) he would have become a UKC with the right of abode under the Immigration Act 1971. This covers patriality through a parental or grandparental connection with the U.K.;

        (ii) his father has become a BC.

    (c) A woman is given 5 years[138] after commencement of the 1981 Act within which she can register on the basis of her marriage to a man who was a UKC and who has, or would have, become a BC - s.8. The marriage must however still subsist; if it has ended, the Secretary of State has a discretion to register - s.8(2).

    (d) Registration because of residence in the U.K., or because of U.K.-related employment e.g. Crown service, before and after commencement of the Act - s.7. Essentially this rule covers those who would have been entitled to UKC or to patriality because of lawful residence and settlement status had the 1971 Act remained in force. Such people are allowed 5 or 6 years (depending on the category) in which to register. For those who were minors on commencement, the 5 year period runs from the age of majority. Registration is an entitlement but it is essential that the immigrant community be made properly aware of the provision.[139]

I. BRITISH DEPENDENT TERRITORIES CITIZENSHIP (BDTC)

Part II of the Act contains identical provisions for the acquisition of this inferior form of citizenship through a connection with a Dependency.[140] The complexity is thus identical and one can sympathise with the relevant administrators[141] and applicants. The holder of this citizenship does not obtain a right of entry into the U.K. but has the no doubt comforting description of 'British' in his passport.[142]

J. BRITISH OVERSEAS CITIZENSHIP (BOC)

Part III of the Act grants this similarly attenuated form of citizenship to those UKCs who did not become BCs or BDTCs on commencement and who can mainly claim a connection with a former British territory. The majority are UKCs, living in the New Commonwealth, who do not have local citizenship. The Foreign Office has estimated that there are roughly 210,000 BOCs who cannot claim another citizenship.[143] Most (about 130,000) live in Malaysia and there are about 39,000 U.K. passport holders (UKPHs) in India who qualify and who are entitled to entry under the voucher system set up in 1968.

BOCs are a residual and contracting category. The generally accepted rules on statelessness[144] mean that their children will normally gain local citizenship by birth abroad. In the meantime, wives and children born within 5 years of commencement of the 1981 Act are entitled to register as BOCs (s.28 and 27 respectively). Thereafter, the Secretary of State has a complete discretion to register minors. The contrast between this and the more circumscribed discretion earlier in the Act emphasises the precarious position of BOCs. They have no right of entry into the U.K. The Government clearly hopes that most will not present any international difficulties and, with luck, be absorbed into their countries of residence. Moreover, and significantly, the right of BCs and BDTCs to resume their citizenship (if they had earlier to renounce it in order to acquire another nationality - ss.13 and 24) is not conceded to BOCs. However, the category is not finite. Not all States are determined to avoid statelessness. Children born in Malaysia and Singapore are likely to be stateless and will therefore request that the Secretary of State register them as BOCs under s.27.[145]

Comment
It is fair to say that "there will be no great difficulty in British overseas citizens living in this country moving on to become citizens of this county"[146] (via registration). However they must be present in the U.K. in the first place. Whilst BDTC and BOC perpetuate, in formal terms, the U.K.'s Commonwealth responsibilities, they are virtually meaningless in municipal law, since they do not carry the right of entry

into the U.K.[147] In this regard, they merely continue the policy of immigration legislation in 1962 and 1968. They are cosmetic concepts designed to mollify local and international opinion. They soon led to sceptical reaction and confusion from the international community, with Canada, France and Germany in 1983 querying the status of the holders.[148] Indeed the U.K., as it found in relation to Ugandan Asians in 1972, may find it difficult to shed its international responsibility by merely awarding passports without a right of entry. For example, if international developments of the Falklands or Ugandan variety reoccur, international law and perhaps U.K. public opinion will force the U.K. to admit its second class citizens.

The more honourable and not unrealistic course would have been

(a) to have conceded BC to those BOCs who have no other citizenship (roughly 210,000);[149]
(b) to have provided a simpler method for the remaining BOCs and all BDTCs to upgrade their status to that of BC after entry into the U.K.; and
(c) to have given them preferential status for admission into the U.K.

K. BRITISH NATIONAL (OVERSEAS)

Under the Act 3 million of Hong Kong's estimated 5.3 million inhabitants became BDTCs.[150] With the U.K.'s lease on the territory due to expire in 1997, it is quite possible that many BDTCs will find life under Chinese rule unbearable. If they then leave, or are expelled, other countries will almost certainly fix responsibility for their settlement on the State named in the passport - the U.K. - no matter what the U.K.'s immigration laws say. Citizenship and its appurtenances are thus a cardinal, if not sole, motive for the U.K.'s negotiations with China and the preliminary agreement, reached between the two countries in 1984,[151] has led to a further amendment to the U.K.'s citizenship laws.

The ranks of BDTC and even BOC are too generous in the Hong Kong context for they are transmissible and can be acquired by registration. A narrower status had to be devised. Thus, under the Hong Kong Act 1985 the Government will be able, by Order in Council, to replace the status of BDTC with that of British National (Overseas) (BN(O)). Under the new scheme BDTCs in Hong Kong will either:

(a) before 1997 choose to adopt BN(O) - this will not be transmissible by descent but will otherwise bear the same incidents as BDTC viz. access to British consular protection, right to register as a BC after residence in the U.K. (s.4, 1981 Act); and the passport will probably state the right of abode in Hong Kong;[152] or

(b) become Chinese nationals; or

(c) if they do not choose or do not qualify for (a) or (b), and if they would otherwise be stateless, become BOCs - though it is not yet clear whether the Government will allow this status to be transmitted to future generations.

The new status of BN(O) may well be introduced gradually, giving the U.K. the opportunity to persuade other countries to accept the new passport. Those who elect BN(O) will not lose BDTC before 1997 and will thus have both.[153]

Comment
The fate of refugees in Hong Kong has yet to be resolved (and probably will be by the continued, painfully slow process of dispersal), as must that of those employed in Hong Kong's civil service. It is unclear how many of the latter will be admitted by the U.K. for settlement. Indeed there are many, important details still to be agreed. In the meantime and as 1997 approaches, pressure and desire to emigrate from Hong Kong are likely to increase. This development will focus the attention of immigration officials on Hong Kong entrants and they may well replace the Indian subcontinent as the officially perceived threat of large-scale illegal immigration. At present Hong Kong BDTCs do not need entry clearance for a visit of less than 6 months, but this can always be changed as happened with visitors from Sri Lanka in 1985.
        The problem facing the U.K. is - how to avoid a potentially high level of immigration from disenchanted BDTCs since international law may, and world opinion certainly will try to, force the U.K. to accept them. The solution is to persuade as many as possible to throw in their lot with China by becoming Chinese citizens. As for the rest, a 'pray for the best' attitude is adopted of offering a short term, symbolic citizenship and leaving the position of future generations unclear. As Uganda showed in the early 1970s, the U.K. may not be able to shed its responsibilities so easily.

L. BRITISH SUBJECTS AND BRITISH PROTECTED PERSONS

This is a miscellaneous category of legacies from Imperial History:

(1) British Subjects without citizenship (s.30)

(a) Since in 1948 India and Pakistan had not yet passed their own nationality laws, the Nationality Act of that year (ss.13 and 16) created a residual category of people who might not acquire citizenship when such laws were passed. The category was one of "transitory

131

existence".[154] There are estimated to be about 50,000, mainly in Sri Lanka.[155]
(b) Wives of British Subjects (BS) who have registered (s.6(1) 1948 Act, s.1 BNA 1965). By 1981 200 had registered.[156]
(c) Ireland. A dying category of people born before 1949 who are citizens of Eire but who exercised their right to retain BS status.[157]

(2) British Protected Persons are those connected with a former trust territory or protectorate (s.38). There are estimated to be 140,000 (about 130,000 in Brunei).[158] They are the most inferior form of U.K.- related citizenship -they do not even qualify to be called Commonwealth citizens (s.37(1)). They are not aliens (s.50) but fall somewhere in the middle.[159]
    The status of these citizens is similar to that of BOCs and BN(O)s - availability of passports and consular facilities, allegiance to the Crown and the right to settlement after 5 years' residence in the U.K. (s.4). However, that right is effectively thwarted since they have no right of entry in the first place.
    The wives of British Subjects (married before 1983) are entitled to register until 1988, but the registration of children is at the complete discretion of the Secretary of State and this may be a potent weapon to control the size of the category. Indeed, the desire to be rid of any responsibility for BSs is reflected in s.35 which (unlike the general U.K. rule) prevents dual nationality, so that a person ceases to be a BS if he acquires any other type of citizenship.

M. COMMONWEALTH CITIZENS (s.37)

BCs, BDTCs, BOCs, BSs and all citizens of the Commonwealth countries in Sch. 3 have the status of Commonwealth citizen.[160] On the other hand, the previously synonymous status of British Subject is now confined to those within ss.30-33. The status of Commonwealth citizen has no practical, long-term[161] significance under the new law but is a sentimental gesture towards the organisation of which the Monarch is head.

N. THE LOSS OF BRITISH CITIZENSHIP

There are two methods - (a) voluntary renunciation; (b) official deprivation.

(a) Renunciation (s.12). Until 1870, the principle nemo potest exuere patriam held powerful sway over British law. Status could not be replaced, in British eyes, by any other citizenship. It was indelible. Thus, if a subject acquired nationality of an enemy state, he committed treason. The Naturalisation Act 1870 made fundamental changes. Not only was a subject allowed to make a declaration of alienage, but British status was lost if naturalisation abroad took place or if a British woman married an alien. The 1948 and 1981 Acts only allow the first, known as a declaration of renunciation. This policy encourages plurality of citizenships. On the other hand, it is qualified in that many countries forbid dual nationality and require a potential citizen to relinquish any other nationality on the acquisition of its own. Any person over 18 (or younger if married) can sign a declaration which becomes valid

(i) when registered by the Secretary of State, and
(ii) provided that the person acquires another nationality within 6 months.

Registration may be denied in times of war.[162] Thus, conscription cannot be avoided and, if a foreign nationality is assumed, a treason charge could follow.[163]

(b) Deprivation (s.40). This only applies to citizenship (BC and BDTC) acquired by registration or naturalisation and is a discretionary power for the Secretary of State. It can be exercised in the following circumstances;

(i) Where there is fraud, false representation or concealment of material fact. A similar but tougher power was introduced in 1914. The Secretary had no discretion and revocation was possible if the respondent was shown not to have been of good character at the time he acquired citizenship.[164] There is a clear possibility of interpreting 'false representation' or 'concealment' in line with the immigration cases. The 'duty of candour' requirement imposed by Zamir has been removed by Khawaja,[165] but silence, for example, in answer to police questioning for naturalisation purposes, could still suffice.
(ii) Where there is disloyalty or disaffection towards the Crown, by act or by speech.[166]
(iii) Where there is detrimental trade or communication with an enemy during war.
(iv) Where a prison sentence in any country[167] of at least 12 months has been imposed within 5 years of acquiring citizenship - but not if deprivation would leave the person stateless.

For all categories, the Secretary of State must be satisfied of an overriding condition, that it is not "conducive to the public good" for the person to retain citizenship (s.40(5)(a)). These provisions are rarely used. Under the 1948 Act there were 10 deprivations.[168] The courts have been more productive since they have ruled that citizenship which has been acquired by fraud etc. is a nullity[169] and therefore deprivation is unnecessary.[170] The reasoning is similar to that which prevailed in the Zamir line of cases (viz. fraud vitiates the citizenship, therefore there is no 'citizenship' which had to be withdrawn) and effectively obviates the need for a committee of inquiry into a deprivation case (see below). Since the current provisions repeat those of the 1948 Act (s.20(2)), it is likely that the same interpretation will be followed. However, references to voidability and voidness ab initio have been deprecated by the House of Lords in Khawaja (above) and it is arguable that:

(a) in citizenship cases, the courts should follow suit,
(b) because the 'facts precedent' to registration or naturalisation are in dispute, the citizenship is prima facie valid unless and until struck down and therefore
(c) an inquiry (below) should be available.

The current provisions do contain some relaxation of prior rules. The 1914 and 1948 Acts, like many countries, permitted deprivation if the citizen lived abroad continuously (meaning more than 7 years outside the Commonwealth).[171] In other words, if a person seeks to become a citizen, he should 'act like one' and reside in his adoptive country. Again, the 1914 power to deprive the former citizen's family of their status was removed in 1948 and this policy is continued. However, it is suggested that the current grounds for deprivation are still undesirable. Grounds (ii) and (iii) are unduly oppressive, since they are subject to no time limit. Moreover, both can be better dealt with by the criminal law,[172] and, insofar as they cannot, they should not be included, for otherwise a naturalised or registered citizen can be punished for unwelcome conduct whereas a 'home grown' citizen cannot. As regards ground (iv), since the State is content with a person's character when citizenship is granted, it should put up with any subsequent, unfavourable consequences and not place the holder under a probationary period additional to the one he had to satisfy in the first place when obtaining citizenship.

On the procedural level, the person is entitled to a semi-formal committee of inquiry, if he so requests, and is thus in a more favourable position than a person deprived of a passport (see below).[173] The committee consists of a chairman "possessing judicial experience"[174] and such other members as the Secretary of State thinks proper. The Secretary of State may give it judicial powers and these can be exercised by one or more members of the Committee.[175] However, the committee's findings do not bind the Secretary of State. There were only 5 such inquiries under the 1948 Act.[176] The paucity of cases and the inherent weaknesses of the grounds for deprivation argue for the abolition of grounds (ii) to (iv).[177] Punishment for ground (i) could be left to prosecution under s.46 with a judicial power to withdraw citizenship after consideration of all the circumstances, along the lines of the power to recommend deportation. It is at least desirable that courts replace committees of inquiry, that their decisions be binding on the Secretary of State and that those decisions be then based on "clear, unequivocal and convincing" evidence.[178]

O. RESUMPTION OF CITIZENSHIP (s.13,24)[179]

This was permitted in 1964. Under current legislation, if BC or BDTC (but not BOC) is renounced in order to acquire another nationality, the applicant is entitled to recover it once only. This can benefit, for example, women returning to the U.K. after the failure of a marriage abroad or expatriots returning to the U.K. on retirement. In further or other cases of renunciation, the Secretary of State has complete discretion to allow resumption and it may be permitted more than once. It is noteworthy that the former provisions of the Status of Aliens Act 1914[180] were more generous, for they allowed the children of parents who had ceased to be British subjects to revert to the status by the making of a declaration within a year of reaching majority (then 21).

P. STATELESSNESS s.36, Sch.2.

Schedule 2 recognises the Act's potential for producing statelessness by a series of provisions to alleviate it. They are principally made necessary by the Act's abolition of ius soli and have been included to fulfil the U.K.'s international obligations.[181] For example, those born in the U.K. to BDTC or BOC parents who would be otherwise stateless are entitled to take their parents' status (Sch. 2, para. 1); those born in the U.K. who have always been stateless (e.g. by failure to register as a BC) and are between the ages of 10 and 22, may become BCs on satisfying 5 years' residence (Sch. 2 para. 3).[182]

Q. COMMENT

(1) "The Bill is an attempt to massage our nationality legislation to suit immigration policy."[183]
   "There is nothing in the Bill that has anything to do with immigration."[184]
   The latter of these statements is manifestly untrue. For example, the abolition of ius soli, the creation of BDTC, BOC

135

and BN(O) and the limitation of ius sanguinis by birth abroad
have much to do with immigration. Yet, as the former statement
hints, the groundwork had already been well laid by prior
immigration legislation. Much of the 1981 Act is concerned
with tailoring nationality law to match the pre-existing
reality of immigration law. Consequently, the ' Act's
immigration implications, though real, are minor. This both
illustrates again the lack of scope which Governments have had
for tightening immigration control since 1971, and must also
question the wisdom of the Government allowing the Bill to be
debated in an atmosphere of alarm and extremism.

By comparison, Canada appreciated the immigration
consequences of citizenship much earlier and turned its back
on the Commonwealth in this respect in 1946. The resulting
simplicity of its provisions contrasts sharply with the U.K.
legislation. Ius soli operates, whilst birth abroad transmits
citizenship provided that one parent is a Canadian citizen and
the child registers or establishes a close connection with
Canada before the age of 28.[185] Apart from the procedural
safeguards which operate, a desirable feature of the
legislation is the clarity and directness of language
employed.

Naturally such comparisons can be simplistic, and special
historical connections will inevitably enmesh a country like
the U.K. which has a legacy of overseas rule.[186] However, it
must be doubtful whether the cost of the bureaucratic
machinery consequent upon the abolition of ius soli and the
alarm caused to resident ethnic communities can be justified
by the relatively small number of children denied citizenship
by birth.

Had the U.K. adopted a realistic definition of citizenship
in 1948 at a time when it was clear that other Commonwealth
countries were likely to do so, the ensuing immigration and
nationality problems and controversy would have been
significantly reduced.[187] By clinging to the concept of
Commonwealth citizenship the U.K. was unable to start afresh
in 1981. In the interim it was forced to adopt restrictive
immigration control and a devaluation of citizenship. It was
then in 1981 influenced both by immigration considerations and
the legacy of Commonwealth obligations. Thus the former
dictated the abolition of ius soli, the substitution of
complex registration provisions and the similarly complex
transitional provisions, whilst the latter led to the creation
of three types of citizenship (BDTC, BOC and BN(O)) which are
of cosmetic, and not substantive, importance. On the other
hand, the concessions to Gibraltar (through Parliamentary
pressure) and to the Falkland Islands (through the events of
1982) indicate the inherently political nature of nationality
laws and the sort of narrow 'kith and kin' citizenship laws
which the U.K., like all other States, is ultimately prepared
to accept.

136

(2) One of the strongest criticisms of the previous law was its complexity. This deficiency has not been remedied.[188] For an issue as fundamental to an individual as his citizenship, the law remains extraordinarily complex, necessitating resort to professional assistance for understanding. Some of the complexity is of course due to the historical context of the Commonwealth, but much stems from the abandonment of ius soli and the fact that the Government began with a narrowly drawn Bill but had to broaden it to accommodate opposition, thus producing subtle refinements. An indication of the complexity is the saving provisions which have had to be made for reducing statelessness[189] and thereby ensuring compliance with the U.K.'s international obligations.

(3) The complexity of the legislation meant that debate on its passage was arcane. Although it had been preceded by Green and White Papers and 4 years of digestion, public understanding was not greatly improved.[190] This helped to fan alarmist and frequently ignorant fears. But the underlying fear arose from the context in which the Bill was promulgated. It came soon after changes in the immigration Rules and in fulfilment of a Government's election manifesto which had promised firm action on immigration.[191] Indicative of the alarm was the dramatic increase in the number of people who acquired citizenship in 1981 and 1982.[192] The majority hailed from the Commonwealth, with the largest groups being Indians, Jamaicans and Pakistanis. The increase was due in part to increased efficiency in the Nationality Division of the Home Office and in part to a clamour to apply before the BNA became operative on 1 January 1983. The complex registration provisions add burdens to an already overloaded Home Office. Indeed, obtaining citizenship is by no means a quick process, involving delays of up to 2 years.[193] Though as the well publicised case of Miss Zola Budd, the South African athlete, revealed in April 1984, exceptional speed is always possible for exceptional cases.[194] The objection to this case lies not in the fact that the athlete benefited, but that other applicants should have to face the Home Office's normally pedestrian pace.

(4) The opportunity was not taken of reviewing the incidents of citizenship. Citizenship has always been used to deny a range of economic and political rights to non-citizens. Today those disabilities are scattered in a variety of statutes. A thoroughgoing reform of citizenship would not merely seek to ally it with the right of entry but would reappraise the purpose of the status and consequently the privileges which should attach to it and those which it is legitimate to deny to aliens. The Green and White Papers of 1977 and 1980 however concentrated, in their brevity, on the immediate and narrower aims of the acquisition of citizenship and its immigration

implications.[195] The excuse that the definition and incidents of the status have always been treated by the law as separable issues is a self-serving and inadequate answer but it is typical of the British traditional preference for piecemeal practicality as opposed to fundamental theoretical review.[196] Typical too was the lame defence that the inclusion of the appurtenances of citizenship smacks of a Bill of Rights and that is both alien to U.K. law and binding on Parliament.[197]

(5) The Act continues the tradition of citizenship and immigration laws by vesting wide discretion in the Secretary of State's hands. In part this is due to the complexity of the legislation, for in debate, when difficult examples were cited, resort was frequently made by the Government to clauses permitting the Secretary a discretion to override technical requirements. Elsewhere, he has a very broad power to "make provision generally for carrying into effect the purposes of" the Act (s.41(1)). A simple and contemporaneous example of this arose with the increase in fees for taking out citizenship.[198] The Secretary's power to impose charges (s.41(2)) is similar to those formerly in s.29 of the 1948 Act but, in line with the overall Government policy of public expenditure savings, the charges payable under s.41(2)(e) (for any search of records made necessary by the application) and (f) (any written opinion supplied about a person's status) are new.[199] Since public servants are involved and the complexity of the current provisions is of the Government's own making, these additions were unfortunate.[200] Moreover, there is no express limitation of reasonableness and, although grossly exorbitant charges might be challenged before the courts,[201] there is still wide room for manoeuvre. Increases in fees ought to have been made subject to an affirmative resolution by Parliament.[202] The 1982 increases meant, for example, that fees for naturalisation stood at £200 for each application, £270 for both spouses and £35 for a minor and at £70 for registration. Following Parliamentary pressure, the fees were reduced in April 1984 (to £160 for naturalisation and £55 for registration).[203] It can be argued however that these fees are still too high and for a family can be a considerable burden. Quite apart from the desirability of reducing the fees, they ought at least to be waived for those receiving state benefits.

In an attempt to placate hostile opinion to the Bill s.44(1) was added,[204] whereby any discretion in the Act must be exercised without regard to race, colour or religion.[205] It is a sad reflection of official policy in recent times that such a clause was not inserted as a matter of course and as the first section of the Act. It is also regrettable that sex discrimination was not added to the list of prohibitions (subject to the transitional provisions), since elsewhere the Government proudly proclaimed the Bill's move to sex equality.

Since there is no obligation on the Secretary of State to supply reasons for his decision, the safeguard of s.44(1) is unlikely to be of much practical use. If it could be established that discrimination had been practised and the applicant denied registration or naturalisation, s.44(3) could potentially apply. This subsection preserves the iurisdiction of the courts to hear proceedings involving "the rights of any person under any provision" of the Act. Many of the Act's provisions bestow rights (e.g. s.1(3)) and they are therefore the preserve of s.44(3); others however confer privileges and these are the preserve of the Secretary of State's discretion. Yet, when that discretion is exercised to grant or refuse any application, it "shall not be subject to appeal to, or review in, any court" (s.44(2)).[206] The only possibilities of challenge are a complaint to the Ombudsman, if his jurisdiction of "maladministration" covers discrimination,[207] an investigation by the Commission for Racial Equality[208] or a Parliamentary question. In between there are some rights which involve a discretionary stage (e.g. under s.7(5) entitlement to registration because of service or employment is subject to the Secretary of State's untrammelled assessment of whether the applicant has a close connection with the U.K.) and therefore a potential conflict between s.44(2) and (3). A similar conflict could arise if a discretionary decision is shown to have been exercised in a discriminatory manner contrary to the general proscription of s.44(1). It could be argued that the right to non-discrimination is superior to s.44(2) and in line with the U.K.'s international respon-sibilities.[209] It is also possible that in times of a more developed public law, the exclusionary rule in s.44(2) could be directly challenged as failing to oust the jurisdiction of the court. There are authorities[210] which could be argued but to apply them in this field would be to reverse a tradition of non-intervention and the courts may well eschew the struggle to do so.

The abundance of discretion is symptomatic of the jealousy with which States guard the prerogative of granting citizenship. Some States, however, have at least improved the procedural aspects of citizenship. Thus, in Canada naturalisation and the renunciation and resumption of citizenship are determined by a citizenship judge whose decision binds the Government and, most importantly, must be accompanied by a statement of reasons.[211] These procedures reflect the awareness of citizenship as an important issue of civil liberties and the recognition that due process is a theme of all such issues. The U.K. however has steadfastly refused to take this course. This is partly due to a wider tradition of executive discretion, to the absence of a Bill of Rights and to the lack of a developed system of administrative law. It is also due to

(a) the link which citizenship has with immigration and hence the unwillingness to concede the potentially uncomfortable implications of natural justice and

(b) the unwillingness to accept that the process of granting citizenship has implications of civil liberties.

(6) On the more positive side, the concept of dual nationality has been retained. The Labour Government's Green Paper raised the options for reforming dual nationality and hinted that voluntary acquisition of another nationality would lead to a loss of BC.[212] During passage of the Bill, reference was frequently made to the inability and undesirability of a person 'serving two countries'. This approach sees citizenship solely in terms of allegiance and the obligation to 'defend one's country' and underestimates the looser and more practical role which citizenship today fulfils. The abolition of dual nationality was ultimately resisted "because it is true that to some extent people can have dual obligations in their hearts ... and also because, as a matter of practice, it seems a workable concept".[213] This approach can be welcomed for recognising the pluralistic nature of modern society and the inevitable insecurity which would be felt within ethnic communities if dual nationality were to be abolished.

(7) As ever the acquisition of British Citizenship will be automatic for the majority of individuals. For the minority they face immense complexity, considerable delay and uncomfortably high expense.

R. PASSPORTS

The hallmark of a passport, if I may use that phrase, is the fact that it is vouched on behalf of Her Majesty and contains within its own covers a request by Her Majesty as Queen or head of the Commonwealth to those to whom the passport may be shown, to render assistance to the bearer. It is, in a sense, a form of currency by which persons may travel from one realm to another.[214]

(1) Importance

Today passports perform various functions. First, they serve as a form of identification at frontiers and, thus, a precondition for modern travel. For, though in principle it is possible to travel outside the U.K. without one,[215] State practice requires it.[216] Second, they conveniently reveal the nationality of the holder so that he can seek assistance and protection from his country's diplomatic representatives overseas.[217] Third, they can reflect the holder's immigration status since visas and entitlement to stay are usually endorsed within the passport.[218] This is a function of increasing importance and sensitivity today in the contact between immigrants and the police or government[219] and in the process of checking for entitlement to State benefits, for example, health treatment. It is soon to be exacerbated by the wider use of machine readable passports which can be checked by computers in the first instance against the holder's immigration record.[220] The potential implications are far-reaching if access to such records were ever to be conceded to other data bases such as police, tax or D.H.S.S. records.

(2) Background

Historically, the grant and withdrawal of passports have been a discretionary process subsumed within the reach of the Royal Prerogative. Since the Monarch could prevent a subject from leaving the Kingdom by the writ of ne exeat regno,[221] it became the practice to grant licences to depart and these survived the Magna Carta (which by cl. 42 made departure from the realm lawful). Legislation during the Napoleonic wars[222] required passports to be obtained before an alien could leave and their issue was placed firmly at the discretion of the Secretary of State. On the other side of the coin, under constitutional law aliens were admitted by leave of the Crown - the very name 'passport' entitled the holder to 'pass the port' of control. Additionally, in Medieval times, aliens were frequently admitted on condition that they reside in a particular town and required leave or a licence of that municipality to travel to others. Thus, leave to enter and roam the country was a discretionary power of the King and Borough. The passport was the chief mechanism of control under the emergency legislation between 1793 and 1816, governing both the alien's entry and his movement within the country.[223] This Executive discretion has survived recent changes in immigration and nationality laws with the absurd result that statutory entitlement to citizenship is not matched by entitlement to a passport.

(3) International practice[224]

The discretion is reflected by the lack of impact of international law in this area. Admittedly it has recognised the right of a person to leave his own country[225] and, since in practice a passport is a prerequisite to travel, it can be argued that a person is entitled to expect one from his own country.[226] However, on the crucial issue of how passports are issued, international law has made no headway. Issuance traditionally lies within the ambit of a State's foreign affairs.[227] It is a simple yet most effective method of curtailing a person's freedom, and States have been unwilling to cede the power to formal requirements of due process. Such willingness must be generated internally. For example, in the U.S. the emergencies of the 1940s and the 'Cold War' of the 1950s led to stringent controls on the issue of passports.[228]

The State Department enjoyed unchallengeable and arbitrary powers.[229] In the late 1950s and more enlightened 1960s the courts began to challenge them on constitutional grounds, notably for infringement of the due process requirement in the Fifth Amendment, and to emphasise the right to travel.[230] Yet the pendulum, as is prone to happen in the political context of the Supreme Court, swung back in the Executive's favour in 1981 when the Court, in a case involving the well travelled litigant, Agee,[231] undid much of its earlier work and ruled in favour of the Government's discretionary power to revoke passports at the expense of the procedural requirements demanded by the Fifth Amendment.

(4) U.K. practice

In the U.K. the imbalance has always lain in favour of the Government. There has been no flirting with procedural or statutory supervision. "The power to grant or withhold a passport in the United Kingdom is one of Her Majesty's Royal Prerogatives and [the Secretary of State] has a discretion to accede to or refuse an application ..."[232]

Application for a passport is a straightforward exercise with forms available at Post Offices.[233] A spouse and children can be included on the applicant's passport and children under 16 can obtain separate passports if supported by their parents. As the provisions of the British Nationality Act 1981 take effect, the difficulties of proof facing those born overseas, or born to non-citizen residents will appear, such as proof of parental, lawful residence (see further, section H (1) above). It is unfortunate that what should be a constitutional entitlement, like a birth certificate, has to be paid for[234] and does not last for life.

The Royal Prerogative in this field is not subject to substantive or procedural qualifications. Thus the refusal to issue and the withdrawal of passports have acquired a certain mystique, frequently associated with the British tradition of secrecy. It would appear that refusal or withdrawal may stem

(a) from the police or a court, during the course of a criminal investigation, so as to prevent the suspect or accused[235] evading jurisdiction;
(b) from a court order for the protection of children threatened with removal from the U.K., contrary to an award of custody, or pending judicial proceedings;[236]
(c) from the Crown so as to obtain reimbursement from a person repatriated to the U.K. at public expense;[237]
(d) from the Crown's untrammelled power. In 1958, this was said to cover "persons whose activities are so notoriously undesirable or dangerous that Parliament would be expected to support the action of the Foreign Secretary".[238] This is slim protection for a power of such unwieldy potential. The fact that few cases

appear to arise is no answer. On the contrary it
questions the very usefulness of the power.

This passport law, or the lack of it, is symptomatic of the
U.K.'s treatment of civil liberties. Thus, a discretionary
power is asserted and its use shrouded in secrecy. Its
continued use is defended by a mixture of references to
tradition and claims to the responsible way in which it is
exercised.[239] The possible controls are more theoretical than
feasible -

(a) Parliamentary accountability is limited since the
    Ministerial reply can refuse to comment or can be
    couched in general terms. Rarely, a case may arouse
    such pressure as to force a more detailed reply but
    even then the substance of the decision can be
    withheld.[240]
(b) The Ombudsman is excluded from investigating the issue
    of passports in the context of national security and
    crime.[241] What remains are non-controversial complaints
    from, for example, bona fide holiday makers over the
    delays in issuing passports; in other words, possible
    maladministration in the decision-making, not the
    merits of the decision.[242]
(c) Judicial review of the royal prerogative does not yet
    extend to assessing the merits or grounds of a case
    but is strictly limited to determining the precise
    scope of the prerogative.[243]
(d) Relief is theoretically possible if the deprived
    citizen intends travel within the E.E.C. Since the
    U.K. does not administer an identity card system,
    passports are essential for travel and must be
    supplied.[244] However, art. 48(3) of the E.E.C. Treaty
    preserves to Member States a wide margin of discretion
    to infringe the paraphernalia of freedom of movement.
    What may have to change, if a case ever arises, is the
    procedural application of art. 48(3). Theoretically,
    by analogy with Directive 64/221 (see chapter 5), the
    lack of appeal and the need to supply reasons could be
    struck down by the Court of Justice. However, in these
    uncharted waters of traditional State prerogative and
    in a case which would have art. 48(3) overtones, it
    will take a bold English court to act. The long
    awaited and delayed implementation of the passport
    union[245] will see the use of a common burgundy-coloured
    passport which will ease travel within the E.E.C. but
    the grant of such passports will remain firmly within
    the competence of each Member State.

(5) Reform
In a society which purports to abide by fundamental human

rights, a passport should automatically accompany citizenship. It would then be a right and should be issued free of charge and, subject to voluntary loss of citizenship and the substitution of updated photographs,[246] for life. The critical question would then become the grant of citizenship and for this an appeal to a judicial tribunal with the normal panoply of natural justice should be available.

It is difficult to think of circumstances where permanent withdrawal of a passport would be justifiable (as opposed to temporary withdrawal, such as for bail or the protection of children). It may be necessary to prevent suspected traitors from leaving but in wartime the Emergency Powers legislation and, in peacetime prosecution under the Official Secrets Acts, are ample to achieve this purpose. There are, of course, circumstances where a Government would <u>like</u> to restrict a person's movement, for example, to prevent an IRA sympathiser from travelling abroad to make political speeches but such sensitivity ought not to justify withdrawal of a passport. Only if the holder's conduct is unlawful should a sanction be applied and for that the general criminal law is available.

----

1   Blackstone, Commentaries, Book I, ch.10.

2   U.S. Constitution 1787, Art. 1, s.8, cl.4.

3   It is thus an important motive for newly formed countries
e.g. the Citizenship Act 1984 (Zimbabwe) which prohibits dual
nationality and gives whites 12 months in which to choose
Zimbabwe nationality or retain British citizenship.

4   Government's Green Paper, 1977, Cmnd. 6795, para. 13.

5   7 Jam. I c.2.

6   As a result of the Dred Scott case, 19 How. 393 (1857).

7   Until then, they could only acquire citizenship by
naturalisation; birth in 'their own' country was insufficient
- Elk v Wilkins 112 U.S. 94. See also the Citizenship Act 1948
(Ceylon) and Pillai v Mudanayake [1953] A.C. 514 for the
indirect discrimination practised against the Indian Tamils;
and the Naturalisation Act 1903 (Australia) which barred
naturalisation to natives of "Asia, Africa or the Islands of
the Pacific, excepting New Zealand".

8   Of the latter, see the treatment of Communists in the U.S.
under the Subversive Activities Control Act 1950 and the
Immigration and Nationality Act 1952 (s.313); Dennis v U.S.
341 U.S. 494.

9   Cf. U.S. Immigration and Nationality Act 1952, s.93 and
British Nationality and New Zealand Citizenship Act 1948; note
that voting rights are still conceded to Commonwealth citizens
in the U.K. and survive the recent reform of the Representation of the People Act 1949 - Home Affairs Committee H.C. 32
(1982-83), paras. 17-39 and the Government's White Paper in
response, Cmnd. 9140. Now s.1(1)(b)(ii) of the Representation
of the People Act 1983.

10   Cf. the recent endorsement by the Supreme Court of
restrictions on aliens in the U.S., Ambach v Norwick 441 U.S.
68 (1979) (which held that a State is entitled to require
public schools' teachers to be U.S. citizens since they
fulfilled a 'governmental function' in educating future
citizens); Sugarman v Dougall 413 U.S. 634 (1973); Foley v
Connelie 435 U.S. 291 (1978); see 92 Harv. L.R. 1516, 31 Stan.
L.R. 1069, 54 Tu.L.Rev. 225, 89 Y.L.J. 940.

11   See Leage, Roman Private Law, 3rd Ed., p.87-90, and
Buckland, Textbook of Roman Law, 3rd Ed., p.86-100 for a
detailed account. As to the further classifications according

to social position, see Gernsey, Social Status and Legal Privilege in the Roman Empire, Part IV.

12 This position had already been reached by the common law before being codified by statute in 1367 - 42 Ed. III c.10.

13 Anon (1562) 73 E.R. 496.

14 Anon (1544) 73 E.R. 872.

15 Hale, Pleas of the Crown, vol. I, ch.10, p.59.

16 But there is no legal entitlement to it, see China Navigation Co. v A.G. [1932] 2 K.B. 197.

17 Calvin's Case (1608) 77 E.R. 377, at p.382 and 407 respectively.

18 See Macdonald's Case (1746-7) 18 State Tr. 860 cf. Joyce v D.P.P. [1946] A.C. 347 where, under later law, the subject had to renounce specifically his citizenship before he could escape a charge of treason.

19 See Cable, Decisive Decisions of U.S. Citizenship.

20 It took an Act of Parliament in 1783 (22 Geo. III c.46) to free natural-born subjects of the indelibility of their citizenship

21 See the discussion in Stoeck v Public Trustee [1921] 2 Ch. 67.

22 Per Macdonald C.B. in Daubigny v Davallon (1794) 145 E.R. 936, at p.937-8.

23 25 Ed. III stat. 1.

24 77 E.R. 377. See Parry, Nationality and Citizenship Laws of the Commonwealth, p.30-40.

25 Ibid., at p.399.

26 Ibid. A.G. v Sands (1669) 21 E.R. 720; Burk v Brown (1742) 26 E.R. 640; Du Hourmelin v Sheldon (1839) 41 E.R. 203. The position was summarised in Sharp v De Sauveur (1871) 41 L.J.Ch. 576.

27 Thornby v Fleetwood (1720) 93 E.R. 545.

28 12 W. III c.2 which barred, inter alia, "any office or place of trust". All Bills of Naturalisation had to contain a

clause reciting the disabilities - 1 Geo. 1 c.4.

29 Chiefly because it was probably not at this time retrospective (thus the applicant's children would remain aliens) and because he was not exempt from paying the higher aliens' taxes. "A denizen is in a kind of middle state, between an alien and natural-born subject, and partakes of both of them." Blackstone, Book I, ch.10, p.374.

30 And it could be made retrospective by the inclusion of a special clause to this effect; Fourdrin v Gowdey (1834) 40 E.R. 146.

31 22 Geo. II c.45 (1749); cf. 14 and 15 Car. II c.15.

32 7 Anne c.5, An Act for Naturalising Foreign Protestants.

33 Select Committee on the Laws Affecting Aliens, (1843) P.P. v.

34 13 Geo. II c.3; cf. 29 Geo. II c.5.

35 12 Car. 2 c.18.

36 10 Anne c.5.

37 14 Geo. III c.84.

38 13 Geo. II c.7.

39 20 Geo. II c.44.

40 26 Geo. II c.26.

41 27 Geo. II c.1.

42 See the Middlesex Case, (1804) 2 Peck. 118, Representation of the People Act 1983, ss.1 and 2; previously at local level, see Municipal Corporation Acts 1835 and 1882, County Electors Act 1888, Local Government Act 1894.

43 Respectively, R v De Mierre (1771) 98 E.R. 463; Anthony v Seger (1789) 161 E.R. 457; Aliens Employment Act 1955.

44 On the Stock Exchange, Weinberger v Inglis [1919] A.C. 606.

45 (1843) P.P. v

46 7 and 8 Vict. c.66.

47 7 Anne c.5, 4 Geo. II c.21, 13 Geo. III c.21.

48 De Geer v Stone (1882) 22 Ch. 243.

49 British Nationality and Status of Aliens Act 1914, s.1(1)(a). Once acquired by birth in one part of the Empire, the status was retained on travel to another e.g. Jephson v Riera (1835) 12 E.R. 598.

50 It can still retain vitality; see Lesa v A.G. [1982] 1 N.Z.L.R. 165 in which the Privy Council held that persons born in West Samoa between 1928 and 1948 were natural-born British subjects and, by statute, were therefore New Zealand citizens. New Zealand was not amused at this Polynesian prospect and promptly reversed the decision by taking away the citizenship of those concerned through the Citizenship (Western Samoa) Act 1982.

51 Re Johnson, Roberts v A.G. [1903] 1 Ch. 821.

52 Cmnd. 2768, p.14.

53 Wartime legislation in the U.K. (1914 and 1916) had already signalled these consequences, since under it naturalisation within the Dominions did not necessarily prevent the person from being regarded as an alien in British eyes, R. v Francis e.p. Markwald [1918] 1 K.B. 617; Markwald v A.G. [1920] 1 Ch. 348.

54 Canadian Citizenship Act 1946, c.15.

55 See Hansard vol. 453, col. 500 ff.

56 Status of Aliens Act 1914, s.3, which provided for an Imperial certificate of naturalisation which was to be recognised throughout the Empire. For an account of the 'common code' and the conflict between imperial idealism and regional immigration policies, see Parry, op. cit. pp.84-86.

57 See J. Mervyn Jones, vol. XXII, BYBIL 122.

58 Immigration Act 1910.

59 British Nationality and Status of Aliens (in New Zealand) Act 1928.

60 Though the 1948 Act was amended on no less than 40 occasions. One of the more important changes was the right of alien women to acquire citizenship on marriage to British subjects without citizenship - BNA 1965.

61 H.C. Debs. 27 April, col. 1227, a short debate on the introduction of the Government's Green Paper on possible changes, Cmnd. 6795.

62 Cmnd. 7987.

63 Following upon objections by the Dependent Territories who could see little merit in being lumped together with the residual category of BOC. As will be seen, the future of Hong Kong has led to a further category of citizenship.

64 H.C. Debs. 28 January 1981, col. 935.

65 S.I. 82/933. It received the Royal Assent on 30 October 1981; its treatment by the Standing Committee was subjected to a guillotine (H.C. Debs. 29 April 1981, col. 792); it is supplemented by secondary legislation - S.I. 1982/986-89, 1004, 1011, 1070.

66 H.C. Debs. 28 January 1981, col. 931.

67 Ibid. For a statement of the link between transmission of citizenship and the right of abode, see H.L. Debs. 13 July 1981, col. 1010-11. Cf. the reported remarks of the Prime Minister, whilst in India, that fears of a flood of immigrants were a justification for the Bill, Times 18 April 1981; and see H.C. Debs. 28 April 1981, col. 646.

68 Defined so as to include the Channel Islands, Isle of Man and Northern Ireland, s.50(1) and in certain circumstances, a U.K. registered ship and aircraft, s.50(7).

69 This would not cover those exempted from immigration control under s.8(3) and (4) of the Immigration Act 1971 (diplomats and armed forces). E.E.C. nationals are in a curious position. If resident for employment, they are entitled under Community law to remain without time limit and are therefore 'settled'. Yet under U.K. practice, the time limit is only usually removed after 4 years (r.144 and Standing Committee F on the Bill, col. 44). Since most E.E.C. States prohibit dual nationality, it is unlikely that many E.E.C. families will wish their children to acquire BC. For those who do, it is similarly unlikely that the Court of Justice would condemn the 4 years' delay as an impediment to the principle of freedom of movement.

70 Shah v Barnet L.B.C. [1983] 2 A.C. 309

71 It will assist those few children whose parents travel frequently abroad but not for long enough to lose their ordinary residence, cf. R v Waltham Forest L.B.C., ex p. Vale,

Times, 25 February 1985.

72 [1980] A.C. 930; reversed by Khawaja [1984] A.C. 74.

73 Cf. s.2(2) British Nationality Act (No.2) 1964.

74 U.N. Convention on Statelessness 1954, art. 2.

75 E.g. Watson v Nikolaisen [1955] 2 Q.B. 286, Wheatley v Waltham Forest L.B. [1979] 2 All E.R. 289.

76 Standing Committee F on the Bill (hereinafter, the Standing Committee), col. 212.

77 Applications for nationality generally necessitate procuring the appropriate form from the Home Office. The Government has resisted the call to make forms available at Post Offices - H.C. Debs. 3 March 1983, col. 367.

78 If the adoption order ceases to have effect, this does not affect the child's citizenship status - s.1(6). An order can only be revoked in two circumstances - on appeal or if an illegitimate child has been adopted by a single, natural parent and both parents subsequently marry.

79 In the latter case, if the child is not caught out by the immigration laws, theoretically he would fall within category (e).

80 There is evidence to suggest that recently the Home Office has been prepared to turn a blind eye to the import of foreign children by childless British couples, Guardian, 7 March 1985.

81 Standing Committee, col. 41.

82 Standing Committee, col. 41. Based on the calculation that in 1979 between 59,000 and 64,000 children were born in the U.K. to parents born outside the U.K. and the assumption that 95% of the children would qualify as citizens because their parents had acquired the status or become settled. (See also H.C. Debs. 8 February 1983, col. 315.)

83 Ibid.

84 R.59-65, 127-131. Indeed, during discussion of the Bill, comments in the Standing Committee were frequently deflected by the excuse that the Rules, yet to be drafted, would tackle the detailed implications of s.1 on children wishing to travel e.g. cols. 94, 96-7. Yet when the Rules were finally debated in 1982 and 1983, the controversy over the provisions on husbands overshadowed the amendments dealing with children.

85 Having abandoned its election commitments to compile a register of incoming dependants and to impose annual quotas.

86 Cf. the New Zealand Citizenship Act 1977 which employs the same distinction, s.7.

87 S.I. 1982/1004, S.I. 1982/1709. The list includes the British Tourist Authority, NATO, the Commonwealth War Graves Commission, the British Council.

88 See De Geer v Stone (1882) 22 Ch. 243, because the ambassador's house was deemed to be part of the kingdom.

89 Principally 25 Ed. III st. 1.

90 Cf. 1343 Pt. Deb. (Rot. Parl. vol. 2, 139) - citizenship to those born of parents in the King's Service.

91 Reference can be made to the European Communities Act 1972, Sch. I, Part III and the Interpretation Act 1978, see H.L. Debs. 7 October 1981, col. 52. For a discussion of the effect of the 1981 Act in the E.E.C. context, see Bonner [1982] Eu.L. Rev. 69-75.

92 Cf. one of the possible conditions for naturalisation in the 1981 Act -"service under an international organisation of which the United Kingdom or Her Majesty's government therein is a member" (Sch. I, para. 1(1)(d)(ii)); and for registration, s.7(4)(b). This more generous provision should have been adopted throughout the Act.

93 A similar requirement exists for Crown Service, s.2(1)(b).

94 Concerted attempts were made in the House of Lords to broaden the exemption but they were resisted lest 'sham' business connections with the U.K. qualify (H.L. Debs. 13 July 1981, col. 1037).

95 Pt. Roll. 17 Ed. III (1343); see De Geer v Stone (1882) 22 Ch. 243, at p.250.

96 De Geer v Stone (1882) 22 Ch. 243.

97 7 Anne c.5, 4 Geo. II c.21, 13 Geo. III c.21.

98 And a declaration of retention before the age of 22, British Nationality and Status of Aliens Act 1922.

99 This qualification is not crucial if a child would be otherwise stateless, Sched. 2, para. 4.

100 This can be extended to 6 years by the Secretary of State in special circumstances (s.3(4)). It is highly unlikely that ignorance of the rule would count as a special circumstance and hence the need for full publicity to be given to the requirement.

101 Thus, residence of the child alone (e.g. for education) does not qualify.

102 Thus restoring the position which operated before 1730; see Parry op. cit., p.61-62.

103 Because, in classical sex discrimination terms, an English mother who went abroad with an alien husband was sub potestate viri, see Duroure v Jones (1791) 100 E.R. 1031.

104 Crown or similar service in the dependent territory may enable registration regardless of conditions (c) and (d). It lies within the Secretary of State's discretion if he "thinks fit", but there must be "special circumstances" - s.4(5). Civil servants, senior police officers and the like who find life in Hong Kong unacceptable in future years are clear potential beneficiaries of this discretion.

105 [1984] A.C. 74, by reversing the effect of Zamir [1980] A.C. 930 in relation to the meaning of entry by deception, see further chapter 8.

106 See Daily Telegraph and Times, 22 May 1985, for the case of Mr. Eric Ho.

107 Strictly speaking, three, since naturalisation by Act of Parliament is still possible e.g. James Hugh Maxwell Naturalisation Act 1975.

108 Payable on application, S.I. 82/1011, regn. 2(2). For details of the procedure, see S.I. 82/986.

109 450 days absence is permitted in relation to the 5 years and 270 to the 3 years; for both only 90 days are allowed in the 12 months preceding the application.

110 Margueritte [1983] Q.B. 180.

111 Or Crown service/marriage to a person in Crown service, during these periods.

112 Welsh, Scottish and Gaelic qualify. A similar requirement for naturalisation by marriage was withdrawn from the Bill.

113 7 Jam. 1 c.2.

114 Cf. the traditional use of written tests in Australia to weed out non-English applicants; now relaxed by the Citizenship Amendment Act 1984. See Gelberg, Jewish Chronicle, 7 July 1911, for an account of how a Home Office Circular requiring the applicant to speak, read and write English reasonably well reduced the number of successful applicants to the U.K.

115 Mr. Enoch Powell M.P., Standing Committee, col. 115.

116 See Parry, op. cit., p.71; De Conway's (Countess) Case (1834) 12 E.R. 522; De Wall's Case (1848) 13 E.R. 666.

117 Gout v Zimmerman (1847) 5 N.C. 440.

118 H.C. Papers vol. 7, 299 (1923).

119 On certain questions relating to the Conflict of Nationality Laws; see British Nationality and Status of Aliens Act 1933, c.49.

120 For a concise account, see Parry, op. cit., p.179

121 Following protests from the ethnic communities, a language test was not included.

122 An immediate consequence of the Act and amended Rules was to require the wife of a British Citizen to obtain entry clearance instead of the previous certificate of patriality (the term 'settled' in the Rules being interpreted to include BCs and thus making r.46-49 and entry clearance applicable) - Brahmbhatt, Times, 17 October 1983.

123 See H.C. Select Committee on the Laws Affecting Aliens (1843) P.P. v

124 Standing Committee col. 692, Junior Home Office Minister. The applicant's immigration record may also be relevant, such as a history of overstaying.

125 Home Secretary H.C. Debs. 2 June 1981, col. 855.

126 Ibid. Cf. the approach of the court in Dowhopoluk v Martin 23 D.L.R. (3d) 42 (1971).

127 Ibid. at col. 856. Cf. the Green Paper, paras. 53-57.

128 Guidelines may be the better approach, for otherwise the State may be tempted to list too many criteria; cf. 8 U.S.C.

para. 1101(f) which spells out many, including habitual drunkards, polygamists, prostitutes and those convicted of crimes involving 'moral turpitude'; and for analysis of this last category see 23 A.L.R. (Fed.) 480.

[129] Lazarov v Secretary of State of Canada 39 D.L.R. (3d) 738 (1973) but cf. the more deferential approach in Dowhopoluk v Martin 23 D.L.R. (3d) 42 (1971).

[130] The Minister's discretion to waive an Immigration Appeal Tribunal decision adverse to the immigrant is a case in point.

[131] H.C. Debs. 2 June 1981, col. 859.

[132] Ibid, col. 828, including 249 for the 'good character' requirement and 190 for the language test. The total number of refusals in 1981 was 895, in 1982 1,121 and in 1983 819.

[133] Ibid, col. 859-860 and H.C. Debs. 4 June 1981, cols. 1117-19.

[134] Cf. the variable attitude of Citizenship Court Judges in Canada; see Richmond, Post-War Immigrants in Canada, p.198.

[135] Which prompted a Government amendment - H.C. Debs. 27 October 1981, col. 768.

[136] A first attempt to extend the benefit was defeated in the Commons, H.C. Debs. 9 July 1982, col. 618.

[137] S.39 and Sch. 4 of the 1981 Act contain consequential amendments to the 1971 Act, the general purpose being to redefine the right of abode in terms of BC; see Fransman (1983) NLJ 691, 727 and 739 for consideration of the inter-relationship. Certificates of patriality become certificates of entitlement -s.39(8).

[138] Originally 2 years, until the Government accepted an amendment to the Bill.

[139] E.g. 'Registration - What it means to you', a CRE publication.

[140] Anguilla, Bermuda, British Antarctic Territory, British Indian Ocean Territory, Cayman Islands, Gibraltar, Hong Kong, Montserrat, Pitcairn, Henderson, Ducie and Oeno Islands, St. Christopher and Nevis, St. Helena and Dependencies, Sovereign bases at Akrotiri and Dhekelia, Turks and Caicos Islands and the Virgin Islands - Sch. 6.

[141] The administrative functions are carried out by the

Governor of the particular territory, to whom all powers, save the Secretary of State's rule-making function, are delegated - s.43.

142 The Government dismissed the suggestion that the status was inferior and preferred to describe it as "a parallel citizenship", H.C. Debs. 28 January 1981, col. 1036.

143 Home Affairs Committee H.C. 158 (1980-81), Evidence p.1-9. The Committee's Report is a detailed account of BOCs.

144 U.N. Convention on the Reduction of Statelessness, 1954.

145 H.A.C. Report, supra, paras. 10, 16. Cf. the registration facilities under s.28 and Sch. 2.

146 Standing Committee, col. 102.

147 Except UKPHs who, though they become BOCs, are entitled to a voucher for entry, since the Government agreed to honour the commitment to them.

148 E.g. Canada refused to admit BOCs because of their apparent lack of a right to return to the country of residence, Guardian, 20 July 1983; for Germany, see Guardian, 20 August 1983.

149 In immigration terms, not all would have elected to enter the U.K. and their rate of entry could have been regulated.

150 The remainder being 1.8 million Chinese residents, 400,000 shorter-term Chinese residents, 20,000 BCs, 95,500 other nationals and 4,500 stateless persons - see H.C. Debs. 25 January 1985, col. 550.

151 Draft Agreement, Cmnd. 9352 (26 September 1984).

152 But the exact phrasing has yet to be resolved with the Chinese, H.C. Debs. 6 February 1985, col. 1071.

153 See H.C. Debs. 21 January 1985, col. 810.

154 Parry, op. cit., p.307.

155 Standing Committee, col. 1692.

156 Ibid, col. 1693.

157 Or who have been in Crown Service and revealed other signs of connection (loosely defined and left to the Secretary of State's discretion) with the U.K., s.31.

158 For a list of Protectorates, see S.I. 82/1070.

159 Similarly, the 1948 legislation did not classify them as aliens but they bore some signs of alienage, principally naturalisation rather than registration as UKCs was open to them. The possibility of statelessness arising for their descendants has necessitated provisions to reduce it - S.I. 82/1070.

160 46 countries are listed, compared to 9 under the 1948 Act.

161 In the short-term it may be relevant to determine whether a person is or was a patrial under the 1971 Act and therefore able to take advantage of the transitional provisions in the 1981 Act.

162 Cf. s.19, 1948 Act. The courts had already implied such a limitation in defiance of the clear wording of the earlier 1914 Act - see Sawyer v Kropp (1916) L.J.K.B. 1446, Ex p. Freyberger (1917) 116 L.T. 237, Vecht v Tay, ibid, 446, Gschwind v Huntington [1918] 2 K.B. 420.

163 See R v Lynch [1903] 1 K.B. 444, Joyce v D.P.P. [1946] A.C. 347.

164 S.7, 1914 Act, abolished in 1948.

165 [1980] A.C. 930; [1984] A.C. 74 respectively.

166 Cf. the tighter provision in the New Zealand Citizenship Act 1977 - if the holder has acquired another citizenship and has acted contrary to the country's interests; yet judicial review to the Supreme Court is available, s.19. And note the U.S. approach which lists proscribed activities with relative, though lengthy, precision - 8 U.S.C. paras. 1451(c) and 1424.

167 Confined to the Dominions in the original 1914 version.

168 Standing Committee, col. 1841; and there were none between 1975 and May 1985, see H.C. Debs. 13 May 1985, col. 11.

169 Mahmood, Times, 2 August 1979, Akhtar [1980] 2 All E.R. 735.

170 63 registrations were consequently deemed nullities under the 1948 provisions, Standing Committee, col. 1842.

171 British Nationality and Status of Aliens Act 1918, s.1. Cf. the U.S. Naturalisation Act 1950, 3 years' residence in the country of birth or former nationality (or 5 years in

156

others) lead to denaturalisation, see now 8 U.S.C. para. 1484.

172 E.g. Statute of Treasons 1351, Incitement to Disaffection Act 1934, unlawful assembly.

173 Withdrawal of a passport can, for practical purposes of travel, achieve the same purpose as deprivation of citizenship. Judicial review of the prerogative power (under which passports are issued) is theoretically possible but would need convincing evidence of an abuse to found a court's jurisdiction.

174 S.40(7), repeating s.20(7) of the 1948 Act. The 1914 version spoke of "high judicial office", s.7(4). For the current procedural Rules, see S.I. 82/988.

175 S.40(8) cf. the 1870 and 1914 versions under which the inquiry "shall have" the powers etc. of a High Court.

176 Standing Committee, col. 1841.

177 Cf. the U.S. where citizenship by birth or naturalisation is protected by the Constitution (14th Amendment) and in principle cannot be withdrawn without the holder's consent, Aroyim v Rusk 387 U.S. 253 (1967).

178 Schneiderman v U.S. 320 U.S. 118 (1943), at p.125.

179 S.10 preserves the right of resumption (BNA 1964 s.1; S.I. 1964/682) for those who had renounced UKC.

180 S.12; not re-enacted in 1948.

181 U.N. Convention on the Reduction of Statelessness, art. 1 (a Contracting State shall grant nationality to a person born in its territory who would be otherwise stateless).

182 And those born abroad to BCs, BDTCs, BOCs or BSs who are stateless (Sch. 2, para. 4) and those who could have benefited under the British Nationality (No. 2) Act 1964 and S.I. 1964/1391.

183 Mr. Steel, M.P., H.C. Debs. 28 January 1981, col. 958.

184 Mr. Gardner M.P., Ibid, col. 961.

185 Canadian Citizenship Act 1976 c.108. The generosity of age 28 is thoroughly reasonable, giving young people the opportunity to travel before deciding to settle in Canada; for the U.S. and the development and future of its nationality laws, see 23 A.J.I.L. p.13 ff.

186 Cf. the detailed consideration of legislation and historical development which faced the court in Levave v Immigration Department [1979] 2 N.Z.L.R. 74 (re the status of L whose father was born in Western Samoa in 1924) and Lesa v A.G. [1982] 1 N.Z.L.R. 165.

187 Principally of course by the denial of entry to predominantly coloured immigrants in the 1950s.

188 "Translating it into the Latin to make it clearer" does not greatly aid comprehension - Bishop of Peterborough, H.L. Debs. 13 July 1981, col. 1003. Applicants for registration or naturalisation now fall into no less than "24 distinct streams", Report on I and N Dept. (Home Office 1984), p.37.

189 S.36 and Sch. 2, principally because of birth in a State, which has abandoned ius soli, to parents whose nationality adheres to ius soli e.g. a person born in the U.K. who has not been able to register as a citizen under s.1, who is between the ages of 10 and 22 and who has always been stateless (Sch. 2, para. 3); a person born outside the U.K. to parents who were BCs, BDTCs, BOC or BS who has always been stateless but has been in the U.K. for 3 years (ibid, para. 4) - though the chances of him entering the U.K. in the first place are slim.

190 Apart from ethnic organisations, it was opposed principally by the churches which launched a concerted and determined attack on the Bill in the House of Lords.

191 It was announced in 1978 and was succeeded by considerable controversy, see chapter 2.

192 Thus, the numbers in 1978 were 25,000, 1979-24,600, 1980-27,500, 1981-48,500, 1982-76,200 - see cmnd. 9009.

193 H.C. Debs. 26 January 1983, col. 455. The average time taken to process applications for naturalisation is 21 months and for registration is 14 months - H.C. Debs. 12 April 1984, col. 312.

194 The Secretary of State's discretion under s.3(1) was used to grant the citizenship because of her father's connection with the U.K. (he was a BC by descent) and because of her exceptional talent and desire to represent the U.K. in athletics - H.C. Debs. 13 April 1984, col. 422.

195 For the Green Paper, "Such privileges [of citizenship] do not stem directly from the law of nationality and so are not dealt with in this document", para. 66.

196 Cf. the more sensible approach in Canada where the Citizenship Act 1976 c.108 sets out the rights of citizens and the disabilities of aliens (s.31).

197 Junior Home Office Minister, H.C. Debs. 28 January 1981, col. 1034-5.

198 In April 1982; see S.I. 82/1011. A motion to revoke them was defeated at H.C. Debs. 24 November 1982, col. 9.

199 It was influenced by the fact that costs of inquiries into applications for citizenship had risen dramatically from £437,000 in 1979-80 to £1.1m in 1980-81 and £1m in 1981-82 - H.C. Debs. 26 January 1983, col. 450-1.

200 Especially since it was announced on 28 July 1983 that the Home Office made a profit of £6.43m in 1982 from nationality fees. See further, 3rd Report of the Home Affairs Committee, British Nationality Fees (1982-83) H.C. 248 which revealed miscalculations by the Home Office such as to produce the profit. For the Government's counter-argument, see H.C. Debs. 11 April 1984, col. 491-2, and its reply to the Committee, cmnd. 9183. In spite of its reply, the fees were speedily reduced (below). See also Mactaggart, Guardian 16 April 1984.

201 On the basis of unreasonableness under Associated Provincial Picture Houses v Wednesbury Corporation [1948] 1 K.B. 223, cf. Backhouse v Lambeth LBC, Times, 14 October 1972.

202 An amendment to this effect was tabled but defeated - H.C. Debs. 4 June 1981, col. 1091.

203 British Nationality (Fees) Regulations 1984, S.I. no. 230; for a debate on the Regulations, see H.C. Debs. 11 April 1984, col. 485. The fee for minors is increased to £55, but one payment continues to cover all minors in a family.

204 Standing Committee, col. 1909.

205 This excludes beliefs which, as a matter of public policy, have not been regarded as 'religion' in official eyes, e.g. the Church of Scientology; Standing Committee, col. 1936.

206 Repeating verbatim s.26 of the 1948 Act.

207 See Standing Committee, col. 1937.

208 Cf. Home Office v CRE [1982] Q.B. 385.

209 U.N. Convention on the Elimination of All Forms of Discrimination, 1966; cmnd. 4108. For an analysis of s.44, see

Bates [1982] P.L. 179.

210 Anisminic v Foreign Compensation Commission [1969] 2 A.C. 147, as interpreted by Re Racal Communications [1981] A.C. 374.

211 Citizenship Act 1976 c.108, s.13; except where the case is declared by the Governor in Council to be prejudicial to security or public order (s.18). Cf. the procedural improvements in the Australian Citizenship Amendment Act 1984.

212 Cmnd. 6795, paras. 61-65. For the many countries, which prohibit dual nationality, this consequence would automatically follow regardless of U.K. law.

213 Mr. Raison M.P., Junior Home Office Minister, Standing Committee col. 181.

214 Per Ashworth J in R v Secretary of State e.p. Bhurosah [1968] 1 QB 266, at 274. Cf. R v Brailsford [1905] 2 KB 730 at p.745.

215 Unlike many countries which require a passport.

216 Unless special provision is made e.g. the E.E.C. in which an identity card will suffice, Reg. 1612/68, art. 3(1). For an illustration of the difficulties, see Justice, 'Going Abroad' (1974) para. 7.

217 Under international law a passport is not essential for this. However, the holder of a U.K. passport can only claim protection, he cannot demand it -China Navigation Co. v A.G. [1932] 2 KB 197.

218 For an account of the subtle endorsements used by the Home Office, see Grant (1979) L.A.G. 155. Such endorsements continue under the British Nationality Act 1981 and are used in the passports of lesser forms of British citizenship such as British Overseas Citizens. They are 'valuable in preventing evasion of control', Home Secretary, H.C. Debs. 12 July 1979, col. 251.

219 E.g. see the report of an apology by Camden L.B.C. which asked a British citizen of Asian origin for her passport before issuing a marriage certificate, Guardian 19 October 1983.

220 Such passports are already issued by some countries, notably the U.S., and the Home Office has installed an experimental computer terminal at Heathrow, H.C. Debs. 26 January 1983, col. 460. More detailed consultation was

promised before their wider use in the U.K. - H.C. Debs. 26 July 1979, col. 415; and it has been decided to introduce such passports by 1987 - H.C. Debs. 24 July 1984, col. 567.

221 Now virtually obsolescent, but for a review and an interesting case of an attempt by a citizen to halt a rugby team's visit to South Africa, see Parsons v Burk [1971] NZLR 244.

222 E.g. s.8 of 38 Geo 3, c.50.

223 E.g. ss. 8-11 of 33 Geo 3, c.4.

224 See generally, Turack, The Passport in International Law, (1972).

225 E.g. Universal Declaration of Human Rights 1948, art. 13(2), U.N. Convention on Civil and Political Rights, 1966, art. 12(2).

226 See Vidal Martins v Uruguay, U.N. Human Rights Committee, Communication R.13/57 (1982), vol. 3 Human Rights Law Jo. p.165 (1982).

227 E.g. Passports Acts 1938-66 (Australia) and see the reliance on foreign affairs as justification for the U.S. decision in Haig v Agee, infra.

228 E.g. the Subversive Activities Control Act 1950, 50 USC 785. Under the Immigration and Nationality Act 1952 (8 USC para. 1185(a)-(b)), it was an offence to leave the U.S. without a passport, and issue of the passport lay in the preserve of the Secretary of State.

229 See 61 Yale L.J. 170 and Hurwitz 20 Clev. St. L. Rev. 271.

230 Kent v Dulles 357 U.S. 116 (1958); Aptheker v Secretary of State 378 U.S. 500 (1964); U.S. v Laub 385 U.S. 475 (1967).

231 Haig v Agee 453 U.S. 280.

232 Lakdawalla [1970] Imm. A.R. 26, at p.31.

233 For a full passport of 10 years, a child's passport of 5 years, a visitor's passport of 1 year.

234 £15 for a 30 page passport, £22.50 for a passport which includes the other spouse and £30 for a 94 page passport. Fees are more understandable for additional or supplementary passports - those needed urgently when a country refuses to accept a passenger whose passport has been stamped by another

country or where the return of a traveller's passport is delayed pending the issue of visas. The number of such passports is not recorded - H.C. Debs. 20 January 1983, col. 207.

235 If an arrest warrant is out or as a condition of bail.

236 But until recently the Passport Office was not necessarily informed of the order with the result that the potential absconder/kidnapper could apply for a new passport! See now Practice Direction [1983] 2 All ER 253. Removal of a child is automatically prohibited in an order for wardship or for custody following divorce. A parent can then lodge a caveat with the Passport Office to prevent the issue of a fresh passport in the child's name and in an emergency the child's name can be added to the 'stop-list' held by immigration officers at ports of entry to prevent removal of the child. The Child Abduction Act 1984 makes it a criminal offence to remove children from the U.K. in certain circumstances.

237 See the statement of the Foreign Office as to this and the other grounds in H.C. Debs. 16 June 1958, col. 860; and of the Home Office in H.C. Debs. 24, July 1984, col. 578 and H.C. Debs. 17 December 1984, col. 8.

238 Ibid.

239 Note the comments of the Home Office Minister on the analogous subject of naturalisation during the passage of the Nationality Bill - Standing Committee F, cols. 692-696.

240 See the debate arising out of the controversy over certain subjects in Rhodesia, H.C. Debs. 14 May 1968, col. 1041-1112.

241 Parliamentary Commissioner Act 1967, Sch. 3, para. 5.

242 E.g. case 3B/950/78, Parliamentary Commissioner, 1st Report 1979-80, H.C. 124, p.80. Although it is sometimes difficult to distinguish at first sight between 'maladministration' and review of the merits - see case 3B/834/78, 4th Report 1978-79, H.C. 302, p.22 - even in that case the PCA dealt only with procedural propriety.

243 See Lakdawalla [1970] Imm. A.R. 26; consistent with a long line of authorities on the prerogative e.g. Musgrove v Chun Teeong Toy [1891] AC 272, Chandler v D.P.P. [1964] AC 763, Blackburn v A.G. [1971] 1 WLR 1037. Cf. the view of Lord Denning in Laker Airways v Department of Trade [1977] 1 QB 643, and the possible scope for review on procedural grounds offered by the House of Lords in Council of Civil Service Unions v Minister for Civil Service [1984] 3 All E.R. 935.

244 Directive 68/360, art. 2(2).

245 For the style and content of such passports see OJC 241/1 (1981), OJC 179/1 (1982).

246 As is done with a child's passport; valid for 5 years but renewable on production of new photographs.

4 ENTRY CLEARANCE

> Firm immigration control is essential to achieve good community relations.[1]

Possession of a visa prior to entry has for long been a feature of immigration controls throughout the world. In principle, it is a sensible requirement, enabling the host State to weed out unacceptable entrants and saving the latter the disappointment of rejection at the port of entry. In practice, it can be a formidable first hurdle for travellers and possession of a visa may not guarantee entry.

In the U.K. a visa system was introduced for aliens during the First World War and retained thereafter. Reciprocal arrangements were gradually reached with many countries for its abolition and by the 1960s visas were not required for most. For Commonwealth citizens, the Commonwealth Immigrants Act 1962 introduced work permits but nothing more. Instead an informal system of prior approval for non-workers was encouraged (entry clearance) and proved successful in some regions, for example, the West Indies and West Africa. Possession of an entry clearance certificate meant automatic entry into the U.K. in most cases. In the Asian subcontinent, however, the system did not flourish and led to the arrival of many claiming to be dependants of those already in the U.K., but whose claim had still to be verified at the port of entry. By 1969 this had produced considerable delays at those ports with claimants examined in frequently chaotic and humiliating conditions.

In 1967 the Wilson Committee closely examined the value of an entry clearance procedure and, though it encouraged its use, decided against its compulsory introduction because "the great majority of aliens ... are free from the visa requirement [and] it would be out of the question to impose on Commonwealth citizens the same requirement under another name".[2]

In November 1968 the Government agreed with this

164

conclusion[3] but, spurred on by the increasing publicity given to the congestion at ports of entry, changed its mind a few months later and, on the eve of its Royal Assent, inserted a clause in the Immigration Appeals Bill requiring an entry clearance certificate for all dependants of Commonwealth citizens.[4] The change, it was said, would not take away rights but was "in substance an administrative one"[5] designed to relieve congestion and "render the scenes at London Airport"[6] obsolete. With all party support in the Commons, it was felt that an entry clearance "would be more humane and lead to improved efficiency".[7]

For many parts of the world, this prediction has been confirmed but, as subsequent developments have shown, in the Asian subcontinent the optimism was quickly proved to be misplaced[8] and the consequences of entry clearance were shown to have been inadequately explored in public in 1969. The defects in the procedure have been well-documented.[9] The most obvious were to move the queues overseas and lengthen them, and then, through the Immigration Act 1971, to switch to overseas the right of appeal against refusal of clearance.[10] The practical difficulties of the entry clearance procedure include: the delays pending first and further interviews, the verification of documents and referral to the Home Office; the distance travelled for interview, the provision of suitable interpreters, uncertainty over the documentation required and its availability in certain countries, the number and training of overseas immigration officers, intrusive questioning of applicants, the burden and standard of proof, the limited advisory services for applicants and the difficulties of making an appeal against refusal. Much of the blame for these difficulties lies, first, with the persistent lack of sufficient entry clearance officers (e.c.os) at British posts abroad despite initial assurances that they would be available.[11] In fact, staff resources have become an in-built mechanism for control and delays in the system.[12] As the Select Committee (1978) commented, "there is now, for all practical purposes, a quota determined by the number of staff and the rate at which the applications are processed".[13] Second, the fear of forged documents and fraudulently obtained certificates prompted the immigration officers at ports of entry to play an increasing role in double-checking claims to admission. This in turn produces delays again at airports and reduces the entry certificate to a presumption in favour, rather than a virtual guarantee, of entry. Third, changes in the Rules have not only widened the category of entrants requiring e.c. but have also tightened the requirements by imposing extra evidential hurdles. Ironically this preoccupation with entry clearance has tempted even temporary visitors to apply for it unnecessarily and thereby choke the system further.

PROCEDURE - OVERSEAS[14]

Entry clearance (e.c.) encompasses:

(1) Visa
Essential for nationals of those countries listed in the Appendix to the Rules and stateless persons.[15] The list covers the Eastern block, much of Africa and Asia (including, since 1973, Pakistan). Visa is essential, regardless of the purpose of entry; obtainable from the U.K. authorities in the alien's own country and is an endorsement in the passport. For all other aliens, a visa is either discretionary or mandatory, depending on the various categories of entry specifed in the Rules.

(2) Letter of consent
Similarly, all other aliens may or must obtain this separate document from the U.K. authorities where they are living, or from the Home Office on their behalf by someone in the U.K.

(3) Entry clearance certificate
(E.c.) - for Commonwealth citizens only. Mandatory in some categories, advisable in others; obtainable in the country of residence and is an endorsement in the passport.
Application is made to British missions abroad, preferably by personal visit and after completion of the appropriate form which itemises the relevant information required.[16] However, since "the legislation does not prescribe any form of application",[17] the application may be in writing or even oral, provided only that a request has been made "in quite unambiguous terms".[18] The applicant will then be given three months' notice of the date of interview with the entry clearance officer.[19] The interview procedure includes the following difficulties:

(a) The small number of British posts in the Asian sub-continent may necessitate a considerable journey for the applicants[20] which must be repeated if a second interview is required. Successive Governments have refused to extend the number of British missions. The cost of premises and staff would of course be considerable and, with the steadily declining fall in the number of immigrants, is now out of the question.
(b) Documentation may be both formal - e.g. birth and marriage certificates, tax claims for dependants - and informal - correspondence between spouses, proof of transfer of money to support dependants. With the possibility of forgery and the publicity given in the U.K. to the "trade in illegal immigration", such documentation is far from conclusive and is often peripheral to the primacy of the interview. Forgery

may be employed for both false and genuine claims -the latter arising under the belief that documentation is essential to a successful application or in order to validate the sponsors' previous behaviour. The so-called "Sylhet tax pattern"[21] is an excellent example, whereby sponsors in the U.K. have claimed tax allowances for non-existent relatives and, when they later seek to import their true relatives, invent documents so as to correspond with their previous claims. The corollary is that such a "pattern" may be automatically assumed by e.c.os when dealing with individual cases.[22] In some countries the requisite documentation (such as registration for births) may not have existed until relatively recently and even then may not be mandatory.[23]

(c) Advisory services can be critical in securing troublefree applications by assisting applicants and warning them of pitfalls. They are of two kinds (1) local agents whose reliability varies from the competent[24] to the exorbitantly priced forgers; and (2) U.K. agencies, chiefly the United Kingdom Immigrants Advisory Service (U.K.I.A.S.). Governments in the Asian sub-continent have been regrettably slow to provide adequate advisory agencies,[25] whilst the U.K. has regrettably failed to fill the gap properly. U.K.I.A.S. operates in India, Pakistan and Bangladesh, but the resources made available to it have been severely limited[26] with the result that U.K.I.A.S. representatives face an unmanageable workload. More fundamentally, the constitutional position of the U.K.I.A.S. leads to an uneasy relationship between it and the Government, for on the one hand it is funded at the discretion of the Home Office[27] yet on the other is frequently a sharp critic of that Office's policy and practice.[28] The suspicion that U.K. Governments have been less than committed to a full and comprehensive service is hard to disprove in the face of the enormous difficulties and the slender resources which the U.K.I.A.S. has had to endure. From the immigrant's perspective, the agency can be seen as uncomfortably close to the Home Office.

(d) The interview. The official policy of strict immigration control, the frequent inadequacy of documentation and the determination to uncover bogus applicants can lead to rigorous interviews in which extremely detailed and personal questions are asked of all the applicants and, for family claims, stories are cross-checked and each applicant cross-examined on the basis of the other's answers - the discrepancy system.[29] The extent of this questioning (e.g. as to the colour of wallpaper or number of light bulbs in the family home) and the consequential intrusion into privacy are well-documented and often-criticised.[30] The well versed cheat will be coached in the answers and will require .extensive interrogation, whereas the genuine and unversed applicant will frequently stumble, yet the latter will inevitably and ironically be embraced by the discrepancy procedure. The procedure has prompted one adjudicator to remark, "It seems to me that the search for 'kitchen sink' discrepancies is becoming almost an obsession ... Decisions are often delayed for months or years for tax enquiries which in my experience at least are rarely, if ever, helpful. And meanwhile documents which can often be helpful (letters, photographs, remittances) are often disparaged or, if they cannot be disparaged, they are ignored".[31] The wisdom of such practice is doubtful in view of (i) its impact on race relations, by colouring the applicant's initial impression of U.K. attitudes, (ii) the breach of conventional standards of privacy and due process. For example, the questioning of children in the U.K. about their parents is tolerated only in criminal investigations subject to safeguards and restrictions on the reliability of their evidence[32] and (iii) the questionmark hanging over its success in sifting out the bogus applications. Studies into cases refused entry clearance, whilst not entirely free from methodological objection, suggest that a significant number of refusals are genuine cases[33] and that a clearer picture is gained if village visits are made to verify applications.[34] Whilst some visits are made by British staff,[35] the Government has been unwilling to provide resources for their increased use, the burden of gaining entry clearance being seen to lie on the applicants rather than the Government. If, however, a purpose of detailed questioning at interviews is to detect bogus applications and if that process is likely to bar some genuine cases, it can be argued that the Government owes at least a moral duty to assist entry for dependants of those already settled in the U.K. and that visits should be stepped up. On the other hand, village visits can be even more intrusive than the standard interview, they are not foolproof, the e.c.os may not be impartial[36] and it is arguable whether the risks of further incursions into privacy are desirable.[37] Much the better solution lies in ameliorating the rigours of the current interview procedure by, for example, the use of tape-recording, a greater role for advisory agencies and relaxations in the burden of proof.

(e) Proof. The onus lies on the applicant to produce

sufficient evidence to satisfy the entry clearance officer that he qualifies for admission within a specific category. In this process, a very wide variety of methods is deployed by the immigration officials from the primitive - photographs of the applicant to gauge age[38] - to the sophisticated - forensic examination of handwriting. This can prompt the applicant to resort to similar expertise e.g. the use of blood tests to establish paternity.[39] The temptation on the officer's part to examine minutely inconsistencies between documents and oral evidence may easily deflect him from considering the evidence "in the round" and the Government has agreed with the Home Affairs Committee that "e.c.os must assess the importance not of resolving conflicting evidence but of the implications of its existence".[40] Similarly, it is now the practice to reach split decisions, whereby part of a family can be admitted, even though one claimant member is rejected, rather than reject the whole family.[41] Both endorsements of principle have come late in the day (1982). In theory, the standard of proof is the civil one of the balance of probabilities but controversy has surrounded the reality. Before 1965, the benefit of the doubt was given to the applicant, but the White Paper of that year,[42] preoccupied with the fear of evasion of control, sharpened the scrutiny and a subsequent study indicated[43] that the higher, criminal standard of proof beyond reasonable doubt operated. Significantly, following a visit to the Asian sub-continent by a Home Office Minister in 1975 in which he urged the use of the civil standard, the refusal rate of entry clearances noticeably declined.[44] Subsequent evidence suggested a return to the higher standard,[45] but it is difficult to generalise, since an appeal may not be lodged or the e.c.o. may not mention the point in his notes of the interview and decision. Since, however, the whole entry clearance procedure is geared towards seeking the truth after a careful investigation of the facts and since politicians, press and public in the U.K. demand strict immigration control, it would be surprising if entry clearance officers were not influenced, at least subconsciously, into adopting the higher standard. The suggestion by Lord Scarman in Khawaja [46]that, in habeas corpus proceedings, there is little difference between the two standards is palpably wrong - as subsequent appeals illustrate[47] and because of the more lenient atmosphere which the civil standard inevitably generates at the interviews. This conflict is to some extent irrelevant since, whichever standard governs, traditional rules of evidence do not apply to entry clearance and thus a wide range of information, including hearsay, can be considered.[48] Ultimately, the applicant's chances will depend on the variable yardsticks of the training, quality and sympathy of the e.c.o. and the applicant's determination to pursue his claim.

Given the difficulties facing an applicant, it is not unreasonable to suggest that the onus of proof be reversed and placed on the e.c.o. so that, once the applicant has adduced prima facie evidence, the e.c.o. should have to disprove the applicant's case by satisfying the criminal standard of proof. After all, if a trade organisation has to satisfy that standard before withdrawing custom from a supplier because the latter's livelihood is at stake,[49] there is surely just such a need when the reunification of a family is at stake. This change would be likely, however, only to intensify the efforts of the e.c.o. in defeating the applicant. No amount of manipulation of evidential and procedural law can match the benefits which would flow from a less paranoid atmosphere about illegal immigration which only Government policy can inspire.

(f) Entry clearance officers. Views again differ sharply, from allegations of bias[50] to the conclusion that they "do a first class job in extremely difficult circumstances".[51] Apart from basic (and short) training, it is now the practice to show e.c.os the U.K.I.A.S. project,[52] which suggested a high refusal rate of genuine applicants, and village visits are seen as "valuable in providing [them with] an insight into the background of applicants".[53] However, as long as the governing legislation is directed so fiercely against immigration and as interviews are not witnessed by an independent third party or tape-recorded, allegations of bias will not be conclusively refuted and e.c.os, like the police in their complaints' system, will not fully enjoy the reputation of impartiality. After persistent prodding, an experiment into the feasibility of tape-recording was eventually conducted in 1978-79, but its introduction was rejected because of the cost and lack of time-saving.[54] One reason was the extra time which would be needed for e.c.os to prepare explanatory statements (for appellate purposes) by referring back to the tape. If, by doing so, the accuracy of decisions is improved, it is to be welcomed and against the delay can be matched the deterrence of spurious appeals in the face of a transcript of the interview. It is indeed ironic that the Government rejects tape-recording because of delay when its own policies have contributed so much to delays.[55]

(g) Delay. The continued length of queues of applicants is an ample indictment of the persistent refusal of U.K. Governments to provide adequate resources to cater for immigration and to take seriously its humanitarian consequences. In addition, the inconclusive result of the interview, requiring further evidence and procedures, frequently extends the process. In Dhaka, for example, in 1981 4,127 (59.7%) of applications were deferred.[56] These deferrals may involve the following matters:

(i) Medical examinations of the immigrant (both permanent and short-term) abroad or the sponsor in the U.K.[57] to eliminate those whose condition is undesirable because, for example, of contagious disease or the likely expense of subsequent medical treatment in the U.K., and to verify the genuineness of the applicant e.g. examination of teeth and bone structure to establish age. This area has witnessed considerable controversy over X-ray and virginity tests. The former were used to gauge the age of applicants under 21. Only estimates of their use was available -in Bangladesh about 480 in 1980, 260 in 1981, in Pakistan about 400 per annum and India about 20.[58] They were first stopped in India, on the official basis that India "is a more sophisticated place generally, in terms of evidence provided [for e.cs]".[59] Significantly it was in India that the strongest official hostility to the tests was voiced. Apart from their intrusive nature, the reliability of X-rays for this purpose is questionable[60] and in the U.K. their use on children is confined to medical treatment. Yet, the Yellowlees Report of April 1980[61] concluded, inter alia, that their employment was ethical. Eventually, the Government quietly abolished them,[62] but on the remarkable basis that at long last it had appreciated their negligible value. As to virginity tests for fiancees, their usefulness rested on assumptions about the cultural climate of the sending countries. After considerable furore amongst immigrant communities and some of the press, they were withdrawn. Objections to both tests on grounds of privacy have been well-rehearsed.[63] They are a discrete and illuminating example of (1) the second class way in which coloured immigration has been regarded by the U.K. and the persistent reluctance of the Government to withdraw their use, despite considerable controversy, (2) the use of secret and administrative practice rather than published Rules to operate them. Both tests sprang up without statutory authority. There was no public discussion of their proposed use or monitoring of their subsequent operation.[64]

(ii) The need to check that the U.K. sponsor can offer adequate maintenance and accommodation to the applicant. For this purpose, a large number of cases are referred to the Home Office,[65] involving further delays of up to 6 or 7 months whilst inquiries are made of other agencies such as the Inland Revenue or Department of Health and Social Security. This prompted the Home Affairs Committee to recommend a limit of 3 months for such inquiries.[66] This modest suggestion was rejected.[67]

(iii) Inadequate documentation or discrepancies in the interview which often require re-interview after intervening investigations. The percentage of re-interviewees in the queues are not known, though will be known soon since statistics on first interviewees have been collected since 1983.[68]

(iv) Re-applicants who are likely to be the more difficult cases requiring extra effort on the part of e.c.os and are likely to increase as immigration figures fall and failures "try again".

Administrative practice is the most potent cause of delays and can be employed to stall or expedite the procedure. Its negative use includes the deployment of e.c.os e.g. the decision to clear a backlog of appeals (via the drafting of explanatory statements) means that e.c.os have to be taken off their normal duties; the establishment and use of priority queues (below) which further delay the main queue; the decision to accelerate re-interview cases. Its potency is illustrated by the positive changes in practice e.g. the making of split decisions, observance of the civil standard of proof[69] and allowing patrials to claim their status here rather than queue overseas.[70]

Future
Figures on the number of e.c. applications and the average length of queues were not published in the annual immigration statistics until 1977 by which time the former, but not the latter, were generally falling. Subsequent data indicate a declining trend:

Applications for Entry Clearance[71]

	Bangladesh	India	Pakistan
1977	4,920	6,300	12,720
1978	6,950	6,260	13,090
1979	7,920	5,870	9,820
1980	7,380	3,740	7,500
1981	5,590	2,820	4,880
1982	6,990	2,170	4,770
1983	9,040	2,810	5,070
1984	8,830	2,760	4,670

Months waited for first interview[72]

		Bangladesh	India (Delhi)		Pakistan
1977	4th quarter	21	5		17
1978		20	5		19
1979		24	10		22
1980		23	10		$21^1/_4$
1981		20	12 (Bombay)		20
1982		16	$14^1/_2$	15	11
1983		20	$7^1/_2$	6	$9^1/_4$
1984	1st quarter	20	10	6	10
	2nd quarter	22	10	6	$10^1/_4$
	3rd quarter	22	$10^1/_2$	6	$10^1/_2$
	4th quarter	23	12	6	$103/_4$

These waiting times refer to the main settlement queue but,
since 1975, various priority queues have been used for those
deemed to benefit from quicker admission. The type of priority
queue differs within the Indian sub-continent but they
generally favour wives with no or young children, U.K.P.Hs,
applicants for patriality, and returning residents.[73] For them
the delays are considerably less e.g. in Bangladesh between 3
weeks and 6 months.[74] This expedient does mean, however, that
the non-priority applicants are pushed further back. They were
further delayed when merged with the former, separate queue
for the least favoured of all - fiances.[75] It is interesting to
note again the part which administrative discretion plays in
the arbitrary length of queues.

The hardship caused by separating families, frequently for
many years, through the practice of the e.c. system is
difficult to defend on any basis. It has been explained by
Governments on the basis of administrative and financial
shortcomings, in spite of assurances on its introduction in
1969 that adequate resources would be made available.[76]
Inhumane though waiting times are, the bulge of entrants in
the 1970s will clearly not be repeated and the number of
applicants is steadily decreasing. The H.A.C. felt able to

173

predict the ending of queues within fixed periods.[77] This optimism was somewhat naive and is already refuted by the latest statistics.[78] It assumed a constant fall in e.c. applications and the maintenance of e.c.os. Yet, the latter have been cut whilst the former have decreased steadily but slowly,[79] with the possibility of an increased ration of re-applicants and hence the more difficult cases. Moreover, the Government's Response[80] to the H.A.C. Report displayed no sign of urgency or encouragement, least of all any regret for the harshness of the e.c. system. It thus rejected the modest commitment of promising not to allow high levels of delay to re-occur, once the present queues have dwindled. Instead, the brief Response concentrated on picking holes in the H.A.C.'s recommendations. It was an uncompromising Response, reflecting the harsh logic of the Home Office Evidence to the H.A.C. namely, that applications are falling, it is relatively easier to enter and therefore there is no need to take action to speed up the process.[81]

Reform
Queues of entrants will ease through the fall in applications rather than Government initiative. Improvements in the system have invariably resulted from pressure groups and publicity and not from that initiative. Such an initiative would hinge on the provision of extra e.c.os and prospects of that are theoretical, whichever of the major parties is in power. Further ways of possible reform include:[82]

(a) Greater flexibility in the use of e.c.os so that when, for example, pressure eases at one point, staff are transferred to another.[83]
(b) A time limit in which e.c. applications must be considered, with financial compensation for non-compliance.[84] The suggestion is a non-starter but would concentrate the minds of the Home Office wonderfully.
(c) E.c. to be conclusive proof of entitlement to enter.
(d) Applications for the settlement of dependants to be initiated by U.K. sponsors, who would have access to a wider range of advisory services and whose accommodation and maintenance criteria could be more readily vetted, leaving only a final assessment of the claimed relationship to be checked subsequently by the e.c.o. The advantages are, however, speculative and would not obviate the official need to examine closely the applicant abroad.
(e) Improvements in the appellate system. The proof of the pudding from the entrant's point of view lies in the opportunity for appealing an e.c.o's decision. The Rules require the applicant to complete the preparation of his case within various time limits.

There is no such temporal restriction on the Home Office. The e.c.o. will prepare an explanatory statement for the hearing before the adjudicator. It is often compiled many months after the interview and without the benefit of a taped interview. Since the procedure is essentially accusatorial, the e.c.o. will understandably emphasise the points in favour of his decision whilst understating or even omitting points in favour of the appellant, with the consequence that the latter's use of them at the hearing may appear disingenuous (as if they had been dreamt up in the interim). Moreover, the final explanatory statement used at the hearing may well be prepared by officials in the U.K. and based on the e.c.o's notes. The appeal is heard in the U.K. and the chances of success for the appellant are slender.[85] Since neither the e.c.o. nor the applicant will appear at the hearing, the adjudicator is faced with a choice between statements and the e.c.o's more experienced and sometimes forthright exposition will often prevail.[86]

A much fuller transcript of the interview with the e.c.o. should be supplied, preferably by tape, and within a time limit. Moreover, the appeal would benefit from becoming inquisitorial in nature and procedure since it would oblige the Home Office to present all relevant information to the adjudicator. The Home Office has acknowledged the difficulty facing an appellant from overseas but, in a most extraordinary exculpation, has pointed to the informal safety net of members of Parliament.[87] The reasoning is disingenuous but not surprising. A further limitation on the system is that an appeal can only be considered on the basis of facts which <u>existed</u> at the time of the original decision.[88]

(f) A register of dependants. It has been mooted regularly. Its purposes are to ascertain a more precise figure of prospective immigration and to require registration within a time limit, possibly linked to an annual quota.[89] The cost of the scheme, its limited usefulness (not all who register would emigrate) and its uneasy impact on the feelings of resident ethnic minorities have contributed to its non-implementation.[90]

(g) Specific annual quotas for each category of applicant. The e.c. system already achieves this informally by priority queues, administrative practice and staffing and the Rules directly by their criteria.[91]

Control at the port of entry

Entry clearance can only be used once and within six months of issue. Under the 1962 Rules, whilst not being a passport to entry,[92] it was in practice a reasonably sound guarantee of untroubled entry. The change came in1965, amidst fears of illegal immigration, when the Home Secretary[93] and the White Paper[94] announced closer scrutiny of the intentions and eligibility of Commonwealth entrants at ports of entry. The overriding power of the immigration officer (i.o.) was endorsed by the Immigration Appeals Tribunal (I.A.T.)[95] and entry clearance (e.c.) assumed its current status - an easily rebuttable presumption in favour of entry.

The i.o. has the power to examine all entrants, to detain them for that purpose[96] and to make a decision on "reasonable inferences" drawn from the examination, which could include the entrant's demeanour, intelligence[97] and conviction under questioning, and "any other information available" to the i.o.[98] Of particular importance to the last is the Home Office Intelligence Unit, information from other agencies such as the police and D.H.S.S., potential use of computers, and even informer's tip-offs. The entrant's corrspondence (e.g. letters between spouses) can, and usually will, be examined to test the real purpose of the entry.[99]

Since the i.o. does not perform a judicial function there is no need "to hold a full-scale inquiry"[100] with the panoply of natural justice. However, he must act fairly, tell the entrant of his suspicions and give him a chance to explain. There are 1,700 i.os in the Immigration Service, only 30 are from ethnic minorities.[101] Initial training lasts for 6 weeks. Late in the day (1984), a place has been found in the training programme for race relations and racism awareness. Since the emphasis of the law and practice is on deterrence of illegal immigrants, it would be surprising if refusal rates were not used as a measure of each i.o's efficiency. The i.o. can refuse leave to enter if "satisfied" on any of the following matters:[102]

(a) False representations were made or material facts concealed so as to obtain e.c., by, for example, claiming a spurious relationship or concealing an intention to stay beyond the terms of leave. The controversial Zamir line of cases[103] has been checked and there is now no duty on the entrant to volunteer information.[104] The onus is therefore clearly on the immigration officer to pose the right questions, since false representations may still be practised by the entrant's silence. Even if the entrant avoids or survives the scrutiny by the i.o., his misrepresentation may be detected later by, for example, contact with the police, D.H.S.S. or during an application for extension of leave and removal is then still possible by administrative direction under Schedule 2.

(b) There has been a change of circumstance since e.c. was obtained; for example, the entrant's intervening

marriage, as in Zamir,[105] or the intervening death of a
U.K. sponsor, as happened in the well-publicised case
of Afia Begum.[106] Again, since the entrant is under no
general duty to reveal facts, the i.o. must be careful
to ask the most pertinent questions. As an exception,
children who have applied within time but are accepted
after attaining majority, may still qualify.[107]

(c) That refusal of entry is conducive to public good
(r.85). This catch-all provision covers not only the
rare but controversial "political" entrant (e.g. a Klu
Klux Klan leader,[108] a left wing agitator,[109] trade union
officials from Communist countries[110]) but the more
mundane whose immigration[111] or criminal record[112] counts
against them. It is "designed to deal with
'undesirables' of all kinds".[113] As Singh illustrates,
it protects the immigration authorities in a neat
cocoon - there the e.c.o. had by mistake granted leave
to enter and the i.o. had spotted it. The court held
that resort to "public good" is inappropriate if the
real intention is to correct an administrative error,
but, since there was evidence that the entrant's
relatives had conspired to effect entry, the power
could be used.[114]

The power, exercised by the Secretary of State
personally (in cases of notoriety such as security) or
by the i.o., is without limit - the circumstances
mentioned in r.85(b) (the passenger's character,
conduct or associations) are only examples.[115] It can
operate as a useful safety net if other powers fail.[116]
It can be questioned whether, with the benefit of
experience, it is not beyond a State to "come clean"
and specify in greater detail whom it considers to be
undesirable. The temptation would be to compile a
lengthy list[117] but at least entrants would know where
they stand and it would be open to Parliament to
reject the list. A more attractive alternative may be
to list the criteria which should govern the use of
the power, along the lines of Rules 156 and 161 on
deportation.[118]

(d) Medical grounds (r.79-82). Two situations may arise
-the visitor seeking medical treatment in the U.K.,
and the visitor rejected because of medical evidence.
The former must produce sufficient evidence to show
that he can pay the full costs[119] and that the visit is
genuine.[120] As regards the latter, the Medical Inspector
has unchallengeable discretion to reject the entrant
as undesirable and, provided that he follows the
precise wording of r.80,[121] the i.o. (or e.c.o.) is
bound to follow his opinion.[122] The opinion cannot be
appealed even if the applicant can produce a contrary,
independent one. The only relief is through "strong

compassionate reasons" (r.80) but this is extremely difficult.[123]

In contrast, the E.E.C. rules attempt to control this power by a list of prohibited illnesses[124] and, it is submitted, modern science should enable a State to spell out the diseases it wishes to prohibit. The E.E.C. model is precise as regards physical diseases but, for mental illness, is necessarily vague and open to interpretation.[125] It is, however, to be commended for the attempt. Such a list would have the advantage of being "precedent facts" necessary for the i.o's decision and potentially judicially reviewable. This is particularly apposite for the second part of r.80 (medical opinion that illness may hinder the entrant's ability to support himself) since the decision-making is inherently speculative.

(e) Criminal record (r.83). Provided that the applicant has been convicted, here or abroad, of one of the specified offences,[126] it does not matter that he has already been punished[127] nor that conviction occurred many years ago. Refusal is mandatory.[128] It applies to entrants from all countries except that, in relation to the E.E.C., interpretation of article 48(3) of the Treaty requires that previous convictions be evidence of a continuing and present threat to public policy, order and security.[129] This is a fairer approach, more accurately reflecting the current threat to the host society, yet the only exception to the Rule ("strong compassionate reason") makes no such allowance. The 1970 version[130] permitted exceptions on "compassionate grounds" but even then the I.A.T. had added the gloss of "strong"[131] and subsequent versions endorsed it. The current terms "are perfectly plain and clear English words"[132] and the only guidance to interpretation is, first, to determine if there are compassionate grounds and second to see if they are strong. Whilst this prevents the I.A.T. from adding further glosses to already narrow words,[133] it heightens the role of the i.o's discretion and his impressionistic approach. A successful appeal on the facts is thus most unlikely. Even if it is, ground (c) above, can be used simultaneously to ensure non-admission, because of the applicant's "character" or "conduct".[134]

(f) Restricted returnability (r.15) i.e. that the passenger cannot be admitted to another country once his stay in the U.K. has terminated. This provision does not apply to those eligible for settlement. If the applicant wishes to seek asylum, his claim will be considered by the Refugee Unit at the Home Office[135] and the provisions of the U.N. Convention (1951)[136] will apply. However, he can only appeal formally if he holds an e.c. or work permit or holds British Citizenship. In other cases, he must depend on the discretion of the Home Office and any public and Parliamentary pressure he can muster may be crucial.

(g) Entry in defiance of a deportation order (r.84). The proper means of redress is to apply overseas for revocation of the order.[137]

These categories are the legacy of traditional grounds of exclusion worldwide - the ill, the criminal and the undesirable. Before a State refines its immigration policy, they are the first to be marked out.[138] The apparent verbosity of the U.K. Rules does not destroy their essentially discretionary nature; "public good" and "medical opinion" are redolent of the sovereign power which the U.K. has always claimed over entry conditions and of the reluctance to confine that power by self-imposed criteria and effective independent scrutiny. The accompanying secrecy means, for example, that it is not the Secretary of State's "practice to publish information about the numbers or kinds of persons whose entry to the U.K. he has certified would not be conducive to public good".[139]

----

1   Home Affairs Committee, Immigration from the Sub-Continent, H.C. 90, Evidence of the Government, H.C. 90-II, at p.1 (hereinafter, H.A.C. Evidence).

2   Cmnd 3387, para 70.

3   H.C. Debs. 13 November 1968, col. 528. The full debate (at col. 417), on the annual renewal of the 1962 Act, offers an interesting insight into the spectrum of Parliamentary opinion on immigration at the time.

4   S.20. The Home Secretary announced the change on 1st May (H.C. Debs. col. 1631) and the new clause was debated on the 15th (H.C. Debs. col. 1791). An advantage of its hasty introduction was the avoidance of a rush of entrants trying to beat the Act.

5   Home Secretary, H.C. Debs. 1 May 1969, col. 1631.

6   Ibid, col. 1633.

7   Ibid, col. 1631.

8   The following discussion concentrates on this area but the difficulties identified have potential impact in any country which threatens large scale or sensitive immigration e.g. the 1982 requirement that Polish applicants for entry clearance apply personally to the British Embassy in Warsaw, thereby delaying the increased number of aspiring entrants, or the requirement of June 1985 that nationals from Sri Lanka obtain visas.

9   See, for example, Select Committee 1978, especially the volume of Evidence; Home Affairs Committee 1982, Evidence, footnote 1, supra; "Where do you keep your string beds?" (1974), Report on Immigration Control Procedures (1977), Runnymede Trust; Report on Immigration Control Procedures, (1985) Commission for Racial Equality (hereinafter, the C.R.E. Report).

10   S.13(3). Provided an entrant has entry clearance, he can appeal in the U.K. even though the clearance is defective - Chanda [1981] Imm. A.R. 88.

11   H.C. Debs. 1 May 1969, col. 1635. The number of e.c.o.s. in India and Pakistan was not increased. Thereafter, they rose from 36 in 1975 to 44 in 1976 but were cut back in the 1980s - with the loss of one e.c.o. in Delhi (1981) and one second secretary and four e.c.os in Pakistan (1982). The loss in Delhi increased the length of the main settlement queue from 9

to 12 months - H.A.C. Evidence, p.132.

12 Their crucial importance is illustrated by the Foreign
Office estimate in 1981 that a further 26 e.c.os would reduce
the maximum delay to 6 months - H.C. Debs. 30 June 1981, col.
321; see further, Guardian, 21 March 1985.

13 Para. 170; coupled with the limited number of British
diplomatic missions.

14 See generally, Select Committee (1978) Evidence p.436ff;
H.A.C. Evidence, Apps. 8-11.

15 But not certain holders of refugee travel documents.

16 E.g. form IM2 for an entry certificate.

17 Brown [1976] Imm. A.R. 119, at p.124; Prajapati [1981]
Imm. A.R. 199; Salmon TH/42851/59 unreported, but see the
account in U.K.I.A.S. Advice newsletter, June 1982 p.19.

18 Ibid; Abdul Malik [1982] Imm. A.R. 183. The need to know
the precise date of the application can become important in
that, once lodged, it does not matter that the applicant has
exceeded the qualifying age before clearance is granted.

19 As to delays, see below.

20 They could include children. A 200-250 mile journey in
India to Delhi would not be untypical. On arrival, the
facilities offered by the British posts may be minimal, see
H.C. Debs. 23 May 1985, cols. 1188-9.

21 Named after the region in Bangladesh where it has been
particularly prevalent. For Dhaka, see Home Affairs Committee
para. 52: generally, see the evidence of the Inland Revenue to
the Select Committee (1978), Evidence p.405 and C.R.E. Report,
paras. 4.4.1-4.6.5.

22 Before 1980, it was even the practice for the Home Office
to supply adjudicators with descriptions of the "pattern" as
part of its submissions on an appeal.

23 E.g. a registration procedure for marriage in most parts
of India was introduced in 1955 (Hindu Marriage Act) and a
uniform procedure for births in the Punjab only in 1969
(Registration of Births and Deaths Act). See further, Select
Committee (1978) Evidence, p.447.

24 There are government-funded agencies in Pakistan
(I.A.S.P.) and Bangladesh (B.I.A.S.), but not India.

25 I.A.S.P. was established in 1974 whilst B.I.A.S. is largely confined to issuing passports.

26 It receives a grant from the Home Office - £778,000 in 1983/84 and £801,000 in 1984/85 - which accounts for 90% of its revenue; for details of this arrangement see H.A.C. Minutes of Evidence, (1985), H.C. 389-i.

27 It is interesting to note that the Government's refusal to fund a second U.K.I.A.S. representative in Sylhet was based on the belief that the existing officer was not devoting his time to what the Government saw as the most relevant work - see Government's Reply to the Home Affairs Committee, 1982, cmnd. 8725, Annex p.9-10.

28 Apart from its regular Newsletter, Annual Reports and letters to the press, see its Bangladesh research project; extract printed in H.A.C. Evidence p.96.

29 Children under 10 years are not interviewed and those between 10 and 14 years only in the presence of a parent or guardian. Cf. the Central Policy Review which suggested, in 1977, that children under 14 years only be present to deal with discrepancies as to their age.

30 For an example see the case of Talish Khan, discussed at H.C. Debs. 26 January, 1979, col. 992. See the account in C.R.E. Report, paras. 4.9.3-4.9.18.

31 Air Vice-Marshall Ayling in Khudeja Bibi, TH/58547/80. See further, C.R.E. Report, paras. 4.7.1-4.8.7.

32 E.g. corroboration, the presence of an independent adult during the interrogation - see para. 13 of the Code of Practice for the detention, treatment and questioning of persons by the police, issued to accompany the Police and Criminal Evidence Act 1984. See the similar double standard which operated in relation to X-rays, below.

33 See U.K.I.A.S. research and Runnymede Trust, supra, footnote 9; the latter suggested that of 58 rejected appeals, 55 had a genuine right of entry.

34 E.g. 180 visits made from Islamabad in 1979 led to entry clearance in one third of the cases - see Altaf [1979-80] Imm. A.R. 141.

35 E.g. 2 per annum in India. For an account of these visits, see C.R.E. Report, paras. 4.20.1-4.20.13.

36 See the facts of Momin Ali [1984] 1 W.L.R. 663, where 4
e.c.os set out on a village visit to confirm suspicions
supplied by informants. They did not go "with an open mind"
(Sir John Donaldson M.R. at p.668) and "were not engaged upon
an independent judicial inquiry" (Fox L.J. at p.673).

37 Government's Response to H.A.C. Cmnd. 8725 p.10. For
example, the U.K.I.A.S. research questioned children between
the ages of 4 and 7 years and used, in part, their spontaneous
reactions to justify the project's findings - see H.A.C.
Evidence p.101. Moreover, since the Secretary of State can
"take into account the totality of the evidence before him",
including hearsay, the problem of village informers can arise,
see Altaf supra.

38 Including the use of Polaroid cameras in Dhaka and
Islamabad, lest the applicants go to commercial photographers
and try to fake their age, see C.R.E. Report, para. 4.16.6.

39 See Guardian, 9 February 1984 for a report of blood tests
which secured the entry of two Bangladeshis to join their
father after a 9 year struggle with the Home Office.

40 Government Response, cmnd. 8725 p.9.

41 Ibid.

42 Cmnd. 2739.

43 "Where do you keep your string beds?", (1974), Runnymede
Trust.

44 See Akram and Elliott, Report on Immigration Control
Procedures, (1977), Runnymede Trust, p.24. For details of, and
a discussion of, the Minister's visit, see H.C. Debs. 23
January 1975, col. 1998.

45 Ibid; the H.A.C. Report, para. 48, impliedly recognised
the prevalence of the higher standard when it blandly
commented that "in some cases ... the benefit of any doubt" is
given to the applicant.

46 [1984] A.C. _74, at p.112; cf. R v Hampshire C.C. ex p.
Ellerton, Times 27 February 1984.

47 Awa, Times 12 March 1983; Miah, Times 19 July 1983; cf.
Momin Ali [1984] 1 W.L.R. 663.

48 Altaf [1979-80] Imm. A.R. 141.

49 R. v Milk Marketing Board, ex p. Austin, Times, 21 March

1983.

50 E.g. H.A.C. para. 47. For examples of e.c.os stereotyping applicants, see C.R.E. Report, e.g. para. 6.15.7, "Many [Ghanaians] are like lost and confused children, ill-prepared for their proposed travels with no particular reason for undertaking them and little or no incentive to return". See further para. 4.29.7.

51 Ibid para. 48. It can be noted that the initial training for e.c.os is 3 weeks, see H.O. Report on the Work of the Immigration and Nationality Department (1984), at p.13.

52 Government Response to H.A.C., p.9.

53 H.A.C. Evidence, App. 10, para. 32.

54 H.A.C., Evidence App. 18 for the Government's arguments. Cf. the reluctance of the Home Office to conduct field trials for the police and its general opposition to the practice -[1983] Crim. L.R. 158, Standing Committee J, 8 March 1983 col. 1162 (on the Police and Criminal Evidence Bill). For a discussion of the issues in that context see Royal Commission on Criminal Procedure, cmnd. 8092 paras. 4.16-4.24.

55 A further review is now under way by the Foreign and Commonwealth Office into the feasibility of tape-recording.

56 H.A.C. Evidence, p.211 (see further p.177).

57 The scheme originated in the White Paper 1965, cmnd. 2739 paras. 27-31. For an historical account, see Evidence to Select Committee (1978) p.397-8.

58 H.A.C. Evidence, p.46-47.

59 Ibid.

60 They can test for maturity rather than age, though it is possible that for the latter environmental factors (e.g. nutrition) are more significant. Accuracy may vary to within 3 or 4 years. See Haque [1974] Imm. A.R. 51. Scientific opinion conflicts over reliability - see the sources mentioned in H.A.C. App. 4.

61 The Medical Examination of Immigrants, Report of Chief Medical Officer, H.O. , published in December 1980.

62 H.C. Debs. 22 February 1982 col. 279.

63 Medical examination can include other invasions of

privacy, e.g. examination of teeth, genitalia, to establish age: see the facts of Re H.K. [1967] 2 Q.B. 617.

64 Cf. the similar way in which the Home Office can regulate prisons e.g. Williams v. Home Office (No. 2) [1981] 1 All E.R. 1211.

65 E.g. 2,482 of the 4,127 deferrals in Dhaka in 1981.

66 Paras. 60, 61.

67 Government Response, Cmnd. 8725, p.10.

68 Ibid. p.8.

69 Note the visit of a Junior Home Office Minister to Asia in 1975 and his reminder to e.c.os of this standard, supra.

70 As happened in Phansopkar [1976] Q.B. 606 when the Court of Appeal ruled that administrative practice could not deny a person's entitlement to enter.

71 For immediate settlement, cmnd. 9544, Table 6.

72 Ibid. Table 5. The waiting times are for interview, thus grant of an e.c. may be made much later and used even later.

73 For Pakistan, see H.A.C. Evidence p.170, Bangladesh p.174, India p.180 and 187. The Select Committee (1978) had recommended narrower priority queues for Asia; and for the West Indies (1976-77) H.C. 180.

74 Cmnd. 9544, Table 5. If an applicant in the priority queue is rejected, any reapplication is allotted to the main queue.

75 Before 1981, fiances had to wait about 5 months longer than the main queue in Pakistan, 13 in Bombay and 8 in New Delhi - H.A.C. Evidence, p.173, 180 and 195 respectively. The merging of them with the main queue in New Delhi in 1981 reduced their delay by 3 months but raised it by 4 for the main queue - H.A.C. Evidence, App. 11, para. 11; see further example cited in Select Committee (1978), para. 62.

76 Supra, footnote 11.

77 Pakistan by the end of 1982, Bangladesh - middle of 1984, India - middle of 1985 - Report, para. 36.

78 Waiting times have increased slightly in Bangladesh, New Delhi and Pakistan in 1984, cmnd. 9544, Table 5.

79 Ibid, Table 6.

80 Cmnd. 8725.

81 H.A.C. Evidence, Q 431-435, Home Office Minister.

82 Of the many see H.A.C. paras. 60-66, Evidence p.54-65; Select Committee (1978) and Evidence 184-7; and C.R.E. Report, esp. ch. 4.

83 H.A.C. para. 133 ff.

84 Select Committee (1978) Evidence, p.413.

85 See H.A.C. Evidence, Appendix 17, p.206 - 6% from Delhi in 1979, 11% from Bombay in 1980; and see the observations of the House of Lords in Khawaja [1984] A.C. 74. The Home Office is still conducting a review of the appellate system. See its discussion document, "Review of Appeals under the Immigration Act 1971", and comments by Justice (December 1981) and the Runnymede Trust, "Pivot of the System - a briefing paper on Immigration Appeals" (1981).

86 For a perfect example, see Alam Bi [1979-80] Imm. A.R. 146, where the adjudicator had cautiously given the benefit of the doubt to the applicant but the Immigration Appeals Tribunal preferred the e.c.o's robust refusal of entry clearance.

87 H.A.C. Evidence, p.147.

88 Kotecha [1983] 2 All E.R. 289; Bastiampillai [1983] 2 All E.R. 844; Weerasuriya [1983] 1 All E.R. 195. For a fuller discussion of the appellate system, see chapter 8.

89 It was frequently mooted during the 1970s. It formed part of the Conservative Party Manifesto in 1979 and resurfaced in the controversy over the current Rules in the 1982-83 Parliamentary session.

90 A Parliamentary Report on the feasibility of a register was generally discouraging, Cmnd. 6698 (1977).

91 E.g. those governing aged dependants, which make their entry extremely difficult (see ch.6).

92 Cmnd. 1716, r.4. It could be overruled on a variety of grounds such as fraud, medical reasons.

93 H.C. Debs. 4 February 1965, col. 1284.

94   Cmnd. 2739. See generally the account in Patterson, Immigration and Race Relations in Britain, 1960-67, p.30 ff.

95   Mustun [1970] Imm. A.R. 97. Once the i.o. is satisfied that the entrant is not eligible under the Rules, he has no discretion to exercise in his favour -Malek [1979-80] Imm. A.R. 111.

96   See Schedule 2 of the 1971 Act. He must decide within 12 hours of examination otherwise the entrant is deemed to have indefinite leave to stay. This potential escape route has, however, been limited so that time will not begin to run provided the i.o. shows signs that he is still pursuing the examination -Pereira [1979-80] Imm. A.R. 58. Under Sch. 2, para. 19, of the Act, the carrier is liable for the cost of the detention and may seek to recover it from the passenger; see Guardian, 11 May 1985, for the practice at Heathrow.

97   E.g. a test of a prospective student's fitness for study, Hussain [1970] 1 W.L.R. 9.

98   R.14.

99   See H.C. Debs. 11 May 1984, col. 483.

100 Per Lord Parker L.C.J., Re H.K. [1967] 2 Q.B. 617, at 629.

101 H.O. Report on the Immigration and Nationality Department (1984), p.8.

102 R.13. The ensuing categories apply to entrants regardless of whether they hold entry clearance (r.76 ff), but crucially those who do can appeal in the U.K: non-holders must appeal from overseas. Mention can also be made of exclusion orders issued under Part II of the Prevention of Terrorism (Temporary Provisions) Act 1984, e.g. to exclude Sinn Fein representatives.

103 [1980] A.C. 930; see ch.8.

104 Khawaja [1984] A.C. 74.

105 Supra.

106 See H.C. Debs. 8 May 1984 col. 738. Mrs. Begum had e.c. but her husband died before she arrived. She was admitted temporarily to sort out his affairs and went into hiding. A year later she was caught by the police and hastily deported. See Entry Clearance (Change of Circumstances) Bill 1984 (Bill no.118) which sought to reverse the case by preserving an e.c. once it had been granted, H.C. Debs. 7 March 1984, col. 854.

107 See the example of Begum, Guardian, 8 October 1982.

108 Or former Nazis, see H.C. Debs. 9 February 1983, col. 363.

109 See the instance of Kwame Ture (formerly the black power leader, Stokeley Carmichael) who was denied entry in January 1984 because, during an earlier visit, he had urged oppressed blacks to consider violent rebellion; see Guardian, 24 January and interview with Ture on Black on Black, Channel 4, 31 January.

110 On the grounds of the propaganda which they might exploit, see the case of 5 such officials refused permission to enter in order to attend a conference in Glasgow - Guardian, 13 February 1984.

111 Osama [1978] Imm. A.R. 8.

112 Scheele [1976] Imm. A.R. 1; Khazrai [1981] Imm. A.R. 9 (possession of opium).

113 Ibid, at p.3.

114 Ajaib Singh [1978] Imm. A.R. 59.

115 See Scheele, supra. For E.E.C. protected persons, the power can only be used within the confines of "public policy" as interpreted by the European Court of Justice, see ch.5.

116 Cf. Palacio [1979-80] Imm. A.R. 178.

117 Cf. the U.S. and its comprehensive catalogue from polygamists to subversives to those entering to engage in any immoral sexual act. For a full list, see 8 U.S.C. para. 1182.

118 Cf. judicial attempts to do so in the deportation field - Nazari [1980] 3 All E.R. 880. An attempt to apply Nazari principles to leave to enter was firmly rejected in Khazrai [1981] Imm. A.R. 9, because (a) the Rules were silent on the matter and by implication excluded their adoption, (b) deportation is more final whereas an entrant can try again. Ground (a) is understandable and preferable; as to (b) this ignores the reality that, once refused, the applicant's details will be well known in the Home Office on any subsequent attempt to enter.

119 R.18; the port medical inspector may assess the likely expense.

120 The fact that he has not sought treatment overseas may be

ground for suspicion, cf. Mohan Singh [1973] Imm. A.R. 9.

121 Sudhakaran [1976] Imm. A.R. 3.

122 Ibid, and AL-Twaidji [1974] Imm. A.R. 34.

123 Some hope was offered by Parvez [1979-80] Imm. A.R. 84 (a fiance admitted in spite of tuberculosis), but the decision is the very limit (Bhatti TH/57482/80(1719)) and must be read in the light of increasing hostility towards fiances.

124 Directive 64/221, Annex . cf. in the U.S., 8 U.S.C. para. 1182(a) (1)-(6) as amended by 75 Stat. 654 (1961), which similarly lists proscribed illnesses.

125 I.e. "profound mental disturbance; manifest conditions of psychotic disturbance with agitation, delirium, hallucinations or confusion". The U.S. is similarly imprecise, supra.

126 Those in Sched. 1, Fugitive Offenders Act 1967 (which covers Commonwealth countries) and Sched. 1, Extradition Act 1870 (which covers those other countries with which the U.K. has signed an extradition treaty).

127 E.g. Langridge [1970] Imm. A.R. 38.

128 Liberto [1975] Imm. A.R. 61 suggested this and the position was made clear in the 1980 Rules, r.74.

129 See ch.5.

130 R.55, cmnd. 4298.

131 Langridge, supra.

132 Palacio [1979-80] Imm. A.R. 178, per Donaldson L.J., at p.181.

133 As happened in Palacio, when the I.A.T. held that the reasons must be "of a totally exceptional and compelling nature".

134 R.85(b), see Palacio, supra.

135 R.73.

136 See ch.5.

137 See ch.8.

138 E.g. Aliens Act 1905, s.1(3); cf. in the U.S. the string

of legislative prohibitions preceding the first comprehensive code of control of 1924, e.g. criminals (1875), lunatics (1882), Chinese (1882), contract labourers (1885), disease carriers (1891), anarchists and epileptics (1903), unaccompanied children (1907), illiterates and alcoholics (1917).

139 H.C. Debs. 14 February 1983, col. 11.

5 PRIMARY IMMIGRANTS

It has been generally recognised that there is a limit to the rate at which any nation can absorb new immigrants without endangering good community relations. The Government are convinced that, at a time when our housing and educational resources and the social services generally are under severe strain, this policy must be not only continued but further strengthened.[1]

A broad distinction can be drawn between three main categories of entrants.

I   Those who are entitled to enter the U.K. as **primary immigrants** - British Citizens, returning residents, United Kingdom Passport Holders under the voucher system and E.E.C. nationals in pursuit of work; and those who may so enter - refugees.
II Those who are entitled to enter the U.K. as **secondary immigrants** because of dependency on sponsors already admitted i.e., spouses, children and, subject to discretionary control of admission, more remote dependants.
III Those who may enter for long-, or short-term purposes - workers, businessmen, students, visitors and holiday-makers.

A further distinction can be made between primary immigrants, being essentially heads of households, and secondary immigrants, being dependants who seek to join them.

The first class, and subject of this chapter, represents the State's assessment of whom it is content to admit unhindered as primary immigrants.

A. BRITISH CITIZENS[2]

The British Nationality Act 1981 sought to do this on a rational basis but it was shackled by the imperial legacy of its 1948 predecessor which means that for many years the transitional provisions will be relevant to preserve Commonwealth rights of patriality under the Immigration Act 1971. Moreover, its abolition of ius soli (s.1) has replaced simplicity with complexity, necessitating a dozen additions to the Rules (59-65, 127-31). For a child born in the U.K. after 1 January 1983 he can, in general, only become a citizen if his parents were citizens or settled in the U.K. at the time of his birth (s.1(1)). Otherwise he must wait for registration after 10 years. If, in the meantime, or after 10 years without registering, he travels abroad, he must obtain leave to re-enter with the following possibilities:

(i) If he has been abroad for less than 2 years, he will be admitted[3] on the same terms as his parents e.g. if he has spent 6 months abroad visiting relatives and is returning to join parent(s) who have become B.Cs, he will be given indefinite leave; similarly if he is returning along with his parents and they are admitted (r.62-4).

(ii) If he has been abroad for more than 2 years, he has no right to re-enter. But if his parents are settled here or wish to settle, he can rely on r.50[4] and gain entry.

The child's immigration rights are thus closely linked to his previous or intended attachment with the U.K. In theory, this sounds sensible. In practical terms, it raises the question of proving his parents' immigration status which could be both embarrassing (for example, if he is in a school party) and time-consuming. Admittedly, the fact that the child had been given leave to remain before his departure "will assist" (r.60) the immigration officer (i.o.) on his return, but this is not conclusive. The i.o. is perfectly entitled to conduct a thorough examination. Provision of a re-entry permit (valid for 2 years) would be a simple precaution and amelioration. Although these rules are of global application, the preponderance of recent coloured immigration and the suspicion with which it is officially regarded mean that coloured entrants will bear the brunt of their application.

B. IRISH CITIZENS AND THE COMMON TRAVEL AREA

A person who has entered the common travel area (the U.K., Irish Republic, Isle of Man and Channel Islands) is generally entitled to move within it without hindrance. There are exceptions to prevent the admission of various undesirable passengers and to prevent the area being used to evade general immigration control by the "back door".[5] Of the former, the Secretary of State may exclude as "conducive to public good"[6] and, more controversially, by an exclusion order under the Prevention of Terrorism (Temporary Provisions) Act 1984.[7]

History, contiguity, practicality and membership of the E.E.C. can justify the favourable treatment accorded Irish citizens, but the insensitive way in which it was handled by the Government during passage of the Commonwealth Immigrants Act 1962 and the British Nationality Act 1981 led to charges of unfair discrimination against both the old and new Commonwealth.[8]

C. RETURNING RESIDENTS[9]

There are three categories:

(a) Commonwealth citizens, who were settled in the U.K. when the Act came into force and who have been settled here within the previous 2 years, are entitled to entry.[10] The 2 years' period cannot be extended and the applicant must have been physically present in the U.K. in 1973.[11] Though "settled" raises the thorny issue of "ordinary residence" (below), this category is a dwindling one since most Commonwealth citizens, here since 1973, will have taken out citizenship or will fall within the next category.

(b) All other passengers are similarly entitled to entry if they had indefinite leave to remain before they departed and if they return within 2 years.[12] Indefinite leave involves the status of settled and that in turn requires 'ordinary residence'. Home Office fears that this category was being abused by people staying abroad for long periods and simply returning briefly every 2 years, led to a change in practice in 1978, whereby entrants were closely scrutinised to see if they had retained 'ordinary residence' in the U.K.[13] This concept is incapable of precise definition,[14] especially since the House of Lords has rejected the view that it means, like domicile, a person's real home.[15] Instead, in the words of Lord Scarman, it "refers to a man's abode in a particular place or country which he has adopted voluntarily and for settled purposes as part of the regular order of his life for the time being, whether of short or of long duration".[16] This approach encourages complexity. For example, ordinary residence can be acquired in more than one country, can be obtained by even a short residence and also retained in spite of lengthy periods abroad.[17] Even before the Shah decision, the difficulty of establishing 'ordinary residence' had proved to be counter-productive for the Home Office (examination of each applicant was time consuming and, significantly, the tougher approach had apparently encouraged entrants who would not otherwise have returned to the U.K.). Consequently, in 1982, the practice was changed to that of pre-1978[18] and entrants are accepted on proof of presence in the U.K. within the previous 2 years. This episode is an illustration of the vigilance of the Home Office in spotting gaps in immigration control and ultimately of a vigilance too rigorously pursued.

(c) To avoid the rigours of an inflexible application of (b), a person who has been abroad for more than 2 years may be admitted "if, for example, he has lived here for most of his life" (r.57). The example has been tightened over the years - in 1962 he needed to have lived here for "some time" and in 1970 for "some considerable time" - and the period has been calculated on a simple mathematical basis. Thus, an applicant who had spent 20 of his 57 years in the U.K. could not qualify, even though the 20 had been as an adult.[19] However, this is clearly only an example, and it is open to the applicant to point to other factors such as family ties in the U.K., since it is the quality rather than quantity of residence which may be important. "Family ties" were specifically mentioned in the 1962 and 1970 Rules and the I.A.T. has restored their subsequent omission.[20] Moreover, it is possible exceptionally for an applicant to justify his prolonged absence successfully on the grounds of illness or other insuperable reason.[21]

Welcome though the decision of Armat Ali is, it is unsatisfactory that potential returning residents should have to rely on the vagaries of tribunal decisions. A possible solution, adopted by some countries, would be the provision of re-entry permits with a generous time limit on their use;[22] it would however, raise the probability of bureaucratic delay in granting the permits.

Those with time limits on their stay who leave the U.K. temporarily (for example, a holiday in the country of origin) have no right to re-enter. The immigration officer may, and in most cases (such as returning students) will, attach the same conditions to the person's leave as when he departed. However, each case is to be judged "in the light of all the relevant circumstances" (r.58). The applicant may be treated as a new entrant or perhaps denied entry because of fresh information about him or because circumstances have changed since his initial entry to the U.K. The commonest causes of complaint here are the lengthy delays and interrogation which the entrant may have to face after even the shortest trip abroad.

D. UNITED KINGDOM PASSPORT HOLDERS (UKPHs)

During its development of many parts of Africa, notably the East and South, the U.K. imported many Asians to man the economy. They proved to be very successful, forming a wealthy, hard-working middle class in between the British and the native blacks. Predictably, on gaining independence, the native population of East Africa took exception to the affluence of the Asians and some States, chiefly Kenya and Uganda, engaged in policies of Africanisation - a ruthless system of positive discrimination favouring native blacks in, for example, positions within the civil service and the issue of trading licences.[23] On independence local citizenship was narrowly regulated. In Kenya, it could be claimed automatically only by the birth of both the applicant and one of his parents in the State.[24] Alternatively, U.K. Citizenship (UKC) could be retained,[25] but not both. Increasingly apprehensive, the majority of Asians opted to retain UKC and were thus free from control on entry into the U.K. under the Commonwealth Immigrants Act 1962. The numbers exercising the right to enter grew from 6,150 in 1965 to 13,600 in 1967 and reached 12,823 in the first two months of 1968 before the Commonwealth Immigrants Act 1968 came into force. That Act extended control to UKCs who could not claim a close connection with the U.K., that connection being the birth or issue of a passport in the U.K. to the applicant, his parent or grandparent.[26] The Asians were effectively brought under immigration control. They became holders of U.K. passports, and no other, but had no automatic right to enter the U.K. There were four avenues of escape -

(a) Category A and B employment vouchers under the 1962 Act were available but no country could claim more than 15% of the A quota and for this purpose all UKPHs were classed together.
(b) Entry as persons of independent means. Very few Asians were able to qualify because of the restrictions placed on the export of their capital from East Africa.
(c) 1,500 special vouchers per annum were issued by the U.K. to heads of households who could then bring in their dependants. This scheme has the advantage of being a non-statutory concession, enabling the U.K. Government to exercise total and unappealable discretion over its operation.[27] The quota was grossly inadequate to cope with the demand[28] and priority categories were drawn up with the 'pressure to depart' and economic hardship as the most favoured.[29] A voucher

195

gives entitlement to enter the U.K. but all dependants[30] require entry clearance and, since 1973[31] voucher holders must comply with the maintenance and accommodation requirements relating to them (in doubtful cases the head of the household may be admitted alone in the first instance to prove that he can offer the necessary support, before his dependants are admitted).[32] This is an unduly restrictive qualification in view of the fact that the U.K. has recognised their entitlement to enter. The problems of establishing the requisite degree of dependency are similar to those in the general entry clearance system. Children may be included up to the age of 25, provided that they are fully dependent and unmarried. This can create extra pressure by preventing older children from seeking employment overseas and prompted the Home Affairs Committee to recommend that all children under 25 be treated as fully dependent.[33] The Government's limited concession to older children extends only to those children who would qualify for a voucher in their own right.[34] The scheme is sex discriminatory since it proceeds on the basis that the head of the household will be the husband but, consistent with earlier jurisprudence,[35] the House of Lords has recently refused to extend the operation of the Sex Discrimination Act 1975 to the voucher scheme.[36]

The vouchers are only available to U.K.P.H.s who can trace a connection with East Africa, who do not hold another citizenship and who do not have an unrestricted right to enter another country. If the applicant is considered medically unfit to act as head of the household, a voucher will be deferred or denied, though the wife may step into his shoes as de facto head. There is no provision allowing an appeal against denial of a voucher.

(d) India agreed to accept a proportion. The U.K. hoped that such people would settle in India, whereas India was more concerned to offer temporary relief before onward journey to the U.K. The form thus issued to applicants reflected the contradiction by including a right to enter the U.K. but also the condition of settlement in India.[37] Subsequently, employment prospects were made difficult for UKPHs in India and many sought to enter the U.K. It is this category which remains the problem today (see below).

As pressure on Asians in East Africa grew, so did the scramble for entry to the U.K. whether with a voucher or not. Those without a voucher led to the well-publicised practice of 'shuttlecocking' unwanted travellers e.g. from Uganda to

France to the U.K. to France to Uganda to the U.K.[38] Twenty five unsuccessful entrants brought a successful complaint before the European Commission of Human Rights, the only legal redress available in the absence of an appeals' system. The Commission boldly concluded that the main body of the Convention could apply even though immigration was separately covered by Protocol 4 (which the U.K. has not signed); that denial of entry to UKPHs was racially discriminatory; that that could amount to degrading treatment within article 3 and that the inability of husbands to join wives in the U.K. (under the 1969 Immigration Rules) could be a breach of the right to family life under article 8.[39] The Commission's Report finally reached the Committee of Ministers in 1977 and no further action was taken. The U.K. had already tried to head off such action by

(a) admitting all the complainants,
(b) progressively raising the number of vouchers from the original 1,500 to 3,000 in 1971, 3,500 in 1972 and to 5,000 in 1975, so that by 1977 the queues in East Africa had disappeared, and
(c) allowing husbands to enter in 1974 and join wives already here.

The significance of the proceedings lies not only in the concrete benefits to the East African Asians concerned but also in the flexible approach which enabled immigrants to use the Convention by the 'back door' application of articles 3 and 8, in spite of the U.K.'s protestations that Protocol 4 was exclusive as regards immigration. The Report gave hope to many subsequent complainants throughout the immigration system, but its reasoning has been challenged by the European Court in 1985 during interpretation of the 1983 Rules.[40]

In August 1972 a more urgent problem of resettlement arose with President Amin's ultimatum to the Asians in Uganda to leave the country in 90 days on the charge of sabotaging the economy.[41] Their property was expropriated and they were allowed to take £50 each out of the country. The emergency was resolved by the U.K.'s willingness to admit 28,000 Asians for settlement immediately.[42] At the time, fierce criticism, bordering on the self-righteous, was directed within the U.K. towards Uganda but it must be remembered that

(a) the U.K. accepted its responsibility only after other members of the Commonwealth, such as India and Canada, had agreed to share the task,[43]
(b) responsibility was not a charitable gesture so much as an obligation under international law (viz. the Asians had U.K. citizenship and nowhere else to go) which the U.K. had done its best to shirk in the Commonwealth Immigrants Act 1968, and

197

(c) the U.K. Government's attempts to obtain compensation
on behalf of the Ugandan UKCs have been protracted and
largely unsuccessful and have caused bitterness in the
Asian community. Under the succeeding Ugandan
Government the Expropriated Properties Act 1982 offers
compensation for those Asians who return to Uganda,
but for those who remain in the U.K. the details are
unclear (s.11). This Act has now enabled the U.K. to
wash its hands of the matter by unrealistically
directing U.K. Asians to exhaust the local remedies
under the Ugandan Act[44] rather than relying on the
U.K.'s diplomatic efforts.

In other parts of East Africa, the increase of vouchers to
5,000 per annum meant that by 1977 the hardship of the queues
had diminished. Instead the difficulties had moved to UKPHs in
India. This is a largely forgotten group of people who may
wait 5 to 6 years before securing entry into the U.K. In the
meantime, by not electing to take out Indian citizenship,[45]
they are unable to enjoy full commercial rights in India.[46]
   There is very little chance of a UKPH being able to visit
the U.K. before a voucher is obtained;[47] for example, to
undergo education or visit relatives. An entry clearance
application is rigorously scrutinised lest the visit be a ruse
for permanent entry. The difficulty was superbly conceded by
the Home Office Minister when he said "It is not totally
impossible for UKPHs to come in".[48]
   Precisely how many are awaiting entry from India has been
the subject of speculation, typical of the uncertainty which
has dogged immigration statistics generally and which can in
turn feed exaggeration. In 1977, the Home Office estimated a
figure of 38,000, including dependants,[49] and in 1982 this had
been revised to 34,000 by the Foreign Office.[50] This stands in
sharp contrast to the Home Affairs Committee who estimated
that at most, 18,000 would in fact wish to enter the U.K.,[51]
though this figure is again speculative and assumes a constant
annual rate of applications whereas most who want to enter the
U.K. are likely to be in the queue already. The true figure is
likely to be much lower.[52] The annual quota of 5,000 was
originally intended primarily for East Africa, but now that
queues there have disappeared, it might be thought humane to
transfer the unused quota to India where about 5,000
applications (not including dependants) await for an annual
quota of 600 vouchers.[53] Governments have consistently refused
to do so, emphasising initially the need to be flexible in
implementing the voucher scheme and later 'the sensible rate
of flow' of immigration which the U.K. can tolerate. The
former reason cannot hold water now that the queues in East
Africa have gone; the latter is assisted by the inflated
claims of 34-39,000 potential applicants and the effect which
their expedited immigration would have on employment and

social conditions and, most crucially, it is suggested, on public opinion in the U.K. Such a defensive attitude ignores, first, the fact that immigration in general is falling and that an increased quota for UKPHs in India need not have a noticeable effect on statistics. Second, the problem of public opinion is not insuperable given political will, after all it was possible to persuade public opinion, if not to welcome, at least to accept the Ugandan Asians in 1972. Third, the considerable hardship and disillusionment to UKPHs who wait for many years for the U.K. Government to honour its commitment cannot benefit race relations, quite apart from the humanitarian considerations. For the Home Office Minister to comment that delay "is a consequence which [UKPHs] might not particularly welcome"[54] indicates the staggering complacency which Governments (of both major parties) have displayed in this area. The H.A.C. recommended that the quota for India be tripled for 2 years thus enabling those in the queue in 1982 to enter by 1985.[55] This modest proposal would make more palatable the setting of a cut-off date after which applications would not normally be accepted (though since UKPHs are ultimately the responsibility of the U.K. such a date would depend upon agreement with the Indian Government to continue to cater for the remainder). It would, moreover, give a clear undertaking to U.K. public opinion that the commitment to this element of immigration statistics is finite.

The Government response to these modest proposals was to use its own weapon - the imprecision of statistical estimates - to criticise the H.A.C.'s detailed and publicly argued figures of 10,000 UKPHs likely to seek to enter the U.K.[56] Its response deserves as much credibility as its own figures. Admittedly, all such estimates are fraught with doubt, but the refusal to increase modestly the annual quota for India is particularly disappointing, if not callous. The Government's policy (both Labour and Conservative) is based on the need for a 'controlled rate compatible with the capacity of the host society to absorb new immigrants'.[57] Yet this ignores the fact that the U.K.'s immigration policy has never been based on a scientific or detailed assessment of what that 'capacity' is.

The more extravagant option would be to abolish quotas. There is no doubt that the number of entrants would increase noticeably, but apart from the humanitarian considerations, 'public apprehension'[58] could, if handled sympathetically by a Government, be assuaged by the prospect of an end to this category of immigration. Moreover, it is more likely to ameliorate race relations problems within the U.K., a matter surely of equal 'public apprehension'. A cut-off date for applications, set some years in advance, would then be defensible and realistic.

The plight of the UKPHs is a sorry tale, stemming from the initial breach of promise in 1968, whereby UKPHs were denied their immediate right of entry in the face of large scale immigration. It illustrates a number of sad features:-

(a) The essentially bipartisan approach of Governments. Neither major party has exerted itself to ameliorate the difficulties and the approach is illustrated by the Select Committee (1978), which recommended the annual publication of figures for quotas but nothing more, and by the failure to recover compensation on behalf of UKPHs for their expropriated property.

(b) The harsh preoccupation with immigration figures which prevents the increase in quota vouchers.

(c) The limited, but nonetheless real, effect of the European Convention on Human Rights which, on the one hand, forced an increase in the annual quota but which, on the other, has failed to assist UKPHs in India.

(d) The ease with which a category of immigrants, UKPHs in India, can be 'forgotten' in the public mind. The British tradition of secrecy, which prevented for so long the publication of the Indian quota until Parliamentary pressure succeeded, is a major factor.

(e) The steadfast refusal of Governments to acknowledge the hardship caused to UKPHs, notably in recent years those in India who, as the H.A.C. observed,

> are temporarily in India. They are not UKPHs from India but from East Africa. They have therefore been subjected to pressures of precisely the type the scheme is designed to relieve, but because they have gone to India, in order to ease the short-term burden on this [sic] country, they find they are viewed by the Home Office as Indian UKPHs suffering less pressure than those in East Africa. It cannot be too strongly emphasised that they are in India because they have suffered such pressures at their most extreme.[59]

(f) The traditionally defensive attitude of the courts. In Amin[60] a woman sought a voucher as head of the household. The scheme only permits a woman to apply if she is widowed, single, divorced or in effect the head of the household because of her husband's illness. The House of Lords could agree that this approach was sex discriminatory but the majority held that a voucher was not a 'facility' or 'service' within s.29(1) of the Sex Discrimination Act 1975 and that in any event the Act covered essentially private rather than public acts performed by the Crown. This narrow interpretation is not untypical of judicial attitudes in both sex discrimination and immigration matters but contrasts sharply with the more expansive approach of the minority, especially since the House was not tied to precedent but faced virgin legal territory. It illustrates once again the broad leeway given by courts to the Executive in immigration matters which smack of foreign affairs, and the need for an incorporation of a Bill of Rights or the European Convention so as to give an impetus to a more positive attitude in favour of the individual.

(g) The saga of East African Asians is a perfect example of how official discretion could have been used positively to assist entry.

E. IMPACT OF THE E.E.C.

Membership of the E.E.C. has compelled the U.K. to adopt a separate set of Rules to govern E.E.C. protected persons. The liberality of these E.E.C. commitments stands in sharp contrast to the strictness of the general immigration law, and the history of their development illustrates the layers of difficulties which have to be peeled away in pursuit of freedom of movement and the benefits which may accrue therefrom.

Freedom of movement of persons is one of the cornerstones of the Treaty of Rome (article 3(c)) and legislation to achieve it was passed expeditiously.[61] Coupled with a considerable and dynamic jurisprudence from the European Court of Justice, it may be seen as one of the few successful legislative achievements of the Community. Ironically, its practical significance is relatively minor. The state of national economies in the 1970s and 1980s has been relatively weak and migration within the Community by E.E.C. nationals has declined rather than expanded. In the U.K. the figures since 1973 (the date of U.K. membership) have been constantly low. 11,340 residence permits were issued in 1974, falling steadily to 6,940 in 1984. Of these about 50% go to workers.[62]

Article 48 is the foundation of the law. It requires that "freedom of movement for workers" be secured and in particular "the abolition of any discrimination based on nationality between workers of the Member States as regards employment remuneration and other conditions of work and employment". Article 48(3) is more illuminating.

[Freedom of movement] shall entail the right, subject to limitations justified on grounds of public policy, public security or public health:

(a) to accept offers of employment actually made;
(b) to move freely within the territory of Member States for this purpose;
(c) to stay in a Member State for the purpose of employment in accordance with the provisions governing

the employment of nationals of that State laid down by law, regulation or administrative action;

(d) to remain in the territory of a Member State after having been employed in that State, subject to conditions which shall be embodied in implementing regulations to be drawn up by the Commission.

These provisions on employment should be read alongside those on the right of establishment (art. 52 ff.) and the freedom to provide services (art. 59 ff.). Although harmonisation has been less successful in these two areas,[63] when all three are taken together, they represent a formidable incursion into a State's sovereign power over immigration. Moreover, art. 51 and its secondary legislation[64] on state benefits play a vital supporting role in underpinning the free movement provisions, since fulfilment of the latter could not be properly attained if its exercise jeopardised entitlement to unemployment, sickness or pension benefits.[65]

Community protection extends to the nationals of any E.E.C. Member State[66] and their families, regardless of the latter's nationality. On the other hand, it does not generally extend to a national returning to his own country.[67] Thus, in the High Court's opinion, it cannot be used as a backdoor method of admitting non-E.E.C. dependants by, for example, a "U.K. national"[68] travelling to and working in France, marrying a non-E.E.C. national and seeking to return as an E.E.C. worker with dependants.[69] Nor can it be claimed unless the applicant moves or seeks to move within the Community.[70]

Since the E.E.C. Treaty is aimed at economic integration, its beneficiaries must be engaged in, or linked with, economic pursuits rather than be visitors or tourists.[71] The E.E.C. entrant must be a worker or in search of work.[72] This is a question for European not national law and has been expansively construed by the Court of Justice so as to cover part-time or poorly paid work below the national average.[73] Similarly, work need not be the primary objective. Thus, a Frenchwoman can use her employment in the U.K. as a means of introducing her Indian husband and it does not matter that that is her main motive provided only

(a) that she is engaged in some economic activity,[74]

(b) that it is genuine in the sense of being a serious pursuit.[75]

There are limits and, if the person is workshy or moving from job to job with no intention of real employment, or is really intent on sponging off the State, he will not be classed as a worker, E.E.C. protection will be forfeited and he may be deported in the interests of public policy.[76]

Subject to these general requirements, any E.E.C. national, regardless of where he has been residing, is

202

entitled to enter the U.K. to take up employment previously arranged[77] or to look for employment.[78] He needs only to establish his identity by an identity card or a passport.[79] Any direct or, more importantly, indirect obstacle in theory breaches Community law. In the U.K. context, this means that leave to enter is not needed,[80] a separate channel is set aside for E.E.C. nationals at ports of entry and the duty to complete landing cards was abolished in 1980 in view of its likely unlawfulness.[81] Similarly, any questioning as to the purpose and duration of the stay could be construed as an unwarranted intrusion into freedom of movement.[82] The European Commission is seeking to go further and to ease or even abolish passport checks.[83] But, like the entry clearance system, States are jealous of their power to determine who is entitled to enter, as France illustrated in August 1983[84] by stopping and turning back coloured entrants from the U.K. In the U.K. context frontier supervision is the backbone of immigration control and, it is argued, if passport checks were abolished,

(a) it would invite abuse since at present the Home Office is faced with "people attempting to gain entry ... by using forged Community documents";[85] and

(b) it would divert official attention to a system of internal control based on identity cards.[86]

At the outset, an E.E.C. national is entitled under the U.K. Rules to remain for 6 months.[87] Once he obtains employment, he is entitled to a residence permit in uniform style throughout the Community.[88] Its duration will depend upon the length of employment. If it is expected to last between 3 and 12 months, the permit will coincide with that period.[89] Anything longer gives entitlement to a permit for 5 years. This is automatically renewable unless the holder has been unemployed for 12 consecutive months during the 5 year period, in which case the renewed permit can be limited to 12 months. Whilst a penalty can be imposed on an E.E.C. national for failure to obtain a residence permit, it must not be such as to impede the free movement of persons, so that

(a) it must be proportionate to the gravity of the offence (as compared to similar offences in the national context)[90] and

(b) in any event it cannot warrant expulsion from the country.[91]

The reason for this is that a residence permit is merely proof of E.E.C. status and does not affect a person's entitlement to remain.[92] Indeed, apart from deportation on the grounds of public policy under art. 48(3),[93] a permit can only be withdrawn if the holder becomes voluntarily unemployed (see below). On the other hand, since Community law does not exclude the power of Member States "to adopt measures enabling the national authorities to have an exact knowledge of population movements affecting their territory",[94] requirements of registration with the police would be permissible. The U.K. does not in fact require it of E.E.C. nationals but does so for non-E.E.C. family members (r.74).

The result of these provisions is twofold. First, there is the unrestricted right of entry for nearly all E.E.C . nationals, save for the limitation of public policy under art. 48(3). The right is untrammelled by the entry clearance procedure, leave to enter, work permits and the stringent paraphernalia of the Immigration Rules. Secondly, as Pieck demonstrates, there is the right to challenge any national obstacle to freedom of movement before the Court of Justice.

Family and Dependants

Applicants within this category may join the sponsoring E.E.C. national, <u>regardless</u> of their own nationality, but they must meet the following four conditions:

> (i) They must fall within the definition laid down by article 10(1) of the basic Regulation 1612/68, which encompasses
>> "(a) his spouse and their descendants who are under the age of 21 years or are dependants;
>> (b) dependent relatives in the ascending line of the worker and his spouse."
> The U.K. Rules adopt a more precise formulation, namely,
>> "the person's spouse, their children under 21, their other children and grandchildren if still dependent, and their dependent parents, grandparents and great-grandparents." (R.68)
> It will be noted that, unlike the general Rules which contain different rules of admission for husbands and wives (r.48, 54), there is no sex discrimination - either spouse can introduce the other.[95] The fact that younger dependants may be either under 21 or dependent is similarly liberal, encompassing, for example, step-children provided that they are part of the family in the sense of dependency, and a dependent daughter of 25. To this end, applicants need only produce an identity card or passport, proof of their relationship with the sponsor and, where relevant, proof of dependence upon him.[96] Moreover the onus lies on the State of origin or previous residence to supply certificates of proof, for failure to do so would be an indirect obstacle to freedom of movement. "Dependence" does not have to be full dependence; it

204

(ii)   is sufficient that the applicant lives under the same roof as the sponsor.[97]
(ii) If the applicants are non-E.E.C. nationals, they must still obtain an entry clearance. However, if they were subjected to unreasonable delays (as in the Indian subcontinent) or unnecessary formalities, they could well establish that these restrictions constituted an indirect obstacle to the fulfilment of article 48.[98] It follows also from Levin[99] that public policy cannot be used to refuse an entry clearance on the basis that the real purposes of the sponsor's work are to evade immigration control and admit his non-E.E.C. family to the country, provided only that he is engaged in some form of real work.
(iii) Consistently with the economic theme of article 48, the sponsor must be employed in the U.K. before the family can join him.[100]
(iv) He must also have "available for his family housing considered as normal for national workers in the region where he is employed".[101] Part VI of the U.K. Rules does not specifically mention this but resort may be had to the general provisions of r.46 (which requires an ability to maintain and accommodate dependants), in the absence of a contrary E.E.C. rule.[102]

Additionally, by virtue of article 10(2) of 1612/68 a Member State must "facilitate the admission" of other family members if they are dependent on the worker or were living "under his roof" before he arrived. The obligation is a loose one. There is no right of entry for such people and requirements (ii)-(iv) above must still be satisfied. The obligation is really one of "easing the way" for entry and thus, if disproportionate obstacles (via the entry clearance procedure for example) confront the applicant, they could well amount to a breach of 10(2). Certainly it prevents a Member State from introducing new barriers. The duty is to lessen rather than increase the difficulty of entry.

Stay
An E.E.C. worker or businessman will be admitted initially for six months. At any time before the expiry of that period, he can apply for a residence permit.[103] The permit is not a condition of his lawful residence but rather proof of his entitlement. Member States are therefore under a duty to supply him with one provided that he produces evidence that he has obtained employment. It can only be refused for reasons of public policy within art. 48(3) (below) or if he has failed to enter employment. R.141 adds "if during that time he has become a charge on public funds". This is not strictly accurate, since a genuinely unemployed E.E.C. national who

205

comes to seek work may be entitled to claim State benefits for a maximum of 3 months.[104] Thus, removal would really be confined to a person who between 3 and 6 months after admission has remained unemployed.

Once issued, the permit can only be withdrawn for reasons of public policy or if the holder has voluntarily ceased employment.[105] Otherwise it is automatically renewable for further 5 year periods.[106] Again, however, emphasising the economic nature of the E.E.C. provisions, if, on the first renewal, the holder has been involuntarily unemployed for any 12 months' period during the 5 years, the renewed permit may be restricted to a shorter period of not less than 12 months.[107]

If the holder of a residence permit has been in the U.K. for 4 years and continues to be employed, in business or a member of the family, he may apply for indefinite leave to remain.[108] Whether he does so or not, Title II of 1612/68 gives him the right, throughout his stay, to equal treatment alongside nationals of the Member State in a broad range of matters including conditions and terms of employment (art. 7(1)), social and tax advantages (7(2)),[109] vocational training (7(3)), trade union membership and benefits (8(1)) and housing (9), which would include for example, eligibility for a place on a housing list.[110] The list is a formidable one and has been strengthened by the following factors:

(a) Forthright jurisprudence from the European Court of Justice. For example, it has been held that "social advantages" within art. 7(2) must be interpreted broadly so as to include all those advantages "which, whether or not linked to a contract of employment, are generally granted to national workers primarily because of their objective status as workers or by virtue of the mere fact of their residence on the national territory and the extension of which to workers who are nationals of other Member States therefore seems suitable to facilitate their mobility within the Community".[111] In the Reina case this meant that discretionary as well as mandatory benefits available from the State were open to E.E.C. claimants on an equal footing. In this expansive approach, the Court of Justice has made ample use of the general prohibition of discrimination on the grounds of nationality (found in article 7 of the Treaty of Rome)[112] to prohibit both the direct barriers to equal treatment such as reserved quotas for a State's own nationals[113] and the more indirect obstacles such as bogus residential requirements which will favour them.[114] Even if discrimination can be objectively justified by the Member State, the discriminatory measures taken must be proportionate to the policy

pursued.[115] This doctrine of proportionality is one of
the most notable developments in the European Court's
jurisprudence and one which, it is suggested, could be
usefully employed in the rest of U.K. immigration
law.
(b) The considerable success, at least by Community
standards, in the harmonisation of social security
laws which ultimately underpin the achievement of free
movement.[116]
(c) The Court's similarly robust treatment of freedom of
services (art. 59) and establishment (art. 52).
Frequently in the absence of legislative harmonisation,[117] the Court has been firm in its condemnation of
indirect barriers to the full implementation of
articles 52 and 59.[118]

The force of these developments has been felt by U.K. courts,
and its success was illustrated by Macmahon[119] where the High
Court had to deal with an Irish worker in England who
subsequently joined a teacher training course and claimed the
right to a mandatory grant from his local authority. The
court, in upholding his application, made it clear that,
provided a person is, or has been, a 'worker' for E.E.C.
purposes, art. 7(3) of 1612/68 gives him the right of equal
access to vocational training, on the same terms as U.K.
nationals. Dillon J. took a leaf out of the European Court's
expansive approach by defining vocational training as "any
training in a school or college which is intended to prepare
or qualify a person for a particular vocation or job, whether
manual or technical or not".[120] The imposition of higher fees
for those who had not been ordinarily resident in the U.K. for
3 years, though not barring admission to a training course,
made it more difficult and therefore amounted to covert
discrimination.[121] This decision is in keeping with the
continued, adventurous approach of the Court of Justice. For
example, in Gravier[122] the Court used art. 128 (which seeks a
common vocational training policy) in conjunction with art. 7
(non-discrimination) to condemn the imposition of registration
fees for E.E.C. students wishing to study the art of strip
cartoons. The enforcement of equality has thus come a long way
and is available (a) to young people seeking to complete their
training as well as to those who have already worked and who
are now seeking advancement, and (b) even, it seems, to those
E.E.C. nationals who have not expressed an intention to work
in the E.E.C. after the training.
    The E.E.C. worker's access to the above social and other
advantages will of course benefit the members of his family.
In their own right, his spouse and children under 21 (or those
of any age who are still dependent on him) are permitted to
take employment, regardless of their nationality.[123] His
children, if residing with him, must be admitted to

"educational, apprenticeship and vocational training courses under the same conditions" as the State's own nationals.[124] This equality extends to "general measures intended to facilitate educational attendance"[125] and to all the rights arising from admission to a course.[126] Thus, such children will be classified in the U.K. as "home students" for the purposes of fees and grants, regardless of how long or brief their residence here has been.[127]

Removal under E.E.C. law

It is here that E.E.C. law has made its most publicised mark. It has produced a variety of cases which have exposed the breadth of the U.K.'s general Rules on deportation and forced their modification for E.E.C. purposes.

If a person fails to qualify for or loses E.E.C. protection under the foregoing Rules, he can be removed under the general deportation powers,[128] for example, if he does not obtain employment within 6 months and becomes a charge on public funds. In principle, the right of his family to remain will lapse along with his. This will particularly affect the non-E.E.C. national members of a family, for at least the E.E.C. members can seek to obtain employment on their own account and thus claim E.E.C. protection in other Member States. Some relief looked possible, following the bold decision of the High Court in Sandhu,[129] in cases where an E.E.C. national divorces his non-E.E.C. spouse or separates from his non-E.E.C. family. Comyn J held that this did not "automatically put an end to the non-E.E.C. national's rights".[130] The ruling overturned the policy of the Home Office, adjudicators and the I.A.T.,[131] who had previously taken the view that divorce, mere separation within the U.K. or a prolonged absence of the E.E.C. national from the U.K. forfeited the non-E.E.C. family's claim to remain. The court ruled that that claim instead depended upon all the circumstances, including the claimant's character, conduct, the duration and genuineness of the marriage and cohabitation, length of time spent in the U.K. and any physical or mental disability.[132] The decision, in spite of its looseness, was a welcome reversal of immigration practice enabling individual circumstances to be reviewed. It was achieved partly by the almost emotive reference to the harsh consequences of the earlier practice whereby "the non-E.E.C. spouse is entirely and utterly and completely and permanently dependent upon the continued affection and cohabitation of the E.E.C. spouse";[133] and partly by an expansive reading of E.E.C. legislation (such as 1612/68, 1251/70 and 73/148), so as to conclude that E.E.C. law gathers the spouse's family "under its cloak". This boldness was remarkable since the E.E.C. law (e.g. art. 3(2) of 1251/70, which allows a family to remain after the spouse's death) is far from conclusive. On the contrary, by specifically mentioning "death", it could easily be interpreted as implicitly excluding other causes such as divorce. Overall, the decision was a useful reminder of the protection available under E.E.C. law if the courts are prepared to embrace the spirit of the Treaty of Rome. It was short-lived. The Court of Appeal, adopting a literal approach to the relevant legislation, overturned the decision.[134] A non-E.E.C. national's rights are derivative from those of an E.E.C. national: if the latter's lapse, so do the former's.[135] O'Connor L.J. left open the position where the spouses separate and the E.E.C. national continues to work, and the Court of Justice has now decided that (1) the non-E.E.C. members of the family do not need to live with the E.E.C. sponsor in order to retain a right of residence, but (2) they will lose that right on divorce or the departure of the sponsor from the country.[136]

Insofar as art.48(3) involves medical grounds for removal or exclusion, the Annex to 64/221 sets out an exhaustive, though inherently imprecise,[137] list of relevant disabilities and diseases. Moreover, they are only relevant at the time of entry or issue of a first residence permit; if the illness arises at a later date, it cannot be used to justify expulsion. Non-medical reasons, however, can apply even if the individual has employment and holds a residence permit. Article 48(3) thus applies across the board as regards "public policy" and "public security", and replaces the "conducive to public good" category in the Immigration Rules for E.E.C. purposes. The Rules wisely eschew the task of defining this category but make no effort to guide the reader.[138] Reference must therefore be made to the considerable jurisprudence of the European Court of Justice which has established the following guidelines:

(i) 48(3) is directly effective.[139] This means that its interpretation is a matter of E.E.C. law over and above national law,[140] the individual has the right to apply for leave to appeal to the Court of Justice from a national decision[141] and consequently unilateral Member State action is impermissible.

(ii) 48(3) is to be interpreted strictly.[142]

(iii) Its use "shall be based exclusively on the personal conduct of the individual concerned".[143] It cannot therefore be employed to further economic policy[144] or as a general warning to other immigrants[145] or as a general deterrent against crime.[146] In Adoui, for example, immigrants were wrongly deported because of alleged involvement in prostitution and because of prostitution's known links with general crime. Yet, for E.E.C. purposes, personal conduct to the detriment of the host State had not been proved. The facts of Van Duyn, the first English case to be referred to the Court of Justice, would seem to be at variance with this proposition since the U.K. was allowed to count mere membership of an undesirable organisation as sufficient for deportation.[147] The case can be seen historically, however, as a first tentative step by the Court in the elucidation of 48(3) and now overtaken by judicial developments,[148] so that membership per se will not suffice. It may be different if the organisation is proscribed within the host State and membership of it is unlawful for the State's own nationals, e.g. the I.R.A.[149]

(iv) There must be equality of treatment between the E.E.C. immigrant and the host nationals. Thus, in Adoui (above) prostitution was not forbidden in Belgium, yet, because non-Belgians participated in it they were deported. This was held to be unlawful discrimination. To justify deportation the Member State must therefore, vis-a-vis its own citizens, employ "repressive measures or other genuine and effective measures"[150] against the particular conduct.

(v) The penalty of deportation must be proportionate to the danger or wrong caused to the Member State. Thus, the mere failure to comply with formalities on entry or residence permits cannot justify the use of 48(3), though lesser penalties, proportionate to similar offences within the State, may be imposed.[151] Breach of the Immigration Rules per se will not suffice for deportation.

(vi) Above all, the personal conduct must entail "a genuine and sufficiently serious threat to the requirements of public policy affecting one of the fundamental interests of society".[152] Past conduct, if sufficiently serious, such as drug pushing, may well be relevant but the Member State must also establish that that conduct still makes the offender a "serious threat".[153] The most significant consequence is that a conviction alone will not be enough.[154] The courts must instead proceed to consider all the facts and background of the case before making a recommendation for deportation.

In summary, a person who falls within the E.E.C. rules, can only be deported if the requirements of art. 48(3) are satisfied. Of the four U.K. powers of deportation (see further, chapter 8) removal for breach of the formalities of immigration control will not be justified,[155] whilst the others can only be exercised if they overlap with the requirements of public policy set out above.

Procedurally the E.E.C. national must be given the same rights of appeal as are available to the host nationals in respect of administrative acts.[156] If there is none, he must be given one. It need not be a court, provided that it is an appellate authority which is independent of the decision-making body. For these purposes, the U.K. system will suffice even though the Home Office appoints and pays for adjudication.[157] An E.E.C. national's appeal will thus follow the path described in Part II of the Immigration Act 1971. Save in cases of urgency, deportation should not be executed before a proper opportunity to lodge an appeal has been allowed.[158] This means that the applicant does not have to leave the U.K. before appealing. Royer and art. 9, 64/221 do not however cover initial refusal of entry, and appeal must, like the entry clearance system, be made from abroad.[159] The deportee must be given "a precise and comprehensive statement of the grounds for the decision",[160] unless this would be contrary to the interests of security,[161] so as to enable him to defend his interests properly. He is entitled to the same assistance and representation as those available "before other national authorities of the same type".[162] In the U.K. the lack of legal aid can be defended on the basis that it is a general rule covering tribunals. So far, article 9 of 64/221 and the Court's pronouncements offer little procedural protection to the deportee and the U.K. procedure falls broadly within the limitations. The only serious prospect for incompatibility concerns court recommendations and the wording of article 9 which seems to forbid deportation "until an opinion has been obtained" from an independent authority. Since the Home Office only implements a court recommendation <u>after</u> it has been made, it is only by construing art. 9 as "except after an opinion has been obtained" that a breach of art. 9 is avoided.[163] This is a restrictive and strained interpretation and ignores the fact that a recommendation may have been made many years before the Home Secretary considers it. Admittedly the recommendation must be sufficiently proximate in time to the deportation order so that no new facts have arisen in the meantime,[164] but this still gives a wide margin of discretion to Member States and, as the facts of Santillo illustrate, it may be very difficult to challenge successfully the continued validity of a recommendation.[165] An application for judicial review is possible but, since the Home Office need not disclose all the information on which it acted, very strong and clear evidence of an irregularity would be required to launch an application. If it is possible to establish a material and favourable change of circumstance, the recommendation will lose its force, the Home Secretary cannot act on it and it is difficult to see how he could lawfully turn to any other basis for deportation since art. 48(3) is narrowly confined.

Provided that the initial decision to deport is properly made, the deportee has no right of re-entry until, semble, a reasonable time has elapsed and only if he can show a material change of circumstance[166] such as to justify a fresh application.

Public Service

States generally deny foreigners the opportunity of participating in the government and administration of the State. Art. 48(4) of the Treaty thus allows employment in "public service" to be reserved for the State's own nationals. Confusion can arise over the precise scope of the exception. In Re Public Employees, Commission v Belgium the Court of Justice spoke of "the exercise of powers conferred by public law and duties designed to safeguard the general interests of the State or other public authorities".[167] This guidance failed to help the parties and on a referral back to the Court,[168] it was held that, for example, a works' supervisor, a night watchman and an architect in local government fell within the public service, whereas nurses, gardeners and skilled workers did not. Such distinctions are not only imprecise but too broad. There are many nationalised industries[169] and facets of central and local government which will be included in art. 48(4) but which pose no security danger and which do not objectively necessitate the "special relationship of allegiance to the State".[170] The exception of 48(4) is simply a blunt recognition of the sensitivity of countries to immigrants and a salutary reminder that freedom of movement can only go so far in the face of parochial interests.

Comment

(a) The impact of the U.K's entry into the E.E.C. on 1 January 1973 has been slight in terms of the number of E.E.C. nationals taking advantage of the freedom of movement by entering the U.K. On the other hand, it is clear that the E.E.C. (especially when Spain and Portugal are admitted to full membership) has replaced the Commonwealth as the primary source of any future labour requirements in the U.K.[171]

(b) The impact upon, and lessons for, immigration law are far more important. The simplicity of article 48 of the Treaty and the overriding force of E.E.C. law have cut a swathe through the U.K. laws, highlighted the latter's rigidity and complexity and necessitated 22 separate Rules out of 177.[172]

(c) Yet even those Rules bear the hallmark of the general U.K. approach to immigration. They are terse and generally unhelpful in failing to reveal the full range of E.E.C. protection. For example, no attempt is made to give guidance on the meaning and scope of art. 48(3), in spite of the considerable European jurisprudence.

(d) The ease of entry for E.E.C. nationals and their dependants contrasts starkly with the rigorous hurdles facing non-E.E.C. entrants, such as the entry clearance procedure, and is reminiscent of the liberal system which existed for Commonwealth citizens under the 1962 Immigration Rules.

(e) The Court of Justice's interpretation of the E.E.C. laws reveals how much can be achieved if the emphasis is placed on the "spirit" of free movement. A broad, expansive interpretation is consistently given to E.E.C. related questions, no less so than in the scope of "social advantages" which must accompany free movement.[173] Thus, the judgment of the High Court in Sandhu[174] can be contrasted with the consistently narrow and restrictive interpretation of the U.K's non-E.E.C. laws, as indeed was typified by the Court of Appeal in Sandhu.

(f) The impact of the E.E.C. also reveals the many layers of obstacles which must be stripped away before real freedom of movement can be achieved. To allow entry is one thing, but to make it genuine and effective the right must exist for the head of the household's family, discrimination within the State must be abolished, ancillary rights of social benefits must be available and deportation confined to a small and carefully supervised category. The strict preconditions for deportation under art. 48(3), when compared to the "conducive to public good" power for all other immigrants, is a forceful example. The net result is illustrated by the benefits which non-E.E.C. nationals can claim by reason of a family connection to an E.E.C. national. Delays are minimal and rights to take employment and settlement follow, as do a variety of social benefits.

(g) Significant though these developments are, the progress towards setting up a European passport union has been severely limited[175] and is a reminder of the jealous prerogative which States have traditionally claimed for defining their own nationals and of the political limitations of international and regional law. A similar jealousy pervades each State's determination to decide for itself who is entitled to E.E.C. protection in the first place, as France forcefully demonstrated in 1983 in its reception of coloured British visitors.[176]

F. ASYLUM AND REFUGEE STATUS

In law a refugee is someone who cannot return to the country of his nationality or habitual residence because of a "well-founded fear of being persecuted for reasons of race, religion, nationality, membership of a particular social group or political opinion".[177] In common parlance the description has expanded to encompass those who flee countries because of famine or other 'natural' disasters. The two meanings must be distinguished for it is only the former which has so far been recognised in international law, and the scale of the latter means that developed countries are unlikely to broaden the legal meaning. The legal status may be granted in broadly two circumstances:

(a) In response to mass expulsions or movements of population, such as the Vietnamese in the late 1970s or the German Jews in the 1930s. The weight of numbers involved means that the task of dispersal necessitates agreement between sympathetic host governments.

(b) On an individual ad hoc basis.

Both can have sensitive foreign policy implications, since refugee status implicitly criticises the standards of the departed country and advertises the comparative virtues of the host society.[178] Thus, the attitude of the Foreign Office will exert a clear, but little publicised influence on whether the Home Office bestows the status cautiously or liberally. Furthermore, in a climate of tough immigration laws, the effect of its regular bestowal on immigration figures will be a crucial factor. That climate creates the traditional arguments against immigration based on economic, racial, cultural and security fears.

With such delicate issues at stake, it is hardly surprising that international law has made little progress in this field other than to create organisations to put pressure on governments[179] and to define the legal rights of a refugee once that status has been secured.[180] The initial and vital decision whether to grant refugee status is, and always has been, the sole prerogative of the granting State. Thus, "the so-called right of asylum is certainly not a right possessed by the alien to demand that the State into whose territory he has entered with the intention of escaping persecution in some other State should grant protection and asylum. For such State need not grant these things".[181] It follows that there are no minimum requirements of natural justice. Each State can devise its own procedures for determining the status.[182]

These issues are illustrated by Simsek,[183] a Turk who sought refugee status by invoking the 1951 Convention Relating to the Status of Refugees before the High Court of Australia. He failed, the court holding that the government had the prerogative power to sign treaties and, unless they were incorporated into domestic law, they gave no rights to the individual. In the U.K. the Convention has been ratified but is only incorporated by virtue of the Immigration Rules (r.73). Its status is therefore ambivalent - binding on the Immigration appeals system[184] but only a guideline before the courts.[185] In any event, as Simsek demonstrated, the Convention gives no procedural relief. Australia had set up a non-statutory Committee to hear applications and to advise, but not order, the Minister for Immigration. That was enough. For the court to imply natural justice "before the Committee, which may have to consider a wide range of confidential information ... and whose conclusions might, if made public, affect good relations with other countries, might well stultify its operations and would not serve the best interests of applicants ...".[186]

The outcome is that a State needs to do little in order to proclaim proudly that its practice accords with the Convention.[187]

U.K. Practice

Although the terms "asylum" and "refugee" are often used synonymously and applied for simultaneously, the following distinctions can be made in U.K. practice:

(a) Refugee status. This is the prized category. The status is made permanent after a probationary period of 1 year and indefinite leave to remain is normally granted after 4 years. Significantly there is no right to settlement given by the U.N. Convention. The former status of asylum was less secure, being subject to a 3 year probationary period and more appropriate for an applicant who was undecided about his future abode and was seeking temporary relief. In 1984 the distinction was abolished and now every successful applicant is given refugee status.[188]

(b) Compassionate circumstances may be used to allow those who cannot claim asylum to remain. It is usually made indefinite after a year. Such cases are rare and heavily dependent upon the strength of public pressure which can be generated.[189]

(c) Exceptional leave to remain may be granted to some whilst they search for another country to go to or to others whilst the situation in their own country improves. The Cypriots who fled to the U.K. in 1974 are the best example of the latter. Their leave to remain was periodically extended until their relatives in Cyprus could "re-establish" themselves. Such people are in a precarious position. Since their leave is "exceptional" and outside the Rules, they cannot qualify for settlement after 4 years. Their children born in the U.K. do not become British Citizens. They are dependent upon the tolerance and concessions of the government and "inhabit a world made shadowy by the workings of the Whitehall bureaucratic machine".[190] For example, in April 1982 some of the Cypriots were given indefinite leave to remain, others were refused because they remained in Cyprus after the Turkish invasion and could be said to have resettled there before going to the U.K.[191] They can qualify for social benefits but not travel documents.[192]

(d) Temporary permission to stay is given to those applying for (a) and (b) since delays in the procedure may easily reach 18 months.

Seekers of asylum will enter in any of the following circumstances:

(i) Where their refugee status is all but secure because of intergovernmental agreement. In this regard the U.N. High Commissioner for Refugees (U.N.H.C.R.) will play a major part by processing applications in transit camps and then distributing them amongst willing governments.[193] The problem here is that such a process can be painstakingly slow,[194] is dependent on the vagaries of political will in the host countries and that will is increasingly dwindling.

(ii) Where they lawfully enter in a recognised category such as visitor or student, and subsequently seek asylum, because of, for example, a change of government in their own country which makes return perilous.[195] The fact that a visitor prefers life in the U.K. will not suffice (see below) and he may be tempted to "gild the lily", but the care and thoroughness with which the Home Office processes applications make the chances of success remote. Moreover, when, as with Poland recently, the government becomes concerned with the number of applicants, it can make it more difficult for visitors to enter in the first place by scrutinising more rigorously entry clearance applications or delaying the process, for example, by requiring a personal visit by the applicant to Warsaw for an entry visa along the lines of the Indian Sub-continent.

(iii) Where they illegally enter and subsequently seek to regularise their status. An illegal entrant is not simply the seaman who jumps ship or the stowaway[196] but also the person who gains entry by deception by, for example, failing to reveal, in answer to the entry clearance officer's questioning, that the real purpose of the visit is to secure asylum.[197] In response to the increase of Polish applications, the government in March 1983[198] instructed entry clearance officers to police entry clearance more strictly. Yet, since there is no right of admission for the purpose of asylum per se, an applicant must inevitably try to deceive the e.c.o. by seeking a short-term visa for a visit. When he applies for asylum and his illegal entry is discovered, he can be detained and removed by administrative direction. This would run counter to the U.N. Convention which specifically prohibits the imposition of penalties on illegal entrants provided that they "come clean" as soon as possible and can show "good cause" for the illegality.[199] It is arguable that the lack of exit visas from his own country or even necessity could suffice as good cause. However, under the normal U.K. Rules there is no legal opportunity for the entrant (or, similarly, overstayer) to raise this issue, since an appeal against removal can only be made overseas.[200] Instead, any potential claim to asylum must be referred to the Home Office regardless of removal powers (r.73) and his representations can be made to it. Since an illegal entrant is invariably detained in the first instance lest he "go to ground" and can be removed once his representations have been considered, it is vital for him to receive advice as to the preparation of his case at an early stage. In the light of the case of Papasoiu, who was discovered accidentally by a British Romanian Society four months after his detention had begun,[201] it is now the practice to inform the U.K. Immigrants Advisory Service of all cases when removal is proposed and no other agency or M.P. has intervened.[202] But the fact remains that his fate is dependent on the variety and strength of pressure which can be exerted on the Home Office rather than on a judicial determination of the merits.

For those who have entered lawfully, no appeal is possible against rejection of asylum per se, but it can be pleaded as part of other proceedings, for example, in an appeal against refusal to vary leave.[203] This omission reveals the limits of public international law. States' practice differs so widely, from pure executive discretion to quasi-judicial committees to judicial determination, as to exclude uniform provisions. Significantly, international obligations of natural justice could involve public and detailed revelations of complaints against States and are therefore unattainable. Since the "proof of the pudding" lies in establishing refugee status rather than its attributes (which the 1951 Convention does cover) and since the U.K. frequently boasts of its generosity in bestowing the status, it is unfortunate that the U.K. has not taken the initiative by establishing separate appellate and procedural rights for its determination. Moreover, asylum may of course overlap with extradition and deportation as conducive to the public good. There is therefore the possibility that administrative powers of removal can be used to prevent the formal proceedings of the former and the loose safeguards of the latter. In Amekrane[204] a Moroccan Air Force Officer fled to Gibraltar after the failure of a coup. His application for asylum was rejected. Although there was no extradition treaty between the U.K. and Morocco, he was returned within 24 hours and subsequently executed. Significantly, the U.K. reached a rapid "friendly settlement" before the European Commission for Human Rights by agreeing to pay £37,500 ex gratia to the deceased's dependants. This settlement avoided not only unwelcome publicity against the U.K. but also the chance for the Commission to rule on the alleged breaches of art. 3 (inhuman treatment), art. 5(4) (right to challenge detention) and art. 8 (right to family life). The need for a separate and automatic right of appeal against refusal of asylum is essential.[205]

Be he legally or illegally in the U.K., the applicant must reconcile himself to a lengthy delay, frequently of between 12 and 18 months. To succeed in his application he must establish the following facts:

(a) A well-founded fear of persecution directed against him or a particular group of which he is a member. The element of "persecution" is crucial and, as a relative term, capable of widely differing interpretations. He must fear "persecution" rather than the application of his country's general criminal law.[206] Thus, Papasoiu claimed that, since it is an offence to leave Romania without permission, he would be persecuted on his return. The Home Office took the view that, whilst such emigration laws are deplorable, they were generally available in Eastern Communist countries and could not therefore amount to persecution. Moreover, to hold to the contrary would make every person in those countries a potential refugee. This reasoning assumes that all such people wish and are financially or practically able to leave and runs counter to legislation relating to international human rights' which specifically allows for the right to leave one's country.[207]

The applicant's activities must have been significant in the sense that the foreign State would be likely to single him out for special punishment on his return.[208] As with extradition law (see chapter 8), it helps the merits of his case and the burden of proof if he can show that he is part of organised opposition to his government rather than a "loner". Additionally, and this is where the U.K.'s foreign policy may be significant, the Home Office may be more sympathetic to those fleeing from what are seen by the Foreign Office to be turbulent and unfriendly, rather than stable, countries.[209] On the other hand, it is clear that mere inconvenience or hardship will not suffice nor will "an individual's dissatisfaction with political or economic conditions in his own country".[210] It is necessary to distinguish between economic and political entrants. Unless the applicant is a well-known "dissident" or can point to easily verifiable prison sentences for "political" crimes, it may be extremely difficult to supply the Home Office with convincing proof of persecution. His claim may rest on unproved allegations and he may be tempted to embellish the truth.[211] There seems to be little room in today's practice for the contrasting liberality of the Home Secretary in 1905 who hoped that "the benefit of the doubt, where any doubt exists, may be given in favour of any immigrants who allege that they are flying from religious or political persecution in disturbed districts, and that in such cases leave to land may be given".[212]

Consequently much will depend upon the strength of pressure brought to bear on the Home Office. The opinion of the U.N. High Commissioner for Refugees may be very influential and the U.K.I.A.S. and expatriot organisations have some role.[213] M.Ps can be very useful in stalling a decision to remove but, as recent history shows, if the Home Office has set its face against admission, it can be unyielding. Thus, in May 1985, when faced with an increased arrival of Tamils from Sri Lanka, the Home Secretary decided that M.Ps should have 24 hours, rather than 4-6 weeks, in which to make representations on behalf of refugee claimants. On the other hand, in the cloistered world of the Home Office, publicity is unwelcome, especially if a decision is portrayed as harsh and contrary to the "British tradition". The media is thus the most important but unpredictable vehicle of pressure.

(b) The persecution must be linked to race, religion etc. An element of discrimination is needed and, as in (a), similar problems of proof will arise. These criteria may overlap with the exceptions to extradition law[214] -indeed these exceptions were specifically tailored in 1870 to cater for political refugees.[215] However, pre 1967 treaties under the 1870 Act refer only to "political" offences[216] and it is possible for a person to face extradition for what he claims to be racially or religiously motivated purposes and for which he should be able to seek asylum.[217] Again, for celebrated artists or scientists, this element of discrimination is more easily proved but for the less esteemed, such as disaffected seamen, it may well be impossible.

(c) There is no other country to which he can travel. Refoulement i.e. return to the frontiers of the country which he fears because of (a) and (b), is forbidden by the Convention,[218] but removal elsewhere is not. Thus, if there is even a "good chance" of his being accepted elsewhere, the U.K. cannot be the "last refuge".[219] The onus is on the applicant to show that he has made efforts to enter countries with which he has had some previous contact. He is thus, in practice, given leave to stay whilst making such efforts.

If the applicant is successful, he will be admitted (r.73), allowed to remain (r.134) or not removed under a deportation order (r.165) as the case may be.

Benefits of Refugee Status

As opposed to the other forms of leave to stay, refugee status brings the benefits of the 1951 U.N. Convention such as rights to employment, social security, housing and education[220] on a par with either nationals or aliens. Most importantly, the refugee is entitled to a standard form travel document, as set out in the Convention.[221] On the other hand, apart from large scale influxes which necessitate governmental assistance,[222] the refugee is traditionally left to "find his feet" unaided. There are no official reception centres, separate training or retraining facilities[223] or monitoring systems to assist his progress, in spite of the considerable material, linguistic and psychological problems of adjustment which he is likely to face.[224] The establishment of the first reception centre in Brixton only in 1983, funded by voluntary refugee organis- ations, amply illustrates the lack of official concern.

Comment

Countries are increasingly hostile to refugees both because of the numbers involved and the perceived pressures which they bring to the host society. For example, littoral States tend to place transit camps close to the border of the country of origin, for if sited further inland they may become more permanent and will occupy valuable space. Such camps can then be used as guerilla bases or objects for attack by the country of origin.[225] The plight of refugees and the apathy of world opinion are typified by the fleeing 'boat people' in south eastern Asia, whose flight is an opportunity for attack by pirates and whose boats may well be pushed out to sea again on arrival.[226] Even West Germany, with its more generous recent history to refugees, has cut its intake of refugees by 80% between 1980 and 1983.[227] The attitude of Western European States has recently been described by the U.N. High Commissioner as "a mood of xenophobia".[228]

As regards the U.K., from the Dutch Protestants in the sixteenth century to the Huguenots in the seventeenth to the Russian Jews in the nineteenth, the belief in this country as the "land of freedom" emerged[229] and the "historically long and proud record of generosity"[230] in granting asylum is still frequently adverted to by governments.[231] Although this century contains examples of generosity, such as the reception of exiles and displaced persons in the aftermath of both World

Wars,[232] the boast has been wearing thin. It has always yielded to national interests when the numbers of refugees become too large. Thus, the continued influx of Russian Jews prompted the Aliens Act 1905; the entry of German Jews in 1936-8 was carefully regulated;[233] Ugandan (1972) and Vietnamese (1979) refugees were admitted only as part of a wider international agreement between Governments; in 1982/3 the gathering pace of Polish applications was checked[234] and the Vietnamese and Chinese stranded in Hong Kong were seen as a problem for the Colony rather than the U.K.[235] References to the U.K's "proud record" have for many years been an exculpatory preface to reminders of the need for "firm immigration control". On an individual basis, when confined to small numbers or distinguished intellectuals, the Government can still afford to be generous and to be seen to be. Once these numbers increase, however, the same preoccupation with immigration statistics emerges, since asylum is one of the few remaining opportunities for primary immigration, and more rigorous scrutiny of applicants takes over. These and other features are illustrated by two recent events:

(a) The controversy which surrounded the removal of the Romanian, Papasoiu, on 16 March 1983. Statistics on refugees were not collected until 1979. In that year, 708 applicants from 25 countries were successful; in 1982, 2,368 (from 30 countries) out of 4,167 were granted (56%).[236] However, of 645 applications from citizens of East European countries, only 74 were allowed (11%).[237] When martial law was declared in Poland in December 1981, the U.K. was at first generous and allowed Polish visitors to remain if they wished for 12 months (subsequently extended for a further 12 months), with no restriction on employment, but only 37 applications were granted for asylum up to 9 March 1983.[238] On that date the generosity was modified. Poles already in the U.K. were allowed to remain for a further 12 months, but subsequent entrants were to be scrutinised more carefully and visas only granted if the e.c.o. was satisfied of the applicant's intention to leave at the end of the visit.[239] The Junior Minister's subsequent explanation makes it perfectly clear that the underlying rationale for the change was the fear of a large increase in the immigration figures.[240] Papasoiu served as a deterrent to others.[241]

The controversy which surrounded the removal indicates both the power and vagaries of publicity. Press and Parliamentary coverage (notably from the Government's own backbenches) kept the Home Office on its toes.[242] On the other hand, on its merits Papasoiu's case was not a strong one, necessitating a broad interpretation of "persecution" and, compared to the many Iranians who were removed after the Islamic Revolution in spite of fierce criticism of its inhumanity, perhaps received undue attention. At least the case enraged Parliamentary and public opinion, but such enragement tends to be sporadic and fortuitously aimed at the nearest object rather than at the overall U.K. context and procedure.

(b) Part of that context is the U.K's recent practice which illustrates that on the scale of liberality, the U.K. operates towards the mean end. There is no longer evidence that applicants are given the benefit of the doubt. It is now extremely difficult to succeed with an asylum application. The change has been possible because of the considerable discretionary power of the Home Office.

This is devastatingly demonstrated by the U.K's reaction to entrants from Sri Lanka in 1985. During 1984 and early 1985 approximately 900 Tamils from Sri Lanka were refused leave to enter, but were allowed to stay temporarily and precariously. The number of arrivals grew (about 1,330 in May[243]) and the Government became alarmed. It was able to call upon the lessons and precedents of recent immigration control in erecting barriers. Firstly, each entrant who raised fears about his safety would be examined on his merits and could exceptionally be granted leave to remain for 12 months if he could show that there was reason to believe that he would suffer 'severe hardship' if he returned[244] (a suitably amorphous term). Second, without warning, M.Ps were told that in future they would have 24 hours rather than 4-6 weeks in which to make representations on behalf of an aspiring entrant. The preoccupation with official haste soon led to the Home Secretary apologising for "a serious failure in communication" involving the removal of a Tamil before representations on his behalf had been heard.[245] Third, and similarly without warning, a visa was required of each Sri Lankan passenger, with the Home Secretary able to point to other West European countries as precedents for the requirement.[246] This episode illustrates not only the role of discretionary power but also the tough and uncompromising approach adopted today towards refugees whenever their number triggers governmental panic, and finally how threadbare the cupboard of liberality to refugees has become.

Some thought might be given to the creation of a separate right of appeal against refusal of asylum,[247] to a new independent panel, composed of Parliamentarians, a lawyer and a representative of the U.N.C.H.R. or similar organisation.[248] The right of appeal should be open to all applicants, including illegal entrants, and each applicant should be told in detail of the reasons for refusal.[249] The benefit of the doubt should be expressly in his favour. The benefits would be more objectivity and openness about the U.K's policies. The obstacle to its implementation would be the Government's traditional and jealously guarded prerogative of formulating asylum priorities and practice. However, it is suggested that "fear of persecution" is capable of more objective determination than the bald guidance currently indicates and should be decided without regard to the U.K's diplomatic relations with the particular foreign State or to any implications for immigration statistics. Alternatively, a generous, annual ceiling on applications should be fixed. The total number of immigrants is, after all, falling and there should be more scope for humane bestowals of asylum. Compared with the average of 100,000 applications per annum to the U.S. the U.K. cannot be regarded as "overrun". More humane decisions are desirable per se but need not lead to an influx of "undesirables". It would still be justifiable to demand a short probationary period before making the status permanent, in which time serious offenders could be removed. From a purely mercenary standpoint, many of the applicants, such as students, can be of economic use.

The reality of public opinion, however, means that such reforms are out of the question. The age of liberality ended 80 years ago and the belief in firm immigration control is too deeply entrenched to be disturbed by magnanimity to 'unknown numbers of refugees'.

----

1 Home Secretary, H.C. Debs. 25 January 1973, col. 653.

2 See further chapter 3.

3 R.63 is mandatory. The 2 year period is paralleled by that for returning residents (see below); it can be broken by even one day's presence in the U.K. The maintenance and accommodation requirements (r.46) do not have to be satisfied. E.c. is not needed but a visa national requires a visa (r.62).

4 This rule is the general one governing children not born in the U.K.

5 See s.9 and Immigration (Control of Entry through Republic of Ireland) Order 1972, S.I. 1610 (as amended, S.I. 1979/730). Thus, an entrant who overstays his leave in the U.K. cannot re-enter via the Republic without obtaining leave of entry - Bouzagou, Times, 4 July 1983. See for a neat account of the provisions, Grant and Martin, Immigration Law and Practice, ch. 4.

6 S.9(4)(a), Immigration Act 1971.

7 See the Review of the Act's Operation by Earl Jellicoe, Cmnd. 8803; H.C. Debs. 7 March 1983, col. 566. For the attitude of the European Commission of Human Rights to the Act, see McVeigh, O'Neill and Evans v. U.K. (1983) 5 E.H.R.R. 71.

8 See Patterson, Immigration and Race Relations in Britain, p.19.

9 R.56-58. On one point of view the status can only be claimed on re-entry; the traveller cannot return in one capacity and subsequently claim it as a basis for extension - Khatoon Ali [1979-80] Imm. A.R. 195. However, such a claim was favourably but obiter treated by the Master of the Rolls in Coomasaru [1983] 1 All E.R. 208.

10 R.56; unless already the subject of a deportation order, r.77.

11 Taneja [1977] Imm. A.R. 9; Hashim [1974] Imm. A.R. 75.

12 R.56. Both conditions must be satisfied - endorsing the interpretation of Tosir Khan [1974] Imm. A.R. 55, of the earlier Rules (Cmnd. 4298, r.48, 49) which used "or".

13 This is an excellent example of the discretionary and secretive way in which immigration control can be altered. For

an account, see C.R.E. Report, paras. 5.15-5.19.

14 E.g. Chopra [1981] Imm. A.R. 70, Joshi [1975] Imm. A.R. 1,
Osama [1978] Imm. A.R. 8, Patel [1979-80] Imm. A.R. 106.

15 Shah [1983] 2 A.C. 309.

16 Ibid, at p.343.

17 For further consideration, see R v Waltham Forest L.B.C.,
ex p., Vale, Times, 25 February 1985; Reed v Clark, Times, 12
April 1985; Hipperson v Electoral Registration Officer etc.,
Times, 2 May 1985.

18 See U.K.I.A.S. Newsletter, vol. 12, no.1. But note the
difficulties posed by Azhar Karim Khan [1982] Imm. A.R. 176,
in relation to diplomats who fall outside the Act (s.8(3)) and
for whom a passport stamp of 'indefinite leave' is
inappropriate.

19 Peart [1979-80] Imm. A.R. 41, cf. Sheikh [1970] Imm. A.R.
143.

20 Costa [1974] Imm. A.R. 69 was overruled for this
suggestion by Peart, supra, but has been reinstated by Armat
Ali [1981] Imm. A.R. 51.

21 Armat Ali.

22 Cf. Canada, Immigration Act 1976 s.25, where such permits
are given for those expecting to be abroad for more than 183
days in a year; and in the U.S., 8 U.S.C. 1203(a)-(c) valid
for 1 year (extendable to 2 years).

23 For example, in Kenya the Trade Licensing Act 1967 and
Immigration Act 1967 (as amended), in Uganda the Trade
(Licensing) Act 1969 and Immigration Act 1969; and note the
facts of Madhwa v City Council of Nairobi [1968] E.A. 406.

24 Constitution of Kenya, chapter 1, arts. 1 and 2.

25 E.g. Uganda Independence Act 1962, s.2; Kenya Independence
Act 1963, ss.2(3), 3; Zanzibar Act 1963, s.2.

26 For a detailed account of the background to and passage of
the Bill, see Steel, 'No Entry'. See also, Cable, 'Whither
Kenyan emigrants'.

27 E.g. Shah [1970] Imm. A.R. 56; R. v E.C.O. Bombay ex p.
Amin [1983] 2 A.C. 818, but see the powerful dissent of Lord
Scarman.

28 The Foreign Office estimated that in 1970 there were about 170,000 UKPHs in East Africa - Select Committee, Evidence p.443 (1970).

29 They were (i) persons under notice to leave Africa, (ii) those barred from employment, (iii) those unable to obtain employment, (iv) those in economic hardship, (v) others, ibid, p.441. Significantly, Kenya ceased in 1969 to issue notices to quit, thus easing the pressure on the U.K.

30 Late in the day (1982) priority was given to applicants over 70 years and to widows with children already in the U.K. and capable of supporting them - H.A.C. App. 11, para. 40.

31 R.38 of H.C. 79; now r.45, 46 of H.C. 169.

32 On the other hand, since 1979 a voucher for the head of the household and the family have been dealt with together rather than separately.

33 Report, para. 118.

34 Cmnd 8725 (1982), p.15.

35 See Kassam [1980] 1 W.L.R. 1037.

36 Amin, supra, by a majority of three to two.

37 Form QF 9, see Select Committee (1970), Evidence p.637.

38 Case 4486/70 before the European Commission of Human Rights.

39 See the text in (1981) 3 E.H.R.R. 76.

40 Abdulaziz, Balkandali and Cabales v U.K., see further chapter 6.

41 For the background, see Tilbe, 'The Ugandan Asian Crisis', (1972 CRRU). Attempts to rely on the U.K.'s international law responsibility for Ugandan Asians surrendered to Parliamentary sovereignty as expressed in the Immigration Act 1971 - Thakrar [1974] Q.B. 684.

42 The Ugandan Resettlement Board was created to supervise the process of integration; cf. the Polish Settlement Act 1947.

43 The United Nations organised the airlift. Many were taken to transit camps in Austria. Some other countries also agreed

to accept some U.K.P.H.s on a temporary basis (e.g. Belgium 400, Greece 100, Italy 950, Morocco 300, Spain 500).

[44] Foreign Office Letter to Ugandan Evacuees Association, 25 April 1983; an attempt to force the U.K. to pursue the claims at governmental level was rejected by the High Court, Times, 8 September 1984. For details of the 1982 Act, see H.C. Debs. 8 May 1984, col. 321. Around 3,000 compensation claims have been lodged, see H.C. Debs. 22 May 1985, col. 458.

[45] If they did, any claim to U.K. protection and a voucher would be lost.

[46] See the evidence of JCWI to the Select Committee (1978) at pp. 226-233; and 411, 412, 416 for an account of the detailed problems which they face.

[47] Or 'short cut the circuit', see Thakrar, supra.

[48] H.A.C. Ev. Q 383. It is illustrated by the case of Patel in 1982 who tried to visit his ailing father in the U.K. The i.o. suspected that the son would seek to remain. Entry clearance was refused and the father died 2 weeks later, Guardian 21 August 1982. He arrived to arrange the funeral and was subsequently allowed to remain, Guardian 5 November 1982. For a successful appeal against refusal of entry, see UKIAS Newsletter, vol. 13, no.2, in which the adjudicator remarked, "Of course with all U.K. passport holders there is a suspicion that they are trying to settle in the U.K. without a voucher, but a 'suspicion' must be supported by tangible evidence".

[49] Evidence to Select Committee, 1978, p.6. This estimate was later proved inaccurate since the average number of dependants per household had been overestimated as 4 rather than the real $1^1/_2$ in 1981 and $3/_4$ in 1982; see H.A.C. App. 17.

[50] Evidence to H.A.C., Appendix, p.210.

[51] Report, para 81.

[52] In fact, the H.A.C. estimated 10,000 as more realistic, para. 84.

[53] H.A.C. Report, para. 72. The figure was withheld by the Government for many years because they were not 'traditionally ... announced' - Select Committee (1978) Q 116. The 'tradition' was finally breached following pressure from members of the H.A.C.

[54] H.A.C. para. 89.

55 Ibid, para. 105.

56 Cmnd. 8725, pps.3, 12. The document as a whole is redolent with defensive postures to what is, it is suggested, a modest H.A.C. Report.

57 Cmnd. 8725, p.13. The H.A.C. implicitly endorses this line of argument by arguing for an increase in quotas rather than the more liberal option of their abandonment.

58 Ibid p.13.

59 H.A.C. para. 88.

60 [1983] 2 A.C. 818.

61 The first Regulation was passed in 1961 (15/61, J.O. 1961, p.1073) and was followed by Directives (38/64, J.O. 1964, 965; 64/221, J.O. 1964, 850). These left a fair measure of discretion to Member States but by 1968 a comprehensive code was drafted for implementation in 1970 (68/360, J.O. 1968, L257/13; 1612/68, J.O. 1968, L257/2). For an account of the history see 6 C.M.L. Rev. 466. For the current provisions, see Wyatt and Dashwood, Part IV; Hartley T.C.; Plender (1983) N.L.J. 37, 90.

62 Cmnd. 9544, Table 11. The number accepted for settlement is similarly low - 2,770 in 1984, Table 18.

63 Progress on the mutual recognition of professional qualifications has, for example, been painfully slow.

64 Principally, reg. 1408/71, J.O. 1971, L149. For a review of the caselaw, see Steiner (1985) 10 Eu.L.Rev. 21.

65 See Niemann [1974] E.C.R. 571.

66 This can include dependencies e.g. the French Overseas Department. See art. 227 Treaty and Hartley at p.44 for a neat table.

67 Unless the context of the E.E.C. legislation suggests the contrary - e.g. it may be possible for a national to invoke the right of establishment so as to force his own country to recognise a training qualification gained in another Member State, see Knoors [1979] E.C.R. 399; cf. Auer [1979] E.C.R. 437.

68 Specially defined for E.E.C. purposes, see art. 227 of the Treaty. The Isle of Man and Channel Islands do not benefit from the right of free movement.

69 Obiter remarks of Forbes J. in Ayub, [1983] 3 C.M.L.R. 140, cf. Sundberg-Weitman, Discrimination on Grounds of Nationality (1969) ch.9 and the possible use of art. 7 of the Treaty, and Giangregorio [1983] 3 C.M.L.R. 472. Note also that the Advocate General in Morson, infra, left the question open.

70 Morson [1982] E.C.R. 3723.

71 Though there is a dispute as to whether tourists can benefit from the articles on provision of services (art. 59 ff.), see Wyatt and Dashwood, p.200; cf. Secchi [1975] 1 C.M.L.R. 383 and Hartley at p.96 ff. In practical terms, the argument is largely academic since the U.K. permits entry of E.E.C. visitors for 6 months (r.20).

72 Art. 1, 1612/68.

73 Levin [1982] E.C.R. 1035.

74 Which is more than token and for which she is paid; Levin, supra; Dona v Mantero [1976] E.C.R. 1333.

75 Levin, supra. This broad interpretation is typical of the Court's attitude in this area but is difficult to square with art. 48 which governs entry for the "purpose" of employment. It should be contrasted with the position of non-E.E.C. entrants whose genuineness is examined thoroughly lest employment be used as a backdoor to settlement.

76 Levin, supra; Secchi [1975] 1 C.M.L.R. 383, cf. Nijssen [1978] Imm. A.R. 226, Giovanni [1977] Imm. A.R. 85.

77 Art. 1, reg. 1612/68.

78 Royer [1976] E.C.R. 499. If he is not, or if he is trying to enter illegally, the normal power of removal under the Immigration Act 1971 can be used. 20 were so removed in 1981, 30 in 1982; see H.C. Debs. 7 March 1983, col. 278.

79 Art. 3(1), 68/360.

80 Pieck [1980] E.C.R. 2171.

81 In the light of Pieck, supra; see H.L. Debs. 6 November 1979, col. 779 for the Government's statement.

82 Written Answer of the European Commission at O.J. C12/3, 17 January 1983.

83 O.J. C3/4, 5 January 1983; for a draft resolution see

C.O.M. (82) 400, and for tourists, E.C. Bulletin Supplement 4/82. See further, O.J. C197/7, 31 July 1982. The European Parliament has frequently called for the abolition of police checks at frontiers, e.g. O.J. C287/93, 9 November 1981.

84 See The Guardian, 3, 4, 5, 6 August 1983.

85 House of Lords Select Committee on the European Communities (1983-84) Fourth Report, H.L. 24, Q4 (Evidence from the Home Office).

86 Ibid, Evidence from the National Council for Civil Liberties, Q 133 ff.

87 E.E.C. law is silent on this, no period being specified in reg. 1612/68. It was intended to be 3 months and some countries e.g. France, so require.

88 Special provision is made for seasonal workers, art. 8, 68/360. For similar provisions on establishment and the provision of services, see 73/148 (O.J. 1973, L172/14).

89 Thus, short-term contracts e.g. for teaching assistants, can neatly avoid the issue of renewal.

90 Watson [1976] E.C.R. 1185, para. 21.

91 Pieck, supra.

92 Royer [1976] E.C.R. 497; Sagulo [1977] E.C.R. 1495; Pieck, supra; Giangregorio [1983] 3 C.M.L.R. 472; Monteil [1984] 1 C.M.L.R. 264.

93 In 1981, 48 were refused, in 1982, 89 - evidence of Home Office to Fourth Report of House of Lords Select Committee on European Communities, H.L. 24 (1983-84).

94 Watson, supra, para. 17.

95 Public policy under art. 48(3) would however prevent the entry of polygamous spouses.

96 Art. 4(3), 68/360.

97 Art. 4(3)(e), 68/360; cf. the difficulties of proving dependency under the general Rules, see chapter 6.

98 Cf. Ayub [1983] 3 C.M.L.R. 140 for the view that a 6 months' delay in Brussels in procuring e.c. was defensible.

99 [1982] E.C.R. 1035

100 Art. 10(1), 1612/68.

101 Ibid. art. 10(3); there is no similar requirement for freedom of establishment or services - 73/148.

102 Hence r.46 could not be used for establishment or services, since it would then be imposing a burden additional to E.E.C. law.

103 Under art 5(1), 64/221, a first residence permit must be issued within 6 months of application. Under r.142, businessmen and the self-employed may be allowed to remain beyond 6 months in order to complete their arrangements.

104 Art. 69, 1408/71.

105 Involuntary unemployment, confirmed by the Department of Health and Social Security, or through accident or illness do not entitle withdrawal, art. 7(1), 68/360.

106 Ibid, art. 6(1)(a). For an affirmation of this point in answer to the Secretary of State, see Giangregorio [1983] 3 C.M.L.R. 472.

107 Ibid, art. 7(2).

108 R.144 and 147 contain a further collection of cases where the applicant is allowed to remain e.g. on retirement.

109 These have been held to include travel vouchers (Cristini v SNCF [1975] E.C.R. 1085) and interest-free loans (Reina [1982] E.C.R. 33).

110 These provisions overlap with the Race Relations Act 1976 to some degree, but go much further since they are intended to place the E.E.C. worker on exactly the same footing as a U.K. worker. For example, residential qualifications, which vis-a-vis the rest of the world may be objectively justifiable under the 1976 Act, cannot apply to E.E.C. nationals. As to the political status of E.E.C. nationals, see Evans (1981) 30 I.C.L.Q. 20, at p.31.

111 Reina, supra, at para. 12. See also, Ugliola [1969] E.C.R. 363, Rosskamp [1972] E.C.R. 1243, Hoeckx and Scrivner, Times, 11 April 1985.

112 See, for example, Commission v French Republic [1974] E.C.R. 359, Dona v Mantero [1976] E.C.R. 1333, Kenny [1978] E.C.R. 1489, Forcheri v Belgium [1984] 1 C.M.L.R. 334, Gravier, Times, 12 March 1985.

113 E.g. Commission v French Republic, supra.

114 Sotgiu [1974] E.C.R. 153, R v I.L.E.A., ex p. Hinde and others [1985] 1 C.M.L.R. 716.

115 E.g. Choquet [1978] E.C.R. 2293.

116 See the early example of Singer [1965] E.C.R. 1191. Article 51 of the Treaty has prompted a bundle of legislation, chief of which is Regulation 1408/71, O.J. L149, 5.7.1971, and in turn a host of cases. See Wyatt and Dashwood, ch.14.

117 The coordination and mutual recognition of professional and trade qualifications has been particularly piecemeal and limited.

118 See, for example, Brockmeulen [1981] E.C.R. 2311, Webb [1981] E.C.R. 3305, Seco v EVI [1982] E.C.R. 223 and the useful collection of decisions cited by Leenen (1980) 12 C.M.L. Rev. 259.

119 Macmahon v D.E.S. [1982] 3 C.M.L.R. 91.

120 Ibid, at para. 17, Judgment. To similar effect, see R v I.L.E.A., ex p. Hinde and others [1985] 1 C.M.L.R. 716, where it was held that "vocational school" in art. 7(3) extends to the professions e.g. medical training, the Law Society.

121 This conclusion is in keeping with Casagrande [1974] E.C.R. 773. It should be noted that, subsequent to the facts of Macmahon, the U.K. conceded home student status to all E.E.C. nationals in higher education regardless of whether they are workers, provided only that they have been resident in the E.E.C. for the preceding 3 years. The difference between the home and overseas rate for students can be considerable, see Students, chapter 7.

122 Times, 12 March 1985.

123 Article 11, 1612/68; e.g. Forcheri v Belgium [1984] 1 C.M.L.R. 334.

124 Ibid, art. 12. As regards schools, see D.E.S. Circular 5/81 to local authorities outlining the duty to provide education for children of E.E.C. workers. "Courses" include special training for the handicapped - Michel S. [1973] E.C.R. 457, and entitlement may continue beyond the age of minority - F v Belgian State [1975] E.C.R. 679.

125 Casagrande [1974] E.C.R. 773, para. 8, Judgment; grants,

fees and criteria of entry would be included here.

126 Alaimo [1975] E.C.R. 109.

127 Education (Mandatory Awards) Regulations 1982, S.I no.954, regs. 9(2)(b), 13(1)(a); Education (Fees and Awards) Regulations 1983, S.I. no. 973, sch. 3.

128 See chapter 8. These powers apply to the extent that the person does not fall within E.E.C. protection. The English courts have ruled that art. 48 of the E.E.C. Treaty does not affect the law of extradition, see Re Budlong and Kember [1980] 2 C.M.L.R. 125.

129 [1982] 2 C.M.L.R. 553.

130 Ibid, at p.557.

131 E.g. Grewal [1979-80] Imm. A.R. 119.

132 In Sandhu, the marriage was in fact genuine and a child had been born in the U.K.

133 At p.561.

134 [1983] 3 C.M.L.R. 131.

135 Logically, the decision of the Court of Appeal means that non-E.E.C. family members cannot use the right of appeal (and the accompanying factors) normally open to family members under r.160-4, but must instead seek the compassion of the Home Office.

136 Diatta v Land Berlin, Times, 12 March 1985. The House of Lords in Sandhu (Times, 10 May 1985) treated this case as decisive of the Sandhu issue and refused to refer it to the Court of Justice.

137 See, for example, the broad definition of mental illness in B.2 of the Annex, cf. similar imprecision in the U.S.-8 U.S.C. 1182/(a)(1)-(6). At least the list is an improvement on the untrammelled discretion of the Medical Officer vis-a-vis non-E.E.C. persons (r.79ff).

138 For an account see Evans [1981] P.L. 497, Plender [1976] Crim. L. Rev. 676.

139 See, for example, Van Duyn v Home Office [1974] E.C.R. 1337; Royer [1976] E.C.R. 497; Dona v Montero [1976] E.C.R. 1333.

140 E.g. Watson and Belmann [1976] E.C.R. 1185.

141 Under art. 177, E.E.C. Treaty; though the decision to refer a question is a discretionary one for the lower courts.

142 E.g. Rutili [1975] E.C.R. 1219.

143 Art. 3(1) of 64/221; this provision being of "direct effect", see Van Duyn, supra.

144 See Rutili, supra.

145 Bonsignore [1975] E.C.R. 297.

146 Adoui [1982] E.C.R. 1665. Art. 48 does not, however, necessarily derogate from powers under the State's domestic criminal law such as extradition (Kember [1980] 1 W.L.R. 1110) or removal under the Backing of Warrants (Republic of Ireland) Act 1965 - Healy, Times 11 May 1984; or the operation of the Prevention of Terrorism (Temporary Provisions) Act 1984.

147 Supra. The U.K. was permitted to exclude the Dutch immigrant because of her membership of the Church of Scientology, even though the organisation was not banned in the U.K. and U.K. nationals were not forbidden from working for it.

148 The case is implicitly inconsistent with Bonsignore, supra and with the cases cited in proposition (vi) below.

149 See Prevention of Terrorism (Temporary Provisions) Act 1984. Cf., for binding over of the State's own nationals, Saunders [1979] E.C.R. 1129.

150 Adoui, para. 8, Judgment. Thus, many political agitators who could be removed relatively easily under the normal powers as "conducive to public good", would not be covered unless the State sought to control them internally.

151 Royer [1976] E.C.R. 499, Pieck [1980] E.C.R. 2171.

152 Bouchereau [1977] E.C.R. 1999, para. 35, Judgment. See also Rutili, Adoui, supra. The test was applied in Kraus [1982] Crim. L.R. 468. For an application of the Bouchereau principles, see Hayes [1981] Imm. A.R. 123.

153 See Kraus, supra. As the case shows, this may be relatively easy to satisfy. But note the striking facts of Monteil [1984] 1 C.M.L.R. 264, where a persistent sex offender had responded to treatment in prison and the I.A.T., applying the Bouchereau principles, held that he presented no current

234

threat to society and therefore deportation was unnecessary.

[154] Art. 3(2) of 64/221.

[155] See Royer, supra.

[156] Art. 8, 64/221, Pecastaing [1980] E.C.R. 691.

[157] See Adoui [1982] E.C.R. 1665.

[158] Royer [1976] E.C.R. 499; Pecastaing, supra. If appeal is not sought, the deportee has generally 15 days in which to leave if he has not been granted a residence permit and 1 month in all other cases, art. 7, 64/221.

[159] Cf. Nijssen [1978] Imm. A.R. 226.

[160] Rutili [1975] E.C.R. 1219, para. 39. See also Dannenberg [1984] 2 W.L.R. 855 as regards court recommendations of deportation.

[161] Art. 6 of 64/221; the special procedure for such cases in the U.K. is thus compatible with E.E.C. requirements, see chapter 8; but only if the case has security implications. To the extent that it raises political issues, such as the U.K.'s interests with another country, the procedure is unlikely to suffice.

[162] Rutili, supra, para. 19.

[163] Some textual versions of art. 9 support this construction and it was seized upon by the Court of Appeal on the reference back of Santillo, see [1981] Q.B. 778.

[164] Santillo [1980] E.C.R. 1585; as happened in Monteil [1984] 1 C.M.L.R. 264.

[165] See [1981] Q.B. 778. The case has been strongly criticised, see Barav (1981) Eu. L.Rev. at p.150ff, O'Keeffe (1982) 14 C.M.L. Rev. at p.42ff.

[166] Adoui [1982] E.C.R. 1665.

[167] [1980] E.C.R. 3881, at para. 10, judgment.

[168] [1982] 3 C.M.L.R. 539.

[169] Witness the Chairmanship of the British Steel Corporation and the National Coal Board in recent years.

[170] Commission v Belgium, supra, para. 10.

171 E.g. the E.E.C. has adopted the International Clearing of Vacancies and Applications for Employment (SEDOC), so that priority is given to workers from other Member States when vacancies arise which cannot be filled locally by the host State - Title IV, Part 2, 1612/68.

172 The benefits of E.E.C. protection can thus lead to attempts to bring cases within its umbrella. For a bold attempt, see Mansukani [1981] Imm. A.R. 184.

173 Art. 7(2), 1612/68.

174 [1982] 2 C.M.L.R. 553.

175 Governments agreed in 1974 that a passport union should be examined and the Commission submitted proposals in 1975 (E.C. Bulletin, Supplement 7/75). The Council of Ministers agreed in 1981 to endeavour to achieve a uniform passport by 1 January 1985 as a first step to a passport union. For a discussion, see Fourth Report, House of Lords Select Committee on the European Communities, 'The Easing of Frontier Formalities', H.L. 24 (1983-84).

176 See press, 3-6 August 1983. France thereby broke an understanding (reached in 1955) allowing 'no passport excursions' of up to 60 hours. It eventually withdrew from the agreement in May 1984, but accepted an alternative and stricter arrangement in July 1984 once it was satisfied that the U.K. would guarantee to accept back any visitors to whom France objected. Similar agreement was reached by the U.K. with Belgium in 1967 and the Netherlands in 1974.

177 Art. 1(A)(2), Convention Relating to the Status of Refugees, 1951, U.N.T.S. vol. 189, p.150; see Cmnd. 9171.

178 E.g. the preference given by Canada to refugees from Czechoslovakia and Poland.

179 International concern took off in 1921 with the League of Nations High Commissioner for Refugees and the pioneering work of its first Commissioner, Nansen. A series of bodies followed - the Intergovernmental Committee on Refugees (1938), International Refugee Organisation (1946), United Nations Relief and Works Agency for Palestine Refugees (1949), United Nations Korean Reconstruction Agency (1950), U.N. High Commissioner for Refugees (1950), Intergovernmental Committee for European Migration (1952).

180 U.N. Convention 1951, supra, and its supporting Protocol of 1967, U.N.T.S. vol. 606, p.267, Cmnd. 3906.

181 Oppenheim's International Law, vol. I, p.618, (7th ed. 1948).

182 For a survey, see Johnson 9 Sydney L.R. (1980) 11.

183 40 A.L.R. 61 (1982).

184 By virtue of s.19, Immigration Act 1971.

185 Because of their approach to the Rules in general e.g. Hosenball [1977] 3 All E.R. 452.

186 At p.68, per Stephen J.

187 For an example, see the stonewalling and complacent approach of the U.K. at H.C. Debs. 11 April 1983 col. 794-5.

188 See H.C. Debs. 17 July 1984, col. 85.

189 E.g. the Starosta family in April 1983, only weeks after the heated controversy over the Romanian Papasoiu (below); see H.C. Debs. 18 April col. 9.

190 Times, 22 February 1983.

191 Even though the 'resettlement' may have been under canvas or in army barracks. See Times, 8 May 1982. Their battle to stay continues.

192 Though applications for these documents from people who cannot obtain passports from their own countries are now more sympathetically considered, H.C. Debs. 17 July 1984, col. 85.

193 E.g. the Vietnamese in Hong Kong and Malaysia; the 10,000 Poles in Austrian centres in 1982. The U.N.'s offices will be particularly helpful in granting travel documents for travel in the first place.

194 E.g. Ugandan Asians who spent 9 years in an Austrian transit camp before the U.N.H.C.R. succeeded, Times, 5 August 1982.

195 The Islamic Revolution in Iran is a recent example.

196 E.g. the notorious Papasoiu (see below) was smuggled into the U.K. in a lorry.

197 This would still amount to a misrepresentation by silence - Khawaja [1984] A.C. 74, Zamir [1980] A.C. 930.

[198] H.C. Debs. 9 March, col. 399.

[199] Art. 31(1).

[200] And the U.N. Convention cannot help, see Musisi, Times, 8 June 1985. For another gap in the appeals' procedure, see Muruganandarajah, 23 July 1984.

[201] H.C. Debs. 31 March 1983 col. 518-9.

[202] Ibid, col. 524 and H.C. Debs. 11 April 1983, col. 313. In 1976, U.K.I.A.S. in cooperation with U.N.H.C.R. appointed a full-time refugee counsellor in recognition of the special difficulties which potential refugees pose.

[203] E.g. Ali [1973] Imm. A.R. 19 and 33; but not as part of an appeal against the destination of removal if the asylum plea has already been considered at the making of the substantive decision. On the other hand, if it has not, an appeal against the destination is a separate process and therefore permissible, see Enwia [1984] 1 W.L.R. 117. The value of the appeal is doubtful, see Select Committee (1978) Evidence, Q 428, where U.K.I.A.S. pointed to 150 appeals without success.

[204] Vol. 16 Y.B.E.C.H.R. 356. Cf. the use of the "conducive to public good" power to deny residence to undesirable refugees, see the case of Bloch, Guardian 30 December 1983.

[205] For the arguments of the Home Office, see its report on the Work of the Immigration and Nationality Department (1984) p.25.

[206] See Doonetas TH/12339/75 (conscription being a general requirement) and Atibo [1978] Imm. A.R. 93.

[207] Art. 13, U.N. Declaration 1948, art. 12, Covenant on Civil & Political Rights 1966.

[208] See Observer, 10 April 1983 re 2 Turkish applicants.

[209] The role of the Foreign Office in influencing the Home Office is shadowed in doubt, but the usefulness of asylum in embarrassing or not embarrassing a foreign State would suggest a large measure of consultation.

[210] Home Office Minister, H.C. Debs. 31 March 1983, col. 461; as the Papasoiu case makes abundantly clear. Cf. Ali [1978] Imm. A.R. 126, an apparently harsh case in which the policy of Africanisation in Kenya had deprived A of his job but which was held not to amount to persecution. Significantly, if it had been so held, the "special voucher" system devised by the

U.K. for U.K.P.Hs would have been thwarted.

211 E.g. Ahmet [1973] Imm. A.R. 1.

212 Regulations for the Administration of the Aliens Act 1905, cmnd. 2879, p.29.

213 In the light of Papasoiu case, they are likely to assume greater significance.

214 The Fugitive Offenders Act 1967 and post 1967 treaties signed in accordance with the Extradition Act 1870: the definition is based on the U.N. Convention of 1951.

215 Following parliamentary pressure. No such leeway was incorporated before 1870.

216 Defined as personal conduct by the defendant as part of organised opposition to the foreign government.

217 The Home Office Working Paper on Extradition (1982) commendably suggests the adoption of the wider definition in any revised extradition law and recent extradition treaties have adopted the asylum definition. See Cmnd. 9421 and further chapter 8.

218 Art. 33(1), U.N. Convention, supra, unless the applicant is a danger to security or is regarded as such because of conviction for a "particularly serious crime", art. 33(2).

219 Two Chilean cases [1977] Imm. A.R. 36.

220 E.g. entitlement to local authority grants and home student fees - S.I. 1983/973, Schedules 2 and 3.

221 Annex. The U.K. has also ratified the European Agreement on the Abolition of Visas for Refugees (1959, Council of Europe, Treaty Series No. 31).

222 E.g. the Ugandan Resettlement Board or the reception centres and dispersement camps set up to cater for the Vietnamese in 1979.

223 For example, the British Council does administer awards given by other bodies but does not sponsor training courses itself, H.C. Debs. 9 March 1983, col. 435.

224 See, for example, the difficulties revealed in the Psychological Problems of Refugees (1983, British Refugee Council). The recent fate of Vietnamese refugees, in contrast to Ugandan Asians in 1972, is an excellent example of the

problems of readjustment and the lack of official support services in preference to voluntary effort and self-help, see Edholm et al, Vietnamese Refugees in Britain (C.R.E. 1983).

225 E.g. Guatemalans (about 35,000) in Southern Mexico, Ugandans (170,000) in the Sudan, Salvadoreans (20,000) in Honduras, Namibians (93,000) in Angola, Kampucheans (200,000) in Thailand, quite apart from the Palestinians in the Middle East.

226 See also the disturbing practice of States returning refugees e.g. Kenya and Tanzania exchanging 30 political refugees in 1984.

227 From 108,000 in 1980 to 20,000 in 1983. See Interior Minister's speech to the United Nations, Times, 22 October 1983.

228 Times, 18 January 1984. See also, Sunday Times, 29 April 1984.

229 E.g. May, Constitutional History of England, vol. 3, p.50 (1906).

230 Select Committee on Race Relations and Immigration (1978), para. 98.

231 See, for example, the remarks of the Secretary of State in H.C. Debs. 22 March 1983, col. 718, H.C. Debs. 17 July 1984, col. 85, and the Minister of State on 31 March 1983 at col. 521.

232 Today's Newspaper obituary columns are a simple indicator of those granted asylum in, for example, the 1920s and 30s.

233 See the accounts by Sherman and Wasserstein.

234 By the strict application of the entry clearance system, H.C. Debs. 9 March 1983, col. 399.

235 The numbers admitted falling from 1,793 in 1981 to 246 in 1982, H.C. Debs. 25 January 1983, col. 367. In 1980 the Colony withdrew its "home base" policy under which refugees could not be turned away if they managed to set foot on the territory. The stark reality of refugee policy is poignantly illustrated by the fact that the U.N. Convention (1951) does not extend to Hong Kong, because of its small size and vulnerability to large-scale illegal immigration (H.C. Debs. 6 March 1984, col. 529, and 27 February 1985, col. 968). Concern has been expressed at the plight of 5,600 Vietnamese held in closed camps in Hong Kong in 1985, see Home Affairs Committee,

Refugees and Asylum (1985), and its Evidence, H.C. 72; H.C. Debs. 14 May 1985, col. 298, 22 May, col. 996, 24 May, col. 1286.

236 H.C. Debs. 28 April 1983, col. 376.

237 H.C. Debs. 30 March 1983, cols. 141-2.

238 H.C. Debs. 30 March 1983, col. 146, although 257 individual applications were lodged during that period (December 1981-28 March 1983).

239 H.C. Debs. 9 March 1983, col. 399.

240 H.C. Debs. 30 March, col. 521ff.

241 This was assisted by the wide publicity which the news of his removal was given in Eastern countries.

242 The Czech family of Starosta was significantly granted compassionate leave to stay soon afterwards - H.C. Debs. 18 April 1983, col. 9.

243 H.C. Debs. 6 June, col. 219.

244 H.C. Debs. 20 May, col. 273.

245 H.C. Debs. 6 June, col. 435.

246 H.C. Debs. 3 June, col. 52. See cmnd. 9539.

247 At present it can only be made as part of some other appeal. Cf. Canada where the applicant is interviewed initially (legal representation being possible) and a report is sent to the Refugee Status Advisory Committee which advises (but cannot direct) the Minister. Appeal against refusal lies to an Appeal Board - s.45, Immigration Act 1976.

248 Adjudicators and the I.A.T. may be seen as too legalistic and, in any event, boasting no particular expertise in this field.

249 This would be in line with resolution 77[31] of September 1977 by the Council of Europe.

6 SECONDARY IMMIGRANTS

> Scores of Japanese and Chinese in Australia for 'Business
> reasons' are rearing large families and their children,
> naturally, are not prohibited immigrants - they do not
> arrive via the Immigration Department. Japanese and
> Chinese merchants, businessmen, wool buyers and traders
> arrive in Australia with wives who are approaching
> motherhood. An astounding revelation ... .[1]

Dependants in this chapter consist of spouses, children, aged
and distressed relatives, fiances and fiancees. A distinct
feature of the Immigration Rules 1980 was the greater use of
"recourse to public funds" as a bar to admission. Such
requirements are common in immigration control - they
underlay, for example, the Aliens Act 1905.[2] They represent
one of the basic objections by the host community to
immigration - the hostility to 'spongers' on the national
wealth - and these objections have been heightened by the
creation of the Welfare State. Although maintenance and public
funds have regularly featured in U.K. controls, the 1980 Rules
showed a hardening of attitude. Sponsors in the U.K. must be
able to offer their dependants adequate accommodation and
maintenance and will be required to give an undertaking in
writing to do so.[3] If supplementary benefits are subsequently
claimed by the dependant, the sponsor may, and usually will,
be required to reimburse the D.H.S.S.[4] and may in appropriate
cases be prosecuted.[5] There is no time limit to this liability
and it will continue until the sponsor loses his factual
responsibility for the dependant.

This concern to ensure the financial independence of
immigrants is rigorously implemented, but has to be tempered
by a recognition of the family unit which common humanity
demands.[6] Thus, when primary immigration was effectively
curtailed in the 1960s, successive Governments have preserved
the right of secondary immigrants to enter; so much so that,
since the beginning of the 1970s, they have constituted by far

the largest section of immigrants. This has meant that, when Governments have looked to imposing stricter controls, secondary immigrants have been their chief target. A considerable number of hurdles have been placed in the path of dependants, of which the most serious are (a) the delay in obtaining admission, especially in its effect on children and aged relatives; (b) proving the claimed relationship; (c) the official perception of husbands and fiances as primary immigrants and the consequent discrimination against them; (d) the precise scope of categories of dependants - for example, the maximum age limit for children, the minimum for parents, the entitlement or otherwise of more distant relatives.

A. MARRIAGE

In immigration terms, this connotes the ability not only to start a family through marriage but also to bring a partner into the country of one's residence. In the U.K., a sharp distinction has been drawn between the rights of women and men.

(1) Wives and fiancees
Men who are citizens of, or settled in, the U.K. have always been allowed to bring in their wives or fiancees,[7] but problems have arisen over proving the genuineness of the relationship and over the delays of the entry clearance system.

Wives and children constitute the major source of permanent immigration today, though the numbers have fallen steadily since 1978.[8] In 1984, 6920 wives were accepted for settlement on arrival, of whom 3360 were from the Indian subcontinent.[9] The statistics indicate that the commitment to wives of men settled in the U.K. is a longstanding one. Indeed, a most extraordinary delay may occur between the admission of the sponsor and the application and admission of his dependants. Roughly one quarter of wives granted entry clearance in the Indian subcontinent in 1981 were married before 1963[10] and roughly three quarters had husbands who entered the U.K. before 1973.[11] This commitment is of course a necessarily dwindling one, but it will be replaced to a degree by a future one, as long as men look overseas for partners and, in particular, the arranged marriage continues.

Conditions
Entry clearance is required, with its attendant difficulties (see chapter 4). The use of priority queues since 1975 has greatly eased the delays for wives with no or young children, but for those joining the main settlement queue they can be considerable and the wisdom of excluding older children from priority status is questionable from humanitarian and race relations' standpoints.

Evidence that the marriage exists between the particular sponsor and the applicant can take various forms. Usually it includes such "indirect" matters as

(i) their passports (subject to the husband establishing that he has a settled status in the U.K.);
(ii) birth certificates;
(iii) family correspondence and
(iv) remittances or tax claims by the husband, although entry clearance officers are on the alert for bogus claims after the so-called Sylhet tax pattern (see chapter 4).

Obviously, greater weight may be given to "direct" evidence that a marriage has taken place,[12] although it may well not be conclusive. For example, the Home Office does not regard the memoranda under the Hindu Marriages Act 1955 (India) as sufficient in themselves.[13] On the other hand, foreign custom and law can be persuasive, for example, that cohabitation raises a presumption of marriage under Mahomedan law.[14]

English law must recognise the validity of the current marriage and, if necessary, of earlier marriages and divorces. A marriage is valid under English law if the formalities of the place of celebration are complied with and the parties have the capacity to marry according to the laws of their domicile.[15] This can have surprising consequences enabling recognition of the marriage of very young children[16] or the marriage by telephone between a man in England and a woman in Pakistan.[17] English courts retain the power to refuse recognition through the use of public policy and it may be that they would do so if the circumstances were seen as particularly offensive to public morality.

The difficulties of establishing a person's domicile are well-known and may have particular relevance for marriages which are potentially, or in fact, polygamous. For most immigrants, the U.K. becomes 'home' and they will acquire the appropriate domicile,[18] as will their U.K. born children even though they may harbour hopes of returning one day to the land of their fathers.[19] A person with an English domicile cannot contract a factually polygamous marriage. If it is potentially polygamous, the position used to be the same. However, Hussain v Hussain[20] partially alleviates the difficulty by upholding a potentially polygamous marriage between a male, English domiciled sponsor and foreign woman, provided that the marriage remains monogamous.[21] It cannot help the reverse situation (a female, English domiciliary marrying a foreign man whose domiciliary law permits polygamy): a subsequent, valid English ceremony would be needed with the consequential embarrassment to the parties. It is to be hoped that the recent suggestion of the Law Commission will be implemented,[22] recognising all potentially polygamous marriages if they remain monogamous.

Problems of proof of domicile are far more likely amongst the first generation immigrants, for example, U.K.P.Hs who were forced to leave Uganda but who seriously wish to return if conditions or enticements to do so[23] improve. Such intentions may well suffice to retain the foreign domicile or resurrect the domicile of origin, in spite of lengthy residence in the U.K., and that domicile[24] can be transmitted as one of dependency to children under 16.[25] Such people could thus enter forms of marriage overseas which are prohibited under English law (for example, on grounds of age, consanguinity or polygamy).

At the other end of the scale, it may become necessary, before deciding whether a current marriage or cohabitation is legally valid or whether a fiancee can enter, to determine the status of an earlier divorce or decree of nullity. The liberality of statute in relation to the former[26] and increasingly of the common law to the latter means that more foreign decrees[27] are recognised and most difficulties concern the financial consequences of recognition.[28] The courts have even recognised non-judicial decrees, such as talaqs obtained in compliance with Pakistan's Muslim Family Law Ordinance 1961,[29] but have pulled back from recognising the most informal methods.[30] Thus, for example, an Indian national, not domiciled in England,[31] who returns to Kashmir and obtains a bare talaq is, under present judicial authority, still married in English eyes and the woman who is his fiancee would have no right to enter as such. If he obtains a more formal talaq, it will probably be recognised but could still be defeated if his spouse had not been given proper notice of the proceedings.[32] The rejection of bare talaqs can be defended on policy grounds if the respondent has a real connection with the U.K. for it is grossly unfair on her to be deprived of normal judicial safeguards by a husband who gets a 'weekend' divorce. If she has no connection, the liberality of the Recognition of Divorces and Legal Separations Act 1971 should dictate recognition. Otherwise, for example, a second wife's immigration status is jeopardised by the non-recognition of an earlier, wholly foreign based divorce.

Female (but not male) cohabitees may also be allowed entry[33] provided that

(i) the relationship with the U.K. sponsor is a permanent one - evidence of foreign custom may be crucial to show this;

(ii) previous marriages of the parties have broken down permanently and no other cohabitees have been admitted already. The concession is not intended to facilitate the entry of a harem.[34]

Fiancees are currently admitted for three months in the first instance[35] and, once the marriage takes place, indefinite leave to stay is granted, if the husband is settled in the U.K.,[36] or a leave to coincide with his leave is granted.[37] The reference to 'settled' may raise the thorny issue of 'ordinary residence'[38] which he must fulfil. The requirement is more liberally interpreted today[39] but still requires a degree of regular physical presence. A particular problem surrounding fiancees has been the distasteful use of virginity tests in the Asian subcontinent in an attempt to ensure the genuineness of the proposed marriage. They not only involved an offensive intrusion of privacy which would not be tolerated generally in the U.K. or most old Commonwealth countries, but represented a cynical exploitation and judgment of a country's moral code by the dubious standards of the U.K.[40]

Overall, however, the simplicity of these entry conditions and their continuance stood in sharp contrast to the hurdles facing husbands and fiances. A call by the Select Committee in 1978[41] to place fiancees under the same criteria as fiances was rejected by the Government on the basis that there was "little evidence of abuse" by women,[42] but this view has now changed in response to the European Court of Human Rights' decision in 1985 in relation to husbands and fiances. Women must now satisfy the "primary purpose" test and are subject to the same 12 months' probationary period as are men (see below). This makes their immigration status and that of their children precarious. Discrimination still exists however, for by s.1 of the 1971 Act the wives and children of Commonwealth citizens who were settled in the U.K. when the Act came into force do not need to satisfy the maintenance and accommodation requirements of r.46.

(2) Husbands and fiances

Husbands and fiances are seen in terms of primary immigration and, for Governments seeking to close all loopholes, are an obvious target. The Rules governing their admission have had a chequered and controversial history, almost leading to the downfall of the Secretary of State in 1982 and culminating in condemnation by the European Court of Human Rights. That history reveals much of attitudes in the U.K. towards immigration generally.

Before 1969 husbands and fiances were admitted as a concession, the latter for 3 months in the first instance pending marriage.[43] As regards the former, a Commonwealth husband was generally admitted if his wife was ordinarily resident in the U.K.,[44] whereas an alien husband was only entitled if his wife was a British subject and for 12 months initially. If she was not, he could only enter if he could prove 'hardship'.[45] By 1969 the Government believed that marriage was being used by Commonwealth citizens on a large scale to evade immigration control, but, like its successors, was unable to put a credible figure on the level of abuse. Thus, the concession for Commonwealth applicants was withdrawn[46] (the position of aliens was unchanged). Entry was only allowed in special circumstances, chiefly, the degree of hardship which would be caused by women having to join their partners abroad.[47] There followed a sordid succession of cases[48] assessing the degree of hardship. Subtle but intangible and hairsplitting distinctions were drawn between hardship and merely considerable inconvenience or discomfort.[49] The spectacle did no credit to the U.K., but it should be noted that the European Commission implicitly supported the policy, pointing out that the women were not barred from marriage and had a choice between staying in the U.K. or joining their partners abroad.[50]

By early 1974 the Home Secretary was aware of the "substantial and continuing new wave of male immigration"[51] which would follow if the Rules were relaxed (though again no figures were mentioned). Shortly afterwards he changed his mind, considering that "the stark and unacceptable nature of the discrimination"[52] outweighed the immigration consequences. He removed the barrier and allowed entry provided that the woman was settled in the U.K.[53] In the next three years, the number of husbands and fiances admitted increased;[54] still small compared to the total immigration but sufficient for the Rules to be tightened again.[55] Fuelled by lurid and extravagant press claims of illegal immigration racketeering, a trade in forged documents and 'brides for purchase', the same Government in 1977 applied a brake, which remains an essential feature of the current Rules.[56] Marriages were in effect placed under probation for a year to ensure their genuineness and to weed out marriages of convenience. The Government believed the abuse to be substantial but was unwilling at first to put a figure on it.[57] Under Parliamentary pressure, the Junior Minister at the Home Office subsequently suggested an annual rate of "several hundred cases".[58] This is telling testimony to the power of the press, to the fickleness and expediency of Governments in immigration matters and the use of statistical imprecision.

The 12 months' period is an arbitrary one.[59] It places the husband in considerable uncertainty because his right to stay lies in suspension. His marriage must not have been terminated during the period, though this is not synonymous with legal termination.[60] A sharp contrast between family and immigration laws emerges since the former generally regards the ceremony and certificate of marriage as conclusive regardless of ulterior motives such as the gaining of entry or citizenship,[61] whereas the latter looks to the reality rather than form of the marriage so as to discover if the marriage is genuine. The possibility arose in 1977 therefore of intrusive questioning by immigration officials as to the state and details of the marriage.[62] The total number of fiances entering from all countries fell by over 1,000 between 1977 and 1980, but significantly by 1,400 for India.[63]

It is an indication of the limited room for manoeuvre facing those who seek tougher immigration control that in 1979 the new Government had to turn to this area. Entry was limited

(i) to the husbands and fiances of United Kingdom Citizens who were born here or one of whose parents was born here, and

(ii) to parties who had already met.[64]

In the Indian subcontinent, the changes had a dramatic effect, applications by husbands and fiances falling from 3,660 in 1979 to 820 in 1980.[65] They inevitably discriminated against the recently arrived and predominantly coloured immigrants by striking at the custom of arranged marriages. As to these, whilst conditions (a) and (b) of the current r.54 (that the marriage was not primarily to gain entry and that each party intends to live together) can at least be defended in the pursuit of immigration control, breach of (c) (the requirement that the parties have met) need not imply illegal entry, and it seemed to Lord Scarman to be "an attack on the social habits and custom of people who have come to this country and who are living according to the customs in which they were brought up".[66] In the context of race relations the requirement is insensitive. Again the Government was unable to estimate the level of abuse of arranged marriages.[67] Admittedly, it is impossible to reach a precise figure but one would normally expect some statistical evidence in similarly controversial areas. The truth may be that, in a field of general political consensus, justification can be sought in shared generalities and fears rather than figures.

The proviso that the woman or one of her parents be born in the U.K. was clearly discriminatory against other women who were, for example, merely settled in the U.K., an impediment to family life and a breach of the European Convention of Human Rights. Pleas to articles 3 (inhumane treatment) and 8 (family life) of the Convention are insufficient, since the European Commission does not, so far, object to a woman having to join her husband abroad.[68] If they are linked to article 14 (non-discrimination), then the proviso can be regarded as indistinguishable from the Commission's ruling in the East African Asians case.[69] More promising is the principle of proportionality. For, if the purpose of this control was to control the exploitation of marriage as a means of primary immigration, the other conditions in the Rules can achieve that, leaving the proviso superfluous. This is especially so since

(a) the Government was unable to quantify the extent of abused marriages and

(b) the proviso prevented settlement however genuine the
particular marriage might be.

In fact the Commission duly ruled against the U.K. in three
test cases in October 1983, but on the grounds that there had
been sex discrimination (arts. 8 and 14) and ineffective
domestic remedies (art. 13) rather than on the basis of racial
discrimination.
   Whilst these proceedings unfolded, controversy over the
proviso grew apace in the U.K. It proved to be a convenient
focal point of attack for opponents of immigration laws. In
1982, the Government, though refusing to admit it publicly,
was sufficiently concerned about the progress of the cases
before the Commission and about unease within its own
backbenches, that it took the opportunity of amending the
proviso as part of a package of changes in the Rules made
necessary by the implementation of the British Nationality Act
1981. The changes, announced in October 1982,[70] allowed
settlement to husbands and fiances of women who were British
Citizens, regardless of how they acquired that status - thus
satisfying one but not two of the cases before the Commission.
It was estimated that the change might lead to an annual
increase of 2,500-3,000 applications.[71] This implication did
not please some of the Government supporters[72] and additional
safeguards were added to placate them - the burden of proof to
lie on the applicant to show that the marriage was genuine and
the probationary period for marriages to be extended to 2
years.[73] The safeguards drove the Labour opposition into real
opposition rather than its earlier expedient abstention and
failed to satisfy the Government's own backbench critics.[74] It
suffered its first defeat since taking office.[75] On reflection
and after much lobbying of its own supporters, the Government
decided to rely on the tacit support of the Opposition,
removed the 2 year probationary period, allowed entry for
husbands and fiances of all British Citizens and passed the
Rules in February 1983.[76]

1983-85 Position (Rr.41-43, 54, 55, 125-6)
Husbands and fiances of British Citizens require entry
clearance. Fiances must fulfil the maintenance and
accommodation requirements and both must satisfy the e.c.o.
that they have met their partners and that the marriage
is/will be genuine.[77] Husbands are admitted for 12 months and
fiances for 3 in the first instance; both are then under
probation for 12 months at the end of which the onus now lies
on them to show that the criteria of r.126[78] are still met.
This shift in the onus of proof has more than counterbalanced
the more liberal aspects of the 1983 Rules. Thus, under the
pre 1983 law the Secretary of State had to satisfy the
Immigration Appeals Tribunal that "first of all, the marriage
is entered into for the primary purpose of evading the

immigration law and rules, and, second, the necessity of there being no intention, or a lack of intention, to live together permanently as man and wife".79 Now the burden lies on the entrant to rebut both these aspects of the marriage and this gives the Home Office a double chance of success. The Home Office regards the current test as "perfectly easy to apply".80 The procedure is as follows,

> A husband or fiance overseas is interviewed in every case before an entry clearance is granted. In many cases his wife or fiancee here is also interviewed. An application has to be made in every case before a husband is granted settlement, and he and his wife will be interviewed wherever there is cause to doubt the bona fides of the application. Home Office staff and interviewing officers, who are experienced in assessing applicants, take into consideration not only the statements of the applicant, his spouse, and of third parties, but also the applicant's immigration history and other relevant information to establish whether the requirements in the rules are satisfied.81

This description is deceptively simple. Firstly, as the court in Bhatia82 has confirmed, the burden lies on the entrant to prove separately that

> (a) the marriage is genuine and
> (b) its primary purpose is not to evade immigration.

(a) need not be conclusive of (b) so the e.c.o. is not tied to the purposes as expressed by the parties but can look further afield. This has particular importance for the arranged marriage and the motives of the parents of the couple. Thus, "an arranged marriage might well be a genuine marriage in the sense that the parties intended to live together, but the primary purpose of the arrangement [by the parents] might still be to secure admission to the U.K.".83 The fact that some marriages have followed this pattern entitles the e.c.o. to treat all claims under (b) with an approach "of caution, perhaps of cautious pessimism".84 Regrettably this stereotyping of applicants from the Indian subcontinent is not untypical in the entry clearance procedure. Second, "If there is no clear evidence either way ... or if the question ... seems evenly balanced, [the applicant] should no longer be given the benefit of the doubt."85 Third, the e.c.o. will undertake a searching examination of the applicant in which the following questions could be asked. "If your fiancee did not live in the U.K., would you still go to her home to live? If you were not able to live with your fiancee in the U.K., would you still marry her? If your family had asked you to marry a local girl, would you have done so?"86 Fourth, there is the difficulty of establishing (a) above, viz. the genuineness of the marriage. If, for example, the letters between the spouses are not 'sufficiently affectionate', the application may be refused.[87] Not surprisingly the changes in 1983 to the Rules have had a significant effect - the 'primary purpose' hurdle now accounts for the majority of e.c. refusals.[88]

Since 1977 the husband will be admitted for 12 months (3 months for fiances) in the first instance and his passport will be stamped with a warning of that situation for official internal information.[89] To an extent his stay may, ironically given the general tenor of immigration and citizenship laws, be determined by his spouse, for she has considerable leverage. Ultimately she can inform the Home Office that "My husband thinks he has got permanent stay in this country" but, "it is just a marriage of convenience for him so he can stay in this country".[90] If the marriage is deemed to be an attempt at evasion of the Rules, deportation as conducive to the public good is possible and probable.[91] Similarly, if the husband fails to satisfy any of the criteria, there is no discretion to waive the requirement.[92] Leave to remain lapses and, if necessary, the man can be deported.[93] Moreover, these dragnet provisions mean

(a) that leave automatically lapses on breakdown of the marriage, even if it was in fact a genuine one, and
(b) that all husbands must comply even if their marriages took place many years before entry.

Sex discrimination was still "absolutely inherent"[94] in the Rules for a settled woman was not able to introduce her partner, unlike a settled man. He had such a right because "By and large, it has been the practice of [Asian] cultures for the women to go where the men go".[95]

Before the European Court of Human Rights the U.K. advanced a more persuasive argument viz. the rules were needed to protect the domestic labour market against illegal male entrants at a time of high unemployment.[96] The Court agreed that protection of jobs was a legitimate aim but ruled that it was insufficient justification for sex discrimination contrary to article 13 of the Convention. The court noted that sex equality was a major goal of the Council of Europe, that a change in the U.K. Rules would only increase male immigration by 2-5,000 and that already 40-70% of female entrants worked, thus refuting the Government's sexual stereotype of the male worker. This part of the judgment was predictable, less so was the more significant ruling that the U.K. failed to offer effective domestic remedies to those who complain of administrative practice. On the other hand, (i) the Court cast doubt on the Commission's opinion in the East African Asians case (which suggested racial discrimination (art. 14) and degrading treatment (art. 3)) by deciding that the U.K.

requirement that the parties to the marriage must have met was not racially discriminatory. (ii) The court reversed the Commission's finding of discrimination, on the basis of birth, against one of the litigants. (iii) It rejected a breach of article 8 (right to family life) since the Convention does not guarantee a right to enter a member state. This again jeopardises the East African Asians case since the Court implies that the Convention cannot be used as a backdoor method of protecting the movement provisions contained in Protocol 4.

The U.K. responded to the ruling[97] by removing the sex discrimination so that all women residents can introduce partners, but predictably imposed the notorious 'primary purpose' test and other criteria in the husband's rules on them and required all sponsors of female entrants to satisfy the maintenance and accommodation requirements (save for the wives of Commonwealth citizens who were settled in the U.K. when the Act came into force). The liberal aspect of these changes is that roughly 2,500 men could benefit by entry. This is more than outweighed by the facts that (i) those men would still have to satisfy the 'primary purpose' test and other criteria, so the figure of successful entrants will be lower. (ii) All wives and fiancees (in 1984, for example, 6,920 and 4,280 respectively were admitted for settlement[98]) must now satisfy the more demanding criteria, which had previously been reserved for men.

Comment

(1) It is quite reasonable for a State to seek to ensure that marriage is not used as a means of evading immigration control and to arm the executive with the power to do so.[99] It is also understandable that sex conditioning and discrimination should lead to the belief that the man is the wage earner and a wife should follow her husband. But several objections can be made to the continued application of this principle in the 1983 Rules. Firstly, it is hypocritical on the one hand, to espouse the principle of equality (Sex Discrimination Act 1975) but on the other, to deny its benefits to all of the population because of minimal immigration benefits. Second, it is hypocritical to object to the custom of arranged marriages yet to put in its place a British perception of morality; in other words, Asian women should not allow their parents to dictate their overseas partners but they should follow those partners in the time-honoured fashion of female subservience.[100]

Third, these Rules are primarily directed towards Asian couples - millions of British Citizens already had the right to bring in partners. It is because they rarely do so that the Government can get away with the Rules. Consequently, the effect on race relations ought to have been acknowledged. Though numbers may be small in relation to the total coloured population, this controversy has served as a forceful reminder to ethnic minorities of the U.K.'s implacable stance against coloured immigration. Moreover, the sight of the Government seeking to appease its right wing and the Official Opposition tamely abstaining in Parliament in 1982 can hardly have furthered support for the principle of racial equality amongst the white population.

Fourth, in the face of principle and of immigration statistics, the size of the 'problem' is small. The Government estimated in 1981 that 70% of Indian women were already British Citizens[101] and thus had the right to bring in marital partners. Of the remainder, there will be some who will not take out citizenship, for example, because they would thereby lose their Indian citizenship (India forbidding dual nationality), but overall the number of 'settled women only' will decrease. Moreover, with the increasing assimilation of Asian women into Western culture, the incidence of arranged marriages will decrease.[102] It is thus extremely doubtful whether the Rules will have anything but a minor effect on immigrant numbers. Fifth, for the Government to argue, as it did,[103] that any amelioration of the position is a matter for the Immigration Act 1971 and not the Nationality Act 1981 (because of which the 1983 Rules were introduced), is specious for

(a) the 1981 Act does have immigration implications,
(b) a change in the Rules would not have offended the 1971 Act since it would have involved, in effect, a concession.

(2) In the context of recent immigration, the issue of husbands and fiances is largely a red herring partly because the numbers remain very small and partly because people, black or white, will always wish to marry and introduce foreigners and, if a society is to be humane, it must always recognise that fact, as indeed the U.K. now does for all British Citizens and residents.[104] In the overall context of immigration, however, the issue has offered an opportunity to vent a gamut of powerful and well-rehearsed emotions. Out come the traditional arguments which have changed little in 500 years. For example, "it is wrong for minority groups constantly to replenish their separateness and their number in the nation".[105] The Parliamentary Debates on the 1983 changes show the same propensity for nationalism, ill-concealed racism, wild speculation and shabby political compromise which have dogged immigration history in the last 20 years. They also indicate the hypocrisy of the major political parties. Thus, it is difficult to take seriously the fulminations of the Labour Opposition, since it was responsible for closing all male entry in 1969, its 'safeguards' of 1977 remain the basis of today's intrusive control and it preferred

unprincipled abstention in the Parliamentary voting on the 1983 Rules.

(3) The current Rules are a modest example of the effect of the European Convention on Human Rights. In context and retrospect, however, they are likely to be seen as a sordid episode in immigration history.

B. CHILDREN

Since 1975 priority queues have operated for younger children. The Select Committee (1978) went further and proposed that "the admission ... of a child ... should normally be limited to children under 12 years of age ...".[106] The aim behind this suggestion is sensible since ideally children should be admitted as quickly as possible to aid their adjustment to the host society. It has not, however, been implemented because

(a) it appeared in a generally unwelcome Report, which, inter alia, raised the politically unacceptable possibility of annual quotas for immigrant categories,[107]
(b) it would have provoked too much resentment and risked a breach of the European Convention[108] and
(c) the number of child entrants was soon to decline. For example, entry clearance applications in the Indian sub-continent have fallen from 14,130 in 1977 to 9,620 in 1984 and the number outstanding from 25,600 to 13,100.[109]

This has not meant that children have escaped the increasing rigours of immigration control. From a cynical standpoint male children are potential primary immigrants. It is quite common for them to remain abroad until quite old. When they seek to come, often approaching the age of majority, official suspicion of bogus applicants inevitably arises and has led to the detailed scrutiny of applications and the crosschecking of stories within the claimed family.[110] The Rules have reflected this concern and, in part reflecting the uncompromising attitude of the Immigration Appeal Tribunal, are now narrowly drawn. They are strikingly so compared to the relative generosity of the 1962 model.[111]

Rule 50 governs the admission of children and for that Rule alone, 'parent' is given an extended meaning. The father of an illegitimate child is included as well as the mother.[112] A step-parent is included, but only if the natural parent is dead. Thus a step-parent by remarriage is unrealistically excluded.[113] An adoptive parent is included, but, whereas the Act refers to a person who has been legally adopted (s.2(1) in relation to patriality), r.50 makes no reference to legally approved adoptions.[114] There are however, two provisos. Firstly, there must have been a genuine transfer of parental responsibility. This may catch the de facto sharing of custody practised in some cultures. It is primarily aimed, as with the Rules on marriage, at deterring adoptions of convenience by parents abroad. An Order of 1973[115] has specified a large number of countries from which "overseas adoptions" will be recognised. Significantly, Bangladesh, India and Pakistan are excluded. For them legal recognition thus depends on the common law and would seem to require the adoptive parents to be domiciled and the child to be ordinarily resident in the country of adoption.[116] However, even if the legal rules of recognition are satisfied, the immigration authorities may still refuse to recognise the adoption if evasion of control is suspected.[117] Secondly the adoption must have taken place because of the natural parents' "inability to care" for the child. This shorthand is a narrower concept than the detailed grounds available for adoption in most countries and can again raise a conflict between family law and immigration rules e.g. an adoption with the consent of the natural parent may be recognised by family law but will not suffice for immigration.

As to the admission of children for the purposes of adoption in the U.K., the Rules make no provision. The Secretary of State has however allowed admission in exceptional circumstances[118] and must follow the terms of his concession.[119] Moreover, there is evidence to suggest that immigration officers at ports of entry have turned a blind eye to childless British residents returning from abroad with a child whom they wish to adopt.[120] For those children admitted temporarily into the U.K., and who then seek adoption, adoption may outweigh the threat of removal since the child's welfare is regarded by a court in adoption proceedings as more important.[121]

Children must generally establish that their sponsors in the U.K. can maintain them - protection of public funds comes before family unity. Entry clearance is needed and involves proving the relationship between applicant and sponsor. Obvious evidence such as a birth certificate, municipal registry or school record may be unavailable and resort must be had to any evidence at hand e.g. letters, evidence of financial support from the parent in the U.K. or testimony of local dignitaries such as a village leader. It is unlikely, however, that any of this evidence will alone suffice - not even the child tax relief which the Inland Revenue has already conceded to the parent.[122] The child must be under 18 and unmarried, and in essence joining or accompanying his parents for settlement in the U.K. The Rules have confirmed the approach of the I.A.T. and require the sponsoring parent to be present as well as settled in the U.K.[123] R.50 sets out the categories of entrants.[124] On a strict interpretation of category (a) both parents need not be living together but could have separated or been divorced. It has been held, however,[125] that the category's purpose is to reunite children with both parents and thus they must be living together. This strict construction is unwarranted since it ignores the reality of divorce and separation, forces the applicant to rely upon Home Office discretion since he cannot readily fit into another category[126] and is a small example of the 'thou shalt not pass' attitude of the I.A.T. This overriding purpose of reuniting families means that one parent cannot accompany the child with the intention of leaving him with the other parent and then return abroad, perhaps to care for other children. The parent's intention must be to settle in the U.K. and that requires ordinary residence.[127] Moreover, since July 1985 (see above in relation to husbands) most female entrants are subject to the same criteria of entry as men, including the 12 months' probationary period. Their children are by necessity placed in the same uncertain position.

In category (e), considerable caselaw has surrounded the meaning of 'sole responsibility'. On the one hand, it is not synonymous with 'legal custody', even if granted by a U.K. court to the U.K. sponsor. More concern for, interest in, and care for, the child are required. Given that an English court will only have awarded custody on proper jurisdictional grounds and based its decision on the paramountcy of the child's welfare, it is both disturbing and remarkable that primacy has been given to immigration Rules. To argue, as the I.A.T. did in Bovell,[128] in favour of immigration primacy is morally questionable and, since most custody decisions are made under Acts of 1971[129] and 1973,[130] in strict constitutional theory those Acts should prevail over the Immigration Act.[131] Unfortunately, the courts have also shown a readiness to concede priority to immigration law and Rules.[132]

On the other hand, "sole responsibility" is not synonymous with absolute responsibility,[133] for otherwise it could never be satisfied. Some degree of shared responsibility is inevitable. Instead the U.K. sponsor must prove "regular, substantial financial contributions and evidence of concern, interest in and role in, the child's welfare and future".[134] This is a question of fact and degree. Thus, the financial contributions must go beyond mere pocket money.[135] Moreover money alone is insufficient. The sponsor must show by letters or visits that he is genuinely interested in the child's upbringing and, above all, that he is consulted over the child's future.[136] The longer the separation between parent and child, the less the chance of establishing sole responsibility.[137] Another relevant factor is the extent to which the other parent abroad has shared the responsibility e.g. how often the child sees that parent or stays with him or receives any maintenance from him.[138]

Category (f) is the only one which permits a child to join a relative other than a parent. It is an excellent example of the extent to which internal guidance can modify the Rules.

Thus, a distinction is drawn[139] between children under 12 seeking to join a parent - for whom entry is normally allowed, and those over 12 joining a parent and all children joining a relative other than a parent - to whom the full terms of category (f) apply and which are extremely difficult to satisfy. In 1968, the Rules referred to "circumstances of a compassionate nature".[140] Most cases concerned the West Indies where children are frequently cared for by relatives or even friends before seeking to join a parent in the U.K. In 1970 the Rules substituted "family or other considerations".[141] The I.A.T. however added the gloss of "serious and compelling"[142] and the 1980 Rules were drafted to reflect that. That gloss is an indication of the rigorous stance of the I.A.T. It examines the child's conditions abroad rather than contrasts the better conditions which life in the U.K. would bring,[143] and looks to see if the child "is being properly cared for".[144] Much will therefore depend on the entry clearance officer's (e.c.o.) perception of the child's circumstances as compared to those generally prevailing in the foreign country and he may be tempted to employ the yardstick of the worst conditions, in which case few will qualify. The child's age and hence his actual or potential ability to look after himself,[145] and whether his circumstances are avoidable[146] will also be relevant. As with aged dependants (below), this process involves the e.c.o. in the unpleasant task of grading personal hardship, such as degrees of overcrowding,[147] and allows for impressionistic decisions. By its narrow interpretation of the Rule and its decisions [148] the I A.T. has mounted a considerable hurdle to entry. The assessment of suffering and hardship to a child reveals the unacceptable face of immigration control.

Children over 18 have usually had to qualify for entry in their own right. Special favour was shown[149] to those aged 18-21 who were still dependent on their U.K. family, but the 1980 Rules severely restricted the opportunity. They can now only qualify for special treatment in the "most exceptional compassionate circumstances" and are lumped together with other dependants under r.52 (below).[150] A concession remains for some daughters (r.51) but was removed from sons in 1980. The hurdles are so many that few daughters will qualify:-

(a) Rr.46 and 47 (accommodation, maintenance and entry clearance requirements) must still be satisfied, the concession is discretionary, and in such 'special' cases the I.A.T. has been reluctant to adopt a generous approach or to interfere with the discretion of the immigration officer.

(b) The daughter must be unmarried and under 21. It is unfortunate that no clear provision is made for the divorced and widowed.[151] It is doubly unfortunate that such daughters are limited to 21, since a divorcee over 21 may well have no one else to turn to but her family in the U.K. As it is she will have to rely upon clearing the most stringent barrier of r.52 (see below).

(c) The applicant must be "fully dependent". This is interpreted strictly. Any dependence overseas on money[152] or in kind[153] bars entitlement.

(d) The daughter's family unit must be in the U.K. and she must have no other close relatives[154] to turn to abroad. The length of separation from that unit will usually be a decisive factor, unless a continuing desire to keep it together can be shown through, for example, the sending of money and letters.[155]

Apart from the sex discrimination in r.51, the age limit for children generally ignores the reality that their dependence may well continue for many years. The strictness of the Rules is to be regretted not only for the individual suffering (e.g. for handicapped children) but also the resentment it can cause in the context of race relations in the U.K. This is particularly so since the harsher 1980 Rules were introduced without any evidence of significant abuse of child entry. They illustrate first, that not even children have escaped the increased stringency of control and second, the generally unsympathetic stance of the appeals' system, which has in part influenced that stringency.

C. OTHER DEPENDANTS (r.52, 53)

It is natural for families to wish to be united with relatives other than wives and children. Separate figures were not kept until recently but the Select Committee (1978) estimated that about 4,000 such relatives were admitted in 1976 of whom a half came from the Indian subcontinent,[156] but by 1984 the number of entry clearances granted to dependent relatives in the Indian subcontinent had fallen to 420.[157] Like all other categories of entrant, these dependants have not escaped the tightening up of the Rules. Indeed they are an illuminating case-study of the way in which the Rules, aided by the I.A.T., have developed over 20 years.

A distinction is drawn between parents/grandparents and other relatives. Originally, little obstacle lay in the path of the former, save the ability of the sponsor to support them,[158] whereas the latter were confronted with tougher hurdles.[159] Over the years, the former have been subjected to the latter's original, more exacting standards whilst the latter have been relegated to leave to enter only in "the most exceptional compassionate circumstances". Thus, in 1962,

(1) Commonwealth parents were admitted easily,
(2) other aged relatives had to be isolated and in need of care,

(3) younger relatives needed compassionate circumstances and
(4) more distant relatives required exceptional circumstances.[160]

In 1968, for aliens, category (2) had to establish "distress" (i.e. a standard of living substantially below that of the native country) and (4) needed "most exceptional compassionate circumstances".[161] In 1970 the age limit for (1) was raised for the Commonwealth but not for aliens.[162] Otherwise the position of Commonwealth relatives was still more favourable. In 1973 stricter criteria applying to aliens were imposed on all.[163] Finally in 1980, category (1) had to be "isolated" and the others were combined into a single category, needing to prove distress and the "most exceptional compassionate circumstances".[164]

Parents and Grandparents
S.1(4) of the Immigration Act 1971 speaks of a sponsor lawfully in, or entering, the U.K. This has been refined by the Rules so that he must be settled or admitted for settlement at the same time as the applicants; he must be physically present in the U.K.,[165] able and willing to maintain and accommodate them.[166]

The categories of applicants are discriminatorily and narrowly defined. Thus, widows of any age can qualify whereas widowers must be over 65. On the other hand, if both parents arrive together it is sufficient that one be over 65. The relationship with the sponsor must be clearly proved as must, where appropriate, the widowed status.[167] "Parent" does not include step-parent[168] or, semble, an adoptive parent.[169] A "widowed mother" cannot include a divorcee[170] or an unmarried mother.[171] Both may experience social and economic hardship and even ostracism if they live in a society which attaches stigma to divorce or illegitimacy, yet they cannot qualify under either part of r.52.[172] Though defensible on a literal interpretation of the Rules, Nisa and Phillips say much of the I.A.T's approach. First, both relied on s.19 of the 1971 Act whereby the Rules are binding on the I.A.T. and thereby justified a strict interpretation,[173] whereas for the courts, it has frequently been held[174] that the rules are not of law but of practice or guidance and can therefore be interpreted more liberally. Second, the decision in Phillips was justified by the sweeping, armchair observation that, since "the propensity [in the Caribbean] towards extra-marital relationships resulting in childbirth cannot have been unknown when the immigration rules were drafted and approved", the lack of reference to unmarried mothers must have been a deliberate omission.

Under r.52, the parents (or grandparents) must be "wholly or mainly dependent" on their children in the U.K. In addition, according to the I.A.T., they must be "necessarily" dependent.[175] Thus, if a parent voluntarily relinquishes employment[176] or sells his assets (if only in order to provide for his children according to local custom)[177] and then becomes dependent on the U.K. sponsor, he is not "necessarily" dependent and cannot qualify. Similarly a degree of self-help on the part of the applicant is expected before necessary dependence can arise.[178] The Rule makes no mention of "necessary" and it was argued in Chavda[179] that the Rule should be given its ordinary meaning and the word not implied. The I.A.T. decided that the Rules were rules of practice and that strict canons of interpretation were therefore misconceived; the Rule's context and purpose could be assessed and this meant that "necessary" should be incorporated. The contrast with the approach in Nisa and Phillips (above) is self-evident and illustrates how the Home Office can be allowed to "have things both ways". If the Rules can be strictly interpreted against the immigrant they will be; if strict construction works to his advantage, then, as general Rules, they can be interpreted more widely to his disadvantage.

The fact and degree of dependence are the crucial questions, not the reasons for which it is given (e.g. through natural family ties).[180] Moreover, it means primarily financial dependence. Emotional dependence can only be relevant as a secondary factor to tip the balance in a doubtful case and even then it has been given an unduly restrictive scope -

> the normal love and affection of a united family is not of itself such emotional dependence. It needs more than that. For instance, and of course this is not comprehensive, suppose one has a lady who has recently been widowed, who has an adult son or daughter who has been living close to her and that adult son or daughter comes to the United Kingdom, then there might well be said in those circumstances to be emotional dependence, because the lady would have been bereft not merely of her husband, but also of the child to whom she would normally have turned for support other than financial support. If in addition she was in part dependent on that child for financial support then the emotional dependence in such circumstances might tip the scale in the decision whether or not she was mainly dependent.[181]

If therefore both parents are living happily together, there will be no emotional dependence on their children, "albeit one can well understand their desire to be near their children, a perfectly normal human desire which all of us have as we get older".[182] These views not only discriminate against the happy family unit (since they imply that it is only when matters go wrong abroad that emotional dependence may come into play) but are also, it is suggested, a sad reflection on the hostile climate to immigration which has been created in recent years, a climate which counts the value of family unity in sterling.

Under the earlier Rules parents needed to prove no more. Other relatives had to go further and show that they were "isolated".[183] Perhaps because of the success of this extra criterion in disqualifying relatives, it was in 1980 applied to parents.[184] Parents had therefore to be "without other close relatives in their own country to turn to", (the reference to "close" relatives was a subtle addition to the previous criterion). The onus of proof is a heavy one and, to a large degree, the I.A.T's conception of moral duty is patronisingly imposed on the relatives overseas. Thus, the fact that there were relatives to whom the applicant might turn overseas was sufficient. It did not matter that they were debarred from responding by social custom[185] or were unable or unwilling to care for the applicant.[186] This was because the overseas relatives only needed to provide "sympathy, companionship and help"[187] or "might be expected to keep in touch"[188] with the applicant. This narrow approach has now been slightly modified by the courts so that "the close relatives must not only have the ability to provide some assistance, but willingness as well".[189]

The category of parents and grandparents is a particularly neat illustration of the gradual tightening of the Rules by successive Governments looking for ways of plugging gaps, however small, in their posture of restrictive control. The 1962 version for Commonwealth citizens thus appears naively comforting - such relatives being entitled to admission "if their children are settled in the U.K. and are able and willing to support them".[190] Whilst the Select Committee (1978) did not find, in relation to the dependence rule, "the standard of proof demanded to be excessive",[191] the additional hurdles erected by the 1980 and subsequent Rules surely make it so. In the lay, if not legal,[192] sense, it can hardly be humane to deny the unification of children and parents. Moreover, the effect of stringent Rules on the morale of ethnic minorities and race relations should not be underestimated.

Other Relatives (r.52)

Parents (save for widowed mothers) and other relatives below 65[193] can only enter if they are "living alone in the most exceptional compassionate circumstances". If this can be established, leave may be given to "sons,[194] daughters, sisters, brothers, uncles and aunts of whatever age".[195] On analogy with the earlier Rules, this category is closed and cannot be extended.[196]

The scope of this provision obviously depends on the particular facts of each case but, as the pre 1980 cases show, it is not easily satisfied. Physical and/or mental illnesses of a severe kind[197] are relevant but usually have to be exacerbated by additional factors such as the lack of financial assistance or physical support overseas, and the U.K. sponsor must establish that he can adequately support the applicant. The applicant can be faced with a catch 22 situation - if the illness is very serious, entry clearance may be refused under the normal medical prohibition (r.79); if it is not, r.52 does not apply. Any decision by the e.c.o. involving the criterion of "compassion" is an impressionistic one and extremely difficult to overturn, requiring the I.A.T. to engage in the same impressionistic and distasteful task of gradating "compassion".[198] Even this possibility has been made more difficult by the insistence that the circumstances be "most exceptional", a requirement which cannot be ignored.[199] As an example of these stringent compassionate circumstances, the earlier concept of "distressed"[200] is used to the effect that applicants must have "a standard of living substantially below that of their own country".[201] It is interpreted in its narrow economic sense and other emotional, social or physical aspects are irrelevant. If taken to mean the lowest standard prevailing in say rural India, then logically few applicants would qualify. Instead the applicant's standard is measured alongside that of his relatives and friends.[202] Since he must also satisfy the general requirement of dependence on the U.K. sponsor, the latter's financial support may ironically undermine the applicant's case[203] by boosting his relative earnings. An unfortunate social result is that it forces relatively wealthy spouses through duty and affection to send their money abroad whereas it might be thought to be more humane and cheaper for the family and a benefit to the Exchequer to allow such relatives into the U.K. The consequential task of proving dependence, isolation, no other relatives to turn to and the most exceptional compassionate circumstances is a daunting one. It is also capricious. Thus, an applicant who satisfies all the other criteria but who happens to be relatively well off is denied entry. The observation of the Home Office to the Select Committee (1978) that the then criteria "are strict ... and there is no reason to suppose that [the number of entrants] will become very substantial"[204] is now something of an understatement. Significantly an attempt in 1980 to subject parents/grand-parents to the 'standard of living' test was dropped on the basis that it was too difficult to prove, but of course it was quite appropriate for other relatives![205] The current criteria illustrate how, over the years, Governments have ruthlessly narrowed even the smallest categories of entrant and produced a separation of families which can only fall very short of inhuman treatment.[206]

----

1   Sydney Truth, 21 August 1932; quoted by Palfreeman, Administration of the White Australia Policy, at p.16.

2   S.1(3)(a). Cf. in the U.S., 8 U.S.C. 1182(a)(15).

3   Supplementary Benefits Act 1976, s.17(1)(c) (as amended by the Social Security Act 1980 Sched. 2, para. 16).

4   Ibid, s.18(3); reversing the effect of R v West London Supplementary Benefits Appeal Tribunal, ex p. Clarke [1975] 1 W.L.R. 1396.

5   Ibid, ss.21, 25.

6   The rights to marry and to family life are well recognised by human rights legislation in international law e.g. art. 16, U.N. Declaration 1948; art. 23, Covenant on Civil and Political Rights, 1966; art. 8, European Convention 1950.

7   Currently rules 48, 44 respectively.

8   Control of Immigration Statistics, Cmnd. 9544, Figure 3 and Table 14.

9   H.O. Statistical Bulletin, Table 4.

10   H.A.C. Evidence, App. 19 para. 4. Further, in 1980 Dhaka dealt with cases of 206 sponsors who entered the U.K. in 1963, 79 in 1967, 63 in 1970 etc. Overall, 50% of Bangladeshi wives were married before 1973 - ibid App. 9. (Some of the delay will of course be due to general entry clearance delays.)

11   Ibid, App. 19, para. 5.

12   It is not essential to pinpoint the precise date of the marriage since the overall question for determination is whether the parties are married, but the discovery of a false date will clearly influence the credibility of their stories - Khanom [1979-80] Imm. A.R. 182.

13   See Select Committee (1978) Evidence p.448 for the background to documentation.

14   See Begum [1978] Imm. A.R. 174; Channo Bi, ibid, 182; Begum [1976] Imm. A.R. 31; Class-Peter [1981] Imm. A.R. 154.

15   See generally, Dicey and Morris, The Conflict of Laws, 10th Ed., Ch. 13.

16   Cf. Mohamed v Knott [1969] 1 Q.B. 1.

17 Akhtar TH/72068/80, since the parties' domicile allowed it, as did Pakistan, the place of celebration.

18 In England and Wales, Scotland or Northern Ireland, there being no 'U.K. domicile'; English domicile will be used in the text for brevity.

19 A mere hope of doing so, without the element of residence, would not suffice to change domicile, see I.R.C. v Duchess of Portland [1982] Ch. 314.

20 [1983] Fam. 26.

21 Under previous practice, the woman was allowed to enter for a short period during which a valid ceremony could be performed.

22 Working Paper No. 83.

23 E.g. Expropriated Properties Act 1982 (Uganda), which offers compensation to U.K.P.Hs who fled the country in the early 1970s.

24 For the tenacity of domicile of origin see Winans v A.G. [1904] A.C. 287, Bowie v Liverpool Royal Infirmary [1930] A.C. 580, and for a more recent confirmation I.R.C. v Bullock [1976] 1 W.L.R. 1178.

25 Domicile and Matrimonial Proceedings Act 1973, s.3.

26 Recognition of Divorces and Legal Separations Act 1971.

27 E.g. Perrini v Perrini [1979] Fam. 84. See Smith (1980) 96 L.Q.R. 380.

28 E.g. Torok v Torok [1973] 3 All E.R. 101. For the Law Commission's proposals here, see its report no. 117, (1981-82) H.C. 514, and for remedy of the difficulty see Part III, Matrimonial and Family Proceedings Act 1984.

29 Quazi v Quazi [1980] A.C. 744. See 96 L.Q.R. 168, 97 L.Q.R. 28; but not talaqs performed in the U.K., see Chaudhary v Chaudhary [1985] 2 W.L.R. 350, Fatima [1984] 3 W.L.R. 659. The I.A.T. had earlier reached the contrary and clearly inaccurate view in the light of the spirit of the 1973 Act - Begum TH/61574/80 (2064). See further Pearl [1984] C.L.J. 49 and 248.

30 A bare talaq in Chaudhary v C, supra. Cf. the informal method of a khula under Thai law; see Ormrod L.J. in Quazi v

Quazi, supra.

31 If he was, he would be caught by s.16 of the Domicile and Matrimonial Proceedings Act 1973.

32 S.8 of the Recognition of Divorces and Legal Separations Act 1971, but the courts are reluctant to invoke this provision unless the spouse has a connection with the U.K. -see Newmarch v Newmarch [1978] Fam. 79, Dickson 28 I.C.L.Q. 132. The whole of the talaq procedure must be performed outside the U.K., see Fatima [1984] 3 W.L.R. 659.

33 Immigration Rules, r.49.

34 See Zahra [1979-80] Imm. A.R. 48.

35 R.44. In 1984, 4,280 were admitted, of whom 3,160 were from India and Pakistan - Home Office Statistical Bulletin, Table 11.

36 R.123.

37 R.124. The position is the same if a woman, here in another temporary capacity, marries - she obtains the same leave as that of her spouse.

38 R.1.

39 Following Shah [1983] 2 A.C. 309.

40 The tests were ultimately withdrawn but not without lengthy delay and controversy. See chapter 4.

41 Report, para. 168.

42 Cmnd. 7287, p.23-4.

43 Cmnd. 3830, r.50 (aliens), Cmnd. 3064, r.32 (Commonwealth).

44 Cmnd. 3064, r.29.

45 Cmnd. 3830, r.43, 44.

46 H.C. Debs. 30 January 1969, col. 367.

47 Cmnd. 4298, r.41, 46.

48 E.g. Hector [1970] Imm. A.R. 41; Dumont, ibid, 119; Kuldip Singh, ibid, 211; cf. Constantinides [1974] Imm. A.R. 30; Ahmet [1973] Imm. A.R. 1; Parvez [1979-80] Imm. A.R. 84.

49 For an excellent example, note the facts of Sadhu Singh [1973] Imm. A.R. 67.

50 Papayianni [1974] Imm. A.R. 7; unlike the E. African Asian cases (see chapter 5) where the dependants had nowhere else to go.

51 H.C. Debs. 28 March 1974, col. 612.

52 H.C. Debs. 27 June 1974, col. 535.

53 Announced in H.C. Debs. 27 June 1974, col. 535; subsequently Cmnds. 5715-18 (1974). In view of the change a Private Member's Bill was withdrawn - Spouses of U.K. Citizens (Equal Treatment) Bill.

54 See Immigration Statistics Cmnd. 8533, Tables 11 and 13(a), and Cmnd. 9544, Table 16. The creation in 1975 of separate, non-priority queues for men did, however, effectively stagger the rate of admission by placing them at the back.

55 H.C. 238-241; debated at H.C. Debs. 24 May 1977, col. 1333; H.L. Debs. 10 May, col. 205; a change described earlier by the Times as one which would be "an advantage for race relations", Times, 28 April 1977.

56 R.126(c)-(f), H.C. 169 (1983).

57 H.C. Debs. 18 February 1977, col. 383.

58 H.C. Debs. 24 May 1977, col. 1354.

59 If the marriage lasts one day longer, the husband is safe from the Rule, though the "conducive to public good" power might be invoked to deport him. The marriage must subsist at the date when the Secretary of State reviews it, not at the time when the immigrant applies to stay - Idrish, Times, 14 July 1984.

60 Confirmed by a Junior Minister at H.L. Debs. 10 May 1977, cols. 221-2.

61 Recently confirmed by the House of Lords in Vervaeke v Smith [1983] 1 A.C. 145; see also Puttick v A.G. [1980] Fam. 1 and in Canada Ciresi v Ahmad [1983] 1 W.W.R. 710 and Fernandez v F [1983] 4 W.W.R. 755. But contrast Asser v Peermohamed [1984] 46 O.R. (2d) 664 and note that the court frowns on an adoption which is designed to improve the child's immigration or nationality status - re H [1982] 3 W.L.R. 501.

62 See the allegations discussed in H.L. Debs. 10 May 1977, cols. 218-9 and the assurance by the Home Office Minister that this would not be allowed to happen. H.C. Debs. 24 May 1977, cols. 1356-7.

63 Cmnd. 8533, Table 11.

64 H.C. 394, r.50, 52; the changes were discussed at H.C. Debs. 14 November 1979, col. 1335, 4 December, col. 975; see further H.C. Debs. 10 March 1980, col. 1010 for a motion of disapproval and H.L. Debs. 20 March 1980, col. 360.

65 Cmnd. 9544, Table 9.

66 Home Affairs Committee on the Immigration Rules and the European Convention, Evidence, para. 110, H.C. 434.

67 Cf. the similar inability in 1982 - H.A.C. Evidence Q.5, response of the Home Office Minister.

68 Papayianni [1974] Imm. A.R. 7, and cf. its approach in X v Sweden 4 E.H.R.R. 408. For a review of the Commission's attitude, see the Home Office brief submitted to the Home Affairs Committee, H.C. 434 (1979-80). Cf. the similar reasoning underlying Re Schmitz [1971] 31 D.L.R. 117, whereby the Canadian Bill of Rights was avoided in the citizenship field.

69 See chapter 4. A view adopted by Lord Scarman, H.C. 434, para. 123; but note that in that case, the men seeking entry were U.K. citizens and had nowhere else to go, factors which clearly swayed the Commission.

70 Cmnd. 8683; debated at H.C. Debs. 11 November, col. 692, H.L. Debs. 18 November, col. 671.

71 Minister in Evidence to H.A.C. Subcommittee H.C. 526, (1981-82) Q.6 and Annex.

72 51 of whom abstained when the draft Rules were debated.

73 Revised Rules H.C. 66, introduced on 6 December 1982.

74 Their objections being that the safeguards were unenforceable and, more fundamentally, any change in the bar on male entry contradicted the Conservative Election Manifesto of 1979 which (p.20) promised "to end the concession, introduced by the Labour Government in 1974, to husbands and fiances".

75 By a majority of 18 - H.C. Debs. 15 December, col. 355.

76 H.C. 169: H.C. Debs. 15 February, col. 180.

77 A fiance who seeks limited leave to enter so as to marry a woman settled here can be admitted, but only if the e.c.o. is satisfied that the parties will leave "shortly after the marriage" - r.43.

78 That the marriage was not entered into primarily for immigration purposes, that it has not been terminated and that the parties intend to live together permanently. The Secretary of State has no discretion to favour an applicant who does not satisfy r.126 - Aksoy, Times, 29 October 1984.

79 Per Lord Lane L.C.J., Mahmud Khan [1983] Q.B. 790, at p.793; see further, Anseereeganoo [1981] Imm. A.R. 30, Class-Peter [1981] Imm. A.R. 154.

80 Junior Home Office Minister, 'Eastern Eye', Channel 4 T.V., 10 January 1984.

81 Junior Home Office Minister, H.C. Debs. 18 November 1982, col. 238. At that time the Rules affected fiances more severely than husbands. Thus, in 1982 in the Indian subcontinent 90 out of 280 decisions on husbands were refused as opposed to 610 of 1220 on fiances - H.C. Debs. 27 January 1984, col. 710.

82 Times, 12 April 1985.

83 Per Forbes J., transcript.

84 Ibid.

85 Internal guidance to e.c.os cited in the C.R.E. Report (1985), at para. 5.9.10. For a further excellent example of such guidance supplementing the Rules, see para. 5.9.7.

86 Ibid., para. 5.9.14; and see para. 5.9.13 for the areas of questioning.

87 See 'Families Divided, Sheep and Goats', Owers, C.I.O. Publishing (1984).

88 See C.R.E. Report (1985), Table 5.3(c) and H.C. Debs. 20 December 1984, col. 538. Moreover, it now applies to wives and fiancees (see below).

89 "360/Husband" which indicates that the holder is subject to a 12 months' limitation.

90 See the case cited in the Guardian, 8 February 1984.

91 E.g. Khan [1983] Q.B. 790; Mohd Malik [1981] Imm. A.R. 134.

92 Unlike the 1977 Rules (H.C. 239) which spoke of "normally", see Sandal [1981] Imm. A.R. 95.

93 As conducive to the public good; for use of the power in these circumstances, see Malik [1981] Imm. A.R. 134; Ullah, [1982] Imm. A.R. 124; Osama [1978] Imm. A.R. 8.

94 H.O. Minister in evidence to H.A.C. Subcommittee 7th Report (1981-2), H.C. 526, Q.48.

95 Ibid, Q.82, 83.

96 Abdulaziz, Balkandali and Cabales v U.K.

97 An amendment to the Rules was placed before Parliament on 15 July 1985 and debated on 23 July.

98 Cmnd. 9544, Tables 3 and 13.

99 Cf. the broad Ministerial discretion in Australia - Unlugenc v Minister for Immigration and Ethnic Affairs (1983) 43 A.L.R. 569; the U.S. determination to root out fraudulent entry via marriage in the 'Gigolo' Act of 1937, 50 Stat. 164.

100 Cf. the argument of the Select Committee (1978) para. 160.

101 Evidence to H.A.C. Subcommittee, supra, Q.42.

102 Not least through the help of the law, note Hirani v Hirani [1983] 4 F.L.R. 232, which adopted a more liberal interpretation of duress so as to justify a decree of nullity.

103 Ibid, Q.82, 83.

104 Thus matching the position in the U.S., see 8 U.S.C. para. 1101(a)(15)(K).

105 Mr. Ronald Butt, Times, 28 October 1982.

106 Report, para. 143.

107 Ibid, para. 172.

108 A small extension of the reasoning in the East African Asians case would have produced a breach of Art. 3 (inhuman

treatment).

109 Cmnd. 9544, Table 7.

110 Which formerly included the use of X-rays; see chapter 4 and Iqbal Haque [1974] Imm. A.R. 51, Miah [1970] Imm. A.R. 185.

111 Cmnd. 1716, paras. 26-28.

112 Generally, he is not included, e.g. s.2(3)(a); see Crew [1982] Imm. A.R. 94, and discussion by Robinson (1984) Statute L.Rev. 113.

113 Thus reflecting Alam [1973] Imm. A.R. 79, though that case reached this conclusion on the interpretation of r.38, which had left 'step-parent' undefined (Cmnd. 4298).

114 Cf. Malik [1970-72] Imm. A.R. 37, which rejected an adoption which was not recognised by Mohamedan law, and Rafiq [1970-72] Imm. A.R. 167, which similarly required an adoption by court order for the purposes of entry under the Commonwealth Immigrants Act 1968.

115 S.I. No. 19, made under s.4(3) Adoption Act 1968.

116 Re Valentines Settlement [1965] Ch. 831, though the common law is notoriously vague here; see Dicey and Morris, The Conflict of Laws, 10th Ed. Ch. 16, part 3.

117 On analogy with marriage (Vervaeke v Smith [1983] 1 A.C. 145), such an adoption is likely to be legal in family law terms and the courts unlikely to use public policy to strike it down, yet insufficient for immigration purposes.

118 If (1) there is a genuine intention to adopt; (2) the child's welfare in the U.K. is assured; (3) a U.K. court would be likely to grant an adoption order in such circumstances and (4) one of the adopting parents is domiciled here.

119 Asif Mahmood Khan [1984] 3 W.L.R. 1337. He cannot therefore incorporate additional criteria without first changing the concessionary policy.

120 See Guardian, 7 March 1985, and the reported comments of the Director of the British Agencies for Adoption and Fostering.

121 See Re H, (1981) 12 Fam. Law 172.

122 For a neat example of the difficulties, see the case of

Talish Khan, H.C. Debs., 26 January 1979, col. 992 where, *inter alia*, the Home Office remained unconvinced of the Revenue's certainty as to the claimed relationship. Press and Parliamentary pressure may in fact be a useful last resort for applicants.

123 R.42 of H.C. 394 (1980) now r.46; endorsing Arshad [1977] Imm. A.R. 19.

124 (a) if both parents are settled in the United Kingdom; or

(b) if both parents are on the same occasion admitted for settlement; or

(c) if one parent is settled in the United Kingdom and the other is on the same occasion admitted for settlement; or

(d) if one parent is dead and the other parent is settled in the United Kingdom or is on the same occasion admitted for settlement; or

(e) if one parent is settled in the United Kingdom or is on the same occasion admitted for settlement and has had the sole responsibility for the child's upbringing; or

(f) if one parent or a relative other than a parent is settled or accepted for settlement in the United Kingdom and there are serious and compelling family or other considerations which make exclusion undesirable - for example, where the other parent is physically or mentally incapable of looking after the child - and suitable arrangements have been made for the child's care.

125 Pinnock [1974] Imm. A.R. 22.

126 (e) and (f) necessarily imply that only one parent is in the U.K.

127 Waheed Akhtar [1981] Imm. A.R. 109.

128 [1973] Imm. A.R. 37.

129 Guardianship of Minors Act 1971.

130 Matrimonial Causes Act 1973.

131 Cf. the earlier rules (Cmnd. 3830, r.40 (1968)) - "Where the marriage has been dissolved and custody awarded to the parent in the U.K. it may also be appropriate to admit the children."

132 See Mohamed Arif [1968] Ch. 643, Re S (minors) (1980) 11 Fam. Law 55, but cf. Re H (1981) 12 Fam. Law 172.

133 E.g. Sloley [1973] Imm. A.R. 54.

[134] Martin [1978] Imm. A.R. 100.

[135] Ibid.

[136] Sloley, supra; Emmanuel [1972] Imm. A.R. 69.

[137] McGillivary [1970] Imm A.R. 63.

[138] Williams [1972] Imm. A.R. 207; Pusey [1972] Imm. A.R. 240. For the internal instructions to e.c.os on the interpretation of 'sole responsibility', see C.R.E. Report (1985), para. 5.5.1.

[139] See C.R.E. Report (1985), para. 5.5.2.

[140] R.40, Cmnd. 3830.

[141] R.43(f), H.C. 79.

[142] Campbell [1972] Imm. A.R. 115: Ravat [1974] Imm. A.R. 79: Dixon TH/1336/75 (843) (1976).

[143] Howard [1972] Imm. A.R. 93: Williams [1972] Imm. A.R. 207.

[144] Thompson [1981] Imm. A.R. 148.

[145] Needham [1973] Imm. A.R. 75.

[146] Pinnock [1977] Imm. A.R. 4; another gloss by the I.A.T.

[147] Holmes [1975] Imm. A.R. 20.

[148] E.g. Thompson, supra.

[149] R.28, Cmnd. 1716 (1962).

[150] Cf. the flexible and more generous E.E.C. provisions. Under art. 10(2) of regulation 1612/68 the worker and spouse may admit their "descendants who are under the age of 21 or are dependants". Cf. Canada which permits "any children who, by reason of age or disability, are, in the opinion of an immigration officer, mainly dependent upon [the parent]", s.2 Immigration Act 1976.

[151] Cf. r.40 of 4298 which specifically included widows (1970).

[152] Bernard [1976] Imm. A.R. 7 (maintenance from a putative father); Cuffy [1976] Imm. A.R. 66.

[153] Cf. Brown [1976] Imm. A.R. 119 (son worked on relatives'

farm and thereby earned his 'keep').

154 They include elder siblings (Steward [1978] Imm. A.R. 32; Nadarajan [1976] Imm. A.R. 144) and probably uncles and aunts.

155 Somerzaul [1970] Imm. A.R. 101. Cf. Bernard, supra.

156 Excluding dependants of U.K.P.Hs, Report para. 148.

157 Cmnd. 9544 Table 7; 360 were refused and 1,100 applications were outstanding.

158 Cmnd. 1716, r.30 (1962).

159 Ibid, r.31

160 Cmnd. 1716, r.30, 31.

161 Cmnd. 3830, r.48.

162 Cmnd. 4298, r.42.

163 H.C. 79, r.45, 46 and H.C. 81 (aliens) r.40, 41.

164 H.C. 394, r.48.

165 R.46; the latter requirement of presence endorsing the gloss required by Manek [1978] Imm. A.R. 131.

166 See Appendix to Government Response to Select Committee (1978) for the method of assessment, Cmnd. 7287.

167 Patel [1970] Imm. A.R. 227.

168 Bagas [1978] Imm. A.R. 85.

169 This follows from the I.A.T's refusal in Bagas, supra, to extend the more liberal rule, now r.50 (which specifically includes adoptive parents for the purposes of admitting children) to the rest of the Rules. Cf. 1968 Rules for aliens in which adoptive parents were specifically covered, Cmnd. 3830 r.45.

170 Nisa [1979-80] Imm. A.R. 20.

171 Phillips [1973] Imm. A.R. 47.

172 R.53 offers a slender chance to those who have remarried.

173 Contrast the approach in Chavda [1978] Imm. A.R. 40, below.

[174] E.g. Hosenball [1977] 3 All E.R. 452.

[175] E.g. Hasan [1976] Imm. A.R. 28, Shukar [1981] Imm. A.R. 58.

[176] Grenade [1978] Imm. A.R. 143.

[177] Zaman [1973] Imm. A.R. 71.

[178] Hasan, supra.

[179] Supra.

[180] Taj Bibi [1981] Imm. A.R. 62.

[181] Bastiampillai [1983] 2 All E.R. 844, per Glidewell J, at p.851.

[182] Ibid.

[183] E.g. r.48 cmnd. 3830.

[184] R.48, H.C. 394.

[185] Ram [1978] Imm. A.R. 123.

[186] Sibal [1973] Imm. A.R. 50.

[187] Kaur [1979-80] Imm. A.R. 76 and compare Jan (1983) N.L.J. p.744, "e.g. companionship, affection, discussion of problems and courses of action, advice and physical help".

[188] Ram, supra.

[189] Per Hodgson J. in Dadibhai (1983), unreported, LEXIS transcript, and see Bastiampillai, supra.

[190] R.30, Cmnd. 1716.

[191] Para. 149.

[192] It remains to be seen whether the concepts of "family", art. 8, and "degrading treatment" art. 3 of the European Convention can encompass this situation. For arguments that they do see Home Affairs Subcommittee H.C. 434, p.40.

[193] Cf. Cmnd. 1716, r.31 which specified 60 for men, 55 for women.

[194] Overruling Bashir [1978] Imm. A.R. 77.

195 Remarkably, on its face the extension does not cover parents (save widowed mothers), though in practice they may be included.

196 E.g. to a sister-in-law, Kaur [1979-80] Imm. A.R. 76, cf. Cmnd. 1716 (1962) r.31 which mentioned more distant relatives such as cousins.

197 Though blindness per se may not suffice, Bashir, supra.

198 E.g. the facts of Sacha [1973] Imm. A.R. 5 where the e.c.o. decided that there were compassionate circumstances but they were not strong enough, cf. Levy [1978] Imm. A.R. 119.

199 See Gheithy [1981] Imm. A.R. 113. This requirement originally only applied to aliens (e.g. r.48 Cmnd. 4298) but in 1973 (r.46 H.C. 79) appeared in the Rules for Commonwealth citizens.

200 H.C. 79, r.46 (1973).

201 "Country" means the place of his ordinary residence, Levy, supra.

202 Mukhopadhyay [1975] Imm. A.R. 42.

203 See Sindhu [1978] Imm. A.R. 147; Kaur, supra.

204 Evidence, p.5.

205 H.C. Debs. 20 February 1980, col. 187 ff.

206 Cf. the East African Asians case, where the European Commission of Human Rights suggested that the separation of spouses may be "inhuman" (art. 3). It is a narrow distinction if this does not apply to a slightly extended concept of the "family".

7 TEMPORARY IMMIGRANTS

> Another method of evading the regulations or escaping the
> restrictions is the "student" dodge. The ease with which
> foreigners have come here under this category is
> remarkable. Moreover even when they are in this country
> the watch kept upon them is so lax that many of them
> remain permanently and take employment in breach of their
> undertaking on entry.[1]

The following categories of persons consist of entrants who
are admitted in a temporary capacity (workers, students and
visitors). For all, the overriding condition that the
applicant be able to maintain and accommodate himself and any
dependants must be satisfied.

A. WORK

(1) Employment
Employment protection remains the rationale of immigration
control. In turn, it generates

(a) often desperate attempts by immigrants to evade that
    control;
(b) equally determined efforts by host States to detect
    evasion and
(c) in particular the careful vetting of secondary
    immigrants (dependants) to ensure that dependence is
    not used as a ruse to admit workers (e.g. by the
    admission of bogus teenage 'sons').

The issue of foreign labour is certain to excite a variety of
emotions in the indigenous population of the receiving
countries. When the influx becomes too high for their comfort,
be it related to the linen trade of the 14th century or the
hotel and shipping industries of the 1970s, opposition is
galvanised. A chorus of denunciation is raised in economic

self-interest, be it overt or concealed behind the 'little England' stance of racial and cultural identity. As such, it transcends international[2] and political boundaries. To the right wing elements the economic advantages of cheap labour are sooner or later outweighed by, as they see it, the cultural and racial disadvantages. To the left idealism is sooner or later displaced by self-interest:[3] employment protection is the litmus test of its supposed international outlook. The attitude within the U.K. to imported labour has now reached one of hawkish proportions with very careful observation kept on the few remaining opportunities for it,[4] even though the total numbers involved are very small.[5]

Against this background, it might be thought that the economic disadvantages of immigration would have been soundly established. Yet the Department of Employment in 1977 concluded that the conflicting theories of advantages and disadvantages had not been resolved.[6] There is no clear evidence that immigration has 'ruined' the economy or caused unemployment. Instead, it would seem that controls have been instituted because of fears of coloured immigration and its cultural and racial consequences, with unproved economic fears acting as an official excuse. In this regard the following facts are significant:

(a) The majority of available work permits are given to aliens rather than Commonwealth citizens;[7]
(b) Two exceptions to the work permit scheme exist primarily for the benefit of the old Commonwealth (those with U.K. ancestry, r.29, and young Commonwealth Citizens seeking a working holiday, r.30);
(c) Only N. America and Europe supply the few seasonal workers required and the latter alone supplies au pairs;
(d) Membership of the E.E.C. requires freedom of movement and, though the influx has been modest and steady,[8] it is clear that if workers are required it is the E.E.C. which will oblige in the future.

Countries may limit immigration across the board by crude numerical restrictions when the level of entry is seen to be too great.[9] Others seek to correlate immigration to the number and kinds of jobs they require.[10] At the beginning of the century the U.K. adopted a policy for aliens which could fulfil either function. For the Commonwealth, the former function was initially chosen (Commonwealth Immigrants Act 1962) but the latter has subsequently prevailed, as it has for aliens (Immigration Act 1971). However, the feature of U.K. control is the secrecy of this development. Policy has been 'hived off' to the Department of Employment with a marked lack of public discussion of what industry and unions require from foreign labour. This has been achieved through the almost wholesale delegation of responsibility for work permits to that Department.[11] The dual controls of quantity and quality then operate through a simple and effective work permit scheme. If demand occurs in a particular industry (as happened in the hotel and catering industries in the 1970s), the supply can be resumed in a carefully calculated and mercenary manner.

For most of this century, the employment of aliens has been controlled. Thus, by 1962 work permits were required from the then Ministry of Labour.[12] The Commonwealth was brought into line in 1962 by a three tier system of permits, called vouchers.[13] The White Paper of 1965 then abolished category C vouchers and cut the annual quota for A and B vouchers to 8,500.[14] The Immigration Act 1971 formally recognised the reality of strict control by replacing vouchers with work permits. The Home Secretary set out the ensuing policy:

> These work permits will not be issued if suitable resident labour is available or if the wages and conditions offered by the employer be less favourable than those obtaining in his area for similar work.[15]

Procedurally, the onus lies on the prospective employer to apply to the Department of Employment for a permit (Form OW1) and to convince the Department of its necessity. The requisite conditions are:

(a) The work must have special characteristics which require foreign labour.[16]

(b) The employer must show that there is no suitable local labour by advertising the post in the appropriate local, national and E.E.C. media,[17] for at least 3 weeks before applying for a permit, and guarantee that, therefore, no resident will be displaced or excluded by the employment of a foreigner. For this purpose, 'local labour' includes applications from E.E.C. nationals. He must show further that the vacancies cannot be filled by an internal promotion or transfer.

(c) The wages must not be lower than those paid to members of the indigenous population. This condition has its roots in the opposition to 'sweated' labour which surfaced as early as the fifteenth century and more recently at the end of the last century.[18]

(d) The minimum qualifying age is usually 23, the maximum is 54 and experience in the employment is essential. The work must in fact require a professional qualification, skill or experience.

These conditions are in themselves rigorous, but the immigrant must also satisfy visa requirements. This means that an immigration officer can override a permit and refuse entry if he discovers a 'good reason' for doing so (r.28). This would include his assessment of the applicant's inability to perform the job or his belief that the permit was obtained by misrepresentation.

Renewal of employment and change of employment

A salient feature of the 1980 Rules was the general prohibition on immigrants who have entered in one capacity from changing to employed status.[19] Thus, for example, students are expected to leave the U.K. on completion of their studies. As for renewal, work permits are normally granted for 12 months in the first instance and can only be renewed (r.116)

    (a) with the support of the employer - a form of tied labour, or
    (b) with the approval of the Department of Employment.

If the job is changed it must usually involve the same type of work as was initially approved. If the applicant has not yet found approved employment, his case for extension may still be considered "in the light of all the relevant circumstances".[20]

Department of Employment

The Immigration Act 1971 makes no reference to the Department of Employment but in the Immigration Rules the Home Office has followed the earlier arrangement for aliens and has delegated complete responsibility for work permits to it. The Department's decision to refuse a permit is invariably final;[21] its discretion is absolute and all-pervasive in employment matters.[22] For example, foreign student health workers fall under the aegis of local health authorities, but, at the conclusion of their training, it is the Department that must approve their employment.

    A cardinal feature of this 'nip and tuck' arrangement is that a Department's decision unlike that of the Home Office is unappealable within the immigration system.[23] The logic is simple. The Home Office has delegated employment decisions to the Department, the latter is not subject to the Immigration Rules and, therefore, there is no right of appeal. The delegation has been upheld, first because the Rules permit it[24] - a self-justifying argument - and, second, because it does not transfer from the Home Office the power to give leave to remain in the U.K., because, even if the Department of Employment approves a work permit, the Home Office can override it.[25] Strictly speaking this is correct, but in practice the power is surrendered since, in the reverse situation, the Home Office will not override the Department's refusal of a permit.[26]

    This arrangement is typically British. Decision-making was transferred many years ago to another Government Department whose decisions are unsupervised and surrounded by secrecy. Subsequent Rules take note of the practice and are endorsed by the courts. From a legal standpoint, it is highly unsatisfactory, for delegation needs specific enabling powers and, since the Rules are not statutory,[27] it is prima facie unlawful. It is saved because of the hybrid nature of the Rules and the willingness of the courts to uphold them. In Pearson,[28] the Court of Appeal was apparently concerned at this latitude given to the Department of Employment and left open the possibility of judicial review. Since the Department's decision is a necessary precondition to a work permit, it would admittedly be possible to challenge the reasonableness of a decision but the chances of adducing sufficient evidence to overturn what is a highly discretionary and sensitive decision, are slim. As to the argument that the Home Secretary has fettered his discretion by agreeing to abide by the Department's rejection of a permit, the Court of Appeal reached the highly dubious conclusion that the words 'should be refused' in the Rules are not mandatory but reserve to the Home Secretary a discretion 'to make an exception'.[29]

Permitted Exceptions

1. R.29 reflects the concept of patriality by entitling a Commonwealth citizen, who can trace a grandparent born in the U.K., to entry clearance without the necessity of a work permit. In abstract, the Rule is sentimental and understandable. In the context of the whole Act, it neatly illustrates the pervading imperial and, in practical terms, racist effect of the law, since the exception by its terms predominantly favours citizens of the old Commonwealth.[30] Thus, in 1984 4,450 Commonwealth entrants were admitted for settlement on this basis, yet only 50 came from Africa and 30 from the Indian sub-continent.[31]
2. Working holidays, r.30 (the admission of young Commonwealth citizens who are enjoying an extended holiday and who wish to take incidental and temporary employment). This concession similarly favours, in practice, young people from the old Commonwealth. On the other hand, it is hedged by carefully drawn safeguards:

    (a) The employment must be incidental to a holiday, not vice versa.[32] The entrant must therefore have financial resources to begin with, which he hopes to supplement by employment from time to time, he must have the means to pay for a return ticket and must not lead the immigration officer to believe that he will resort to public funds.
    (b) The 1980 Rules[33] reduced the maximum period of stay from 5 to 2 years.

(c) Only applicants between the ages of 17 and 25 are eligible.

3. Au pairs between 17 and 25 (r.26).[34] Before 1970, there was no specific provision for au pairs, and so reliance had to be placed on the last mentioned exception. The current provision is again racist, but this time explicit since it is specifically for the benefit of applicants from Western Europe.[35] That it is a European tradition cannot absolve it from the charge that 'it is a nasty little provision'.[36]

4. A miscellaneous category dictated by diplomatic considerations, religious tolerance, practicality, reciprocity and, until recently, in the medical field, by the U.K.'s needs (r.31, 33, 117). However, although a work permit is not required entry clearance must be obtained. The National Health Service has for long relied heavily upon the import of overseas doctors. There are currently about 18,000. They too have had to face increasing internal demands for tighter controls as the U.K. has become self-sufficient in doctors and dentists. Under a scheme introduced by the General Medical Council in 1979 such doctors were given the opportunity of limited registration to train in the U.K. for 5 years. In order to gain full registration thereafter they needed 2 years' experience as registrars. Yet, with cuts in the N.H.S. and unemployment amongst doctors, the opportunities for appointment as registrars and thereby of remaining in the U.K. were sharply reduced. In the meantime overseas doctors have in general been used to fill the least popular jobs.[37] Disquiet in the native medical professions over the possible surplus of doctors and dentists led in 1985 to an abrupt[38] and decisive change in the rules for entry of non-E.E.C. applicants. Thus, (a) foreign doctors and dentists who want to be general practitioners must satisfy the rules for the self-employed (see below). These require, inter alia, an investment of at least £150,000 in the practice and that there be "a genuine need" for the applicant's services (r.35). (b) Those who seek employment (principally in the N.H.S.) need work permits. (c) Entry for training is allowed without a work permit for 12 months (renewable annually to a maximum of 4 years) provided that the trainee satisfies the i.o. that he intends to leave the U.K. at the end of his training (r.25A and 110A) and that he registers with the police. This episode not only illustrates many of the hallmarks of immigration control but also reveals the ruthless efficiency with which that control can now be exercised.

5. Writers and artists, but not entertainers[39] such as popular singers, who need work permits and whose visits are carefully monitored by U.K. trades unions[40] (r.39, 121).

Comment

The work permit scheme is a rigorous method of control for the immigration of non-E.E.C. workers. The additional and simple safeguard of making it an offence for an employer to engage an immigrant unlawfully, an option urged by the E.E.C. Commission[41] and adopted in some other countries,[42] has so far been resisted. Given the existing, informal mechanisms of internal control, it is unlikely that such a change would herald dramatic success in the detection of unlawful employment such as to outweigh the consequential unease which would be felt by ethnic communities at yet further supervision. Liberal reform is out of the question. Unemployment has too great a hold on political and public opinion and, in any event, the E.E.C. is seen in official eyes as the source of any future labour requirements. Indeed, the current system is a neat and striking contrast with the reality of freedom of movement which the E.E.C. Treaty demands, and illustrates how strict U.K. immigration control has 'come of age' since the liberality of the 1950s.

(2) Business

Businessmen and the self-employed are usually economically welcome in host countries, and in the U.K., for many years, were given more favourable treatment than employees.[43] The U.K. still allows them to enter but the gradual tightening of the Rules has made the process far less welcoming.[44] Whereas the pre-1980 Rules were couched in general terms and depended on the totality of the circumstances,[45] the current requirements are detailed and severe:

(a) Entry clearance and its accompanying rigours must be overcome.[46]
(b) The applicant's commitment to the business must be genuine in terms of need for his services, his responsibility for the business and his proposed effort. For this purpose he must invest, since 1980, a fixed figure.[47]
(c) The money must be under the control of the applicant and not, for example, that of his family[48] and the control must be direct and exclusive. He cannot therefore rely on a cultural tradition of family support overseas: ready cash is the test.[49] On the other hand, it is possible for a family in the U.K. to send the money abroad (a possibility facilitated by the easing of exchange control restrictions since 1980). In that case, the overriding requirements of r.13 (e.g. that there has been no fraud or change in circumstances, see chapter 3) can assume importance in detecting collusion and lack of candour.[50]
(d) The applicant's economic venture must create new jobs for people settled here.

(e) The applicant must demonstrate that he is obtaining a real share in the business (i.e. through investment and profits). It must not be disguised employment.[51]

(f) On extension of leave to stay, vetting of these requirements is continued.[52] For all these criteria, conclusive evidence in the nature of bank statements, company accounts and forecasts are needed.

The scientific estimation of a person's financial means and prospects in the Rules of 1980 and 1983 makes them easier to interpret[53] and avoids the previous guesswork,[54] but in the very process of specification the criteria have become very demanding and illustrate the rigour of current immigration control.[55] The previous liberality accorded to middle class businessmen has been affected by that same economic fear of immigration which has affected the admission of employees.[56]

B. STUDENTS

The pursuit of scholarship has always been recognised worldwide as a legitimate ground for allowing immigration and in this regard the U.K., with its imperial history, has assumed a prominent role. Many countries, both within and without the Commonwealth, have looked to the U.K. to fill the gaps in their educational systems.[57] Indeed in 1982 the U.K. ranked fifth in the league table of host countries for overseas students.[58] Over half of those in the U.K. came from the Middle East and Asia and one quarter from States with less than 5 million inhabitants.[59] In all, the Third World and Commonwealth accounted for over 80%.[60]

Education is a small field in which the U.K. can, at a modest price, assist other and, notably, developing countries. In return, it can reap intangible but significant benefits educationally, culturally and, in the long term, perhaps, diplomatically and commercially.[61] Moreover, since time limits are attached to a student's stay, this area is not one of primary immigration. On the other hand, students appear in the overall immigration figures and, for Governments who wish to impose strict control, they are an obvious and easy target. The history of the Rules relating to them is, indeed, a microcosm of the progressively tougher attitude to immigration generally. For example, the U.K's concern to maintain its paternal role as educator of the Commonwealth was reflected in the 1962 Rules which proclaimed that "the Government are anxious to welcome Commonwealth citizens coming to this country for study"[62] and that, for those to whom it applied, "an entry clearance will be readily issued".[63] By 1970, the "anxiety" had disappeared and the Government could merely "welcome" prospective students.[64] Today's Rules portray no hints of friendliness but instead contain robust and tightly drawn criteria. With each set of Rules, the hurdles of entry have been progressively heightened and the real or potential loopholes closed. It should not be assumed, however, that today's restrictions on foreign students are the preserve of the Home Office and the Rules. On the contrary, responsibility for control is shared between a number of Government Departments - the Treasury, the Foreign Office, especially the Overseas Aid Department, the Departments of Employment, of Education and Science, of Trade and Industry (in terms of awards and industrial training) and the Home Office. This is because the main deterrent to overseas students in recent years has been financial contraints.

A higher fee for overseas students in further education than for home students was first adopted in 1967 and in 1979 the gap was widened considerably. In line with its policies on public spending, the Government announced that for the 1979-80 academic session fees for overseas students were to be increased by 30% so as to reflect the full costs of tuition.[65] The number of overseas students in higher and further education fell sharply, from 88,000 in 1979-80 to 55,600 in 1983-84.[66] It would appear that developing countries, both Commonwealth and non-Commonwealth, suffered most.[67] Whilst there are other factors which can explain the fall, such as the world economic depression and exchange rates, it seems clear that the introduction of full cost fees played a major role. It is significant to note again the bipartisan responsibility, for although the Conservative Government wielded the sharp axe in 1979, its Labour predecessor had already cleared a path by introducing a differential fee in 1967 and raising it in 1976. Like other areas of immigration the U.K's attitude to foreign students has been shaped by a lack of coherent planning - many were allowed to enter, abuses were controlled and then indiscriminate (in this case, financial) barriers were erected.

Conditions of entry
The 1962 Act expressly excluded from control those wishing to enter for study and the ensuing Rules adopted a relaxed approach with no reference to the financial means of the student and no prohibition on vacation employment. In the following 20 years, the determined efforts of Governments to curb all loopholes in immigration and the evasion, or at least belief that there was evasion, of control by bogus students have produced narrow Rules. For example, before 1980 visitors to the U.K. were allowed to apply for leave to remain in a different capacity such as a student, but since 1980 "persons admitted as visitors or ... for other temporary purposes have no claim to remain here for any other purpose" (r.99). Essentially the Rules permit the entry of a bona fide student for a course of study which will occupy a substantial part of his time, without recourse to public funds or employment.

284

Subject to maintenance requirements, his dependants will be admitted.

Entry clearance was earmarked in 1962 only for those who had not yet finalised their study arrangements. In 1970, it was said to be preferable for all students and in 1973 and the current Rules,[68] it is mandatory for all.[69] To gain clearance the applicant must establish:

(1) A genuine purpose of study - subjective element

Since the Labour Government's White Paper of 1965, the Rules have concentrated on the need "to prevent people admitted on the pretext of a ... course of study from obtaining permanent settlement".[70] Consequently, the applicant must satisfy the entry clearance officer (e.c.o.) that, at the time of the application,[71] his real intention is to pursue a course of study and not, for example, to enter employment in the U.K. Mere suspicion by the e.c.o. is insufficient to warrant refusal[72] but will inevitably prompt a detailed examination not merely of the applicant but also his family connections with the U.K. and even his prospects in his own country. Difficulties can arise if the applicant quite genuinely intends to study but also intends to seek employment in the U.K. once the study has ended. The earlier Rules referred to the "primary purpose" of study[73] and this led to difficulties similar to those faced by husbands and fiances (see chapter 6).[74] Applicants were in a perilous position before an e.c.o.- if they expressed interest in remaining here at the conclusion of studies, the e.c.o's suspicions would be roused and a searching examination would follow: if they concealed such interest and it emerged later during investigation, attempted deception would be the e.c.o's automatic conclusion.

Since 1973 the position has been partly simplified, to the detriment of the applicant, by the omission of "primary purpose"; instead, refusal will follow if the e.c.o. is not satisfied that the applicant will "leave the country on completion"[75] of the course. Thus, however genuine the prospective student be, where the e.c.o. asks him what he will do on completion of the course, any reference to hopes of staying are likely to sink the application.[76] Moreover, the above-mentioned dilemma remains - he may still harbour hopes of an extension of stay, yet must not deceive the officer.[77]

(2) Objective genuineness

The e.c.o. must be satisfied that the applicant's abilities and background make him a genuine student.[78] Cases have isolated various factors:-

(a) The applicant's economic and social background in relation to the proposed course. As the Immigration Appeals Tribunal cynically observed, a rickshaw puller wanting to study Egyptian scarabs in the British Museum would immediately arouse suspicion.[79]

(b) The financial means at his disposal and whether the course fees have already been paid.

(c) Whether he holds a return ticket.

(d) The presence of relatives in the U.K., for they may be a motive to try to stay permanently.

(e) Whether the applicant has sought to attend similar courses in his own country.

(f) The employment prospects for the applicant on return to his country of origin. The pursuit of knowledge for its own sake may be unobjectionable for a wealthy student who has no incentive to remain in the U.K.[80] but for more modest applicants the e.c.o. will enquire whether the proposed course will be recognised by local employers and thereby economically useful to the applicant.[81] For this purpose he has a discretion to discover local conditions and his assessment, as the 'man on the spot', will be difficult to overturn on appeal.

(g) Academic ability. Whilst it is clear that the educational institution has the prerogative of assessing candidates and that the e.c.o. ought not to usurp it, the prerogative does not prevent him from challenging the applicant's general academic standard in view of the possibility of bogus applicants[82] and bogus institutions[83] and of the frequently unreliable aptitude and linguistic tests which bona fide institutions have employed.[84] The arrangement is defensible only as long as the e.c.o. confines his scrutiny to the glaringly doubtful cases.

In addition, internal guidance alerts e.c.os to various circumstances[85] the general requirement of r.13 (see chapter 4) must be satisfied so that deception or concealment of material facts such as the presence of relatives in the U.K.,[86] can justify refusal. Similarly forbidden by r.13 is the ruse of entering as a visitor with the intention of applying for student status at a later date.[87] More generally, since 1980 the Rules have prevented immigrants from switching categories, thus, for example, a non-E.E.C. immigrant employee cannot subsequently change to student status.

(3) The Course

Under the earlier Rules, the educational institution was loosely described and, wittingly or not, overseas applicants could find themselves students at bogus, private colleges offering, for example, secretarial or 'English language courses at a college in the south of England'.[88] Since 1973 the institution must be recognised as bona fide by the Home Office. The British Council offers a convenient list of colleges which are likely to meet with approval but the Home Office retains the ultimate and untrammelled power of vetting. Consequently the 'college' has no formal redress against non-recognition.[89] The proposed course of study must 'occupy the whole or a substantial part of' the applicant's time (r.21). Since 1962, 'As a general rule' the applicant must propose to spend 'not less than 15 hours a week in organised daytime study' and the institution may be called upon to confirm this. The Secretary of State clearly retains a discretion[90] and, provided the applicant can show that the level of work is intensive and substantial, in terms of field work or private research,[91] many post-graduate courses for example, will qualify. Correspondence courses per se will not suffice (r.22), unless forming part of a wider organised instruction;[92] nor will training, such as a solicitor's articles of clerkship.[93]

Problems may arise for the applicant who wishes to attend not one but a succession of institutions, for example, a child of 8 who intends to proceed from school to university before returning abroad. R.21 requires that he be accepted for a 'course of study', in this example, at a school and r.22 excludes him if he does not intend to leave at the completion 'of it'. If therefore r.22 is confined to the initial course of study at school, the fact that he intends to stay on for higher education will lead to the refusal of an entry clearance. This narrow and literally correct interpretation of the Rules was that adopted by the Home Office[94] until a majority of the Court of Appeal, no doubt influenced by the need to encourage overseas students to public schools, ruled that the 'course of study' in r.22 was wider than that in r.21.[95] It entailed a coherent programme of education which could include more than one institution provided that the applicant could reasonably be expected to complete it.

Since education in the U.K. is still seen as desirable by many nationalities and since the educational system in turn benefits from the admission of overseas students, the decision is an encouraging one. In practice, at school level, it only helps applicants from wealthy families, but its effect is more widespread at the higher levels of education. Thus, applicants to a university who ultimately wish to proceed to a more advanced or practically orientated course will benefit. However, the genuineness of applications will always remain a hurdle. A wealthy applicant or one whose relatives, as in Kharrazi, are able to offer a motive or a bond that he will return after his education will still have a clear advantage. Poorer applicants, with, in Home Office eyes, a greater incentive to stay in the U.K. run the risk of planning a lengthy education and at the same time being penalised for their honesty by detailed interrogation.

In legal terms, the decision in Kharrazi is a rare victory for immigrants and neatly illustrates

(a) how before the I.A.T. the Rules are binding, yet not before the courts and

(b) how easily the courts can modify the interpretation of those Rules if they choose to do so.

Educational institutions enjoy almost a free hand in the process of selecting overseas candidates. Many rely upon British Council supervision of language tests. However, educational or other requirements which are arbitrary and discriminate against foreign applicants and which cannot be objectively justified may infringe the Race Relations Act 1976.[96]

(4) Maintenance

The possibility of a student supplementing his income by employment during vacations was removed in the 1973 Rules, and the current requirements (r.21) that the student be able to maintain and accommodate himself without recourse to 'public funds' were added in 1980. An applicant must produce clear and full evidence (e.g. the production of bank statements) of satisfactory means either under his or his family's direct control.[97] Consequently, the fact that fees for the proposed course have already been paid is very relevant.[98]

Exceptional admissions

Under r.24, the immigration officer has a wide discretion[99] to admit someone temporarily who manages to show that he genuinely wants to be a student and will leave at the end of his studies (added in 1983) but who cannot at present satisfy the preceding detailed requirements. The applicant can apply subsequently to regularise his position when the requirements have been met.

Dependants

They are a further example of the tightening restrictions in 1980 since a wife and children can only be admitted 'if they can be maintained and accommodated without recourse to public funds', (r.25). Furthermore, the gap whereby such dependants could take employment and help to maintain the student has been closed and the prohibition on taking employment is mandatory. Sex equality has never applied here. The wife, but not a husband, of a student qualifies as a dependant and it is clear that the Sex Discrimination Act 1975 is of no avail.[100]

The strictness of these Rules, the rigour with which they are applied coupled with the stiff increase in overseas fees in 1979 and the inability of students' dependants to take employment mean that money represents the critical hurdle to applicants who lack real wealth or their Government's sponsorship.

Stay

A student is allowed to remain for an 'appropriate period'[101] depending upon the length of the proposed course and his means (r.24). In view of the ever increasing job shortage for home-based students, the immigrant's opportunity of securing employment to bolster his income, by, for example, night work or vacation employment was removed in the 1973 Rules. More significantly, his dependants have been similarly denied, since 1980, by a restriction on their employment. Their position can be parlous. For example, if a wife is beaten by her student husband, social or religious custom may force her to submit in silence. Legally, proceedings for domestic injunctions or divorce will deprive her of the right to remain, the right being dependent on the husband. De facto separation will normally be impossible because of her similar financial dependency and, in any case, entitlement to state benefits is specifically prohibited by the Rules.

Renewal of student status

This is permissible provided that the applicant continues to satisfy the conditions for entry, in particular those relating to accommodation and self-maintenance (r.107).[102] Although the educational institution is under no duty to submit details of the student's attendance record, the student must.[103] The Rules are silent as to how the applicant's academic competence should be assessed. The I.A.T. has filled the gap since "the students' rules presuppose that a student's qualifications are adequate for the course he seeks to take" and thus, "prolonged lack of examination success is to be taken into account".[104] The risk of the Secretary of State encroaching upon the prerogative of the educational institution in assessing academic worthiness is clear, though it is also clear that he must have regard to that prerogative and, in cases to date, the academic failure has been so obviously abysmal as not to threaten such encroachment.[105]

Under the 1973 Rules renewal of student status did not oblige the student to prove that he intended to leave the country at the conclusion of his course.[106] The 1980 version filled that gap. R.107 speaks of 'the end of his studies'. In the light of Kharrazi,[107] 'studies' need not be confined to a current course but may be equated to a longer educational programme. If this involves changing courses, a fresh application to the Home Office must be made[108] and, if the students appear to be moving from one course to another 'without any intention of bringing their studies to a close', extension will be refused (r.108). As a guideline, more than four years spent on short courses will lead to refusal. A 'short course' is described as one of less than 2 years or a longer one which is broken off before completion. Thus, after 2 two-year or unfinished courses, extension for a third can be refused. However, this is a general rule and refusal may come

289

earlier, for example, after 3 six-month courses. The only clear precondition in r.108 is that the student 'appears' to the Home Office to be switching courses for the ulterior motive.

Comment

Two observations can be made here. Firstly, the official preoccupation with public expenditure savings has submerged the issue of principle - whether the U.K., as still one of the richest countries of the world, should take more positive and costly steps to resume its earlier and prominent role as a provider of education. Second, recent events show that not even students have escaped the gradual but inexorable tightening of immigration control, with its usual panoply of methods

C. VISITORS

In 1984 roughly 7.7 million passengers (excluding E.E.C. nationals) were admitted to the U.K.[109] The vast majority were temporary visitors for purposes of pleasure or short-term business and were admitted for a period of 6 months. Some require visas, notably those from Eastern countries,[110] and all must show the means both to maintain themselves without recourse to public funds and to pay for their return journey (r.17). Most entered, and will continue to enter, without difficulty. Indeed, in 1984 only 17,355 (excluding E.E.C. nationals) were refused leave to enter. Since, however, recent immigration control has been instituted in order to deal with coloured entrants, it is to them that most attention is paid by the immigration authorities. There is a marked difference between them and visitors from the Old Commonwealth in refusal rates, in those granted admission for less than the usual 6 months[111] and in those detained at ports of entry.[112] In each, the coloured entrants predominate. For example, in 1984 the general figures for admission reveal the following differences in the ratio of passengers refused entry to those admitted:[113]

Passport holder	Total admitted	Total admitted as visitors	Total refused leave to enter
Algeria	21,700	14,400	527
Australia	337,000	229,000	89
Bangladesh	24,400	7,110	432
Canada	440,000	315,000	49
Ghana	34,100	18,300	1,521
India	235,000	124,000	2,044
Nigeria	169,000	85,100	2,707
Pakistan	105,000	58,600	1,415
South Africa	131,000	90,900	55
Sri Lanka	30,200	15,400	474
U.S.A.	2,810,000	1,940,000	738

Quite simply, immigration officers are on the alert for passengers who claim, for example, to be visitors but who are likely to try to stay permanently. The official view that a 'pressure to immigrate' exists in poorer countries means that most of these passengers are coloured entrants. It may be questioned however whether this observable fact can justify the rigour with which officials perform their duties in relation to coloured entrants.[114] Immigration debate is littered[115] with examples of the rigorous welcome which awaits coloured passengers at ports of entry. In its Annual Report for 1982-83, the United Kingdom Immigrants Advisory Service identified three categories of visitors whom it felt were "particularly harshly treated" under the present policies:

[1] It remains exceedingly difficult for elderly dependants of immigrants settled in this country to visit them where the immigration authorities are not convinced that there is an 'incentive to return.' Almost by definition, this means that any elderly grandparent seeking to visit families settled in the United Kingdom from India, Pakistan or Bangladesh, whose standard of living in the Indian sub-continent is not notably higher than that of their families in this country, is likely to be refused admission. Similarly, [2] single parents of West Indian origin find it extremely difficult to bring their children to this country because of the Rule which provides that children should be allowed to enter only when both parents are living in the United Kingdom or entering for settlement. [3] Students from third world countries who are not of an obviously opulent appearance find it difficult to enter the United Kingdom for holidays, even where evidence can be produced that they are engaged in a university course to which they expect to return.

Procedure
"Visitors need not apply for entry clearance but may do so in order to ascertain in advance whether they are eligible for admission to the United Kingdom."[116] Such applications however, can exacerbate the congestion at some British posts and are discouraged. Indeed, possession of one may, ironically, arouse the suspicions of the i.o. at the port of entry. In any event, entry clearance is not a guarantee of a right to enter. It may still be vetted and overruled by the immigration officer at the port of entry.[117] With or without entry clearance, the crucial consideration for the officer is to determine the real purpose of the applicant's journey. For example, is the lady from Bangladesh really on a bona fide visit to see her grandchildren or does she hope to settle permanently? Once the i.o. is not satisfied that the entrant will leave at the end of the visit, he has no discretion to grant leave to enter.[118]

To discover the real purpose a wide range of background factors will be considered. For example, the following:-

(a) The status of the applicant. Thus, U.K.P.H.s awaiting the issue of a special voucher may be tempted to short-circuit the scheme by arriving as visitors, since, once admitted, they are not generally removed (because many other countries will not accept their passports).[119] All U.K.P.H.s, however genuine their motive as visitor, fall immediately under suspicion and are likely to face considerable difficulty in securing entry. So too are non-U.K.P.H. relatives of a U.K. resident who do not appear to have an incentive to return overseas on conclusion of their visit. Parents and aged relatives are the main sufferers here, leading frequently to prolonged, if not humiliating, interrogation.[120]

(b) The immigration history of the applicant, such as previous refusals of entry clearance[121] or previous attempts to leave his native country permanently.[122]

(c) An incentive to return abroad. The applicant's family and financial background will be relevant. Thus, a wealthy man could well wish to visit the U.K. just to see "the maze at Hampton Court",[123] but when considerable resources are spent by a poor family for a visit, the i.o. is entitled "to consider carefully the reasons for the expenditure"[124] and e.c.os "should be particularly on their guard".[125] Similarly, the existence of property, employment or close family relatives abroad may be indicators of genuineness. As the C.R.E. has suggested, there is a clear danger that the e.c.os and i.os concentrate on discovering 'incentives' and ignore or undervalue the applicant's 'intention'.[126]

(d) Correspondingly, the strength of the applicant's connection with the U.K. via, for example, relatives. The integrity of, and assurances (e.g. the offer of accommodation and financial maintenance) by, a U.K. resident may tip the balance in the applicant's favour, but cannot be the sole determining factor.[127]

(e) The applicant's response to questioning. If asked whether he would like to remain in the U.K. if, for example, his U.K. relatives wanted him to, he can be placed in a dilemma - to deny the possibility can be unconvincing or emotionally painful, whereas to admit it may encourage the i.o.'s suspicions.[128] There is a distinction between those who intend to remain indefinitely and who are therefore barred and those who wish to do so but only if it is legally possible. However the distinction is easier to state than to draw at a busy port of entry where language difficulties may exacerbate the difficulties.[129]

Like policing, control at ports of entry can never be exercised with scientific precision and there is much scope for the experience and 'sixth sense' of the individual officer. The dangers which they pose for arbitrary action or prejudice are self-evident.

Leave to enter is normally granted to a visitor for 6 months, though lesser periods may be appropriate so as to coincide with a return flight, or the conclusion of the purpose of the visit or a time limit on the visitor's absence from his native country or because the i.o. has doubts about the passenger's motives. All visits "must have a finite end",[130] and since 1980 the Rules lay down a maximum of 1 year.[131] Another option for the i.o. is to refuse leave to enter but to allow temporary admission. The passenger can then be subjected to stiff conditions (such as place of residence) and, since no leave has in law been given, he cannot apply for an extension. The official determination to deter potential settlers has featured in the written undertakings, which the visitor and/or the U.K. sponsor may give, that the visitor will not subsequently seek an extension of his initial leave to enter. It is a short step for the immigration officer to pressure the parties into signing an undertaking whereby they purport to forfeit their statutory right (s.3(3), 1971 Act) to apply for an extension. Following the case of a 90 year old Indian woman who was only admitted for a visit to see her son after she had agreed not to apply, under r.103 and 104, for an extension of her visit,[132] the Home Office issued and, unusually, published, new guidance to i.os. so that undertakings would only be sought in exceptional circumstances.[133] This small incident is illustrative of the administrative and hence unpublicised, flexibility for tightening control which the Rules offer.

The difficulties frequently faced by short-term visitors, as described in this chapter, are an understandable consequence of the development of immigration law in the last twenty years. That development has reflected a climate of public opinion which is determined to close all loopholes for immigrants and, where possible, to discourage entry.

----
1   Lane, The Alien Menace, (1932) p.9.

2   For contemporary examples, note how economic recession has prompted countries to react against their imported labour (e.g. Australia, France, Germany, Nigeria and the United States).

3   E.g. in 1965 the Labour Government abolished category C vouchers and between 1974 and 1977 it reduced the number of work permits by 44% (e.g. in the hotel and catering industry from 18,000 in 1975 to 4,100 in 1978).

4   Witness the almost passionate interest shown by the Select Committee (1978) in the relatively small numbers employed in hotels and catering and as nurses; or the rigorous rationing of concerts for visiting orchestras. In turn, the desperation of the immigrant to secure a work permit was recently reflected in the allegation of forged permits available for sale from the Department of Employment, see Mail on Sunday, 22 and 29 January 1984.

5   E.g. 5,040 permits for 12 months and 8,060 for less than 12 months were issued in 1984, and for figures over recent years, see Cmnd. 9544, Table 12.

6   Select Committee (1978) Evidence, p.281. A Report by the Department in 1970 similarly reached no firm conclusion; see Jones and Smith, The Economic Impact of Immigration, (1970). See also the encouraging position in Australia, Times 27 June 1985.

7   Ibid, p.237. In 1984 15,350 permits out of the 18,910 total went to foreigners (excluding Pakistan), Cmnd. 9544, Table 12.

8   Since 1976, the annual number of residence permits issued to E.E.C. nationals has fluctuated between 8,440 and 6,620, Cmnd. 9544, Table 11.

9   E.g. U.S. Acts of 1921, 1924 and 1952 setting annual quotas on the number of immigrants.

10   E.g. Canada; see the account by Richmond, Post-War Immigrants in Canada, (1967).

11   Cf. 8 U.S.C. s.212(a)(14) where a certificate is required from the Department of Labor.

12   Aliens Order 1953; art. 4.

13 But note the system of affidavits which was employed in the 1930s in relation to Cypriots whereby a Cypriot worker had to produce an affidavit signed by a sponsor in the U.K., guaranteeing to find him employment - see V. Psarias, "Greek Cypriot Immigration in Greater Manchester" (1979) M.Phil., Bradford University.

14 Cmnd. 2739.

15 Vol. 846 H.C. Debs. col. 1358. The details are set out by the Department of Employment in a series of leaflets OW1-24. See also its Evidence to the Select Committee (1978) at p.237.

16 Lest 'everyday jobs' be devised to facilitate entry e.g. Caballero [1974] Imm. A.R. 13.

17 He must give full details of such advertisements and their results and supply copies of them to the Department.

18 See chapter 2.

19 The earlier Rules said that refusal of a change of status would 'normally' follow (e.g. r.5, H.C. 82). Considerable caselaw developed on the meaning of 'normally' -Pearson, [1978] Imm. A.R. 212, Sarwar [1978] Imm. A.R. 190; Nicolaides [1978] Imm. A.R. 67; Moussa [1976] Imm. A.R. 78; Stillwaggon [1975] Imm. A.R. 132. The cases demanded exceptional circumstances and change was extremely difficult to obtain. The 1980 Rules thus made little difference in practice.

20 See Vethamony [1981] Imm. A.R. 144. Those circumstances include any compassionate reasons and whether the applicant has made concerted efforts to find replacement work.

21 E.g. Chow Tom [1975] Imm. A.R. 137.

22 E.g. Chulvi [1976] Imm. A.R. 133. Note also the series of forms and criteria which it has been able to formulate.

23 Pearson [1978] Imm. A.R. 212, Latiff [1970] Imm. A.R. 76. For judicial review, see below.

24 Thus seeking to distinguish the rule against improper delegation illustrated by Lavender v Minister of Housing [1970] 1 W.L.R. 1231. See Chow Tom, supra.

25 See Brizmohun [1970] Imm. A.R. 122; Munasinghe [1975] Imm. A.R. 79.

26 Unless a very exceptional case can be established along the lines of Vethamony, supra.

27 See Hosenball [1977] 3 All E.R. 452.

28 [1978] Imm. A.R. 212, at p.225.

29 Ibid.

30   The Select Committee (1978) suggested that the grandparental link is too remote, para. 129. The Home Office sought to deflect the racially discriminatory effect by pointing to the 'increasingly large number' of applicants from the new Commonwealth who are seeking to benefit from r.29, but the figures reveal that they are minimal, ibid, Evidence q.59, 60.

31 Cmnd. 9544, Table 3.

32   Clipsham [1970] Imm. A.R. 35, Grant [1974] Imm. A.R. 64, Gunatilake [1975] Imm. A.R. 23, Munasinghe [1975] Imm. A.R. 79.

33 R.30 H.C. 394.

34   The application must be genuine, Ramjane [1973] Imm. A.R. 84.

35   This restriction (introduced in 1980, r.26) can be seen as an endorsement of practice, since few Commonwealth applicants succeeded - 140 between 1973 and 1976 compared with 23,028 other foreign nationals for the same period.

36   Home Affairs Committee on the Rules and the European Convention, H.C. 434 (1979-80) q. 112, per Lord Scarman.

37   For an account, see Smith, Overseas Doctors in the National Health Service, (1980).

38   The new rules were announced in Parliament on 26 March 1985 (H.C. Debs. col. 228) and took effect on 1 April. The rules are contained in H.C. 293.

39   Stillwaggon [1975] Imm. A.R. 132. On the other hand, a composer of music may qualify as a 'writer', Ahart [1981] Imm. A.R. 76.

40   Extending to classical orchestras, under the watchful eye of the Musicians' Union.

41   See the Commission's proposal, discussed at vol. 933 H.C. Debs col. 1995; and in the European Parliament, O.J. Debates no. 234, p.37 (10 October 1978).

42 E.g. Canadian Immigration Act 1976 s.97; and see also in the U.S. the Immigration Reform and Control Bill 1983 directed principally against Mexicans.

43 The 1962 and 1966 Rules were positive. Such people "should be admitted freely" - r.23 of Cmnds 1716 (1962) and 3064 (1966).

44 Rules 35-37, H.C. 169 (1983).

45 Joseph [1977] Imm. A.R. 70.

46 E.g. he must not be likely to resort to public funds, he must be able to accommodate himself and the immigration officer will assess the genuineness of the application. Before 1980, 2 months' stay was possible without entry clearance.

47 £100,000 in 1980 (H.C. 394, r.35), now £150,000 (H.C. 169, r.35).

48 Enforcing Jones [1978] Imm. A.R. 161. He must have the power of 'unfettered disposition' Peikazadi [1979-80] Imm. A.R. 191. Haji [1978] Imm. A.R. 26 rejected support by bank loans, but cf. Peikazadi.

49 Cf. Chiew [1981] Imm. A.R. 102, Ally [1970] Imm. A.R. 258.

50 Cf. Parekh [1976] Imm. A.R. 84.

51 Pritpal Singh [1970] Imm. A.R. 154, Dias [1976] Imm. A.R. 126.

52 Rules 119, 120; e.g. evidence that new jobs have in fact been created. The former provisions (H.C. 80, r.21) whereby a person admitted in another capacity could apply to stay on in business have been dropped (r.118).

53 Cf. for persons of independent means the earlier phrase 'self-sufficiency' and the line of cases it produced e.g. Evgeniou [1978] Imm. A.R. 89.

54 E.g. Stawczykowska [1970] Imm. A.R. 220.

55 Even those of independent means have now to satisfy minimum financial targets (capital of £150,000 or income of £15,000) and either a close connection with the U.K. (which can include periods of residence - Zandfani, Times, 21 December 1984), or that admission would be in the general interests of the U.K. - r.38.

56 Once again compare the liberality of the E.E.C., see chapter 5.

57 E.g. many countries until very recently lacked adequate courses for legal training - those in the Caribbean, Hong Kong, Malaysia, Nigeria.

58 A policy for Overseas Students, Overseas Students Trust (1982) para. 2.39 and supporting Appendix A. The Report is generally an excellent source of statistics. See further the British Council's statistics on overseas students and the Department of Education and Science Bulletins.

59 Ibid., para. 2.11.

60 Ibid. The Commonwealth form 53% and seven countries account for over 50% -Greece, Iran, Iraq, Hong Kong, Malaysia, Nigeria and U.S.A.

61 Witness the many leaders of Commonwealth countries who received part of their education in the U.K.

62 R.9, Cmnd. 1716.

63 Ibid, r.11.

64 R.18, Cmnd. 4298.

65 Full-cost fees were announced in a White Paper on Expenditure, Cmnd. 7746, para. 33. Such a step had been suggested much earlier by the Expenditure Committee, H.C. 96-1, 1973-74, para. 158. For 1984-85 the fee for home students at universities was £500, compared to £3,150 for overseas arts students, £4,150 (science) and £7,650 (medicine).

66 See D.E.S. Statistical Bulletins, Education Statistics for the U.K. 1984 Edition and British Council Statistics.

67 D.E.S. Statistical Bulletin, 9/83, Tables 2 and 3.

68 H.C. 169, r.21 (1983).

69 Save for a limited class of entrant who can be admitted temporarily, pending final arrangements for study, r.24, infra.

70 Para. 22, Cmnd. 2739.

71 C v. E.C.O. Hong Kong [1976] Imm. A.R. 165; Kharrazi

298

[1980] 3 All E.R. 373.

72 The suspicion must be 'reasonable', see Bhambra [1973] Imm. A.R. 14, Goffar [1975] Imm. A.R. 142.

73 Cmnd. 4298, para. 19.

74 Perween Khan [1972] 1 W.L.R. 1058 and see Mo Szu Ti [1982] Imm. A.R. 65, cf. Shaikh [1981] 3 All E.R. 29.

75 Islam [1974] Imm. A.R. 83.

76 Patel [1983] Imm. A.R. 76 - according to Dillon L.J. a person "who only intends to leave if by no lawful means can he avoid it" can be regarded by the Secretary of State as someone who does not intend to leave at the end of his studies.

77 For this unreal distinction, see Mo Szu Ti, supra, at p.71.

78 Although Khan [1975] Imm. A.R. 26 rejected this gloss of realism, it is clear that any proper assessment of genuineness must, at least incidentally, have resort to factors of realism, see Goffar, supra; Islam, supra.

79 Islam, supra.

80 Cf. Islam, supra.

81 Ghosh [1976] Imm. A.R. 60.

82 See the extreme facts of Hussain [1970] 1 W.L.R. 9 (where the entrant could not write 'the cat sat on the mat') and Sae-Heng [1979-80] Imm. A.R. 69.

83 Still a preoccupation of the Home Office, see the concern expressed by the Minister in Guardian, 3 November 1983.

84 See Virdee [1972] Imm. A.R. 215.

85 See C.R.E. Report (1985), paras. 7.6.3-6.

86 See Qureshi [1977] Imm. A.R. 113.

87 Owusu [1976] Imm. A.R. 101. Subsequently endorsed by the 1980 Rules - H.C. 394 r.90; see Mahmoudi [1981] Imm. A.R. 130.

88 See Kpoma [1973] Imm. A.R. 25.

89 Cf. the U.S. which, in keeping with the litigious nature of its citizens, provides for a system of approval and a right

of appeal - 8 C.F.R. 214.3 and 4, and see Blackwell College of Business v Attorney-General 454 Fed. (2d) 928 (1971).

90 Wedad [1979-80] Imm. A.R. 27.

91 Amusu [1974] Imm. A.R. 16.

92 Ibid.

93 Wedad, supra. cf. obiter remarks in Patel [1983] Imm. A.R. 76, which extend 'studies' to vocational training such as Bar School; and note the broad approach in the E.E.C. context e.g. Gravier, Times, 12 March 1985.

94 See further Rashid [1976] Imm. A.R. 12 where it was held that education for 15 years was not the intention of the Rules.

95 Kharrazi [1980] 3 All E.R. 373.

96 Cf. Bohon-Mitchell v Council of Legal Education [1978] I.R.L.R. 525.

97 Puri [1972] Imm. A.R. 21, Bhagat [1972] Imm. A.R. 189, Ayettey [1972] Imm. A.R. 261. It is therefore sufficient if his family can support him, cf. the stricter position for visitors - Chiew, [1981] Imm. A.R. 102.

98 Puri, ibid.

99 Confirmed by the House of Lords in relation to the corresponding, earlier rule in Alexander v I.A.T. [1982] 2 All E.R. 766.

100 Kassam [1980] 2 All E.R. 330; cf. to like effect, Amin [1983] 2 A.C. 818. Contrast the benefit of E.E.C. status (chapter 5).

101 Under the 1973 Rules a fixed period of 12 months, r.21 H.C. 79, r.12 H.C. 80.

102 Breaches of conditions of stay are dealt with severely and it cannot help the student legally (though it may assist an application for compassionate treatment) that his dependants have a separate legal entitlement to remain, Glean [1972] Imm. A.R. 84.

103 Previously lax attendance cannot be remedied by regular attendance prior to the application for extension - Juma [1974] Imm. A.R. 96. Now reflected in r.107 ('has given regular attendance').

104 Amer [1979-80] Imm. A.R. 87; endorsed by Gerami [1981] Imm. A.R. 187.

105 E.g. Amer, supra.

106 See Shaikh [1981] 3 All E.R. 29.

107 [1980] 3 All E.R. 373.

108 Thaker [1976] Imm. A.R. 114; cf. Sidique [1976] Imm. A.R. 69.

109 Cmnd. 9544, Table 10. E.E.C. nationals numbered around 5 million. Excluded from the total are those with the right of abode, seamen, armed forces, those who landed but did not pass through immigration control and those who entered via the Common Travel Area.

110 Countries are listed in the Appendix to the Rules and since June 1985, include citizens of Sir Lanka - Cmnd. 9539..

111 Admitted on Code 3 rather than the usual code 5N - C.R.E. Report, paras. 6.9.2-6.

112 See H.A.C. Evidence, p.85-6, and C.R.E. Report (1985), ch.6.

113 Cmnd. 9544, Table 1.

114 For a detailed discussion of this 'pressure to immigrate', see C.R.E. Report, paras. 6.14-17.

115 For a milder example, see the alleged treatment meted out to a coloured police officer (who had the right of abode and a British passport) at Portsmouth on his return from France. The alleged interview went as follows - Immigration Officer, "You have got to fill in a form every time you come into Britain." Entrant "Surely not. I didn't see any other British citizens filling in the forms." I.o. "You are coloured so you must fill in a form. Now don't argue with me." ... I.o. "Before you go let me tell you we don't want many of your kind in my country." E "Would you care to elaborate on your last remark?" I.o. "You must be bloody thick." E "Can you tell me your name?" I.o. "Bugger off. In future make sure you don't travel on the boat where I am the immigration officer." E "Why, what would you do? Throw me overboard?" I.o. "I'll give you hell. I promise that." - H.C. Debs. 27 July 1979, col. 1268, at 1275. For recent examples, see those cited at H.C. Debs. 5 March 1984, col. 659ff.

116 Home Office Minister, H.C. Debs. 29 February 1984, col. 222.

117 Confirmed in Mustun [1970] Imm. A.R. 97. Now r.17. In addition an e.c. can only be used once, Andronicou [1974] Imm. A.R. 87.

118 Malek [1979-80] Imm. A.R. 111.

119 Din [1978] Imm. A.R. 56, Patel [1978] Imm. A.R. 154.

120 E.g. Patel, supra, Manmohan Singh [1975] Imm. A.R. 118.

121 E.g. Sadiq [1978] Imm. A.R. 115.

122 Hanks [1976] Imm. A.R. 74.

123 Manmohan Singh [1975] Imm. A.R. 118.

124 Ibid.

125 Internal instructions, C.R.E. Report, para. 6.6.2.

126 See the many examples in ch.6 of its Report.

127 Kumar [1978] Imm. A.R. 185.

128 See Bhagat Singh [1978] Imm. A.R. 134, Sobanjo [1978] Imm. A.R. 22.

129 E.g. Lai [1974] Imm. A.R. 98. A similar dilemma may arise if the applicant says too much e.g. Baldacchino [1970] Imm. A.R. 14, Ramjane [1973] Imm. A.R. 84.

130 Hashim [1982] Imm. A.R. 113.

131 Ibid; now rr.20, 103. Thus excluding the earlier possibility of a lengthy stay in order to look after grandchildren, for example, whilst their parents work or study e.g. Nourai [1978] Imm. A.R. 200, Obeyesekere [1976] Imm. A.R. 16, Shamonda [1975] Imm. A.R. 16, Hamilton [1974] Imm. A.R. 43, Afoakwah [1970] Imm. A.R. 17.

132 Raised by Mr. Greville Janner M.P.; see Guardian, 17 November 1983 and 26 January 1984, H.C. Debs., 14 November 1983, col. 280 and 17 November, col. 513.

133 For the text see L.A.G. (1984) p.44 and note C.R.E. Report, paras. 6.24.1-3; cf. s.18, Immigration Act 1976 (Canada) which makes specific provision for a deposit of money as a guarantee of obedience to the terms of entry.

8 REMOVAL OF IMMIGRANTS

Part I   Deportation

If only it were true that provided the immigrant felt
happy and secure in his new country everything would be
all right. But in sober fact it is the psychology of the
home population of the original inhabitants which is the
chief problem. By making immigrants comfortable you may
placate them but at the same time infuriate the older
population, who see immigrants getting what they regard as
unfair advantages.[1]

There are five ways in which immigrants can be removed[2] from
the U.K.-

    A   deportation,
    B   administrative direction,
    C   extradition,
    D   binding over on condition of departure,
    E   removal of the mentally ill.

Methods A and B are the most important, the former having a
long pedigree, the latter being a relative newcomer but
nonetheless important for that. A is dealt with in Part I of
this chapter, the remainder, along with appeals, in Part II.

PART I

Principle
Under customary[3] public international law, it is clear that a
State has the right to expel foreigners from its territory as
it sees fit. How and when it chooses to do so is a matter for
municipal law. As the Supreme Court of the United States
observed in 1892: "The right to exclude or expel all aliens,
or any class of aliens, absolutely or upon certain conditions,
in war or in peace, [is] an inherent and inalienable right of
every sovereign and independent nation..."[4] Whilst the U.K.
has always observed this principle, opinion has differed as to

whether the power of expulsion could be exercised by royal prerogative as well as by statute. Magna Charta in 1225[5] gave alien merchants the right to enter and leave the Realm and, although aliens were removed in the thirteenth and succeeding centuries, sometimes en masse,[6] the evidence for removal by prerogative power of the Crown is unconvincing.[7] Statute was the preferred mode.[8] Even if such a prerogative had existed, it is arguable that by the end of the eighteenth century it had fallen into desuetude[9] and thus necessitated the flurry of statutory powers for removal surrounding the Napoleonic Wars. In spite of the specific retention of prerogative powers in s.33(5) of the Immigration Act 1971, it is clear that they have no role today in expulsion. The matter has been taken over by statute.[10]

It follows from this sovereign discretion that such procedural safeguards as due process have no preordained role to play in the removal of aliens, not even in the face of written constitutions or Bills of Rights.[11] For example, under s.18 of the Migration Act 1958 in Australia, "the Minister may order the deportation" of prohibited immigrants and the courts have held that there is no need to imply a requirement of natural justice.[12] As a country's municipal public law develops, it may be possible to import limited forms of judicial review,[13] but, beyond that only if a state grants procedural safeguards _ex gratia_ is it possible to speak of "rights" in deportation.

The 1971 Act does grant some procedural safeguards and substantive guidelines, but the traditional element of executive discretion is well preserved and still a striking feature of the Rules. With the emphasis of recent law on the exclusion of unwanted immigrants it is hardly surprising that official attention since 1971 has increasingly been directed towards internal control in order to remove those who have slipped through entry control. In this process resort has been placed on a tightening of the Rules. This policy has been demonstrated in several ways, for example since 1980 by the more stringent instruction to immigrants not to resort to public funds during their stay in the U.K.; by the sympathy and connivance of the courts, as shown in their readiness to recommend deportation following conviction and their development of the power to remove illegal entrants by administrative direction; by a wide range of measures designed for a closer supervision of resident immigrants, such as the exchange of information between, and the increasing involvement of, various Government Departments and the checking of passports for a variety of purposes. These last-mentioned measures are certain to develop further and in the short-term will be the major area of controversy in immigration control as Governments strive to portray a tough image towards immigrants.

A. DEPORTATION

Until 1793 expulsion of aliens was organised on an ad hoc basis, directed towards identifiable categories such as Jews, religious dissidents, enemy aliens or particular traders. The modern law took shape in that year and the Act heralded a see-saw of removal powers until 1826.[14] It permitted the removal of aliens in two circumstances. First, breach of the immigration controls, such as failure to make a declaration of personal details at the port of entry, entitled a court to order removal of the alien (s.3). Second, a Royal Proclamation could order the departure of any alien; and there were no limitations on its use (s.15).[15] An alien who breached a Proclamation could be convicted and deported by order of a court (s.16) or, if he apprehended that the alien would not obey the Proclamation, the Secretary of State could issue a warrant directing removal, subject to an appeal to the Privy Council (s.17).[16] The latter was in essence a form of pre-emptive administrative procedure for removal. Succeeding Acts placed greater emphasis on the use of Royal Proclamations during the Napoleonic Wars. Aliens suspected of being "dangerous" could be detained indefinitely or removed by order of the Secretary of State[17] and by 1802 even that limitation had been removed, the discretion being absolute and the precedent for the 1914 and 1971 Acts set. The use of Royal Proclamations continued until 1826, though from 1816 to 1826 expulsion was infrequent.[18] Thereafter immigration control was concentrated upon the recording of details and no power to deport was re-enacted, save for an Act of 1848[19] which lasted for two years and under which no alien was removed. In fact from 1825 to 1905 no alien was expelled under immigration legislation.[20]

The Aliens Act 1905 revived the Secretary of State's power to expel but only

(a) after a conviction for an imprisonable offence and a recommendation by the court, or
(b) a judicial finding within one year of entry that the alien was destitute or living in overcrowded and insanitary conditions, or
(c) in the case of extradition.

The precondition of a conviction is a significant indicator of the comparatively liberal and legalistic procedure under the Act. But this was swept away with the emergency legislation of 1914 (Aliens Restriction Act) which ceded to the Crown complete discretion in the field and this was retained after the War.[21] The Aliens Orders made under this general legislation formed the basis of the current law. For example, removal for the "public good" was instituted,[22] upheld by the court[23] and ultimately incorporated into the 1971 Act (s.3(5)(b)). No appeal was allowed until 1956 when aliens were given the opportunity to make representations to the Chief Metropolitan Magistrate, who in turn advised the Home Secretary.[24] Under the Commonwealth Immigrants Act 1962, Commonwealth citizens could only be deported after a court recommendation (s.7). The White Paper 1965, preoccupied with the need to control unlawful immigration, proposed that they should be removed for evasion of control. In 1971 the broader powers of deportation, which had governed aliens for most of the century, were extended to cover Commonwealth citizens as well.

The Power
The power to deport may arise in four circumstances:

(1) if the person has failed to comply with a condition attached to his leave to enter or remains beyond the authorised time;

(2) if the Secretary of State deems the person's deportation to be conducive to the public good;

(3) if the person is the wife or the child under 18 of a person ordered to be deported;

(4) if the person, after reaching the age of 17, is convicted of an offence for which he is punishable with imprisonment and the court recommends deportation.[25]

It is important to note that deportation is a two-stage procedure, consisting of a decision by the Secretary of State (or recommendation by a court) which may be confirmed by the making of an order.[26] Various consequences flow from this distinction. First, a formal appeal lies only against the decision (or recommendation). Second, whether and when the Secretary of State decides to implement a decision (or recommendation) by making a deportation order is entirely a matter for his discretion.[27] Third, consequently, an applicant can only make informal representations at the second stage and it is here that the intervention of Members of Parliament, lobby groups and publicity campaigns frequently, and sometimes successfully, play their part.[28] Fourth, once an order is made, legal challenge is only possible by judicial review; but, even if successful, it will defeat the deportation order and not the decision. It is thus open to the Secretary of State to make a new order in compliance with the observations of the court. Admittedly this avoids the decision being defeated by a mere technicality at the "order" stage,[29] but given the difficulties facing immigrants in challenging a deportation decision and the resources of the Home Office, it is surely reasonable to demand administrative competence and legality and that, if the High Court sees fit to review an order, the

decision itself should lapse. Here again the limited
effectiveness of judicial review is exposed.

General Considerations
Rules 156 and 161 usefully list the more important and common
factors relevant to deportation decisions. However, the lists
are only illustrative and neither the Secretary of State nor
the deportee are confined to it. Over and above this stand the
general principles of r.154 which emphasise that, whilst each
case depends upon its individual merits, the public interest
is an important consideration. Since part of that interest
lies in firm immigration control and, as r.154 indicates, in
consistent decision-making, the balance will frequently tend
towards deportation.[30] For example, in Anand,[31] the I.A.T.
feared that the effect of immigration rules would be rendered
"nugatory" if the applicant's personal and commercial success
were to overcome deportation. The same fear, albeit in less
emotive terms, always lurks in the background and enables
r.154 to play a critical, residuary role in individual
decisions by outweighing personal and compassionate factors.

(1) Breach of Conditions or overstaying[32]
In spite of the care which immigration officers employ to
ensure the admission of only trustworthy entrants and their
preoccupation with the risk of overstaying, it has not been
possible to quantify the extent of overstaying.[33] The
introduction of computers and machine readable passports in
all countries will eventually produce a clearer picture. In
the meantime, this category of deportation leads to the
highest number of deportation orders of all categories:[34]

	1981	1982	1983	1984
orders made	1345	1389	1591	1438
orders enforced	249	282	267	300

Moreover, recent years have seen a dramatic rise in its use.
Thus, orders rose steadily from 116 in 1974 to 544 in 1979,
but with the harder attitude adopted by the Home Office the
number leapt to 1,553 in 1980. As more resources and official
energies are spent in tracking down overstayers the figures
are most unlikely to fall. On the contrary, they offer a
useful talisman by which Governments can proclaim their
efficiency in safeguarding the public interest.
    In principle, this power may overlap with court
recommendations for deportation (see below), since both
misdemeanours are criminal offences and punishable with
imprisonment.[35] Prosecution for overstaying, however, was
hampered by a ruling in 1973 that the offence was not a
continuing one and that prosecution had to be commenced within
three years of the offence.[36] In 1982 the House of Lords went
further and effectively halted prosecutions by ruling that the

offence under s.24(1)(b)(i) can only be committed on the day after the immigrant's leave expires and only if he is shown to have been aware of that fact on that day.[37]

Much greater use has been made of deportation under the Immigration Rules, with appeals in the normal way to the adjudicator. In principle it may be argued that this procedure is fairer to the immigrant than a prosecution since the immigration apparatus can take into account wider circumstances than the court and is more likely to be sympathetic to the immigrant. However, it should be noted that

(a) as Nazari[38] has reaffirmed, the courts are also under a duty to consider a broad range of factors before making a recommendation for deportation;

(b) at the secondary level of the deportation process, the Home Secretary must still weigh all the relevant factors before implementing a court recommendation;

(c) in contrast, the immigration appellate authorities offer comparatively little hope for the immigrant, given the determination of successive Governments to enforce immigration control strictly and the progressive and subtle tightening of the Rules.[39]

Before 1970, the power to deport for breach of conditions was confined to aliens (Commonwealth citizens being liable only to court recommendations) and, when extended to all non-patrials, could only be used if the immigrant had <u>persistently</u> contravened the conditions.[40] However, since 1980 the Immigration Rules have required simply a failure to comply with, or contravention of, "a condition" of his leave.[41] Since the power to deport is a discretionary one and all the relevant circumstances must be weighed,[42] it does not mean that minor infringements will justify its use (for example, the intermittent failure to report to the police), yet the potential scope of the power is unfettered and the willingness of the appellate system to control its excessive use is an unpredictable safeguard. Most significantly in that regard, in 1973 the equivalent of the current second sentence of the Rule ("Full account is to be taken of all the relevant circumstances ...") opened with the conjunction "But",[43] thus emphasising that, whilst deportation was the normal course, all factors had to be considered. Its omission in 1980 was a subtle yet significant change which has deprived the second sentence of emphasis. Allied to the overriding role of r.15[44] (which refers to the public interest, the need for consistent decision-making and which generally works in favour of deportation) the current provisions mean that a deportation order is usually inevitable for breach of conditions of leave or overstaying. Many will leave before the order is enforced, whilst for others attempts will be made to exert pressure on the Secretary of State to stay execution.

R.156 lists the factors to be taken into account when considering the appropriateness of deportation. They are self-explanatory e.g. the age, personal history, and domestic circumstances of the immigrant. The factor of 'compassionate circumstances' in rules 154 and 156 must be of a personal nature and does not embrace the effect of deportation on people other than the deportee - the effect of the removal of a Sikh priest on the local ethnic community cannot therefore qualify.[44] This is an unfortunate gloss on simple words which can easily bear a more expansive meaning.

Comment

It is right that overstaying and breach of conditions face the ultimate sanction of deportation, for otherwise obedience to the Rules could evaporate. Against this must be balanced the ruthless way in which abuse is detected and the personal hardship which removal, often many years after entry, can cause. The means already exist within r.156 for a humane balance to be achieved but this depends upon the will and direction of the Home Office. Yet the official zeal for detecting overstaying is undoubted[45] and has generated special administrative agencies.[46] It is reflected by the development of computers and machine readable passports, whereby entrants can be checked against departures, to detect overstayers, the close consultation between the Immigration Service and other Government agencies such as the Police, D.H.S.S. and Inland Revenue, and the occasional use of search warrant raids.[47] All such internal controls are the practical effect of the removal provisions and it is that broader effect, in social and race relations terms, by which the bald legal provisions should be judged.

(2) Conducive to the public good

This broad category has many legislative precedents as regards aliens[48] but was only extended to cover Commonwealth citizens in 1971. At worst, it epitomises the ultimate discretionary power which the Crown has always claimed as the sole arbiter of the expulsion of aliens. At best, the current formulation represents a slight improvement upon the Draconian and unchallengeable powers, which the Crown has claimed in times of national emergency, by providing a right of appeal, albeit a limited one in certain circumstances.

The formulation of the power in s.3(5)(b) - "if the Secretary of State deems..." - readily indicates its discretionary nature. There is no requirement of reasonable suspicion or mere suspicion or even the favourite expression of the Rules - "satisfies". The Act does however distinguish between cases of a security or political nature and all others which affect the public good. The former are subject to a special non-statutory procedure, whereas the latter can be appealed to the Immigration Appeal Tribunal.[49] It is the former category which has attracted controversy in spite of its comparatively infrequent use, whereas the latter is used far more frequently and unobtrusively.

Recent use of the power has been as follows:[50]

	1981	1982	1983	1984
orders made	140	60	86	119
orders enforced	113	74	65	83

(a) Security and political cases

Such cases are rare, so rare as to question the usefulness of this type of deportation, especially in view of the extreme criticism and publicity which usually surround them.[51] The cases fall into three categories[52] where deportation is deemed to be conducive to the public good:

(i) Because of national security

Of these, the notorious case of Agee and Hosenball is an example.[53] Much of the controversy here stems from the fact that deportation will often be a preventive act, based in part on speculation as to the deportee's activities. For, if a breach of national security has occurred, the criminal law, in particular the Official Secrets Acts, could be used. The dangers of undue and untested speculation become clear when the appeals' procedure is considered (see below). The theoretical attraction of using the power to expel speedily and quietly security risks instead of using a full-blown criminal trial is matched by the publicity which inevitably surrounds the use of the power.[54]

(ii) Because of relations between the U.K. and any other country

A particular incentive to use deportation here is the avoidance of extradition with its attendant judicial proceedings and the possible defence of "political offence".[55] Alternatively, an extradition agreement may not exist between the U.K. and the country which the Home Secretary seeks to assuage by deportation.[56] As will be seen below, if deportation is chosen, little or nothing, apart from the bare facts, needs to be divulged to the deportee. The temptation is understandable but, if accepted, flies in the face of the spirit of the law and makes a mockery of extradition safeguards. As early as 1913, the Foreign Office advised its Consuls in the U.S. that such a practice "is to be discouraged" and that a removal power is not to be used "for purposes for which it was never intended, when it seems convenient to do so".[57] Yet, in the light of Soblen[58] and Hosenball,[59] the Home Secretary's decision to use deportation in preference to extradition, can only be successfully challenged in

the very rare case when the deportee is able to prove
mala fides on the Secretary's part so as to constitute
an abuse of power.[60]

(iii) Because of other reasons of a political nature
The previous two categories are relatively narrow when
compared with the immense breadth of this residual
category. It can embrace a wide range of political
undesirables from a Klu Klux Klan leader to a
left-wing extremist to members of unusual religions,[61]
with little effective control and accountability over
its use. The case of Dutschke, a student who allegedly
made political speeches in defiance of an undertaking
not to engage in political activities, prompted one
commentator to remark that "in matters of deportation,
Home Secretaries have accustomed themselves to having
their way and having it without the need to give
reasons".[62] Moreover, the pretext for deportation must
inevitably be speculative fears of relatively minor
political danger and embarrassment. For, if serious
subversion is involved, either the criminal law or, at
least, category (1) above will be used. It must be
doubted whether lesser acts such as speeches can ever
justify removal from a democratic society and, most of
all, in the light of the limited appeal rights, in
such an autocratic way.

(b) Other cases conducive to the public good
These can be appealed to the I.A.T., occur far more frequently
than category (a) and yet arouse disproportionately less
criticism and comment. The power is a residuary one called
into play to catch those "undesirables" who overcome, or who
are not specifically covered by, the other Rules. An important
example of the former are convicted persons whom the courts do
not recommend for deportation[63] but whose convictions will have
been routinely passed on by the police to the Home Office. In
conjunction with r.157, deportation can still be ordered at
the Secretary of State's discretion.[64] All the circumstances
known to him must be taken into account and may well include
some not placed before the court or others which have arisen
since the date of sentence. The process thus places the
immigrant in double jeopardy. If he evades a court
recommendation, he still has the Home Office hurdle to leap
even though the court may have deliberately refrained from
making a recommendation. Although a decision is appealable, it
will take a strong I.A.T. to overturn the removal of someone
who has already been convicted of a criminal offence and
against whom further unsavoury facts are likely to have been
amassed by the Home Office. The power adds further fuel to the
argument that the judicial power to recommend deportation be
abolished and the matter left in the Secretary of State's
hands. However, it is suggested that, whether a court or the

311

Home Secretary instigates deportation, it is still a consequence of the immigrant's original crime and that it is fairer to subject the issue to the normal procedural safeguards of a criminal trial. Whichever view is preferred, the present position cannot be regarded with equanimity when it in effect allows the authorities to take "two bites of the cherry".

As regards those who are not prima facie covered by the other Rules, this power of deportation epitomises the historical prerogative of a State to remove aliens at will. It entitles the Secretary of State to try for deportation whatever the other detailed Rules may say, if he deems a person's presence here to be undesirable. This may have unfortunate consequences. First, it depends upon the policy of the incumbent Secretary of State who will determine which category of immigrants should be deported. Second, because of the discretion which surrounds its use, an immigrant faces a most difficult task in overturning the Secretary's decision on appeal to the I.A.T. Third, because of the lack of statutory control, judicial review of the decision is most unlikely.

The scope and flexibility of the power are admirably illustrated by the way in which it has been used to enforce the rules governing admission of spouses. In the case of Ullah,[65] the breakdown of a marriage led to a decision to deport the non-patrial husband on the basis of public good. The decision was unsuccessfully challenged in the High Court and Court of Appeal. The husband's argument that the power had not been intended for use in these circumstances was rebutted by the sequitur that, because the power is unfettered by statutory restrictions, there was no room for judicial review of its usage. Sections 3(5)(a) and (b) were held to be separable and to give the Secretary of State alternative powers. When tied to the restrictive policy on the entry of husbands, wives, and fiancees, the power has far-reaching implications and has been increasingly used in this area in recent years.[66] Admittedly the Secretary of State must consider all the circumstances, including those listed in r.141, but extremely strong compassionate considerations will be needed to overcome the fact that the spouse has lost his status to remain. It can similarly be used where either the Rules make no specific mention of deportation[67] or where the immigrant's conduct, though complying with the Rules, has strayed from the current ideal of a well-behaved immigrant; for example, a businessman or student whose moral or financial behaviour, though lawful, is deprecated. It is, in other words, a catch-all provision which can expand as need demands.

Comment

Deportation in this field attracts very little publicity compared to security and political cases, yet it is used far more frequently and has a far wider potential. The security field is, after all, limited by its very terms, whereas the non-security aspect of "public good" can stretch to meet newly-felt needs and policies over which, because of the silence of the Rules and the courts, there is no effective control.

(3) Family Deportations

The 1971 Act (s.3(5)(c)) saw the introduction of a specific power to deport the family of a deportee up to 8 weeks after the deportee had left the U.K.[68] The run-of-the-mill case is that of deportation following the husband's conviction and subsequent deportation (see (4) below) or his breach of conditions of stay (see (1) above). In principle, the power can be justified because the family's permission to enter and remain will have depended upon the lawful status of the husband. If that is removed, so should theirs. From an economic standpoint, it is more than likely, especially in view of the normal role of the husband as breadwinner, that the rest of his family will have to resort to State benefits and thus it is fair that they too be removed. On the other hand, there is the danger that the sins of the deportee will be unduly visited upon the "innocent" members of a family, especially if they have been in the U.K. for some time and have established strong connections here. The Rules do permit such factors to be taken into account, but the position of the family is inevitably precarious.

(a) The "family"

The family is defined for these purposes as the wife (but not the husband) and children under 18 years of age of the deportee (s.5(4)). To meet cases of polygamy, more than one wife may be included; a child who has been adopted de facto as opposed to legally, as is the case in the concept of the extended family sometimes practised by West Indian and Asian cultures, may be treated as the child of the 'adopter'.

The temptation to judge the family's appeal alongside the merits of the deportee's case (a form of guilt by association) is obvious but has been held impermissible by the Court of Appeal: each applicant requires separate consideration and the Secretary of State must consider the merits of each case.[69]

(b) Wives

All relevant factors known to the Secretary of State must be taken into account before he reaches his decision. It is thus very much in the applicant's interests to produce all the necessary evidence in support of her claim. Rule 161 contains a list of the more important items and of these the ability of the deportee's family to look after themselves "for the foreseeable future" without recourse to public funds is of the greatest significance. If, as is most likely, the deportee is the family's breadwinner, the family will be forced to turn to relatives and friends for support. These in turn must produce clear evidence of their financial ability to look after the family. Indeed, the extent and strength of the family's ties with others in the U.K. is a common thread running through the factors in r.161 and will normally be essential for a successful application. Alongside this, other factors such as the future open to the family if forced overseas will be of secondary importance. Indeed, the belief that a family unit is better kept together is likely to be a far more potent factor in favour of deportation.[70] Overall, r.141 can play a decisive role in favouring the public interest in firm immigration control at the expense of personal considerations.[71] If the wife has qualified for settlement in her own right, she has a claim, but not an entitlement, to remain and will not normally be deported (r.162). Such cases will, of course, be rare in view of the difficulty facing a woman in entering via her independent or business means or work permit under the current Rules. For those that do arise, it is regrettable that no absolute right to remain is conceded when, after all, the woman has qualified for settled status "under her own steam". If the wife has been living apart from the husband, "it will not normally be right" to deport her and any children.[72] Although this concession is couched in general terms, it is of limited practical value. First, there is no definition of "living apart": but, since motive and genuineness will be relevant, a recent separation may well be seen as a thinly disguised attempt to avoid the possibility of deportation. Second, there will be few women who will find the adequate means to support themselves and any children by living apart from their spouses and thus the reference to public funds in r.146 will assume priority. If, third, the woman has been obliged to remain in the family home it may be argued that the spouses have formed separate households under the same roof.[73] For the majority of women, forced by economic circumstances or cultural tradition to remain with their spouses, great hardship may ensue if in fact the marriage has broken down. If they "come into the open" by, for example, invoking the protection of the police, family law[74] or state benefits, they risk deportation. Whereas, if they remain with the spouse, they face continued personal discomfort and deportation along with him.

Children

Children cease to be regarded as members of a family at the age of 18 years[75] and must therefore seek to regularise their position in this country in their own right. Some concessions are allowed to those under 18 years who will not "normally" be deported[76] in the following circumstances:

> (i) Where the child has spent some years in the U.K. and is close to the age of 18 years. Apart from the

314

obvious imprecision of "some years",[77] it is likely
that time in itself will not suffice in the face of
the influence which a blatant breach of the Rules by
the principal deportee will have on the I.A.T.[78]

(ii) Where he has left the family home, found employment
and established himself independently. Proof of
financial independence is essential.

(iii) Where he has married between the age of 16 and 18
years.[79] The marriage must have taken place "before the
deportation came into prospect".[80] This is designed to
exclude marriages of convenience and, given the
Government's determination to expose them, all such
marriages will be closely scrutinised.

However, there is no entitlement for children in these
categories to remain. Of crucial importance to all will be the
arrangements for the future maintenance of the child,
especially if both parents are to be deported. Since the
burden of supporting and, where relevant, educating the child
should not be passed to the U.K. taxpayer, the arrangements
must be "realistic".[81] Even if this is satisfied, all the
circumstances are considered and speculation as to the child's
future may well count against him, for example, that he will
be better if deported along with his family unit or that the
disruption which deportation will cause to his education will
be temporary.[82] This same reasoning is seen at work even if the
children have an independent right to remain by birth in the
U.K. (before 1983).[83] As British citizens they cannot be
removed but the Home Office relies on natural family ties
compelling the parents to take the children with them rather
than leaving them in, for example, the care of a local
authority.

(c) The Order
A right of appeal against a deportation decision lies to the
I.A.T.[84] but, whether exercised or not, it is open to the
family to leave voluntarily before an order is made, in which
case the Secretary may assist with the travelling expenses.[85]
The order lasts as long as the order against the principal
deportee lasts, or until its subject "ceases to belong to his
family". For a child this will automatically occur at the age
of 18 years regardless of whether or not he remains a part of
the family unit and he can thus attempt to re-enter the U.K.
For wives, on the other hand, this will only arise if the
marriage comes to an end.[86]

Comment
In many cases, these deportations are quite defensible. For
example, the family of a student has no other reason for being
in the U.K. than to live with the student during his studies.
If his permission to remain is withdrawn, so should theirs.

Difficulties arise over long term sponsors and the over-zealous application of immigration control to them (for example, the broad definition of "illegal entrant" or the ready deportation for convictions). The spouse could be detected or convicted many years after entry and his "innocent" family too readily removed. Though the power is sex discriminatory, it has been endorsed by the European Commission of Human Rights.[87]

Section 3(5)(c) is the least used of the deportation powers:[88]

	1981	1982	1983	1984
orders made	6	8	5	1
orders enforced	8	2	3	0

Instead economic and emotional pressure and the threat of the power mean that most dependants will naturally leave along with the deportee.

(4) Court recommendations[89]

Deportation following a conviction has a lengthy legislative history. In the aliens' legislation of 1793-1816 it was confined to offences relating to immigration control such as failure to comply with formalities on entry.[90] It was the courts which had the power to order imprisonment for the offence or immediate removal or imprisonment followed by removal. Under the Aliens Act 1905 the power covered all imprisonable offences and the division of responsibility was clearly established, the Secretary of State having the discretionary power to deport following a court conviction.[91] This scheme was a regular feature of Aliens Orders thereafter.[92] It was extended to Commonwealth citizens in 1962 and it now covers most non-patrials.[93]

This power of removal ranks second to Category (1) in the number of deportation orders made but produces the highest number of orders which are enforced:[94]

	1981	1982	1983	1984
court recommendations	820	826	844	929
orders made	704	529	560	660
orders enforced	576	508	479	535

Deportation in this category is not intended to be a substitute for the normal sentencing powers[95] and, thus, although the Home Secretary can in theory make a deportation order before the sentence is served, in practice he waits until it has been. To do otherwise would risk lowering respect for the law, and it is seen as preferable for the offender to "pay his due to the host society" before his removal from the country.

The current procedure is carefully, if not cunningly,

worded and has taken account of difficulties caused by earlier versions. It enables the court, when sentencing a defendant for an imprisonable offence, to recommend to the Home Secretary that a deportation order be made. The defendant must be at least 17 years old at the date of <u>conviction</u>.[96] Thus, the frequently lengthy delays in the criminal process will not thwart the deportation of those below 17 years at the arrest or committal stage. It also follows that offences committed years earlier can warrant a recommendation provided that the accused reaches 17 years by the date of conviction. Moreover, as long as the offence is theoretically punishable by imprisonment, it does not matter

    (a) that the court did not in fact so sentence the defendant - it may even have given him an absolute discharge.[97] Rehabilitative sentences such as probation may be adjudged to be inconsistent with a recommendation since they presuppose that the offender is not beyond redemption.[98] However, unlike the 1970 Rules,[99] the current Rules contain no specific presumption to this effect. Allied to judicial doubts as to the rehabilitative effectiveness of such sentences and the well-known pressures of overcrowding on the penal system, the presumption can be easily outweighed in favour of deportation. At the other extreme, a sentence to life imprisonment need not prevent a recommendation.[100]

    (b) that the court was prevented from sending the defendant to prison because of legislative restrictions on the sentencing of first or young offenders.[101] In keeping with this, the explicit presumption in the 1970 Rules against deporting first offenders has been removed.[102]

    (c) that the court did not in fact convict the defendant, provided only that the offence charged was in fact committed by him.[103]

The court which sentences the offender need not be the same as that which convicted him, as would happen if a magistrates' court commits the case to the Crown Court for sentence. In every case the accused is entitled to 7 days' notice in writing that a recommendation may be made,[104] though there is no set procedure for issuing such a notice; it could be given by the police earlier or by the magistrates' court at remand or committal. Legal representation (and aid, if necessary) is usually essential.[105]

    The requirement of notice does at least recognise implicitly that a recommendation for deportation is a separate process from that of normal sentencing. If it were otherwise, a recommendation might be made almost automatically or relegated to an afterthought or the principal sentence might be reduced so as to expedite the deportation.[106] Evidence that this happens, especially before magistrates' courts,[107] has prompted superior courts to issue reminders[108] that a recommendation must not be part of the sentence but is instead a separable issue to be considered after "full inquiry into all the circumstances".[109] Moreover, since the Home Secretary may decide not to uphold the recommendation at the end of the day, it is important that the defendant be sentenced in the normal way.

Factors

Whilst each case will depend on its circumstances, several common threads have emerged. "This country has no need for criminals of other nationalities"[110] is a sentiment underlying all recommendations, especially those by magistrates' courts, and it will frequently override all other factors. Thus, the greater the seriousness of the offence and the longer the defendant's criminal record, the greater will be the chances of a recommendation. In the hierarchy of judicial disapproval, persons convicted of offences involving violence, fraud and, in particular, drugs, are customarily recommended for deportation; but lesser offences may well suffice, especially if premeditated or seen as part of a "wave" of immigrant crime.[111] Breaches of the immigration law will normally justify a recommendation if deliberate or blatant.[112] The defendant's clear criminal record and the leniency of the sentence imposed on him do not rule out a recommendation - the presumption of earlier Rules,[113] which specifically earmarked first offenders and borstal training as normally incompatible with recommendations, no longer appears.

Against these factors the following will be balanced

(a) The defendant's age, character and previous good record (as an employee, for example). The Court of Appeal has made it clear, however, that, when assessing the potential detriment to the U.K. of allowing him to remain, the fact that he "has been living on social security is not a factor which should be taken into account in deciding whether to make a recommendation for deportation".[114] This is a remarkably favourable ruling to the defendant and it is hard to believe that social security will be so readily ignored by courts of first instance[115] in times of high unemployment. They may be tempted to conceal their reliance on this factor by emphasising the gravity of the crime and other detrimental circumstances.

(b) Most persuasively of all, the extent and strength of the defendant's and his family's[116] connections with the U.K., such as the time spent here, a commitment to complete a course of study or his children's attachment to the educational system, language and

culture. Whilst the disruption caused to these
connections by a recommendation is a relevant
consideration, the prospects for the family abroad
will only be considered if their personal circumstances are in serious straits.[117]

The economic consequences, such as the standard of living in
prospect for the family abroad, are not considered and, in
keeping with the courts' concern not to become overtly
involved in political issues, it is clear that the political
consequences, such as possible persecution facing the
immigrant abroad, are a matter squarely for the Home
Secretary.[118] For the court is concerned

> simply with the crime committed and the individual's past
> record and the question as to what is their effect on
> [this country]. It does not embark, and indeed is in no
> position to embark, upon the issue as to what is likely to
> be his life if he goes back to the country of his origin.
> That is a matter for the Home Secretary.[119]

Such political matters have always rested in the lap of
Government Departments as part of their overall foreign policy
and the courts have in turn stepped aside.[120] This judicial
approach adds further weight to the view that the courts'
power to recommend deportation be abolished and the whole
issue left to the Home Secretary.

Appeals against a recommendation, like those against
conviction and sentence, lie to a superior court and it is
only when they have been exhausted (or the time limit for
appeal has expired)[121] that the second stage of the process may
arise - the making of a deportation order by the Secretary of
State. Before doing so, he must consider all the relevant
factors brought to his notice by his staff[122] and the deportee
and r.156 lists the usual ones. There is no specific reference
to the future overseas which the immigrant would face if an
order is made.[123] To the extent that this may embrace political
persecution, it will overlap with the Government's policy on
political asylum[124] - a policy which is neither clear nor
necessarily a sympathetic one. Above all, the decision is a
discretionary one for the Secretary of State. Thus, full and
carefully drafted representations from the applicant, family,
friends and pressure groups are essential. Of some aid at this
final stage can be the efforts of Members of Parliament and
publicity campaigns.[125] In the majority of cases, however,
representations will be doomed to failure and the Secretary of
State may try to persuade the immigrant to leave voluntarily.[126]
Voluntary departure avoids the issuance of a deportation order
(but it will prohibit re-entry) and may be a better course for
"young or first offenders".[127] On the other hand, if the Home
Office is determined to make an example of the defendant or

impress upon him the gravity of his misconduct, it can opt for a deportation order and it will be most difficult for him to persuade the Secretary that voluntary departure is more appropriate.[128]

Under the earlier rules for aliens,[129] the fact that a court did not recommend deportation or that a recommendation was quashed by a superior court did not oust the Secretary of State's power to make a deportation order as being "conducive to the public good". This alternative now applies to all immigrants and permits the Secretary of State to deport or curtail the person's leave of stay and, on expiry, prohibit his re-entry.[130] Such a decision depends upon all the circumstances and, in particular, the overriding design of r.154. Although the immigrant has a right of appeal against the decision to deport, the fact remains that he faces a double hurdle - even if he dissuades the court from making a recommendation, he can still be deported by the Secretary of State. It may well be fairer either to abolish the court's function in the deportation process and leave the matter to the Secretary or to make the court the sole arbiter of deportation following conviction. Either would be preferable to the double jeopardy which an offender currently faces.

Detention whilst a recommendation is considered

If the defendant is given a custodial sentence, consideration of the recommendation is suspended until he has served the term. The Home Office will then consider the matter in the light of the defendant's representations and the list of factors in r.156. Significantly, that list does not specifically refer either to any "material" change in circumstances which may have occurred since the recommendation was made or to whether the defendant is still a danger to society. Whilst both will doubtless be raised, it is regrettable that their importance is not highlighted, unlike the position of E.E.C. nationals, for whom both criteria have first to be satisfied.[131]

Even if the defendant has not been sentenced to imprisonment, it may be many weeks before he is deported. The time limits for appealing against the recommendation and, then possibly, against the country to which he is to be removed, must first expire.[132] Reports on the immigrant will have to be collected, any representations considered (and here the intervention of a Member of Parliament can be an effective brake on the procedure) and arrangements made for his removal.[133] The possibility that too many deportees, given non-custodial sentences, were detained pending consideration of a recommendation arose from the courts' reluctance to order the temporary release of the immigrant and from lacunae in the law.[134] The former was tackled by a Home Office Circular in 1978[135] which in effect urged courts to consider more seriously the possibility of ordering the defendant's release along the lines of the provisions of the Bail Act 1976.[136] Whether consequentially or not, the number of persons given non-custodial sentences but detained fell from 265 in 1978 to 134 in 1981.[137] The latter has been improved by Schedule 10 of the Criminal Justice Act 1982 which amends Schedule 3 of the Immigration Act and makes it clear that the court has the power to order release, subject to the attachment of restrictions as to residence and reporting to the police.[138] Whilst clarifying the powers of the court, the Act is silent as to the criteria to be used in their exercise and reliance must therefore still be placed on the 1978 Circular and its reference to the Bail Act. It is unfortunate that the opportunity was not taken of setting down specific guidelines.[139] If the court refuses to release, the Secretary of State can do so and, since the 1982 Act, can attach similar restrictions.[140] If the deportee is given a custodial sentence, he will remain in detention after serving it, whilst the recommendation is considered, unless the court or Secretary of State otherwise direct.[141] The possibility that individuals are unnecessarily detained pending consideration of, and arrangements for, deportation still remains and prompted the Divisional Court in Hardial Singh[142] to issue a sharp and welcome warning to the Home Office to exercise all reasonable expedition to remove the deportee. It hinted that, if an unreasonable time is taken, a writ of habeas corpus would be appropriate.

Comment

The court's power to recommend deportation is open to several objections.[143] First, the courts, especially magistrates, may be too ready to make recommendations.[144] Second, the few attempts at self-imposed guidelines, such as those put forward by the Court of Appeal in Nazari,[145] have resulted in ineffectual platitudes. Third, there is undue duplication since the Home Secretary will consider the matter, whether the court makes a recommendation or not. Fourth, in doing so, he is able to make a thorough review of a wider range of circumstances. On the other hand, (1) the courts can act as a first sieve. Moreover, (2) it may be too sweeping to criticise their readiness to deport, for Nazari and Serry[146] show that they are capable of self-restraint. (3) If the courts' role were to be abolished, all cases would be referred to the Home Office and the danger of creating a presumption in favour of deportation might arise, without the check of a court.

It is suggested that the courts' involvement be retained as a first hurdle to sift out the obviously non-deportable cases, but with some modifications. First, the Secretary of State should lose the power to deport those for whom the court does not make a recommendation. Second, guidelines along the model of r.156 should be distilled from the jurisprudence and laid down in statutory form for use by the Courts. They should include a presumption against deportation. Third, deportation should only be possible for an offence committed within three years of entry.[147] Fourth, it should be possible to compile a list of deportable offences.[148] Fifth, those recommended for deportation should have the right to appeal to the Immigration Appeals Tribunal against the Home Secretary's decision to uphold a recommendation. This is particularly important since the Secretary considers wider matters than those before the court and is at present the final arbiter of them. This procedure may appear lengthy and cumbersome, but it should be noted that the current procedure may involve considerable delays whilst representations and lobbying are undertaken. Moreover, the more rights of appeal available to the immigrant, the fairer is the system; this is especially so since a recommendation may be upheld some years after it was made (at the end of a prison sentence) and it is thus just to hold a fresh hearing with a right of appeal. This would, incidentally, reflect E.E.C. law under which a recommendation will cease to have effect if circumstances have changed during the period of sentence and if it is not sufficiently proximate in time.[149]

Procedure following a deportation decision (other than a court recommendation)

The immigrant is given notice of the decision and of his right of appeal.[150] Whether he appeals or not, he may, at the Secretary of State's discretion, be released subject to conditions[151] (restricting his residence or requiring him to report to the police) or he may be detained.[152] If the latter is chosen and the immigrant decides to appeal, he has the right to apply to the adjudicator for bail.[153]

(a) Appeal

Although each category of deportee enjoys a right of appeal, its form differs as follows:

category	appeal forum
breach of conditions etc.	adjudicator - s.15(7)[154]
conducive to public good	generally I.A.T. - s.15(7)(a) security, political cases to Advisory panel - r.150
family deportations	I.A.T. - s.15(7)(b)
court recommendation	higher court - s.6
country of destination	adjudicator - s.17

The last category covers the immigrant against whom a deportation order has been, or is about to be, made,[155] who objects to the country to which he is to be deported and who wishes to be sent elsewhere. This right of appeal cannot be exercised as a pretext for disputing the deportation itself.[156] The normal practice is to return the immigrant to the country of his own nationality or that which most recently gave him travel documents.[157] The onus lies on him to show that another country will accept him[158] and there is no obligation on the Home Office to find him an alternative.[159] Whilst the earlier Rules obliged him to prove cogent and compelling reasons before the travel directions could be overturned,[160] the current Rules are not so limited. However, regard must be had to "the public interest generally and to any additional expense that may fall on public funds" if the travel directions are to be amended (r.169). This latter consideration can place the deportee in extreme difficulty; it may well take considerable time to arrange a visa for travel to a different country, necessitating adjournments, and, meanwhile, the public expense of his detention will work against him[161] and in favour of immediate deportation to the country originally specified in the Secretary of State's directions. The "public interest" can include the U.K.'s foreign policy of comity towards other countries, the need not to allow undue concessions to infringers of immigration law[162] and the overriding principle of consistency in decision-making under r.154, which will all tend toward swift removal.

Appeal in security cases

The Act makes no provision for appeal in these cases[163] but, in the face of Parliamentary pressure, the Rules incorporated[164] an appeal to an advisory panel, modelled on that which hears serious security cases against civil servants.[165] "Appeal" is a misnomer since the immigrant is not informed of the evidence against him or the reasons for the decision; instead, the nature of the allegations will be divulged as far as is possible.[166] Consequently, he is not permitted to cross-examine his accusers. The proceedings take place in camera. Legal representation is not allowed, though curiously a lawyer friend can accompany him. Most significantly, the panel can only offer advice to the Secretary of State and he is under no obligation to follow its opinion.

The procedure was branded as a prima facie breach of natural justice by the Court of Appeal in the Hosenball case.[167] However, in the words of Lord Denning,

> Great as is the public interest in the freedom of the individual and the doing of justice to him, nevertheless in the last resort it must take second place to the security of the country itself... There is a conflict here between the interests of national security on the one hand and the freedom of the individual on the other. The balance between these two is not for a court of law. It is for the Home Secretary.[168]

The conclusion is quite in keeping with the judiciary's reluctance to interfere in matters of national security but no more defensible because of that.[169] It is the hallmark of the rule of law that the courts should be the final arbiter in disputes between the interests of the State and of individual liberty. A litmus test of a society's determination to uphold civil liberties is the willingness to apply traditional criteria, such as the common law principle of natural justice, in just that type of hard case of which security appeals are an example. Such an approach by the Court of Appeal would not have involved a direct conflict with statute or even statutory rules[170] since the court itself recognised that "[Immigration Rules] are rules of practice laid down for the guidance of immigration officers and tribunals".[171] Moreover, it would not have forced the court to examine the merits of the case but would have compelled the Secretary of State to revise the procedures.

In fairness to the court, the responsibility for reform lies with the Secretary of State and Parliament. Furthermore, judicial deference to Government in security cases is common in other countries, including those that boast written constitutions, Bills of Rights and more active courts.[172] The E.E.C. rules stop short of such cases. Indeed, it is extraordinary how wide is the berth which democratic Governments have traditionally given to cases which hint of security implications and how readily carefully constructed and traditional legal safeguards are discarded on the assumption, rather than proof, that they are inappropriate. This is reflected by the terms of the European Convention of Human Rights in which the right to have the lawfulness of one's detention reviewed by a court is apparently specifically excluded.[173] In fact, in Caprino v U.K.[174] the Commission of Human Rights took the view that art. 5(1)(f) did not exclude the review of detention pending deportation as opposed to the deportation decision itself. However, with one dissentor, the Commission held that the applicant had not exhausted domestic remedies i.e. judicial review or habeas corpus, and that therefore the complaint was inadmissible. Decided at the time of Zamir[175] and related cases, when both forms of review were all but hypothetical, the Commission's decision is unrealistic; but, for the future, the ruling that detention pending deportation is still subject to Art. 5(4) of the Convention is potentially significant since, if the English courts, in the light of Khawaja,[176] still refuse to interfere with the deportation decision,[177] the Commission will be faced squarely with the scope of its earlier ruling in Caprino.

It is submitted that appeals in security related cases should be heard by a High Court judge, that the appellant should be entitled to the normal rules and protection of the criminal procedure (with the proviso that hearings may take place in camera) and that the judge's decision, if adverse to the Secretary of State, should be binding on him. The use of a senior judge would bring a visible degree of independence and, in view of the small number of cases involved, would not overburden the judiciary. To the objection that sensitive information might have to be revealed to the appellant, it can be answered that the general criminal law should be relied upon to defend the State rather than the back-door method of a secretive deportation procedure.

Appeal in non-security cases
These appeals lie direct to the I.A.T. In comparison with the security cases, this is by far the larger category of deportation as 'conducive to the public good', covering, for example, bogus marriages and those convicted but not recommended for deportation. Although each case must be seriously considered, the absence of guidance as to its use and the remoteness of judicial review[178] mean that the deportee's chances of success on appeal are slim[179] and that his best remedy may lie in publicity campaigns.

(b) The deportation order
The deportation decision can only be confirmed by the making of an order after the appellate system has run its course and after the Secretary of State has received a summary of the facts and any other relevant information, whether or not it was available to the appellate authorities.[180] This is the immigrant's last chance of influencing the Secretary's discretion to sign an order and it is here that the level and variety of pressures through, for example, Members of Parliament, may be crucial.[181] Whether and when an order is made are matters solely for the Secretary's discretion.[182] If, for example, such pressures are successful, the order can be suspended, reviewed regularly and replaced by restrictions as to residence etc. under Schedule 3, para. 2(5).[183]

(c) Duration of the order
An order lasts until it is revoked by the Secretary of State or, in family deportations, until the marriage ends or the children reach 18 years. Thus, if the deportee returns during its validity, he may be removed by virtue of it and his right of appeal is limited to claiming a legal right to remain, such as British citizenship or marriage.[184] On the other hand, since the Secretary's decision to remove is discretionary, the deportee can make representations and the Secretary is bound to consider them, though the overriding need to enforce immigration control will normally defeat the representations. Apart from this slender possibility, the only alternative open to the deportee is to apply for revocation of the order.[185] Application is made to the nearest entry clearance officer or direct to the Home Office but cannot be made whilst the person is in the U.K.[186] Although revocation was possible for aliens before 1971[187] and for Commonwealth citizens under the 1962 Act,[188] the issue was left entirely to the Secretary of State's

discretion. Since 1973 the factors relevant to revocation have been spelt out in some detail in the Rules and they include – the grounds and circumstances of the original deportation order, such as whether the deportee was a blatant or persistent transgressor of the law. This gives scope for the appellate authorities to express moral indignation at the deportee's conduct. His immigration history will be reviewed and evidence of "studied disregard or defiance of immigration control"[189] will rarely be outweighed by other factors favourable to him, for example,

> (i) any compassionate circumstances such as the presence of dependants in the U.K. or, if the deportee is young or enfeebled, the lack of support for him overseas;
> (ii) any material change of circumstance since the original order was made;
> (iii) passage of time since the order was made.[190]

Under the 1973 Rules a review was conducted after 3 years. The current Rules make no mention either of a review or of a fixed period before revocation is possible, but specifically provide that revocation within 3 years is only possible in the most exceptional circumstances. It is thus solely a matter for the Secretary of State's discretion and, given the importance of the need for immigration control, the passage of time will only stand a reasonable chance of success if allied to other favourable factors such as the youth of the deportee when originally removed or his previous and subsequent good record or family connections in the U.K.

If revocation is refused, the deportee is allowed to appeal[191] but only from outside the U.K. However, the Secretary of State is in turn empowered to veto personally an appeal if he deems it to be conducive to public good. The veto is not tied to interests of national security and thus extends too widely. It is another example of the overriding discretion of the Home Office.

Even if the applicant is successful, revocation does not entitle him to enter the U.K. but merely to reapply for admission in the normal way, with all that that entails.[192]

Exceptions
The following are excluded from liability to deportation:

> (a) Patrials or, to be more precise, British Citizens,[193] even if they hold dual nationality.[194] All lesser forms of citizenship under the Nationality Act 1981 are included in the deportation procedure.[195]
> (b) Persons able to claim diplomatic immunity under the Diplomatic Privileges Act 1964.[196] This immunity is very wide and includes any member of a mission, which is defined as the "head of the mission and the members of

the staff of the mission",[197] his family and anyone who forms part of his household. For this purpose, the "family" has been given a generous interpretation, covering, for example, the mother or sister of a bachelor or widower.[198] The only condition is that the applicant can claim to be a part of the agent's household[199] at the date of the decision to deport, even though he may have entered the U.K. in another capacity.[200] In cases of doubt, a certificate from the Foreign Secretary is conclusive as regards entitlement to immunity.[201] This broad interpretation is a direct result of Treaty obligations and reflects the historically perceived benefits of diplomatic relations. A diplomatic agent can of course be declared persona non grata and removed in that way; but this is a recourse generally reserved for cases of security or retaliation in kind.

(c) Irish and Commonwealth citizens who were ordinarily resident in the U.K. in 1973 when the Immigration Act came into force and who have been ordinarily resident here for 5 years before the deportation decision is made.[202] This type of concession dates back to the 1962 Act[203] and is a dwindling exemption since most of those affected will have regularised their position by taking out patriality or, now, citizenship. The incentive to do so is strong since, without holding patriality or citizenship, such people are in a precarious position -free from deportation but not entitled to re-enter the U.K. at will. For those who have not so regularised their status, for example, because they would lose their current overseas citizenship by doing so, the onus is clearly on them to establish their entitlement.[204] The imprecise, though after Shah,[205] liberal, concept of "ordinary residence" must be satisfied for the precise requisite period.[206] The exception only applies to Irish or Commonwealth citizens and thus, if a country, like Pakistan, leaves the Commonwealth, its citizens in the U.K. will lose the benefit of s.7 unless they become British citizens.[207] If not they must rely upon the unpredictable generosity of Home Office discretion to forego deportation.[208]

(d) Refugees.[209] In reaching a decision here full account must be taken of the Convention Relating to the Status of Refugees (1951),[210] to which the U.K. is a party. Consequently, if a refugee has entered the U.K. lawfully he will not be expelled "save on grounds of national security or public order".[211] If he has entered illegally but can explain the necessity for doing so, he should not incur penalties[212] and may be allowed to stay as a refugee or given time to seek admission to another country. Significantly, the I.A.T. has held that "control of immigration is necessary for the maintenance of public order".[213] Even if a deportation order is made, whether against a refugee or not, it is still open to the deportee to raise the issue of likely persecution if deported to a particular country[214] and the 1951 Convention forbids his return to that country unless there are "reasonable grounds for regarding [him] as a danger to security... or [if he] having been convicted by a final judgment of a particularly serious crime, constitutes a danger to the community".[215] Interestingly, Rule 165 does not mention these exceptional cases permitting expulsion. Its prohibition is without reservation; but the real hurdle is to qualify for the refugee status or to adduce evidence of persecution. It is today extremely difficult for an individual to satisfy r.153 or 165. The Home Office demands a high standard of evidence and tends towards a narrow exercise of its discretion.[216]

----

1   Richard Crossman, The Diaries of a Cabinet Minister, vol. 2, p.773 (1976).

2   These methods involve compulsion by the State. Under s.29 of the Immigration Act 1971, public funds can be made available to assist the voluntary repatriation of immigrants. Two schemes are operated - one by the Home Office and the other by the Department of Health and Social Security. Few immigrants are tempted by them - 139 under the former scheme in 1980-81 at a cost of £78,500 and 36 under the latter in 1982 at a cost of £16,000. See H.C. Debs. 11 February 1982 col. 426, 22 March col. 235, 17 May 1982 col. 13, 16 June col. 187. The schemes have been reviewed by the Home Office, see H.C. Debs. 19 January 1984 col. 421. For figures for 1980-84, see H.C. Debs. 23 May 1985, col. 508.

3   Treaties may of course impose restraints, e.g. Title III, Chapter 1 of E.E.C. Treaty; U.N. Convention on the Status of Refugees; extradition treaties.

4   Per Mr. Justice Gray in Fong Yue Ting v U.S. 149 U.S. 698, at 711; cf. Pochi v Minister for Immigration (1983) 43 A.L.R. 261 which makes it clear that the power of deportation applies to all aliens in Australia no matter how absorbed into the community they have become. A striking example of sovereign power was Nigeria's decision in January 1983 to give illegal immigrants (nearly 2 million) 2 weeks in which to leave.

5   9 Henry III c.30.

6   E.g. the expulsion of the Jews in 1290.

7   See R v Symons (1814) 2 Stra. Madras Reports 93, at 103. Academic opinion inclined to the same view, whereas the Government protested its existence. For the opposing views, see Vol. 6 British Digest of International Law, p.83-97.

8   E.g. 3 Henry V, c.3 (1415) ordering the departure, on pain of death, of all Bretons, who were not denizens.

9   Cf. the writ of ne exeat regno, the scope of which has been held to have withered by non-use, Felton v Callis [1969] 1 Q.B. 200.

10   See the general principle of A.G. v De Keyser's Royal Hotel [1920] A.C. 508. For a discussion of the prerogative, see Vincenzi [1985] P.L. 93.

11   E.g. Turner v Williams 194 U.S. 279, in which the First Amendment (freedom of expression) was jettisoned in favour of

legislation providing for the exclusion and removal of political agitators.

12 Salemi (1977) 14 A.L.R. 1; Capello (1980) 49 F.L.R. 40; Safadi (1981) 38 A.L.R. 399; Haj-Ismail (1982) 40 A.L.R. 341; Arslan (1984) 55 A.L.R. 361; Kioa (1984) 55 A.L.R. 669. The Administrative Appeals Tribunal must observe natural justice, but the content is variable, see Barbaro (1982) 44 A.L.R. 690; and if the Tribunal makes a recommendation to the Minister, he is then under a duty to observe natural justice, Barbaro (1983) 46 A.L.R. 123.

13 E.g. Safadi, ibid, at 403-4, Tagle (1983) 48 A.L.R. 566; cf. the residuary role of the 'Wednesbury Corporation principles' in English law (Associated Provincial Picture Houses Ltd. v Wednesbury Corporation [1948] 1 K.B. 223) and the recent concept of 'legitimate expectation' which brought success to the individual in A.G. of Hong Kong v Ng Yuen Shiu [1983] 2 A.C. 629, and Asif Khan [1984] 1 W.L.R. 1337.

14 Geo 3, c.4, followed by harsher provisions in 1798, 38 Geo 3, c.50, c.77; and replaced by a more relaxed scheme in 42 Geo 3, c.92 (1802). The 1802 Act was repealed the following year and the earlier 1798 model revived, 43 Geo 3, c.155. In 1814 the less restrictive 1802 model was brought back, 54 Geo 3, c.155, whereas in 1815 the stricter 1803 version replaced it, 55 Geo 3, c.54. In 1816 the 1802 model returned, 56 Geo 3, c.86. The 1826 Act then concentrated on compiling information, 7 Geo 4, c.54.

15 This twofold classification still underlies the current law, viz. court recommendations and deportation decisions by the Secretary of State.

16 See also ss.1-3 of the 1802 Act, 42 Geo 3, c.92.

17 S.16, 38 Geo 3, c.50 (1798).

18 Parliamentary Debs. 2nd Series, vol. 10, col. 1338.

19 11 Vict. c.20. It was passed through fear of foreigners fomenting civil unrest.

20 Parliamentary Papers 688, vol. 33, 227. However, extradition and removal of lunatics were possible - Extradition Act 1870, Lunacy Act 1890.

21 By the simple device of applying the 1914 Act outside wartime conditions - s.1, Aliens Restriction (Amendment) Act 1919.

22 E.g. Aliens Order 1919, Art. 12(1); Aliens Order 1953, Art. 20.

23 Venicoff [1920] 3 K.B.. 72.

24 H.C. Debs. 2 August 1956, col. 174. The change was introduced following the U.K.'s commitment to the European Convention on Establishment. In 1965 the Government was able to observe that the Secretary had always followed the Magistrate's advice (White Paper, cmnd. 2739, para. 26).

25 Immigration Act, s.3(5) and (6); Immigration Rules (1983 H.C. 169) 148-171. The Secretary of State may seek to deport on more than one basis - Veena Ahluwalia [1979-80] Imm. A.R. 1. Separate provisions govern E.E.C. protected persons, since account must be taken of Art. 48(3) of the E.E.C. Treaty; see ch. 5.

26 Clearly illustrated by the facts and decision in Mehmet [1978] Imm. A.R. 46. Cf. the similar procedural division in the U.S. - Title 8 U.S.C. para 1252.

27 S.5(1) Yuksel [1976] Imm. A.R. 91. The Secretary of State has a similarly broad discretion as to when the order itself should be implemented. Thus, he need not suspend it whilst an appeal is pursued under the European Convention on Human Rights; see Fernandes [1981] Imm. A.R.1 and cf. Kirkwood, [1984] 2 All E.R. 390 in relation to extradition (see Warbrick [1984] P.L. 539).

28 Witness the celebrated case of the Pereira family in May 1984.

29 See Mehmet, supra.

30 E.g. Jordan [1970] Imm. A.R. 201.

31 [1978] Imm. A.R. 36.

32 R.158. Conditions could include those on employment, for example, or registration with the police.

33 H.A.C., Evidence, Q 507.

34 Control of Immigration: Statistics (1984), Cmnd. 9544, Table 20.

35 S.24(1)(b).

36 Gurdev Singh [1973] 1 W.L.R. 1444. In contrast, under the Commonwealth Immigrants Act 1962 overstaying was expressly

made a continuing offence, s.4(1).

37 Grant v Borg [1982] 2 All E.R. 257. An unsuccessful attempt to reverse the decision by making the offence a continuing one was made in the legislative Chamber of that House soon afterwards during the passage of the Criminal Justice Bill, see H.L. Debs. 23 July 1982, col. 1094. See also the Immigration Offences (Amendment) Bill 1984, H.C. Debs. 6 April 1984, col. 1323.

38 [1980] 3 All E.R. 880, in relation to court recommendations (see below).

39 See Grant and Martin, 230-232 for an account of successful cases.

40 Cmnd. 4295, r.41 (1970), H.C. 80, r.42 (1973).

41 R.143, H.C. 394 (1980), r.158, H.C. 169 (1983).

42 R.154 is thus relevant.

43 H.C. 80, r.42.

44 Bakhtaur Singh, Times 15 December 1984, reversing the first instance approach in Times 12 March 1984, and affirming Darshan Singh Sohal [1981] Imm. A.R. 20, which reserved such circumstances for the Secretary of State's discretion.

45 The preoccupation of the 1965 White Paper (cmnd. 2739) with evasion of control can be seen as the source of this.

46 The Overstayers Tracing and Intelligence Section, the Joint Overstayers Exercise Unit, the Immigration Service Intelligence Unit at Harmondsworth.

47 See Gordon, 'Passport Raids', for a collection of sources, at ch. 3. For a recent example, see H.C. Debs. 25 May 1984, col. 580, and see also H.C. Debs. 30 March 1984, col. 305.

48 Its legislative roots lie in wartime emergency statutes - see the succession of Acts surrounding the Napoleonic Wars, footnote 14 above. It resurfaced in the Aliens Restriction Act 1914 and was a regular feature of peacetime legislation thereafter. See para 20 of Aliens Order 1953 and for an early example see Venicoff [1920] 3 K.B. 72.

49 S.15(7)(a).

50 Cmnd. 9544, Table 20.

51 In the ten years up to May 1985 there were only 8 deportation orders based on national security (2 in 1977, 6 in 1984) - H.C. Debs. 13 May 1985, col. 10.

52 S.15(3).

53 [1977] 3 All E.R. 452. See H.C. Debs. 18 November, 1976, col. 1567. The appellants became well-known but unsuccessful litigants, not merely in England, but in Scotland - Agee v Lord Adv. (1977) S.L.T. (Notes) 54 and in the U.S. - Haig v Agee 453 U.S. 280 (1981); see further under appeals, below.

54 E.g. the publicity which surrounded the first special appeal under the Act by Caprino, which named the members of the review panel (Times, 23 January 1975) and which raised the matter in Parliament. The deportation decision was quickly revoked (Times 25 January). On the other hand, if public opinion is sympathetic to the Secretary of State, the power can be used with remarkable speed, e.g. the removal of Libyans in March 1984 following public order disturbances. The Libyans chose not to exercise their right to make representations against deportation, H.C. Debs. 11 May 1984, col. 485.

55 Under extradition treaties, a person will not be extradited if, by doing so, he will be returned to a country to stand trial for a "political offence", Extradition Act 1870 s.4. Considerable jurisprudence exists as to the meaning of "political offence", see below.

56 Similarly, the countries may not be signatories to the various Treaties which have sprung up in recent years for the return of terrorists, hijackers, drug offenders and so forth.

57 F.O. 368/379. For an account of a case where the power appears to have been used to avoid more formal proceedings, see Gill, Guardian 27 December 1984.

58 [1963] 2 Q.B. 243; see O'Higgins 27 M.L.R. 521.

59 Supra.

60 For the reverse situation, deportation rather than extradition from abroad, see R v Guildford Justice e.p. Healy [1983] 1 W.L.R. 108, where it was unsuccessfully alleged that the British police had connived with their U.S. counterparts to engineer the deportation rather than extradition of the accused back to the U.K; and R v Mackeson (1981) 75 Cr. App. R. 24 where it was successfully argued, resulting remarkably in the Court of Appeal quashing a conviction subsequent to a deportation from Zimbabwe; cf. R v Hartley [1978] 2 N.Z.L.R. 199 and see Warbrick [1983] P.L. 269. The Mackeson case was

subsequently disapproved of by R v Plymouth Justices, ex p. Driver [1985] 2 All E.R. 681, and it is submitted that the reasoning in that case is more persuasive and certainly more in keeping with the courts' traditional reserve.

61 E.g. the Church of Scientology. The blanket ban on this organisation was lifted in 1980 (H.C. Debs. 16 July, col. 578) but the conducive to public good power is still available for individual cases.

62 Marshall [1971] P.L. 2. For a debate on the case, see H.L. Debs. 20 January 1971, col. 522.

63 The 1973 Rules specifically mentioned this category, r.50 of H.C. 82, r.43 of H.C. 80. Its primacy is unlikely to have changed in spite of the current omission. For an example, see Mitchell [1981] Imm. A.R. 140, in which the 'public interest' demanded that a convicted robber be removed. The power can also be used , for example, against illegal entrants - Butt [1979-80] Imm. A.R. 82.

64 See, for example, Bashir [1978] Imm. A.R. 150; Butt supra.

65 [1982] Imm. A.R. 124. See also, Mohd Malik [1981] Imm. A.R. 134. Though the precise reasons for using the power must be spelt out - Ahmud Khan [1982] Imm. A.R. 134.

66 It may be compounded by the eagerness of Home Office officials to use it, see Ramnial (1983) L.Soc.Gaz., p.30.

67 For example, where E.E.C. protection is lost but there is no specific power of removal.

68 Under the earlier law, the same result could be achieved under the general discretionary powers of aliens' legislation, or as "conducive to public good". Much of the hostility to s.3(5)(c) was due to the specific inclusion of this tradition and to the inclusion of Commonwealth citizens within it.

69 Yau Yak Wah [1982] Imm. A.R. 16, for otherwise the Secretary does not exercise his discretion at all and judicial review will be available.

70 See, for example, Ozter [1978] Imm. A.R. 137.

71 See the excellent example of Anand [1978] Imm. A.R. 36.

72 R. 162.

73 Cf. the position in divorce under the Matrimonial Causes Act 1973, s.2(6); see Mouncer v Mouncer [1972] 1 All E.R. 289,

Santos v Santos [1972] Fam. 247, Bromley's Family Law, 6th Ed. at p.225.

74 E.g. orders under the Domestic Proceedings and Magistrates' Courts Act 1978.

75 S.5(4). As to proof of "belonging to a family", see s.15(6).

76 R.163.

77 Three years were held insufficient on the facts in Ozter [1978] Imm. A.R. 137.

78 For a perfect example of this, see Anand [1978] Imm. A.R. 36. Strictly speaking the child's case should be treated separately; see Yau Yak Wah [1982] Imm. A.R. 16.

79 16 years being the minimum age for marriage in England, Marriage Act 1949, s.2.

80 R.163.

81 Ibid.

82 See Ozter [1978] Imm. A.R. 137.

83 On that date the British Nationality Act 1981 came into force and under its provisions the acquisition of citizenship by ius soli has been abolished.

84 S.15(7)(b).

85 S.5(6); a considerable inducement and an indication of the determined policy of the Act.

86 R.164.

87 See A.M. v Denmark, case 9490/81 where it was held not to be a breach of Art. 8(2) to remove a family, since the wife could be expected to accompany her husband abroad.

88 Home Office Statistical Bulletin, Table 14 and Cmnd. 9544, Table 20.

89 S.6 and Rules 156, 157.

90 For example, s.3 of 33 Geo. 3 c.4, s.7 of 42 Geo 3 c.92.

91 S.3(1)(a).

92 Aliens Order 1920 art.12, Aliens Order 1953, art 20.

93 For the exceptions see below. For cases under the 1962 Act, see Shyllon 34 M.L.R. 135, at p.142-146.

94 Home Office Statistical Bulletin, Table 14 and Cmnd. 9544, Table 20.

95 See, for example, R v Edgehill [1963] 1 All E.R. 181; Nazari [1980] 3 All E.R. 880.

96 S.3(6). In cases of doubt as to his age, e.g. forged birth certificate, the court is empowered to consider any evidence as to his true age (s.6(3)(a)).

97 See the case of Thondup, Guardian, 8 November 1977.

98 Nembhard [1963] Crim L.R. 447, Castelli [1976] Crim. L.R. 387.

99 R.40 of Cmnd 4295, 4297, which specifically mentioned borstal training.

100 S.6(4), specifically reversing the previous, contrary judicial assumption expressed in Assa Singh [1965] Crim. L.R. 297.

101 S.6(3)(b). Such restrictions are contained in s.1 and generally Part I of Criminal Justice Act 1982.

102 Rule 39 of Cmnd 4295, 4297. The changes forcefully emphasise that the scope of deportation is meant to be very wide.

103 S.6(3), e.g. a special verdict, a failed alternative verdict.

104 S.6(2).

105 It was encouraged in Mulroy [1963] Crim. L.R. 431; Edgehill, infra; Antypas (1973) 57 Cr. App. R. 207.

106 E.g. Tillman [1965] Crim. L.R. 615; Labbe [1966] Crim. L.R. 56; Yont [1967] Crim. L.R. 546.

107 See Zellick [1973] Crim. L.R. 612. See further, Robertson, Guardian, 25 August 1980 and Blom-Cooper, Guardian, 15 September 1980.

108 Edgehill [1963] 1 All E.R. 181, Assa Singh [1965] Crim. L.R. 297; Nazari [1980] 3 All E.R. 880.

109 Per Lawton L.J. in Nazari, at p.885. This case is a welcome, if overdue, exposition of guidelines in this area. Endorsed by Williams v Smith (1982) S.L.T. 163; compare similar judicial guidance in Australia - Re Georges (1978) 22 A.L.R. 667.

110 Ibid.

111 For example, the notoriety in the mid-1970s of London as a paradise for visiting shoplifters and the judiciary's determination to stamp it out. On the other hand, a serious offence need not justify a recommendation if it was an isolated incident committed under, for example, emotional pressure - Tshuma (1981) 3 Cr. App. R. (S) 97.

112 E.g. Baidoo [1971] Crim. L.R. 293.

113 Rules 39 and 40 of Cmnd 4295, 4297 (1970).

114 Per LLoyd J. in Serry (1980) 2 Cr. App. R. (S) 336; cf. Docherty [1963] Crim. L.R. 106.

115 See the view of the Recorder in Serry, cited by Lloyd J. Moreover, the observation is only relevant to the courts; social security is still a factor which the Home Secretary may consider.

116 This is especially important, since they too may be deported after him; see above. The factor has always been important, e.g. Friedman (1914) 10 Cr. App. R. 72; Gilbert (1921) 16 Cr. App. R. 34. On the other hand, the fact that his family cannot be deported (e.g. because of citizenship) may count in his favour since it may be unwise to split the family unit, see Barbaro (1982) 46 A.L.R. 123.

117 Walters [1978] Crim. L.R. 175, Thoseby and Krawszyk (1979) Cr. App. R. (S) 280. For example, where the wife is mentally ill and there is no family support abroad; cf. Tabag v Minister for Immigration (1983) 45 A.L.R. 705.

118 Caird (1970) 54 Cr. App. R. 499; Uddin [1971] Crim. L.R. 663; Nazari [1980] 3 All E.R. 880.

119 Caird, supra, per Sachs L.J. at p.510.

120 Cf. the similar position on asylum and the recognition of States.

121 S.6(6), being 21 days if a magistrates' court made the recommendation, and 28 days if a higher court.

[122] This could include the evidence supplied by informers, though such information should obviously be treated with caution, especially since the deportee cannot at this stage challenge it, cf. Suardana (1980) 49 F.L.R. 8 and the procedure for review in Australia.

[123] In spite of the fact that the court may have specifically referred this factor to the Secretary's domain, see above.

[124] See chapter 5.

[125] E.g. the well publicised case of the Pereira family in March, April and May, 1984.

[126] R.156. Cf. a similar but limited system of voluntary departure in the U.S. - 8 U.S.C. 1254(e).

[127] Ibid. A further inducement is the power of the Secretary to pay the expenses of the defendant's and his family's removal, s.5(6). From the Home Office's point of view that also avoids the need to make a separate order against the defendant's family.

[128] Csenyi [1975] Imm. A.R. 92.

[129] R.37, Cmnd 4297 (1970).

[130] R.157.

[131] See Santillo [1980] E.C.R. 1585 and see chapter 5.

[132] Being 3 weeks for the former and 2 for the latter, Crown Court Rules 1971, r.7(3), Immigration Appeals (Procedure) Rules 1984, r.4(10)(b), respectively. As to appeals against the country of destination, they can only take place when the Secretary of State has decided on the particular country, see generally Enwia [1984] 1 W.L.R. 117.

[133] Ministerial reply, H.C. Debs. 19 February 1981, col. 190.

[134] See Burgess, (1979) N.L.J. 235.

[135] No. 113/1978.

[136] The Bail Act does not apply to the Immigration Act, but the Circular asked courts to bear its provisions in mind and especially the desirability of bail unless the risks of absconding or of further offences outweigh it.

[137] H.L. Debs. 23 July 1982, col. 1143, see further H.C. Debs.

25 February 1985, col. 29.

138 The Schedule contains detailed provisions for the rearrest of persons who breach such restrictions whilst released, paras. 7 to 10. The tortuous drafting of the Schedule results in Schedule 3 of the Immigration Act being irritatingly cumbersome.

139 Contrast the guidelines for release pending appeals to adjudicators and the I.A.T. - Immigration Act, Schedule 2, para. 30.

140 Schedule 10, para. 1(c). Under the previous law, the Secretary could order release but had no power to attach restrictions, thus making release almost impossible.

141 1971 Act, Schedule 3 para 2(1). It makes no difference that another court has allowed bail - Giambi [1982] 1 W.L.R. 535. Incidentally, if an immigrant is remanded in custody on one charge and simultaneously detained under the Act, the latter period of detention does now reduce any sentence for the former -s.34 Criminal Justice Act 1982.

142 [1984] 1 All E.R. 983. For suggestions that deportees who are willing to depart are nevertheless unnecessarily detained, see A Law Unto Themselves, (1985), Prison Reform Trust and Joint Council for the Welfare of Immigrants.

143 See, for example, the Wilson Committee, Cmnd 3387 (1967), which recommended its abolition.

144 See the criticism voiced against the speedy trial, conviction and recommendation for deportation, of Iranian protesters in 1980 - Robertson, Guardian 25 August 1980, Blom-Cooper, Guardian 15 September 1980.

145 [1980] 3 All E.R. 880.

146 (1980) 2 Cr. App. R. (S) 336.

147 Cf. Migration Act 1958 (Australia), s.13(a) which specifies 5 years. To tie deportation to a minimum length of sentence, as in the U.S. (8 U.S.C. 1251(a)(4)), might, on the other hand, only encourage British judges to award them.

148 There is a danger of Draconian overelaboration of offences. Cf. the expansive concept of 'moral turpitude' in the U.S., ibid and see 23 Am.L.R. (Fed.) 480 for an account.

149 Santillo [1980] E.C.R. 1585. See the excellent example of Monteil [1984] 1 C.M.L.R. 264 where M had nine convictions in

4 years but, since imprisonment had cured him, there was no longer any personal conduct under art. 48(3) of the Treaty so as to justify deportation.

[150] S.18 and Appeals (Notices) Regulations 1984.

[151] Sch. 3, para. 2(5). This decision will depend on factors relevant to bail such as the risks of absconding or of further offences, the strength of family ties and character references.

[152] Ibid, para. 2(2).

[153] Sch. 2, para. 29. In this case, however, para. 30 lays down statutory guidance as to the factors to be considered.

[154] Except that if an appeal against a family deportation is concurrently brought, both will be heard by the I.A.T. - s.15(8).

[155] S.17(3) and (1) respectively. S.17 also covers those refused leave to enter or those here in breach of a deportation order. If notice of the proposed removal directions is given whilst an appeal against a deportation decision is being made, the immigrant must contest those directions in the same appeal; if they are given after his appeal has been heard, he can lodge a separate appeal to the adjudicator.

[156] Ali [1973] Imm. A.R. 33, Muruganandarajah, Times 23 July 1984.

[157] R.169.

[158] Derricks [1970] Imm. A.R. 109.

[159] Croning [1970] Imm. A.R. 51.

[160] R.46 of Cmnd 4295 (1970).

[161] Kroohs [1978] Imm. A.R. 75. The deportee is most likely to be in detention since the bail provisions of Schedule 2 para. 29 of the Act cannot operate during an appeal against destination without the consent of the Secretary of State -para 30. If the deportee is unhappy over the handling of his case or detention (but not the decision on the merits), he can complain to the Ombudsman, but this need not halt his removal and does not guarantee recompense.

[162] Mustafa [1979-80] Imm. A.R. 32.

163 S.15(3). The Immigration Appeals Act 1969 allowed one either to an adjudicator or to a specially constituted I.A.T. (s.9).

164 R.35, H.C. 80 (1973). Now r.150. See H.C. Debs. 15 June 1971, cols 369-397 for a description of the procedure.

165 Known as the "Three Wise Men". See Street, "Freedom, the Individual and the Law" 5th Ed, p.236-247 for a description and critique. For membership of the immigration panel, see H.C. Debs. 8 May 1984, col. 281.

166 R.150. Cf. a similar exception for security cases in the E.E.C., Directive 64/221, art. 6, and the Canadian Immigration Act 1976 s.40 (appellant will not be informed of the evidence if it is prejudicial to national security).

167 R v Secretary of State for the Home Department ex p. Hosenball [1977] 3 All E.R. 452.

168 At p.460-461. The European Commission of Human Rights reached a similar conclusion in rejecting the application of Hosenball's fellow deportee, Agee -case 7729/76.

169 E.g. Venicoff [1920] 3 K.B. 72, Soblen [1963] 2 Q.B. 243.

170 Even if it had, the common law is clearly able "to supply the omission of the legislature" - Cooper v Wandsworth Board of Works (1863) 14 C.B. (N.S.) 180 at 190, 194. Cf. the analogy of the Prison Rules where the courts have recently been prepared to incorporate elements of natural justice - St. Germain [1979] Q.B. 425, Fox-Taylor [1982] 1 All E.R. 646, Mealy, Times 14 November 1981, Anderson [1984] Q.B. 778, Tarrant [1985] Q.B. 251.

171 Per Lord Denning at p.459.

172 E.g. the procedure of the Special Advisory Board in Canada in security cases, Immigration Act 1976, s.83. See further Prata v Minister of Manpower and Immigration (1975) 52 D.L.R. (3d) 383, where the Supreme Court of Canada ruled that a Ministerial certificate excluding a hearing in security cases, was valid in spite of the applicant's pleas to natural justice and the Canadian Bill of Rights. The decision was endorsed and extended by the Immigration Act 1978. For the U.S., note Kleindienst v U.S. 408 U.S. 753 (1972).

173 Art. 5(1)(f).

174 Case 6871/75.

175 [1980] A.C. 930, see Part II of this chapter.

176 [1984] A.C. 74.

177 And it is highly unlikely that the timidity of the courts will be changed by Khawaja. If an immigrant sought "to go behind the record" in habeas corpus proceedings, the Home Secretary's justification of "security considerations" or similar generalities, will doubtless satisfy the court.

178 Ramnial, (1983) L.Soc.Gaz. 30.

179 In 1980, of 76 appeals lodged, 11 were successful, H.C. Debs. 24 July 1981, col. 264; in 1982 of 53 appeals, 8 were successful, H.C. Debs. 7 March 1983, col. 278.

180 R.167.

181 The lodging of a complaint with the European Commission of Human Rights is one method of staying execution, especially if supported by a M.P. The Court of Appeal however has noticed this ploy and held that the Home Office is entitled to ignore it - Fernandes, [1981] Imm. A.R. 1. Cf. to similar effect, Kirkwood [1984] 2 All E.R. 390.

182 Yuksel [1976] Imm. A.R. 91. Although, following Hardial Singh [1984] 1 All E.R. 983, he must probably reach a decision within a reasonable time.

183 See the concession granted to some Cypriots in the 1970s - Mustafa [1979-80] Imm. A.R. 32.

184 R.168.

185 S.15(1)(b), r.170, 171.

186 S.15(5).

187 Aliens Order 1953, art. 29.

188 S.9(3), Commonwealth Immigrants Act.

189 Sanusi [1975] Imm. A.R. 114, cf. Dervish [1970] Imm. A.R. 48.

190 E.g. Udoh [1970] Imm. A.R. 89, under the 1962 Act in which 2 years' atonement sufficed.

191 S.15(5). The Home Office, in its discussion paper the Review of Appeals under the Immigration Act 1971, has suggested that the right of appeal against a refusal to revoke

342

a deportation order should be withdrawn, partly because there are very few and partly because very few are successful. Both reasons are, it is suggested, shabby.

192 See chapter 4.

193 S.3(5) as amended by the British Nationality Act 1981, Sch. 4. A deportation order will similarly cease to have effect if the deportee achieves this status.

194 Romano [1963] Crim. L.R. 638.

195 Cf. the earlier Rules (e.g. r.31 of Cmnd 4297) where a British Protected Person was excluded.

196 S.8(3) Immigration Act, r.149. The 1964 Act incorporated the Vienna Convention on Diplomatic Relations, including the definition of those so entitled.

197 Convention, art. 1.

198 Gupta [1979-80] Imm. A.R. 52.

199 This is a question of fact in which the degree of dependence will play a significant role.

200 Gupta, supra.

201 S.4 of the 1964 Act.

202 S.7 of the 1971 Act, r.149. The crucial date is that of the decision, not the order. Ahmet Mehmet [1977] Imm. A.R. 68, Rehman [1978] Imm. A.R. 80.

203 S.7(2), 1962 Act.

204 S.7(5), 1971 Act.

205 [1983] 2 A.C. 309.

206 O'Connor [1977] Imm. A.R. 29. As a palliative, ordinary residence will not be negatived by overstaying (s.7(2)), though it will be by other breaches of immigration law - Bangoo [1976] Crim. L.R. 746.

207 Rehman, supra; Pakistan Act 1973, Sched. 3, para. 1.

208 In practice, the Home Office frequently regard those from Pakistan as still Commonwealth citizens for the purpose of deportation, but this is by no means a binding concession.

209 Rules 153 and 165.

210 U.N.T.S., vol. 139, p.137, see Cmnd 9171. In contrast to earlier Immigration Rules (e.g. H.C. 82, r.56) no mention is made of other international agreements, notably the Convention on Stateless Persons (1954 U.N.T.S., vol. 360, p.117). The omission is not critical since its terms are almost identical to those of the 1951 Convention.

211 Ibid, art. 32(1).

212 Art. 31(1).

213 Kelzani [1978] Imm. A.R. 193.

214 R.165.

215 Art. 33(2).

216 See further chapter 5.

Part II   Other Methods of Removal and Appeals

B. REMOVAL BY ADMINISTRATIVE DIRECTION AND ILLEGAL ENTRANTS

This power is particularly concerned with the removal of
illegal entrants. The Select Committee (1978) identified four
methods of illegal entry:

   (a) the use of false documents before the entry clearance
       officer,
   (b) the use of false documents at the port of entry,
   (c) covert entry,
   (d) overstaying.[1]

It is with (a) to (c) that this section is concerned, for, by
virtue of Schedule 2 of the Act, those refused leave to enter,
illegal entrants and certain offending seamen and aircrews can
be removed immediately or detained pending arrangements for
removal. Appeal against removal can only be made from
overseas.[2] The procedure is a flexible, speedy and relatively
untrammelled power of removal with obvious advantages over the
more formal deportation or prosecution procedures.[3] Its
advantages are not without justification. If a person clearly
does not fall within a category of permissible entrants or if
he enters by stealth, his expeditious removal will save the
public purse, is fairer to those who have applied properly and
lawfully and may perhaps discourage imitators. The merits are
not quite so obvious if, years after entry, an illegality is
discovered and he is removed forthwith. Yet that is the
position which has been reached, partly through the increasing
stringency of the laws and mainly through judicial
interpretation. The resulting definition of "illegal entrant"
provoked fierce criticism and led to a notable judicial
somersault.

This process must be viewed against the background of a
ruthless determination by Governments since 1965,[4] and
especially since the mid-1970s, to detect illegal entrants.
This is due in part to the lack of a ready alternative target
for a Government which wishes to be seen as displaying a tough
attitude towards immigration. The fervour has been regularly
fanned by media coverage, with, for example, references to
illegal immigration rackets.[5]

This development is illustrated by the record of the
numbers of illegal immigrants detected and dealt with each
year under Schedule 2 of the Act:[6]

	those detected	those dealt with[7]
1974	140	110
1975	188	186
1976	394	349
1977	809	778
1978	934	883
1979	990	963
1980	1620	1528
1981	994	1050
1982	1257	1140
1983	830	983
1984	958	822

Background

In 1905,[8] immigration officers were placed under the duty to prevent the landing of "undesirable" aliens and in 1920 this was extended[9] to cover those who had avoided entry at the designated ports. In contrast, Commonwealth entrants remained free from control until 1962 and the Act of that year can be seen, in retrospect, as a tentative and modest attempt to combat unlawful immigration. For, although Commonwealth citizens could be refused admission at the port of entry and thereby removed, they were under no duty to appear before immigration officials. Arrival by "beach at night" became an attractive proposition, especially since, if the immigrant remained undetected for 24 hours, he could not be prosecuted.[10] The ensuing publicity of bewildered, sea-soaked immigrants, the alleged profitable rackets in this trade based on the Continent and the indignation at such blatant flouting of the spirit of immigration control led to the crucial provision in the Commonwealth Immigrants Act 1968 whereby a Commonwealth citizen was required to submit to immigration control.[11] If he failed to do so, the authorities were given 28 days in which to apprehend and remove him administratively.[12] If they failed to do so in time, prosecution was possible followed by a court recommendation for deportation. However, the current offence of overstaying is not a continuing offence (unlike the earlier 1962 version) and thus prosecution cannot be brought after 3 years.[13] The 1971 Act removed the 28 days' limit to the exercise of the removal powers,[14] and the right of appeal whilst still in the U.K. (inserted by the Immigration Appeals Act 1969[15]) was replaced by a right of appeal from overseas, with all the attendant difficulties.[16]

By virtue of the 1971 Act, if a person is suspected of illegal entry,

(a) he may be granted temporary admission, pending consideration of his case and with the obligation to return to the port of entry at a certain date,[17] or

(b) he may be detained whilst his case is considered,[18] or

(c) he may be removed from the U.K. immediately after he has been refused leave to enter.[19]

Which method is chosen not only depends on the particular circumstances (e.g. prompt intervention by a M.P., reliable indications that the entrant will not go "underground"), but also on the overall Home Office policy.[20]

For those who have already unlawfully entered the United Kingdom, various powers are available to detect and deal with them. S.24(2) of the Immigration Act 1971 gives a constable or immigration officer the power to arrest without warrant a person who has, or whom he, with reasonable cause, suspects to have, committed a range of offences in s.24(1) such as overstaying or illegal entry.[21] There is however no power to enter premises without a warrant for this purpose. In addition para. 17(1) of Schedule 2 authorises a constable or immigration officer to arrest without warrant a person who has physically entered the U.K. but who has not been examined by an officer and given <u>leave</u> to enter. A warrant can also be obtained to search for such people (para. 17(2)) and the warrant can be exercised by any constable.[22] There is some evidence to suggest that, contrary to the normal practice in relation to search warrants, para. 17(2) is interpreted so as not to require the person sought to be named in the warrant.[23] The result is that such warrants become 'general warrants' without the degree of specificity which is normally required of search warrants and can be directed at premises where immigrants are known to be working but without naming or describing the particular person sought.[24] On the other hand, in an important curb on police powers the House of Lords has ruled that a person does not affend s.26(1)(c) of the Act (offence, inter alia, to misrepresent an investigating officer) unless the official is acting specifically in pursuit of the Act's procedures, as opposed to a case where the official is merely making inquiries.[25]

The basis for removing unlawful entrants administratively many years after their entry was thus laid by the 1971 Act. Its retrospective application by the House of Lords[26] to those who had entered earlier, but who could no longer be prosecuted under the earlier Acts, was a foretaste of judicial hostility towards illegal entrants. The decision led in 1974 to an amnesty for such people, which could be claimed up to the end of 1978.[27] It was in the second half of the decade that attention was turned to ports of entry and to those who gained admission by deception. In a series of cases,[28] the courts willingly upheld the use of the removal power in these circumstances[29] and rejected habeas corpus as a method of reviewing the legality of its use.[30] This development coincided with increasing determination by the Home Office and police to detect illegal entrants. The judicial process culminated in the notorious case of Zamir.[31] The appellant, when 15, applied to join his father in the U.K. Entry clearance was granted when he was 18[32] and already married. He did not reveal the marriage[33] and, on arrival, was given indefinite leave to stay. Two years later his wife applied to join him, the marriage was revealed, the Home Office checked the appellant's entry clearance and detained him pending removal. Zamir sought the writ of habeas corpus - the only alternative being an appeal from overseas under the immigration provisions. Early in his judgment Lord Wilberforce indicated his likely conclusion by noting that in the Home Office's opinion Zamir had obtained entry clearance by the use of a forged birth certificate. The observation was not strictly necessary and, after all, gave precedence to the "opinion" of an immigration officer, but it is quite typical of the way in which judgments in immigration cases are coloured.

The appellant argued that the status of illegal entrants depended on the existence of certain objectively determined facts and that the courts have the power to review whether those facts exist. The House of Lords hammered what appeared to be the final nail in the coffin of habeas corpus by rejecting judicial review of precedent facts and confining the courts' role to the well-known principles of Associated Provincial Picture Houses v Wednesbury Corporation.[34] The reasons for this conclusion appeared to be,

> (a) the cases before Zamir had moved towards this position and the House of Lords lacked the will to reverse the trend,
> (b) the nature and process of the immigration system necessitated such limited review, the immigration officer being in the best position to weigh evidence by interview and assessment of documents and therefore deserving a margin of appreciation,
> (c) it followed that the immigration officer was performing an administrative not judicial or quasi-judicial function under the Immigration Rules (which are, after all, rules of practice rather than law) and therefore the Wednesbury limits were appropriate,
> (d) immigration law offered its own appellate system which had the power to review findings of fact[35] and, not least,
> (e) if Zamir's argument was accepted, the floodgates of appeals to the court could open, not just in immigration but in other areas of decision-making.

The confinement of habeas corpus to the parameters of the Wednesbury principles makes the writ a dead letter for practical purposes, since rarely will it be possible to produce sufficient evidence to show, for example, that the immigration officer has acted as no reasonable officer would.

Moreover, this reverses the traditional rule in habeas corpus proceedings that the burden of proof lies on the detainer.[36] The application of Wednesbury would appear to conclude the appeal, since Zamir had failed to disclose a material fact and therefore the officer had reasonable grounds to reach his decision. However, Zamir raised a second issue, viz., what duty to reveal facts is owed by an entrant to an immigration officer? On this point, Lord Wilberforce's opinion made the case a cause celèbre.

Zamir argued that he was under a duty to answer questions but not to volunteer information and, since the officer hadn't asked him if he was married, he was under no duty to tell him. Lord Wilberforce replied:

... an alien seeking entry to the United Kingdom owes a positive duty of candour on all material facts which denote a change of circumstances since the issue of the entry clearance. He is seeking a privilege; he alone is, as to most such matters, aware of the facts: the decision to allow him to enter, and he knows this, is based upon a broad appreciation by immigration officers of a complex of considerations, and this appreciation can only be made fairly and humanely if, on his side, the entrant acts with openness and frankness.[37]

Underlying His Lordship's judgment can be seen the element of deterrence against illegal entrants, forcing them to be candid, and indeed deception can be practised by silence in the face of questioning.[38] However, there is a difference between an entrant who deliberately keeps silent on an important point and one who is ignorant of its importance and innocently fails to mention it. To include the latter makes Lord Wilberforce's reference to "humanely" inappropriate, especially when the "innocent silence" may be discovered years afterwards.[39] From the Home Office's standpoint, the result is most convenient. It judges what are material facts and, provided it has reasonable grounds for it, its decision is unchallengeable. If the entrant is fraudulent, he is removed. If he is innocent but the error is discovered later, he too is removed.[40] Moreover, the Home Office can discover these facts almost at leisure. They may come to light many years after the immigrant entered and will destroy his, and possibly his dependants', right to remain.[41] The ruling tends to focus attention away from the ports of entry and onto internal control, adding extra spice to search warrant raids and the regular contact of immigrants with Government Departments such as the police, Inland Revenue and D.H.S.S. In other words, if an illegal entrant slips through the net, he would, throughout his residence, face the possibility of fortuitous discovery and hence expeditious removal. Allied to an increasing number of reported cases of passport checks for a variety of

administrative purposes,[42] the decision of Zamir caused
considerable consternation and insecurity in immigrant
communities and was seen as further, but this time strikingly
overt, judicial backing for the tightening of immigration
control. Shortly afterwards, the Court of Appeal qualified its
effect and endorsed the Home Office's policy that the
entrant's silence must be in relation to a material fact which
would have affected the immigration officer's decision.[43] The
hostility to the Zamir decision continued however, coincided
with the increased focus on ethnic minorities in the early
1980s and finally paid off in that the House of Lords, having
refused leave to appeal in Khawaja, remarkably allowed it in
Khera,[44] changed its mind on Khawaja and thus reviewed its
earlier ruling of Zamir, within three years. After lengthy
argument, their Lordships (including Lord Wilberforce)
unanimously reversed Zamir,[45] restoring judicial review of
"precedent fact" in place of the Wednesbury Corporation
principles and, as part of the courts' determination as to who
is an "illegal entrant", retracting the "duty of candour"
requirement.[46]

The House of Lords was crucially helped towards its
conclusions by the unusual facts of Khera viz. the applicant
applied for entry clearance whilst a minor, entered over the
age of 18 but had married before doing so and had not
disclosed that fact.[47] However, of the four possible occasions
on which he was alleged to have refused disclosure, the Home
Office initially relied on the first three but later withdrew
that reliance. The fourth could not therefore have been a
factor in the immigration officer's decision and could not
have formed part of any "reasonable grounds" for his decision.
The issue of whether Khera ought to have revealed the
information on the fourth occasion thus fell squarely to be
decided.[48]

With the exception of Lord Wilberforce, whose speech
appears reluctantly apologetic,[49] the speeches in the House of
Lords adopt a rigorous, civil libertarian approach, surprising
for immigration cases. To Lord Bridge, the case called "for a
robust exercise of the judicial function in safeguarding the
citizen's rights".[50] A forceful impetus in this direction was
the recognition that, if removed from the U.K. as an illegal
entrant, perhaps after many years of residence, the applicant
is forced to appeal from overseas (s.16) and "has no realistic
prospect of prosecuting it with success".[51]

The decision breathes new life into habeas corpus. It
makes clear that the writ of action is open to immigrants, for
"Every person within the jurisdiction enjoys the equal
protection of our laws".[52] Furthermore, it restates the
procedural process whereby the burden lies on the applicant to
raise a prima facie case before the burden passes to the
detainer. As to the standard of proof, civil or criminal, Lord
Scarman remarkably cut at the heart of the judicial process

and dismissed the distinction as "largely a matter of words"[53] but ultimately seemed to recognise the distinction by favouring later "the high degree of probability"[54] appropriate to the seriousness of habeas corpus proceedings. The onus is clearly therefore upon the immigrant's counsel to stress to the court the need to be satisfied fully of the executive's justification for the detention.[55] Although Khera was only detained for 2 weeks, on release his residence was restricted and, with important consequences for future habeas corpus applications, the case proceeded "as if the appellant were still detained".[56] Lord Bridge distinguished between the "power to refuse leave to enter and thereupon to order removal" and the "power to order removal of an illegal entrant after entry", confining the former to a lesser standard of judicial review, presumably the Wednesbury principles, and by implication to a lesser standard of proof.[57] He was swayed by the injustice of abruptly depriving the latter of the apparent legal status he thought he had obtained. The distinction is, logically, difficult to justify. If the entrant is not, objectively, an illegal immigrant, it ought not to matter for the purposes of judicial review that he is detected at the port of entry or years later. The precondition of objective facts remains for both. In practice, however, the difference is significant since it may be far more difficult for the person at the port of entry to organise advice and legal representation before removal. It may indeed encourage the Home Office to act more expeditiously in removing him.[58]

At first sight the decision opens up a Pandora's box of legal opportunities for alleged illegal entrants[59] and, if entry took place some years ago, it may be difficult for the Home Office to produce sufficient convincing evidence to challenge the lawfulness of an earlier entry. On the other hand, the applicant may also face considerable evidential hurdles. He will in most cases have only his word against the affidavits and testimony of the Home Office and successful habeas corpus proceedings or judicial review will hinge on whether a court believes him. For, it will be rare when a court will "require the attendance for cross-examination of a deponent from overseas",[60] such as an entry clearance officer. It may be appropriate, however, for the entrant to be summoned for cross-examination.[61] Furthermore, it is clear that the applicant's silence or non-disclosure of a material fact in answer to a direct question will still constitute misrepresentation. Thus, "the silence of the appellant Khawaja about the fact of his marriage to Mrs. Butt and the fact that she had accompanied him on the flight to Manchester were, in my view, capable of constituting deception even if he had not told any direct lies to the immigration officer".[62] This approach was implicitly endorsed by the other judges since Khawaja's appeal was rejected out of hand, and it comes close to a duty of candour. It would appear that if, in the court's opinion, the circumstances are strongly suspicious, silence will still be seen as deception and disproving this impression will remain difficult. In less obvious cases, Khawaja is likely to sharpen the scrutiny of entrants by entry clearance officers and immigration officers which Zamir had potentially relaxed, for the onus is on them to ask the right questions of immigrants in order that any silence may operate as deception.

The current position appears to be as follows:

(a) the duty of candour has gone yet deception by silence is still possible;

(b) for those stopped on entry, appeal from overseas is the usual remedy but judicial review may be possible if organised in time;

(c) for those detected some time after entry, judicial review is a stronger possibility but they may face acute evidential hurdles;

(d) as to those who enter lawfully and then obtain an unlawful variation of leave to remain or who enter unlawfully and get an apparently lawful variation, Schedule 2, para. 9 of the 1971 Act (which permits removal) applies "Where an illegal entrant is not given leave to enter or remain ..." Earlier cases had ruled that any illegality nullifies what follows e.g. a leave to enter obtained unlawfully is a nullity and cannot be rectified by a subsequent variation. Lord Bridge in Khawaja rejected this approach[63] and it is arguable that a person who, for example, enters lawfully, obtains an unlawful variation and then re-enters the U.K. has in fact leave to do so - it is not a nullity - and that prosecution not administrative removal is the correct course for the Home Office.[64] However, Lord Bridge analysed an illegal entrant as (i) someone who practises deception such that (ii) the deception leads to the granting of leave and it is quite arguable that the example above satisfies this analysis, regardless of semantics over nullity. In fact, in Lapinid[65] the Court of Appeal has already evaded this difficulty by holding that para. 9 must be read as "Where a person known to be an illegal entrant". Consequently leave given to an entrant who is not known to be an illegal entrant will not jeopardise para. 9. This is an ill-concealed method of reintroducing nullity but one which is likely to appeal to the courts. One thing is clear, the decision in Khawaja has not stemmed the flow of jurisprudence in this area as the courts struggle to explore and cope with the consequences, some even "unpalatable", of Khawaja.

(e) the House of Lords specifically left open the case where X innocently enters or remains because of fraud

practised by a third party.[66] The Court of Appeal has
ruled in Khan[67] that X is an illegal entrant and can be
removed, but it is difficult to reconcile this
decision with Khawaja.[68]

Summary

An alleged illegal entrant may have three opportunities to
challenge a decision to remove him - appeal from overseas,
judicial review on Wednesbury principles, habeas corpus or
judicial review to examine the existence of "precedent facts".
The decision in Khawaja is important not so much for its
practical effect (considerable evidential difficulties still
remain for the entrant) but, more generally, for revealing the
role and scope which the courts can fulfil in the immigration
field if they are prepared and pressured to do so.[69] If Zamir
had arisen in the 1960s or mid-1970s, it is highly unlikely
that the House of Lords would have reversed itself within
three years. The fact that it did is linked, it is suggested,
first, to the degree to which public, political and academic
awareness of immigration as an issue of civil liberties has
developed; second, to the influence of increased sensitivity
surrounding the state of race relations in the 1980s; third,
and most importantly, immigration is a declining problem. It
can, as with the issue of husbands and fiances, arouse fierce
emotions, but, objectively, the "problem" is coming to an end
and there is correspondingly more room for liberality and due
process. This is perhaps best signified by the decision of the
Home Office not to argue for a "duty of candour" before the
House of Lords in Khawaja. Perhaps it could not believe its
luck in obtaining the Zamir ruling and felt that to have
pressed the point would have been unwise. From the Office's
point of view, the ruling in Khawaja is not crucial. The
ability to stem or delay immigration remains through the
enforcement of the Rules and administrative policy, such as
the staffing of, and instructions to, e.c.o.s.

Comment

In the United States a distinction is drawn between the
removal of those seeking to enter and those who have entered.
For, "aliens who have once passed through our gates, even
illegally, may be expelled only after proceedings conforming
to traditional standards of fairness encompassed in due
process of law ... But an alien on the threshold of initial
entry stands on a different footing".[70] As regards the former,
a hearing takes place before a special inquiry officer and
this can be appealed to the Board of Immigration Appeals.[71] In
the 1950s, the courts showed themselves to be willing to
entertain, in addition, a variety of petitions to challenge
the removal decision.[72] Since 1961 the procedure has been
streamlined so that a final order can only be challenged by a
petition to the U.S. Court of Appeals.[73] As regards the latter

(those excluded at entry), the U.S. Courts traditionally adopted an approach close to that which obtained in the U.K. before Zamir. Thus, in Shaughnessy v Mezei[74] the applicant who had lived for 25 years in the U.S. was denied re-entry and the decision of the Executive was held to be immune from challenge by the writ of habeas corpus (save for an obvious error on the face of the record). Judicial activity in the 1950s again led to broader review through declaratory judgments,[75] but since 1961 it has been confined to habeas corpus proceedings.[76] On the other hand, before the prospects of habeas corpus arise, the applicant is still entitled to challenge an exclusion order before a special inquiry officer (at which he may be represented) and the Board of Immigration Appeals.[77] Moreover, entry by fraud will not lead to removal if the entrant was otherwise admissible and is the spouse, parent or child of a U.S. citizen.[78] In the U.K., by comparison, the definition of illegal entry extends beyond the port of entry to cover those who entered perhaps many years previously, whilst on the procedural level, appeal against removal lies from overseas -a process recognised as virtually worthless by the House of Lords in Khawaja. At the very least, an appeal to an adjudicator should be permitted within the U.K., as in the deportation process. Since such a change would still leave cases within the immigration system, it is submitted that prosecution, with the conventional safeguards of the criminal process, would better reflect the gravity of removal and inject more natural justice into the procedure.

Partly because of the unfairness to those who patiently seek to enter lawfully and partly because of the pre-occupation of successive Governments with the need to control numbers, illegal entrants have been singled out for special treatment. That policy has been fuelled by the media for which the prospect of illegal immigration has long claimed a particular fascination, from salacious tales of "brides for hire" to scaremongering revelations of European immigration rackets. The zeal for discovering illegalities and the lack of public sympathy are not new phenomena, but appeared during the Second World War to deter Jewish refugees.[79] In recent years they have been reflected in:-

(a) An energetic official attitude aimed at rapid removal of suspected illegal entrants and typified by the case in 1983 of a child, believed by the Home Office to be an illegal entrant and in the care of a local authority,[80] who was removed from a local authority institution at 6.00 a.m. for a flight later in the day.[81] To co-ordinate efforts at detecting unlawful immigrants, an Immigration Service Intelligence and Investigation Unit operates in Harmondsworth and a section in the Immigration and Nationality Department deals specifically with overstayers (Overstayers

Tracing and Intelligence Section, O.T.I.S.). A Suspect Index is available to immigration officers and lists those who should be refused entry or whose entry should be treated with caution.

(b) The great importance placed on the mechanisms of internal control, notably the police through stop and search encounters,[82] search warrant raids[83] and information from Government agencies such as the Inland Revenue and Department of Health and Social Security.[84]

(c) The aid of the computer. One was installed in 1981 at the immigration service intelligence unit at Harmondsworth, to provide information on the "abuse, or attempted abuse, of the immigration laws";[85] it includes names of those who have tried to evade the laws or who have been deported, those who are suspected of abuse and addresses which the Home Office associates with abuse.[86] There are over 300,000 names stored but with no independent supervision of the criteria for inclusion.[87] In the future, this system of detection will be improved when all ports of entry are equipped with a computer terminal and, as more countries adopt the machine readable passport, data which can then be linked more easily to the list of suspected illegal entrants.[88] The full potential of computers will be realised when all arrivals and departures are recorded and matched against each other.

(d) The power of the Home Office to make arrangements for the detention of alleged illegal entrants pending removal.[89] Harmondsworth has since 1971 used a private contractor, Securicor,[90] to supervise the detention. The details of its contract are not known.[91] It is not a police force and is not therefore subject to the normal guidance over detention conditions such as the Police Disciplinary Code.[92] Many other immigrants are detained in local prisons. Between 1972 and 1982 they fluctuated between 700 and 1400.[93] Detention under Schedule 2 of the Act will not bring the detainees before the courts, yet they are treated, within the Prison Department, in the same way as remand prisoners and therefore experience the same degrading and unacceptable conditions which obtain throughout the U.K.'s prison system. Detention may last for over a year and periods of six months have not been uncommon. The same fate, incidentally, usually awaits those who have been convicted by the courts, who may or may not have served prison sentences and who have been recommended for deportation. It may even encompass those who are willing to leave under supervised

355

departure but for whom the Home Office prefers the
certainty (hence delay) of a deportation order.[94]
Against this background, the absence of a Bill of
Rights is unfortunate since it would be difficult to
argue successfully that a power to make arrangements
for detention entitles the creation of what is in
essence, a private prison force, free from
accountability and the usual safeguards of due process
or that persons can be held in prison by administrative fiat without recourse to the courts or other
appellate procedures and without the proper
opportunity of bail.[95] . The current organisation is a
perfect illustration of the second class system of
justice which faces immigrants not only in the U.K.
but in most countries and which stems from their
classification as a group qualifying only for limited
privileges and not rights. The prosecution rather than
administrative removal of illegal entrants would do
much to redress this position in the procedural area
(e.g. bail, detention conditions, evidential matters,
legal aid and representation) by bringing them within
the fold of due process. Such a change would reflect
the more crucial reform - a change in Government
attitude signalling less political and, in time,
public obloquy towards illegal immigrants. As matters
stand, the plight of detained immigrants ranks even
lower in official and public concern than that of
immigrants generally.

C. EXTRADITION

Although there is no customary rule of public international
law requiring the surrender by one country to another of
criminals and fugitives from justice, States have traditionally provided for such surrender in bilateral treaties and,
more recently, in multilateral treaties. Those involving the
Crown have a lengthy history, dating from at least the
thirteenth century.[96] The modern law was inspired by a House of
Commons Select Committee of 1868[97] and, as regards non-
Commonwealth countries, is found in the Extradition Acts
1870-1935.[98] To apply there must exist a treaty, bilateral or
multilateral, between the U.K. and the requesting country,[99]
which has been endorsed by Order in Council, and the offence,
for which the person is wanted, must fall within the terms of
the particular treaty - generally the more serious offences.[100]
Proceedings are brought before a magistrates' court. It must
be shown that the offence would constitute a crime in England[101]
and that the requesting State has sufficient evidence against
the accused to base a prima facie case.[102] Depending on the
treaty, it is possible for British citizens to be extradited.[103]
Extradition will not however be permitted "if the offence

... is one of a political character" or if the accused can show that the request for extradition "has been made with a view to try or punish him for an offence of a political character".[104] Considerable judicial uncertainty has surrounded the precise scope of this exception. At one time, it seemed that the accused's action must be part of an organised political party's opposition to the Government of the requesting State,[105] but, more recently, the House of Lords has equated the exception to political asylum[106] thus including cases where the accused is likely to suffer on return because of his race, religion, nationality or political opinion. This wider interpretation not only accords with the original purpose of the exception in 1870[107] but matches the approach adopted in the Fugitive Offenders Act 1967[108] and in the immigration rules.[109] The 1870 Act has accordingly been modified for some purposes[110] and it is now the practice to include the "asylum" definition in all recent treaties under the 1870 Act.[111] The symmetry of extradition and asylum is thus complete. In addition, recent years have seen the U.K. participate in various multilateral Conventions which permit the surrender of individuals for specific crimes, even though no extradition treaty exists vis-a-vis the requesting State.[112] The possibility of allowing such treaties on a bilateral basis ("ad hoc" extraditions) has been suggested by the recent, but little discussed, Home Office Working Party.[113] Unless hedged by very careful safeguards (inadequately discussed in the Report) this development could readily undermine the traditional fabric of extradition arrangements. The Report also moots for example, the abolition of the "prima facie case" requirement (which the requesting State must establish before the magistrates' court and which is often a considerable stumbling block to extradition) and the amelioration of the speciality role (whereby the accused should not be prosecuted for any offence other than the one for which he was surrendered).[114] The tenor of the Report is generally hostile to the rigidity of current extradition laws and, in this, reflects the attitude of many Western Governments which have sought to relax the barriers since the 1970s and which regard the U.K.'s arrangements as too onerous. Its theme points towards a relaxation of inconvenient hurdles to extradition. The House of Lords has already relaxed one aspect of extradition law viz. the double criminality rule whereby it had to be shown that the alleged crime would constitute an offence under the law of the requesting State, similar to an offence under English law. The House has ruled that generally the magistrates' court is concerned solely to enquire whether there is enough evidence to justify committal of the person for trial in England and has no need to investigate what the position would be under foreign law.[115]

Since extradition is a formal, judicial, costly and potentially lengthy procedure, it may be tempting to avoid its technicalities by using the more flexible deportation power of "conducive to the public good". The courts have traditionally set their face against reviewing the exercise of this power,[116] save perhaps if there is evidence of bad faith on the part of the Home Secretary. Admittedly, it will be extremely difficult to produce such clear evidence, but, if it can be , it would be open to the court to strike down "extradition by the back door".[117]

D. BINDING OVER

A Crown Court may require as a condition of binding over that the defendant leave the U.K. for a specified period.[118] It can even be used against a British citizen, unlike deportation, and it is possible that defendants may be pressurised into leaving by threat of a custodial sentence in the alternative.[119] The result would be deportation "by the back door", in circumstances where deportation is either legally impossible or factually inappropriate. However,

(a) the defendant must agree to the condition, because such an order is not permanent and thus, he can choose to return to the U.K. and face the consequences of breaching the order;[120]
(b) it is implicit that some other country be prepared to accept him, for example, because of his dual nationality, prior residence or ancestral connections;[121]
(c) in 1982 the Court of Appeal pre-empted any extension of the order by warning that it "should be used very sparingly";[122]
(d) resolving an earlier doubt the Court of Appeal held that it had jurisdiction in the matter, ensuring therefore that future cases are appealable.

The power was used with some frequency in the 1950s essentially because, until 1962, the courts had no power to deport Commonwealth citizens.[123] It returned amidst a blaze of publicity in 1982 following the first instance decision in Williams.[124] The effect of that press comment may not have been lost on the Court of Appeal in that case and the Court's decision restricts the scope of the power. It is a useful power, the dangers of which have been exaggerated and the employment of which must necessarily be rare.

E. REMOVAL OF MENTAL PATIENTS AND PRISONERS

Under s.86 of the Mental Health Act 1983[125] the Secretary of State may order the removal of certain patients[126] detained in hospital for treatment of mental illness provided:

358

(a) that proper arrangements for the patient's care and treatment abroad have been made, and
(b) that removal is in the patient's interests.

Since 1982 the Secretary must have the approval of a Mental Health Review Tribunal before making an order.[127] Between 1973 and 1979, 53 patients were so removed.[128]

This area receives very little publicity and is briefly mentioned in textbooks on mental health law. Little is known of its operation. Some indication was given by the Royal Commission which preceded the 1983 Act. Thus, the provision is designed to cater for those who are "irrationally opposed to their removal" or who "are unable to express a view" and for whom the Secretary of State and a Review Tribunal consider removal to be the best course. It can also be used "to enable patients to be kept under escort on their journey home if this is necessary".[129]

Repatriation of Prisoners

Under the Council of Europe's Convention on the transfer of Sentenced Persons,[130] it is provided that States may surrender prisoners to fellow signatory States in order that they serve out their sentences in their country of nationality. The Convention was opened for signature in March 1983 and the U.K. signed in August 1983. The Repatriation of Prisoners Act 1984 incorporates the Convention.[131] The transfer of a prisoner needs his consent and that of the two States involved. It is to be hoped that the relatively prompt incorporation of the Convention will open the way for ad hoc treaties (for which the Act provides) with other non-signatory countries.[132]

APPEALS

Under the Aliens Act 1905 an aspiring immigrant was able to appeal to the immigration board of the port of entry if he was refused leave to land. The boards were manned by persons of "magisterial, business or administrative experience", who were approved by the Home Secretary (s.2 of the 1905 Act).[133] The issue upon which most appeals turned was whether the immigrant would be adequately maintained, either by relatives already in the U.K. or by the firm offer of employment. Medical fitness was the other important, but less common, issue.[134] The procedure was expeditious, most appeals being heard before the carrying ship had left the port. Yet a surprisingly high number of appeals (38%) were successful.[135] The wartime aliens' legislation removed this scheme and no statutory procedure was reinstated until the Immigration Appeals Act 1969.[136] That Act stemmed from the recommendations of the Wilson Committee and was designed to assuage concern over recent immigration legislation by clothing the entry procedure with the apparel of natural justice.

The appellate machinery is now prescribed in Part II of the Immigration Act 1971 and its mechanics in secondary legislation.[137] A two-stage procedure operates, with, in most cases, an appeal to an adjudicator in the first instance and to the Immigration Appeal Tribunal (I.A.T.) thereafter. The number of appeals heard by adjudicators in 1983 was 14,057 and by the I.A.T., 796.[138] The overall success rate of appeals is 12% but varies according to the category of appeal.[139] The procedure before an adjudicator is a complete rehearing of the case and the appeal is allowed if he considers that either the original decision was not in accordance with the law or Rules or the Secretary of State's discretion should have been exercised differently (s.19(1)).[140] The major grounds for appeal from an adjudicator to the I.A.T. are "an arguable point of law" or the appellant's fear of persecution if removed to a named country.[141] This brief description[142] conceals a number of complexities. Thus, most rights of appeal can be exercised whilst the immigrant is in the U.K. but there are some, principally appeals against refusal of entry clearance, which must be launched abroad.[143] The time limits for appeal in the first instance vary according to the type of appeal and the appellate authority can vary them in special circumstances.[144] In some situations appeal lies directly to the I.A.T.[145] Finally there are some decisions which cannot be appealed, for example, the refusal of a work permit or a special voucher.[146]

Apart from the foregoing complexity, a number of criticisms can be levelled against the current system and a selection follows:

(1) If, as the Wilson Committee believed,[147] an appellate structure is needed to ensure that justice is seen to be done, it is unfortunate that the Home Office draws up the rules, appoints the adjudicators and is invariably a party to the proceedings.

(2) Some passengers have to appeal from overseas, for example, when denied entry clearance or when excluded at a port of entry for lack of entry clearance, and they are not allowed to appeal at the hearing.[148] Similarly, in the U.S. a lesser standard of due process applies to those who have not yet entered the U.S. (exclusion hearings) than to those well established residents who are to be removed (deportation proceedings).[149] It is argued that the former stand only at the doorway to the Constitution and therefore cannot benefit in full from its guarantees.[150] In the U.K. system a more pragmatic approach, based on convenience, has been adopted. For it is unrealistic, it is argued, to expect most appellants to come to the U.K. to fight the appeal, whilst an appeals system overseas would be expensive to operate and would not obviate the making of inquiries and the taking of evidence in the U.K. Moreover, if those excluded at ports of entry were allowed to

remain pending appeal, the gaols would fill. In any case, "a most generous system of entry as a result of the intervention of a Member of Parliament"[151] operates whereby temporary admission can often be given to an immigrant. This is however a purely discretionary leave to stay and not a right to remain pending an appeal. It is arguable that at least those who can afford to stay in the U.K. pending the appeal or those who have previous residential or familial connections with the U.K. ought to be allowed to remain pending appeal. As to the feared pressure on gaols, it is not (see below) beyond the ability of the Home Office to reduce delays in the appeals' system considerably. As for those who are detained after entry (perhaps some years later) and threatened with removal by administrative means, they also do not have a right of appeal. The official argument is that a right, exercisable in the U.K., would place such people in a better position than those genuine appellants who have to fight the refusal of entry clearance from overseas. Strictly speaking this is correct, but in reality it implies that a large number of immigrants, being aware of the rigours of immigration control, would nevertheless take the risk of travelling to the U.K. in the knowledge that they could appeal here. It is suggested that this official fear is exaggerated.

Even if the current approach of appeals from overseas is accepted, it behoves the law to make very special provision for an appellant who cannot appear in person. Indications are that the provisions are inadequate.[152] Thus, the main evidence before the adjudicator will usually be the explanatory statement setting out the e.c.o's decision. Yet, that statement will not have been prepared by the original e.c.o. but by other, Home office staff, frequently long after the event, and his colleague may be unduly influenced in his drafting by the occasionally strong language used by the e.c.o. in his notes;[153] those notes are not attached to the explanatory statement and there is no tape-recording of the interview with the immigrant.[154] The statement itself will stress the inconsistencies in the appellant's story to the dilution, if not exclusion, of his arguments. It is natural to expect a closing of ranks to protect an e.c.o's decision and, given the exclusionary thrust of the legislation, the tendency may be to avoid losing a case by, if necessary, refusing to admit a mistake.[155] These factors assume considerable importance when it is recalled that the immigrant will not be present at the appeal to rebut the statement and that the burden of proof usually lies upon him. Indeed, officials are specifically advised to couch their decisions in the negative (e.g. "I am not satisfied ...") rather than give a specific reason so that the burden remains on the immigrant.[156] Moreover it should be noted that the hearing is adversarial not inquisitorial in nature and that, for example, the Home Office is not under an obligation to disclose helpful information to the appellant, or to make any further inquiries with a view to aiding his case.[157]

(3) The appellate authority may receive any relevant evidence notwithstanding that it "would be inadmissible in a court of law".[158] This can work to the individual's detriment if, for example, gossip acquired by an e.c.o. on a village visit or the uncorroborated assertions in a letter of denunciation are given too much credence.

(4) There is no statutory right of appeal from the I.A.T. to the courts.[159] An appeal does lie to the I.A.T. from an adjudicator but only if the I.A.T. decides that a question of law is involved.[160] Dissatisfaction with the I.A.T's narrow approach to this issue has contributed to an increase in the number of applications to the High Court for judicial review.[161] Provision of a right of appeal to the courts would be a first, modest step towards improving the appearance of the system.

(5) There is no right of appeal against the denial of asylum per se, though the plea can be made as part of an appeal on other grounds (e.g. against refusal to vary a leave, the directions for a deportee's removal).[162] As for judicial review, the courts have given the Secretary of State's discretion a wide berth.[163]

(6) The time limit of 14 days for lodging an appeal[164] is too restricted, since it runs from the date of the decision and not the time when notice of the decision is received by the individual. In contrast there is a lack of time limits on the Home Office for preparing a case for the hearing.

(7) Since an appeal is a rehearing of the issue that was before the immigration officer, the appellate authority is usually confined to a fresh[165] consideration of those facts which existed at the time of the i.o's decision.[166] Facts which have arisen since the decision cannot normally be adduced and must instead form the basis of a new application for entry, with the attendant delay. For otherwise, it is argued, appeals would be never ending. This approach can obviously cause hardship and inconvenience and complex jurisprudence has developed over its precise scope. Thus, exceptional circumstances can justify reception of the new facts.[167] So also if there is new evidence of facts which were in existence at the time of the original decision but which were not brought to the i.o's attention;[168] or if the subsequent information is both material and strictly relevant to the original decision.[169] On the other hand, if the new evidence concerns facts which were not originally in existence or if it in effect alters the terms of the original application, a new application should be lodged.[170]

In 1981 the Home Office published a discussion document on the appeals system. The outcome, as shown in a debate in 1985 on the amended Appeals' Regulations, [171] is an interesting insight into Government tactics. The document put forward a number of important proposals to reduce delays in the appellate system, e.g. removing the rights of a short-term visitor to appeal against the refusal of an extension of stay, of e.c. and work permit holders to be given leave to appeal from an adjudicator to the I.A.T. [172] Whilst the proposals were being digested and comments were being received, the Home Office and adjudicators made "magnificent efforts" [173] to reduce the delays (the list dropping from 16,350 in 1979 to 9,500 in 1984), with the result that the need for the proposed streamlining had evaporated. This then enabled the Government to boast of having rejected "all the radical proposals in our consultation document"; [174] of having therefore broadly agreed with representations from J.C.W.I. and others; and of having endorsed the system set up by the Opposition in 1969. This camouflage results in the continuation of an imperfect system but also shows again the extent to which administrative change and effort can be used positively to improve immigration control. The very fact that these proposals mooted the abolition of rights emphasises the second class nature of the system (Parliament may make certain criminal offences triable summarily rather than on indictment, but it does not abolish the trial) and that immigration control is seen as naturally lying in the ambit of executive discretion rather than justiciable rights.

----

1   Report, Para. 72.

2   Whereas those holding entry clearance can appeal within the U.K.

3   Illegal immigrants can be prosecuted under s.24 and recommended for deportation, or deported as "conducive to the public good"; both procedures can be appealed against in the U.K. For an excellent review of the removal power, see Nicol, "Illegal Entrants", Joint Council for the Welfare of Immigrants and Runnymede Trust. The Secretary of State has in effect an unfettered discretion as to which power of removal to use (deportation or administrative removal) - Mustafa, Times 22 February 1984 - for, though a court could in theory review his decision on the basis of bad faith or gross unreasonableness, in practice the supporting evidence is unlikely to be at hand, especially since the Secretary need not give his reasons.

4   The date of the Labour Government's White Paper (cmnd. 2739) which singled out evasion of control for particular attention.

5   E.g. "The schooling of an illegal immigrant", Guardian, 25 April 1977.

6   Cmnd. 9544, Table 19, and Home Office Statistical Bulletins, Table 13.

7   By removal, voluntary departure, grant of permission to stay or dealt with as other categories e.g. deportees.

8   Aliens Act s.1(1).

9   Aliens Order 1920, art. 3(5), as amended

10 Sched. 1, para. 1(2). This loophole was confirmed by the House of Lords in D.P.P. v Bhagwan [1972] A.C. 60 and became known as the "Bhagwan gap". For an example, see Ahsan [1969] 2 Q.B. 222.

11 S.3. The White Paper of 1965 (Cmnd 2739) had already promised stricter action.

12 S.4.

13 See Grant v Borg [1982] 2 All E.R. 257. Cf. a similar problem of interpretation under the Immigration Act 1964 (New Zealand) - Malungahu [1981] 1 N.Z.L.R. 668.

14 Sched. 2, paras. 8, 9.

15 S.5, but not brought into force before the 1971 Act became operative.

16 See appeals and Khawaja, infra.

17 Sch. 2, para. 21.

18 After 7 days, he may apply to an adjudicator for bail, ibid, para. 22.

19 Ibid., paras. 8 and 9.

20 For an indication of the Secretary of State's discretion, see Mustafa, Times 22 February 1984.

21 A similar arrest power exists against a person who has secured or facilitated the illegal entry of others; for a constable it stems from s.24 Police and Criminal Evidence Act 1984 (being an arrestable offence), for an immigration officer from s.25(3) of the 1971 Act.

22 Sch. 2, para. 17(2), as amended by Schedule 7, Part I, Police and Criminal Evidence Act 1984.

23 See Gordon, "Passport Raids and Checks", p.37-38. For arguments that this interpretation is unjustifiable, see Macdonald (1981) N.L.J. 768.

24 Contrast the classic condemnation of general warrants in Entick v Carrington (1765) 19 State Tr. 1029. Cf. the similar position in the U.S. where warrants to search for illegal aliens need not specify names, Blackie's House of Beef Inc. v Castillo 659 F. 2d 1211 (1981).

25 R v Clarke, Times 21 June 1985, rejecting the Crown's "breathtaking" (Lord Scarman) assertion of power.

26 Azam [1974] A.C. 18.

27 See H.C. Debs., 11 April 1974, col. 637.

28 For a useful summary, see Lord Wilberforce in Khawaja, infra, at p.102. A flavour of the development can be gathered from Begum [1978] Imm. A.R. 107; Claveria, ibid, 176 (esp. 179-80); Hussain [1978] 1 W.L.R. 700; Choudhary, ibid, 1177, Goordin [1981] Imm. A.R. 24. For an account of Claveria, see C.R.E. Report (1985), paras. 8.4.4-6.

29 The argument that the power was confined to "beach

arrivals" was strongly put in Zamir and Khera, infra, but firmly rejected by the House of Lords.

30 Cf. a similar devaluation of habeas corpus in the U.S. in Knauff v Shaughnessy 338 U.S. 537 (1950) and Shaughnessy v U.S. 73 S. Ct. 625 (1953) where the Supreme Court refused to use the writ to challenge decisions of the Attorney General provided that there was no error on the face of the record; and see also Ekiu v U.S. 142 U.S. 651 (1892).

31 [1980] A.C. 930. See Levin (1980) L.A.G. 178.

32 An indication of the delays within the entry clearance procedure.

33 This cancelled out his entitlement to enter under the Rules, since children must be unmarried, r.50.

34 [1948] 1 K.B. 223; thus, provided the Home Office has acted reasonably and within the bounds of natural justice, no challenge is possible. For a review of habeas corpus, see Newdick [1982] P.L. 89.

35 Though from overseas with all the difficulties which Khawaja infra, later pointed out.

36 Cf. the excellent example of Ahsan [1969] 2 Q.B. 222.

37 At p.950. In the Divisional Court, Lord Widgery described the duty to disclose as "a modest step forward in the law on this topic" - [1979] Q.B. 688, at 694.

38 Cf. in the criminal process, the dicta in Rice v Connolly [1966] 2 Q.B. 414.

39 The conclusion that 'innocent' people are caught as well is not, it must be said, without parallels elsewhere; for offences concerning passports, see Chajutin v Whitehead [1938] 1 All E.R. 159 and compare Naumovska v Minister for Immigration (1982) 41 A.L.R. 635 (though the Federal Court did concede a wider role for judicial review than that postulated by Lord Wilberforce).

40 With the remote prospect of succeeding on an appeal from overseas.

41 For an excellent example of the lingering, illegal status, see Nawaz v Lord Advocate (1983) S.L.T. 653 (N entered by deception in 1971 and was detained in 1981).

42 E.g. Gordon, Passport Raids and Checks, Storey (1984)

43 Jayakody [1982] 1 W.L.R. 405. Relief was also possible if
the immigration officer had made a mistake (Ram [1979] 1
W.L.R. 148) or could be deemed to have waived a requirement
(Mangoo Khan [1980] 1 W.L.R. 569).

44 On granting leave to appeal, Lord Bridge commented,
significantly, "we all know that Zamir has come in for a good
deal of criticism". And as Lord Scarman observed, the decision
had "created a furore in the legal profession", Wilberforce
Memorial Lecture, University of Hull, 27 May 1983.

45 [1984] A.C. 74. See [1983] P.L. 213. Meanwhile Zamir
continued his battle before the European Commission of Human
Rights - 5 E.H.R.R. 242.

46 The questions to be decided by the House are neatly
summarised by Lord Scarman at p.106 C-D.

47 Facts similar to those of Zamir.

48 The facts of Khawaja contained a similar issue of failure
to reveal facts but, since his entry "smacked of deception",
their Lordships were able to dismiss the appeal peremptorily.

49 Note his technical distinguishing of Zamir, at p99-100.

50 At p.122.

51 Per Lord Bridge, at p.120. See also Lord Fraser, at
p.97-98, who, having denied that the right of appeal was
worthless, admitted that success was rare. Note also the
critical comments about this system of appeals in Hussain,
Times, 23 June 1982.

52 Per Lord Scarman, at p.111.

53 At p.112.

54 At p.113. Lord Bridge was persuaded to the same view,
p.124-25. See also Lord Templeman, p.128, and cf. Ellerton,
Times, 27 February 1984.

55 A prompt example of this can be seen in Miah, Times, 19
July 1983 where the Home Office failed to satisfy the
Divisional Court that there had been deception. See also Momin
Ali [1984] 1 All E.R. 1009, where the Home Office failed to
discharge the burden of proving deception on the immigrant's
part.

56 Per Lord Fraser at p.93.

57 P.122. See also Lord Templeman at 127-28. The distinction
has been applied in Kwabena, Times 28 May 1985, so that
Wednesbury principles of review apply to those refused leave
at a port of entry.

58 R.87 permits an entrant the opportunity of telephoning
friends or relatives or his diplomatic representative before
removal. Unpublished internal instructions however deny such
contact when the Secretary of State proposes to remove a
person on security or political grounds. The instructions are
under review; see Guardian, 9 February 1984.

59 Its ruling on the burden of proof had rapid effect, see
Awa, Times, 12 March 1983, Miah, Times, 19 July 1983.
Moreover, it helps those 'innocent' wives of illegal entrants,
who though innocent of their spouses' illegality, could
previously be similarly removed as illegal entrants. The
Federal Court of Australia had already refused to follow Zamir
on the issue of judicial review - see Naumovska (1982) 41
A.L.R. 635.

60 Per Lord Bridge, at p.125. For a neat summary of these
difficulties, see Lord Templeman at p.128.

61 See Manuel, Times, 21 March 1984.

62 Per Lord Fraser, at p.97. On the other hand, it has been
held that the mere production of a false passport, without
more, does not amount to a false representation, Addo, Times
18 April 1985.

63 At p.118-9. See also Addo, supra.

64 See Macdonald (1983) N.L.J. 475

65 [1984] 1 W.L.R. 1269.

66 For example, work permits fraudulently obtained by an
employment agency and innocently used by immigrant employees,
as happened to Filipinos in the 1970s (see Nicol, op. cit.
p.38) or a fiancee who enters in good faith to marry a man who
is subsequently classified as an illegal entrant.

67 [1977] 1 W.L.R. 1466, where a husband used the passport of
his second wife to help to admit his illiterate third wife.

68 Lord Bridge, at p.119, was particularly sceptical of
Khan's validity and the Home Office subsequently changed its
mind on a similar case and allowed the wife to remain,

Guardian, 11 July 1983. Cf. the Canadian Immigration Act 1976, s.27(1)(e), (2)(g) which specifically covers this possibility.

[69] Cf. the court's willingness later in 1983 in Hardial Singh [1984] 1 All E.R. 983, to threaten the grant of habeas corpus in order to expedite the Home Office's decision on the fate of a deportee; and in 1984 to grant bail to an immigrant detained for 8 months - Patel (Guardian, 17 April 1984).

[70] Shaughnessy v Mezei 345 U.S. 206 (1953), at p.212, per Mr. Justice Clark.

[71] 8 U.S.C. para. 1252.

[72] E.g. Shaughnessy v Pedreiro (1955) 349 U.S. 48.

[73] 8 U.S.C. para. 1105a (75 Stat. 651, 1961).

[74] (1953) 345 U.S. 206.

[75] Brownell v Tom We Shung (1956) 352 U.S. 180.

[76] 75 Stat. 653.

[77] 8 C.F.R. 236.

[78] 8 U.S.C. para. 1251(f).

[79] See the excellent account by Wasserstein, Britain and the Jews of Europe 1939-1945.

[80] Bradford local authority had assumed parental rights over the child.

[81] The intervention of an M.P. led to the child's last-minute removal from the plane.

[82] Likely to be more frequent in view of Part I of the Police and Criminal Evidence Act 1984.

[83] See Gordon, "Passport Raids and Checks", ch.3 (1981). For recent lists of joint search warrant operations involving the police and immigration officers, see H.C. Debs., 28 July 1982, col. 528; 11 May 1983, col. 297; 30 March 1984, col. 305. The procedures were tightened up following criticism, see H.C. Debs. 12 December 1980, col. 517.

[84] For an account of the contact between the Home Office and D.H.S.S., see C.R.E. Report (1985), paras. 8.10.1-3. See also, Gordon, Policing Immigration (1985), pp.26-27.

85 H.C. Debs. 11 April 1983, col. 314. For a list of immigration computers, see H.C. Debs. 27 March 1984, col. 121 and H.O. Report on Immigration and Nationality Department (1984), pp.42-44. For a discussion, see Gordon, supra, pp.46-51.

86 Ibid.

87 Immigration was significantly excluded from protection under the original version of the Data Protection Bill 1983 (1982-83) cl. 28(1)(d), but, following an amendment in the House of Lords, it was deleted from the list of exceptions in the 1984 Act.

88 At present, only the U.S. has adopted it; there are 18,000 names on the U.K.'s main warning list, see further H.C. Debs. 11 April 1983, col. 315. The U.K. has decided to go ahead with machine readable passports. See Government Response (cmnd. 8682) to the Foreign Affairs Committee which had recommended that development be suspended. For details of the proposed scheme, see H.C. Debs. 24 July 1984, col. 567.

89 The 1971 Act, Sched. 2, para. 16.

90 At other ports, the British Transport Police, Harbour Board or local police are used.

91 For example, the fees paid to it, H.C. Debs. 14 April 1983, col. 437, 18 April 1983, col. 9.

92 It is subject to a code of practice on bail and detention but this is not published.

93 Prison Statistics (England and Wales) 1982, Cmnd. 9027, Table 6.2.

94 See A Chronicle of Wasted Time: The Cost of Home Office inefficiency (1985), Prison Reform Trust and J.C.W.1.

95 For an attempt to extend the full provision of bail to those held under the Act, see Immigration (Bail) Bill 1985, H.L. 165.

96 See the evidence cited by O'Higgins, 13 Indian Yb.I.Aff.78 (1964).

97 Select Committee on Extradition, 1868 C.393; and endorsed by a Royal Commission Cd. 2039 (1878).

98 The Fugitive Offenders Act 1967 covers the Commonwealth and, unlike the 1870 Act, does not depend on a separate treaty

with the requesting State. For Ireland, see the Backing of Warrants (Republic of Ireland) Act 1965.

99 For a list of treaty arrangements see Halsbury's Laws, 4th Ed. vol. 18, para. 208 and for the Commonwealth, covered by the 1967 Act, see para. 253.

100 Ibid paras. 215, 257. The vintage of some treaties and the subsequent development of the criminal laws in the U.K. and the requesting State can lead to considerable difficulty in interpretation, e.g. Zezza [1983] 1 A.C. 46. On occasion offences are added to the list e.g. Taking of Hostages Act 1982, s.3.

101 See R v Governor of Holloway Prison, ex p. Jennings [1983] 1 A.C. 624.

102 S.10, 1870 Act.

103 E.g. the current treaty with the United States - S.I 1976 no. 2144, sched. 1, art. 1.

104 1870 Act, s.3(1). Semble, that he must show "substantial grounds" for such a fear - Fernandes [1971] 1 W.L.R. 989, dealing with the 1967 Act. Even if the accused fails and is committed by the court, the Secretary of State has the power to refuse to surrender him - 1870 Act, s.11, as interpreted by Atkinson [1971] A.C. 197, Kotronis, ibid, 250.

105 See Castioni [1891] 1 Q.B. 149, Meunier [1894] 2 Q.B. 415.

106 Schtraks [1964] A.C. 556, and see Cheng [1973] A.C. 931.

107 Inserted to assist political refugees from, notably, Eastern Europe.

108 S.4(1), which is based on the European Convention on Extradition (1957).

109 See Rr. 73, 134 and 165.

110 Suppression of Terrorism Act 1978, s.2.

111 Para. 6.9, Home Office Working Party, "A review of the Law and Practice of Extradition in the U.K.", H.O. 1982.

112 For example, the Internationally Protected Persons Act 1978 and S.I 1979/453, incorporating a Convention designed to permit the surrender of those who commit violent acts, such as the kidnapping of diplomatic agents. See the similar powers in relation to aircraft offences e.g. Tokyo Convention Act 1967,

Hijacking Act 1971, Protection of Aircraft Act 1973.

[113] Supra. It contains a wide ranging survey of the field of extradition. A Green Paper has responded favourably to the Report, Cmnd. 9421.

[114] Chapter 4 and 10 respectively. Another significant change under consideration is the relaxation in the rules of evidence for extradition proceedings.

[115] Nielsen [1984] A.C. 606; U.S. Govt. v M^ccaffery [1984] 1 W.L.R. 867.

[116] Venicoff [1920] 3 K.B. 72; Soblen [1963] 2 Q.B. 243; Hosenball [1977] 3 All E.R. 452.

[117] Mackeson (1982) 75 Cr. App. Rep. 24, per Lane, L.C.J. at p.30; however, the Mackeson approach has not been followed in Driver [1985] 2 All E.R. 681.

[118] For an illuminating account and criticism of the power, see O'Higgins [1963] Crim. L.R. 680.

[119] Such a threat does not vitiate the order, R v. Veater [1981] 1 W.L.R. 567.

[120] As happened, for example, in R v. Saunders [1980] Q.B. 72; the defendant's attempt to claim protection under E.E.C. law was rejected by the Court of Justice on the basis that a Member State is entitled to invoke penal measures against its own nationals without infringing the Treaty of Rome.

[121] See the exceptional facts of R v. Hodges (1967) 51 Cr. App. R. 361.

[122] R v. Williams [1982] 1 W.L.R. 1398, per Lane, L.C.J., at p.1403.

[123] As examples of the power, see R v. McCarten [1958] 1 W.L.R 933 (discussed at [1958] Crim. L.R. 734, [1960] Crim. L.R. 113), R v. Flaherty [1958] Crim. L.R. 556, and of its limitations - R v. Ayu [1958] 1 W.L.R. 1264.

[124] Supra.

[125] Replacing s.90 Mental Health Act 1959.

[126] Those who are not British citizens or Commonwealth citizens with the right of abode.

[127] By virtue of Mental Health (Amendment) Act 1982, s.35(2)

now s.86 of the 1983 Act.

[128] H.C. Debs. 21 April 1980, col. 9.

[129] The Review of the Mental Health Act 1959, Cmnd. 7320 para. 8.26.

[130] Eu. Treaty Series no. 112. The Convention comes into operation when 3 States have ratified it.

[131] For an account of its provisions and purpose, see H.L. Debs. 2 December 1983, col. 751.

[132] Which would undoubtedly bring greater benefit to British Citizens in view of the poor conditions (even by British standards) which prevail in many foreign prisons; see, for example, Observer, 20 March 1983, Times, 21 June 1983.

[133] For an account of the system, see Cohen (1984) L.A.G. 13.

[134] E.g. trachoma was a common affliction amongst Armenian and Syrian entrants in 1909.

[135] See Appendix II, para. 9 of the Wilson Committee, infra. This was no doubt due in part to the fact that in 1911 expatriate Jews (the Bnai Brith) organised a legal aid scheme to assist the appeals of Jewish entrants.

[136] Appendix III to the Wilson Committee relates the experimental appeals system which operated with little success between 1932 and 1936 and which allowed a limited class of deportees to make representations to an Advisory Committee. Also, in 1956 a practice was adopted of referring certain deportation cases to the Chief Metropolitan Magistrate.

[137] The Immigration Appeals (Notices) Rules 1984, S.I, no. 2040, and the Immigration Appeals (Procedure) Rules 1984, S.I, no. 2041.

[138] Report on the Immigration and Nationality Department (Home Office, 1984), Tables 8.1-3.

[139] See Tables 10.1-7 in C.R.E. Report (1985).

[140] The adjudicator is strictly confined to these grounds, see Yuksel [1976] Imm.A.R. 91.

[141] S.I. 1984/2041, r.14(2). For the other grounds, see s.22(5) of the Act.

[142] For a full account, see Immigration Law and Practice in

the United Kingdom, I.A. Macdonald, ch.11 and Immigration Law and Practice, Grant, L. and Martin, I. ch.14.

[143] Ss.13(3), 15(5) and 16(2).

[144] S.I. 1984/2041, rr.4, 11(4); but not on an appeal from the adjudicator to the I.A.T., ibid, r.15 and see Armstrong [1977] Imm.A.R. 80; Ashrafi [1981] Imm.A.R. 34.

[145] S.15(7).

[146] For a list of the categories, see Macdonald, supra, at p.273.

[147] Cmnd. 3387, para. 84.

[148] Not surprisingly the success rate is low, see App. 17 to H.A.C. Report (e.g. 6% in Delhi in 1979).

[149] Under the Immigration and Nationality Act 1952; 8 U.S.C. para. 1226(a).

[150] E.g. London v Plasencia (1982) 459 U.S. 21. See the useful annotation at 74 L.Ed.2d 1066.

[151] Junior Minister at the Home Office, H.C. Debs. 4 February 1985, col. 717ff.

[152] Contrast the Wilson Committee, supra, which had optimistically underestimated the difficulties of overseas' appeals, para. 124.

[153] Instead Home Office staff are instructed to fillet "jargon or comment which might indicate less than an objective approach"; instructions quoted by the C.R.E. Report (1985), para. 10.11.4.

[154] Cf. the criticism levelled at the inadequacy of these notes by the court in Govinden, Times 12 July 1985.

[155] Note the investigation of the Ombudsman in case C460/83 in the First Report of the Parliamentary Commissioner for Administration. 1984-85, H.C. 150, p.63.

[156] C.R.E. Report, para. 10.8.2.

[157] Cf. Kioa v Minister for Immigration and Ethnic Affairs (1984) 53 A.L.R. 658.

[158] S.I. 1984/2041, r.29(1).

159 Cf. Immigration Act 1976 (Canada), s.84, which allows an appeal from the Immigration Appeal Board to the Federal Court on any question of law; and, in similar vein, Administrative Appeals Tribunal Act 1975 (Australia), s.44, and see Deniz v Minister for Immigration (1984) 51 A.L.R. 645.

160 Singh [1978] Imm.A.R. 140. Many appeals are prevented by this limitation.

161 E.g. Mehmet [1977] Imm.A.R. 56.

162 However, if a court recommends deportation there is no such right of appeal, see Muruganandarajah, Times 23 July 1984.

163 Santis and Bugdaycay, Times 11 July 1985.

164 Paras. 4 and 15, S.I. 1984/2041.

165 Peterkin [1970] Imm.A.R. 253.

166 Abdullah [1973] Imm.A.R. 57; Patel [1975] Imm.A.R. 95; Mohammed [1978] Imm.A.R. 168; Weerasuriya [1983] 1 All E.R. 195; Bastiampillai [1983] 2 All E.R. 844; Kotecha [1983] 2 All E.R. 289; Hubbard, Times 16 July 1985. It follows logically that an appeal can be heard even if the appellant has died before the hearing, see Hashma Bi, TH/108489/83.

167 E.g. the lengthy delay which an appellant would face if compelled to make a fresh application for entry, Huda [1976] Imm.A.R. 109, Thaker [1976] Imm.A.R. 114; or ill health of the applicants, Thakerar [1974] Imm.A.R. 60.

168 Rashid [1978] Imm.A.R. 71; Mohammed, supra.

169 Thaker, supra; Ashraf [1979-80] Imm.A.R. 45; Amirbeaggi, Times 25 May 1982.

170 Thaker, supra.

171 H.C. Debs. 4 February 1985, col. 705.

172 Review of Appeals under the Immigration Act 1971, (Home Office, 1981). For other detailed proposals, see U.K.I.A.S. Annual Report 1983-4, p.6; see also, 'Pivot of the System' - a briefing paper on Immigration Appeals, Runnymede Trust (1981).

173 Junior Minister, H.C. Debs. col. 720.

174 Ibid.

9 CONCLUSIONS

> This House believes that the operation of the Immigration Rules provides the right basis for a firm and fair immigration control which combines a necessary scrutiny of entitlement to settle here with respect and support for family life and proper treatment of visitors to this country.[1]

Most of this book has been concerned with coloured entrants for the simple reason that the U.K.'s recent laws have been designed primarily to control them. For a nation which has been responsible for a massive negro slave trade and which has a history of imperial domination, it is hardly surprising that attitudes of prejudice have found their way into the framing and administration of immigration law. In the broader historical context, however, a similar prejudice and very similar legal techniques have been employed against all unwelcome immigrants, be they the Jews of the thirteenth century, Protestants of the sixteenth or the undesirables from France during the Napoleonic Wars. It is in terms of internal race relations that coloured immigration offers singular characteristics, which will continue far beyond those which surrounded earlier immigrants.

In the international context, the days of large scale immigration have ended permanently. Countries are as xenophobic as ever and laws have been adopted to reflect that mood. In this context, the laws and practices of the United Kingdom are unexceptional;[2] but none the more admirable for that. Indeed, it is submitted that the U.K. should have taken a lead in according immigrants legal protection more in keeping with that it dispenses, and proclaims to dispense, to its native population. To do this, immigration must first be seen in terms of rights rather than privileges.

A. RIGHTS FOR IMMIGRANTS

Why should a U.K. Government give rights to immigrants and seek to uphold them? However it is dressed up, the primary answer is a matter of common humanity and justice based on universal or natural law precepts. The clearest examples are the grant of asylum and the reunification of families. But the belief in common humanity and justice has a much wider impact since it dictates that concern for civil liberties should not be thrown out of the window simply because foreigners are involved.

Second, and logically, fairness towards immigrants indicates the strength of the host country's attachment to such values. Contemporary examples include the second class system of due process given to immigrants threatened with removal under the administrative powers of Schedule 2 to the 1971 Act. As an American judge has remarked

> Our law, may and rightly does, place more restrictions on the alien than on the citizen. But basic fairness in hearing procedures does not vary with the status of the accused. If the procedures used to judge this alien are fair and just, no good reason can be given why they should not be extended to simplify the condemnation of citizens. If they would be unfair to citizens, we cannot defend the fairness of them when applied to the more helpless and handicapped alien.[3]

Third, some justification can be founded on the historical and hence emotional attachment to the Commonwealth - the sense of duty to be fair as head of the organisation. Thus, Commonwealth citizens were free from immigration control until 1962 and thereafter certain preferential treatment was initially accorded them.[4]

Fourth, and more practically, the historical recognition of the value of aliens to the economy can be matched by a desire to reward them with fair treatment. Thus, in earlier centuries aliens were admitted under Royal patronage and rewarded with citizenship and trading privileges.

Fifth, and more recently, the need to treat immigrants fairly has been linked with race relations, the argument running that denial of basic rights and the discriminatory practices at ports of entry can only hamper the chances of internal racial harmony.

Sixth, some justifications are imposed by diplomatic pressure, for example, the U.K.'s reception of Ugandan (1972) and Vietnamese (1979) refugees and the concession over the citizenship status of Gibraltarians in 1981.

Finally, some justifications are self-imposed by international obligation, the striking example in recent years being the European Economic Community and, to the Government's embarrassment, the European convention of Human Rights.

To argue for rights for immigrants is not to argue for an open-door policy towards immigration but for an injection of flexibility and due process.

As has been suggested elsewhere in this book, many improvements to the rules and practice could be made without jeopardising an overriding policy of firm control.[5] Realistically, however, the future lies in favour of a tightening rather than relaxation of immigration laws.

(1) As to relaxation
Limited steps will be taken in the E.E.C. context. The possibility of a passport union was raised by Member States in 1974[6] and agreed in 1981,[7] under which States will issue a common form passport. The next step of abolishing frontier controls is less likely. It may make sense in Continental Europe where internal control (via identity cards) is commonplace but in the U.K. the simple waving of a claret-coloured passport on entry defies centuries of normal immigration controls, which have concentrated on the point of entry. The more likely step will be the relaxation of passport checks.[8]

Elsewhere, pressure groups and the ingenuity of lawyers will continue to produce success for the immigrant in skirmishes before the I.A.T., the courts and the Home Secretary's discretion, but the wider policy battles such as the advantages of the speedy admission of U.K.P.H.s were lost in the 1960s. Public opinion is so hostile to immigration and politicians are so wary of antagonising that hostility by espousing the immigrant's cause too forcefully that any relaxation in controls will be only superficial or pyrrhic. The only serious cloud on the Government's horizon is the need to reach a settlement with China over the transfer of sovereignty over Hong Kong, so that the U.K. can wash its hands of the colony both legally and morally. If the transfer does not take place smoothly in 1997, the U.K. may, as it found in the 1960s in East Africa, face considerable pressure to acknowledge a moral, if not legal, obligation to assist refugees.

(2) As to tightening
The decision of the European Court of Human Rights in May 1985 on the entry conditions for husbands and fiances[9] forced the U.K. to choose predictably the ignoble path of compliance with the ruling. For although settled women can now introduce their partners (to comply with the ruling), this change is more than offset by subjecting female entrants to the same rigorous conditions as male entrants (principally the 'primary purpose' test).[10] The possibility of any further and significant strengthening of controls on entry is slender partly because

the Government already has at its disposal ample powers and partly because, in terms of numbers, the 'storm is over' and applications by coloured secondary immigrants are steadily falling.[11] Conversely, this does not mean that the U.K. will relax its guard. The official logic is - the queues of entrants are falling and the position is improved, therefore there is no need to improve matters. It is typified by the following exchange over the possibility of expediting the admission of U.K.P.H.s from India.

> (Mr Lyon) Is it not better if the children are going to come that we get them here so that they can get into the schools quicker to get them settled in here that much faster, and in those circumstances it is probably better from everybody's point of view to get the queue ended?
> (Mr Raison, Minister) Well, it will make life easier once the queue is ended. In some ways from our point of view it is simply a question of whether we can suddenly provide the additional resources you are asking for to deal with the problem which, as the figures show, clearly appears on any view to be receding fairly rapidly. It just does not seem to me there is a powerful case for producing additional resources, given the way things are going.
> (Mr Lyon) Would it not be better to get it finished in the next couple of years rather than spinning it out longer?
> (Mr Raison) As I said before, on immigration matters you have to judge on the balance between the immediate interests of the would-be immigrant and other interests which we cannot ignore and, as I say, it seems to me the picture on the immigrants is quite an encouraging one: the queue is taking much less time which presumably will please them. I would have thought that was not something not to take into consideration.[12]

Those 'other interests' include the temporary but sharp increase in the immigration statistics which would follow any acceleration in the entry clearance process and the feared reaction of U.K. public opinion. In truth, the justification employed is one of political convenience and reveals the uncompromising U.K. policy towards immigrants and the lack of moral courage and humanitarian concern which Governments have consistently displayed since 1962 and on many previous occasions in immigration history. As the Labour Minister of Labour observed in 1948, when confronted by news of the first post-war batch of immigrants from the Caribbean, "I hope no encouragement will be given to others to follow their example ... If they suffer any inconvenience, the blame will be on those who sent them and not on those who receive them".[13]

The future trend of immigration control lies rather in the deployment of internal mechanisms and a selection follows.

B. INTERNAL DISABILITIES PLACED ON IMMIGRANTS

(1) Civic and legal rights

Those which involve civic and legal rights have a long history and stem from the status of citizenship. Historically, the alien's inability to own real property was the most important. Disputes over the inheritance of property (usually involving the question of whether the claimant was a British subject) led to early and regular involvement by the courts.[14] The disabilities were largely removed by the Naturalisation Act 1870, though special provisions will naturally operate during wartime[15] to control enemy aliens.[16]

Today few civic and legal disabilities remain. An alien can hold and transmit "real and personal property of every description".[17] He can use the courts and is triable in the same manner as if he were a British Citizen.[18] He is not entitled to vote or serve on a jury, but the Representation of the People Act 1949 granted voting rights to all British subjects and thus included Commonwealth citizens and citizens of the Irish Republic. The latter concession in recent troubled times has aroused controversy and pressure for abolition. The former is of course circumscribed by the hurdle of immigration control and the need to register on the electoral roll. The subject arose recently during the Home Affairs Committee's Report into the working of the 1949 Act but calls to abolish the concession were rejected.[19]

(2) Employment disabilities

Aliens remain disqualified from pursuing a miscellaneous range of occupations such as Member of Parliament,[20] an office of trust or certain positions in the civil service,[21] or a pilot.[22] Accordingly, the scope of the race relations' legislation can be excluded from covering employment in the service of the Crown or any designated public body.[23]

(3) Health services

In 1981 the Government announced its intention to introduce charges for overseas visitors who used the National Health Service. This was partly because it was "not self-evident" that such people should be entitled to free treatment and partly because of the "fairly widespread abuse by foreigners who come to this country suffering from an existing complaint and then claim free treatment on the grounds that they have fallen ill while here".[24] The Government hoped to recoup £6 million from the charges. The first reason is a powerful one in principle whilst the second has little evidential support. The difficulty was the context in which the charges were to be introduced. It is one thing to introduce them at the inception of the N.H.S. and quite another to do so after 35 years in view of the inevitable effect which it would have on race relations. The Government implicitly recognised this at the outset by volunteering a series of exceptions to the scheme - wives and children of those settled in the U.K., those resident for 3 years and those admitted for settlement. After reflection the residential requirement was reduced to 1 year[25] and the charges came into operation on 1 October 1982.[26]

They have not fulfilled the Government's expectations partly because many overseas visitors are excluded through reciprocal arrangements with other countries, or through the other exceptions in the Regulations, and partly because of the unwillingness on the part of certain health authorities to operate the scheme rigorously.[27] It must be seriously questioned whether the exercise has been worthwhile financially[28] and more importantly in terms of race relations. The scheme is a modern expression of a long held fear - that immigrants are responsible for milking national resources. It is hardly surprising that such a fear and such a scheme exist. It is, however, a sober reminder of the limitations of the civil liberties' and race relations' movements.

(4) Identity checks

The Select Committee Report (1978) greatly fuelled the official concern to detect illegal entry and brought the issue of internal controls into the public arena. The intervening years have seen two developments in this direction. Firstly, there have been increasing reports of formal[29] and informal[30] passport checks. Second, the storage of computer-based information has increased the opportunities of detecting illegal entrants. The Immigration Service itself has experimented with the use of computers and this has developed to the stage where machine readable passports are approaching[31] and intelligence on suspected unlawful entrants is regularly stored on computers.[32] Following fears for race relations, the Government withdrew immigration from the list of exempted material under the Data Protection Bill;[33] the concession is of relatively limited importance however, since if immigration information is held for other exempted purposes - principally the detection of crime - it too is exempted. This is easy to satisfy since most of the computer-based data already developed have been designed with the purpose of detecting breaches of the immigration laws. When this is added to the existing Police National Computer[34] and the computer systems already in use for a growing number of police forces, the amendment to the Bill was of slight importance.

The geography of the U.K. lends itself well to immigration control at the port of entry and, apart from national emergencies (1793, 1914 and 1939), the U.K. has traditionally set its face against identity cards, the system naturally favoured by States with land frontiers. Yet it is an indication of the official determination to root out illegal immigration that the incidence of internal passport checks has increased considerably in recent years. It is significant that immigrants were amongst the initial recipients of the plastic national insurance cards launched by the D.H.S.S. in January 1984.[35] Moreover, the Police and Criminal Evidence Act 1984 (section 1) extends, on a national basis, the powers of the police to stop and search individuals and vehicles. These measures may well amount to a surreptitious and creeping form of control by identity checks, illustrated by the award of damages in 1984 to an Indian applicant under the Race Relations Act 1976 who had been asked to produce his passport by the D.H.S.S. as a matter of course.[36] These developments show no signs of abating and, whilst Governments have not formally approved of identity cards, they have not exerted themselves to prevent their informal adoption.

(5) Racial Disadvantage and Discrimination

These disabilities, increasingly well-documented, show no signs of amelioration[37] and will continue to weigh more heavily with the U.K.'s ethnic population than the immigration laws. The effect of uncompromising immigration laws should not however be underestimated for they have played a part in breeding resentment amongst the immigrant community and in reinforcing for the host population a stereotype of 'unwelcome foreigners'.

C. CONCLUSION

A Parliamentary debate in 1984[38] is a fitting end to this book for it illustrates many of the themes of British immigration and the bleak outlook for aspiring immigrants and shows that little is new in debate on the subject. Indeed, most of the themes can be found in earlier centuries. The debate arose on an Opposition motion criticising the immigration Rules for their "devastating and oppressive effect on family life".

(a) There are many examples to support the motion. The refusal rates for entry clearance in the Indian sub-continent are still very high, the queue in Bangladesh has lengthened, aged visitors (particularly since 1980) frequently face a distressing inquisition at ports of entry, the admission of husbands and fiances has been relaxed with one hand but tightened with the other[39] and female partners were subjected to similar criteria in 1985. The official response remains inflexible. As regards male spouses, for example, "We are not prepared to allow marriage to be used as a route to immigration ... Having tightened up on work permits to prevent young men coming here on to the labour market, we cannot allow the same young men to come here by using marriage as a device. That would be the ultimate absurdity and we shall not perpetrate it".[40]

The result of all the measures is a second class system for coloured entrants. As was pointed out, "There are no circumstances in which the Minister would allow his letters to his wife, intimate love letters, to be read by an official".[41] Yet that is a consequence of the entry clearance procedure, a procedure which is claimed "to support family life".[42]

(b) Much of the tough policy has been achieved by the customary use of internal and unpublicised guidance passed to entry clearance officers. Publication of such instructions has been resisted lest it "instruct people on how they might evade control"[43] -an argument which would logically prevent the publication of most official policy. The frequent quotation of the instructions in the Report of the Commission for Racial Equality[44] may now lead to publication of the revised instructions.

(c) The debate revealed the traditionally broad and hence predictable spectrum of opinion - from the right wing bluntness to conservative stonewalling to hypocritical liberal sentiment - and the perennial styles of argument.[45] Firstly, the explicit approach which speaks of "tolerant English people" receiving millions of immigrants with different cultures and habits and concludes that "England, this dear country, has from time to time done some shameful things in its history, but her treatment of immigrants is not one of them".[46] Second, the use of a few cases (of foreign husbands going abroad and leaving their resident families to rely on the State for support) to build a stereotype of immigrant spongers.[47] Third, the reliance upon native hostility and racist troublemakers to justify control. Thus, "without firm control, people will fear for their jobs and there will be others ready to play on those fears and, by stirring up resentment against newcomers, to destroy the efforts of those working for harmony in our society and for good community relations".[48] Fourth, the argument by extremes, that "if we drastically reduced the rules on husbands and grandparents" unacceptably large numbers of immigrants would enter.[49] Of course rules do not have to be changed "drastically" in order to reflect a greater degree of fairness and humanity, but this style of scaremongering is typical in immigration debate and its success reveals what little middle ground exists, which would permit at least some relaxation within an overall context of firm control.

(d) Indeed, the debate was virtually devoid of encouragement for immigrants or of constructive approaches. Instead it was reduced to each side scoring political points off the other.

(e) The Labour Party speakers revealed some of the misunderstanding and much of the blatant hypocrisy which has bedevilled recent U.K. policy. Thus, the shadow spokesman wished "the country to return to the sort of principles on which it used to operate and from which the Government have departed so cruelly and heartlessly".[50] This must refer to the days of the open-door policy (for the Commonwealth before 1962 and for aliens before 1905), since the history of British immigration shows that once control has been instituted, it has worked with little humanity. In fact, the speaker related his statement to the U.K.'s policy on the admission of Jewish refugees at the time of the Second World War - yet this was a policy which bore many of the hallmarks of today's attitude and which in many ways may be regarded as more reprehensible.[51]

On the contrary, by launching an attack on the Government's policy, the Opposition rightly exposed itself to the charge of hypocrisy.[52] For the separation of families by narrowly drawn Rules, lengthy queues in the Asian sub-continent, intrusive questioning and the zealous use of removal powers have transcended political ideologies. Reminders of this bi-partisan attitude cannot be dismissed by the Labour spokesman as "taradiddle",[53] for they question the sincerity of the Opposition's concern for justice in immigration matters. It is not only the freedom of being in Opposition which permits the Labour Party to bring its motion but also the knowledge that the era of large-scale immigration is over and a Party can afford the luxury of being seen to be generous towards immigrants. To ethnic minorities this farrago can only deepen their cynicism, especially since the Opposition was careful not to spell out its detailed policies. Politicians may care about individual immigration cases, but they, like the general public, have shown no inclination or effort to relax the strict laws of immigration control. For they have realised during this century that such a cause attracts few votes for any political party intent on electoral success.

Whereas, historically, the ending of wars, economic expansion and, most of all, underpopulation, have enabled the U.K. to relax sooner or later its immigration laws, no such opportunity is in prospect today. The overriding need for strict control will always, unfortunately, outweigh the infrequent calls for individual justice.

----

1   Motion approved by the House of Commons on 5 March 1984 –
H.C. Debs. col. 708.

2   In many respects they are less severe, cf. the blatantly
racist policies which the U.S., Canada and Australia have
promulgated in this century.

3   Justice Jackson, dissenting, in Shaughnessy v U.S. ex rel.
Mezei 345 U.S. 206, at 275 (1953).

4   E.g. in relation to the admission of aged dependants and
to the powers of deportation.

5   Note also the many recommendations in the C.R.E. Report on
Immigration Control Procedures (1985). Contrast however the
view of the Home Affairs Committee (6th Report, 1984-85, H.C.
277) to criticisms levelled against the Immigration Service.

6   Summit meeting, 9-10 December 1974.

7   O.J. C241 19 September 1981.

8   By separate channels of entry at all ports for E.E.C.
nationals and occasional spot checks rather than the routine
inspection of passports, E.C. Commission (82)400. The former
was approved and the latter disapproved by the House of Lords
Select Committee on the European Communities (Fourth Report,
H.L. 24, 1983-84). At present, the average time for
negotiating passport control is 6 seconds for British
Citizens, 12-15 for E.E.C. nationals and 45-85 for all others,
ibid, Q 65.

9   Abdulaziz, Balkandali and Cabales v U.K.

10 The new rules were discussed at H.C. Debs. 23 July 1985.
All sponsors must now also satisfy the maintenance and
accommodation requirements. To avoid further charges of sex
discrimination, s.1(5) of the 1971 Act will have to be amended
(under which the wives of Commonwealth citizens already
settled in the U.K. have a right of unimpeded entry).

11 E.g. the threat by the Conservative Party in 1979 to
introduce a register of dependants in the Asia sub-continent
was quietly dropped, see the tacit admission by the Home
Office Minister to the Home Affairs Committee, op. cit., Q
461-464.

12 Ibid, Q 432-433.

13 H.C. Debs. 8 June 1948, col. 1851-52.

[14] E.g. Calvin's case (1608) 77 E.R. 377; Duroure v Jones (1791) 100 E.R. 1031; De Geer v Stone (1882) 22 Ch. 243.

[15] E.g. Trading with the Enemy Act 1939. For the effect on property, see Williams on Title (4th Ed.) p.172-3; for contractual dealings, see Chitty on Contracts (25th Ed.) Vol. I, paras. 720-4.

[16] For a consideration of the scope of enemy alien at common law, see Fridman (1955) 4 I.C.L.Q. 613.

[17] British Nationality and Status of Aliens Act 1914, s.17. He cannot however own a British ship directly (s.17, (3)), but can do so indirectly by taking shares in the owning company.

[18] Ibid. s.18.

[19] H.C. 32 (1982-83); Government's response, Cmnd. 9140. See now the Representation of the People Act 1983.

[20] Act of Settlement 1700, s.3, 12 and 13 Will III c.2.

[21] Though a Ministerial certificate may allow aliens to serve in the civil service, provided that no suitably qualified British labour is available, Aliens' Employment Act 1955, s.1. Cf. a similar protection for jobs involving public policy in the U.S. - Sugarman v Dougall (1973) 413 U.S. 634, expanded in Cabell v Chavez-Salido (1982) 454 U.S. 432.

[22] Aliens Restriction (Amendment) Act 1919, s.4.

[23] Race Relations Act 1976, s.75(5); S.I. 1977/1774. The latter contains a list of such bodies which may discriminate on the basis of birth, nationality, descent or residence. It includes the Bank of England, the Civil Aviation Authority and some national galleries and museums. The Civil Service Commission General Regulations 1978 (reg. 12) list the excluded posts within Government, see H.A.C. on Racial Disadvantage, (1980-81) H.C. 424-II, p.385-8.

[24] Secretary of State for Social Services, H.C. Debs. 12 March 1981, col. 1015.

[25] H.C. Debs. 22 February 1982, col. 593.

[26] For the detail, see National Health Service (Charges to Overseas Visitors) (No.2) Regulations, S.I. 1982/863 - replacing and amending the earlier Regulations, S.I. 1982/795. The charges were increased by S.I. 1983/302.

27 Because of the unsavoury questioning of patients (see health circular H.C. (82) 15) or because of the administrative costs of running the scheme (see Bath District Health Authority's decision to end the scheme after 7 months' operation produced only 9 fee-paying patients, Guardian, 21 July 1983). The apparent failure of some health authorities to collect the charges led to Ministerial concern - H.C. Debs. 16 November 1983, col. 500.

28 Rough figures for the first year of collection indicated a paltry average revenue of £1,794 for each district health authority, H.C. Debs. 16 November 1983, col. 499-504.

29 E.g. as a result of N.H.S. charges to overseas visitors.

30 E.g. by an education authority in Newham (Guardian 31 October 1981), by a register office in Camden before issuing a marriage certificate (Guardian, 19 October 1983), by the D.H.S.S. for entitlement to benefits, by some employers. For a detailed account, see Gordon, Passport Raids and Checks, ch.4.

31 Already in use as regards the U.S. and adopted in principle by the U.K. - H.C. Debs. 13 March 1981, col. 436; operational in 1987 - see H.C. Debs. 24 July 1984, col. 567.

32 E.g. At Harmondsworth, by the compilation of an index of suspects. See further pp.42-43 of Report on the work of I.N.D. (Home Office, 1984) for an account of the computer systems.

33 H.L. Debs. 24 October 1983, col. 105.

34 See The Police Use of Computers, Technical Authors Group of Scotland (1982).

35 See the press 10 January 1984.

36 Guardian, 11 February 1984.

37 For a recent study, see Black and White Britain (Heinemann and Policy Studies Institute, 1984).

38 H.C. Debs. 5 March 1984, col. 659-708.

39 In 1983 by broadening the category of women permitted to admit their partners but by unrealistically requiring the applicant to convince the immigration officer that the 'primary purpose' of the marriage is not to obtain entry to the U.K. (r.41).

40 Home Office Minister, col. 670.

[41] Col. 696.

[42] Minister, col. 667.

[43] Ibid., col. 671.

[44] Report of Investigation into Immigration Control Procedures (1985 C.R.E.).

[45] Compare the similar variety of opinion which the Immigration Reform and Control Bill sparked in the U.S. in 1983 and 1984.

[46] Col. 682.

[47] Col. 679.

[48] Col. 667.

[49] Col. 701.

[50] Col. 665.

[51] See the accounts by Sherman and Wasserstein, op. cit.

[52] And eased the Government's task by enabling it to argue, 'we are only continuing the policies which you operated', see col. 666-8, 671-2.

[53] Col. 695.

BIBLIOGRAPHY

Principal Statutes

Aliens Act 1905

Aliens Restriction Act 1914

Aliens Restriction (Amendment) Act 1919

British Nationality Act 1948

Commonwealth Immigrants Act 1962

Commonwealth Immigrants Act 1968

Immigration Appeals Act 1969

Immigration Act 1971

British Nationality Act 1981

Principal Rules

Regulations 1906 Cmnd. 2879

Aliens Order 1920, S.I. 448

Aliens Order 1953, S.I. 1671

Instructions to Immigration Officers, 1962, Cmnd. 1716

Instructions to Immigration Officers, 1966, Cmnd. 3064

Draft Instructions - aliens, 1968, Cmnd. 3830

Draft Instructions - Commonwealth, 1969, Cmnd. 3951

Draft Instructions - aliens, 1969, Cmnd. 3952

Control on entry - Commonwealth, 1970, Cmnd. 4298

Control on entry - aliens, 1970, Cmnd. 4296

Control after entry - Commonwealth, 1970, Cmnd. 4295

Control after entry - aliens, 1970, Cmnd. 4297

Control on entry - Commonwealth, 1973, H.C. 79

Control on entry - aliens, 1973, H.C. 81

Control after entry - Commonwealth, 1973, H.C. 80

Control after entry - aliens, 1973, H.C. 82

Proposals for change - 1979, Cmnd. 7750

Immigration Rules, 1980, H.C. 394

Proposals for change, 1982, Cmnd. 8683

Revised Rules, 1982, H.C. 66

Current Immigration Rules, 1983, H.C. 169

Immigration Appeals (Notices) Regulations, S.I. 1984/2040

Immigration Appeals (Procedure) Rules, S.I. 1984/2041

Principal Government Publications

Annual Reports of the Inspector under the Aliens Act 1905, cd. 3473 (1907), 4102 (1908), 4683 (1909), 5261 (1910), 5789 (1911), 6169 (1912-13), 6841 (1913), 7345 (1914), 7969 (1914-16)

Board of Trade, Memorandum on Immigration of Foreigners into the U.K., P.P., 1887 vol. LXXIX

Commonwealth Immigrants Advisory Council Reports - 1963 (Cmnd. 2119), 1964 (Cmnd. 2266), 1964 (Cmnd. 2458), 1965 (Cmnd. 2796)

Educational Disadvantage and Educational Needs of Immigrants, (1974) Cmnd. 5720

Education, Science and Arts Committee (Commons) - First Report, on Overseas Student Fees, H.C. 552 (1979-80), Government Reply, Cmnd. 8011

Education, Science and Arts Committee (Commons) - Fifth Report, Funding and Organisation of courses in Higher Education, H.C. 787 (1979-80)

Home Affairs Committee - First Report, Proposed New Immigration Rules and the European Convention on Human Rights (1979-80) H.C. 434

Home Affairs Committee - Second Report, Numbers and Legal Status of Future British Overseas Citizens without other Citizenship (1980-81) H.C. 158

Home Affairs Committee - Second Report, Racial Disadvantage (1980-81) H.C. 424

Home Affairs Committee - Fifth Report, Immigration from the Indian Sub-Continent (1981-82) H.C. 90-I and Evidence H.C. 90-II; Government Response, Cmnd 8725 (1982)

Home Affairs Committee - Seventh Report, Revised Immigration Rules (1981-82) H.C. 526

Home Affairs Committee, Refugees and Asylum (1985) H.C. 72

Home Office, The Work of the Immigration and Nationality Department (1984)

Immigration from the Commonwealth (1965) Cmnd. 2739.

Report of Committee on Immigration Appeals (Wilson Committee), (1967) Cmnd. 3387

Report of Parliamentary Group on the feasibility and usefulness of a Register of Dependants (1977) Cmnd. 6698

Review of the Operation of the Prevention of Terrorism Act (1982) Cmnd. 8803

Royal Commission on Labour (1892) Cd. 6795

Royal Commission on Alien Immigration, (1903) Cd. 1741, Evidence Cd. 1742

Select Committee (Commons) on Immigration and Emigration, P.P., 1888 vol. XI, 1889 Vol. X

Select Committee (Lords) on the Sweating System, P.P., 1888 vol. XX, XXI, 1889 vol. XIII, XVI, 1890 vol. XVII

Select Committee on the European Communities - The Easing of Frontier Formalities (1983-84) H.L. 24

Select Committee on Race Relations and Immigration - Control of Commonwealth Immigration (1969-70) H.C. 205-I, II

Select Committee on Race Relations and Immigration - First Report, Immigration (1977-78) H.C. 303-I and Evidence 303-II

Uganda Resettlement Board, Final Report (1974) Cmnd. 5594

Statistics

Control of Immigration Statistics, United Kingdom, Home Office, Cmnd. 5603 (1973), 6064 (1974), 6504 (1975), 6883 (1976), 7160 (1977), 7565 (1978), 7875 (1979), 8199 (1980), 8533 (1981), 8944 (1982), 9246 (1983), 9544 (1984)

Statistical Bulletins, Home Office, Quarterly

Office of Population Censuses and Surveys

Journals

Immigrants and Minorities, Frank Cass

Legal Action Bulletin

United Kingdom Immigrants Advisory Service newsletter, and Annual Reports

Runnymede Trust, Bulletins and Annual Reports

Books - General

Akram, M., Where do you keep your string beds? (1974) Runnymede Trust

Akram, M., Elliott, J., Appeal dismissed: report of the investigation into immigration control procedures in the Indian sub-continent, (1977) Runnymede Trust

Bannister, J., England under the Jews, (1907) London

Banton, M., The Coloured Quarter, (1955) Cape

Banton, M., White and Coloured: the behaviour of British people towards coloured immigrants, (1959) Cape

Benewick, R., Political Violence and Public Order (1969) Penguin

Bethel, N., The Last Secret: Forcible Repatriation to Russia 1944-7, (1974) Deutsch

Bird, J.C., Control of Enemy Alien Civilians in Great Britain 1914-1918, (1981) Ph.D. London University

Bland, A.E., Brown, P.A., Tawney, R.H., English Economic History, Select Documents (1914) Bell

Brocklebank-Fowler, C., Bland, C., Farmer, T., Commonwealth Immigrants, (1965) Bow Publications

Chapeltown, C.A.B., Immigrants and the Welfare State, (1983) N.A.C.A.B.

Collins, W., Coloured Minorities in Britain, (1957) Butterworths

Commission for Racial Equality, Immigration Control Procedures: Report of a Formal Investigation, (1985)

Constantine, L., Colour Bar, (1954) Stanley Paul

Crossman, R., Diaries of a Cabinet Minister, 3 vols. (1975-77) Hamilton and Cape

Cumpston, I.M., Indians Overseas in British Territories, (1953) O.U.P.

Cunningham, W., Alien Immigrants to England, 2nd Ed. (1897) Frank Cass

Daniel, W.W., Racial Discrimination in England, (1968) Penguin

Davies, W.E., Law Relating to Aliens, (1932) Stevens

Davison, R.B., West Indian Migrants: social and economic facts of migration from the West Indies, (1962) O.U.P.

Davison, R.B., Commonwealth Immigrants, (1964) O.U.P.

Davison, R.B., Black British: Immigrants to England, (1966) O.U.P.

Desai, R., Indian Immigrants in Britain, (1963) O.U.P.

Dummett, A., A New Immigration Policy, (1978) Runnymede Trust

Economist Intelligence Unit, Studies on Immigration from the Commonwealth, Nos.1-5, (1961-63)

Edwards, P., Walvin, J., Black Personalities in the Era of the Slave Trade, (1983) Macmillan

Emigration in the Victorian Age, selected materials, (1973) Gregg Int. Publishers

Evans-Gordon, W., The Alien Immigrant, (1903) Heinemann

Eversley, D., Sukedo, P., The Dependants of the Coloured Commonwealth Population of England and Wales, (1969) I.R.R.

Foot, P., Immigration and Race in British Politics, (1965) Penguin

Foot, P., The Rise of Enoch Powell, (1969) Cornmarket Press

Fraser, C.F., Control of Aliens in the British Commonwealth of Nations (1940) Hogarth

Fryer, P., Staying Power: The History of Black People in Britain, (1984) Pluto

Gainer, B., The Alien Invasion, (1972) Heinemann

Garrard, J.A., The English and Immigration, 1880-1910, (1971) O.U.P.

Gartner, L.P., The Jewish Immigrant in England, 1870-1914, (1960) Allen and Unwin

Gilbert, V. F., Tatla, D.S., Immigrants, minorities and race relations: a bibliography of theses and dissertations, (1984) Mansell

Gillman, P. and L., Collar the lot: how Britain interned and expelled its Wartime Refugees, (1980) Quartet

Gordon, P., Passport Raids and Checks: Britain's Internal Immigration Controls, (1981) Runnymede Trust

Gordon, P., White Law: racism in the police, courts and prisons, (1983) Pluto

Gordon, P., Policing Immigration, (1985) Pluto

Griffith, J.A.G. et al, Coloured Immigrants in Britain, (1960) O.U.P.

Griffith, J.A.G., Politics of the Judiciary, (1981) 2nd Ed. Fontana

Handsworth Law Centre, Immigration Law Handbook, (1980)

Henriques, H.S.Q., The Return of the Jews to England, (1905) Macmillan

Henriques, H.S.Q., Law of Aliens and Naturalisation, (1906) Butterworths

Henriques, H.S.Q., The Jews and English Law, (1908) Bibliophile Press

Hepple, B., Race, Jobs and the Law in Britain, (1970) Penguin

Hiro, D., Black British, White British, (1972) Eyre and Spottiswode

Holmes, C., (ed), Immigrants and Minorities in British Society, (1978) Allen and Unwin

Humphrey, D., Ward, M., Passports and Politics, (1974) Penguin

Jackson, J.A., The Irish in Britain, (1963) Routledge & Kegan Paul

James, C.L.R., The Atlantic Slave Trade, reprinted in The Future in the Present, (1977) Allison and Busby

James, C.L.R., Fighting Racism in World War II, (1980) Monad Press

Johnson, S.C., History of Emigration, from the U.K. to N. America, (1913) Routledge

Johnston, H.J.M., British Emigration Policy 1815-1830, (1972) Clarendon

Jones, C., Immigration and Social Policy in Britain, (1977) Tavistock

Jones, K., Smith, A.D., The Economic Impact of Commonwealth Immigration, (1970) C.U.P.

Klug, F., Racist Attacks, (1982) Runnymede Trust

Koch, E., Deemed Suspect: a wartime blunder, (1980) Methuen

Lafitte, F., The Internment of Aliens, (1940) Penguin

Lane, A.H., The Alien Menace - a statement of the case, (1932) Boswell

Layton-Henry, Z., The Politics of Race in Britain, (1984) Allen and Unwin

Lester, A., Bindman, G., Race and Law, (1972) Penguin

Lipson, E., Economic History of England, 3 vols., (1956) Black

Little, K., Negroes in Britain, (1947) Routledge and Kegan Paul

Lunn, K., ed., Hosts, Immigrants and Minorities: Historical Responses to Newcomers in British Society 1870-1914, (1980) Dawson

Macmillan, H., The End of the Day, (1973) Macmillan

Mamdani, M., From Citizen to Refugee: Ugandan Asians come to Britain, (1973) Pinter

Moore, R., Wallace, T., Slamming the Door: the administration of immigration control, (1975) Robertson

Neame, L.E., The Asiatic Danger in the Colonies, (1907) Routledge

Newsam, F., The Home Office, (1954) Allen and Unwin

Nicol, A., Illegal Entrants, (1981) Runnymede Trust and Joint Council for the Welfare of Immigrants

Nicolson, C., Strangers to England; immigration to England 1100-1945, (1974) Wayland

Page, A., War and Alien Enemies, (1914) Stevens

Pannell, N., Brockway, F., Immigration - What is the answer? (1965) Routledge and Kegan Paul

Patterson, S., Dark Strangers, (1963) Tavistock

Patterson, S., Immigration and Race Relations in Britain 1960-67, (1969) I.R.R./O.U.P.

Peach, G.C.K., West Indian Migration to Britain: A Social Geography, (1968) I.R.R./O.U.P.

Pellew, J., The Home Office 1848-1914, (1982) Heinemann

Perry, T.W., Public Opinions, propaganda and politics in eighteenth-century England: a study of the Jew Bill 1753, (1962) Harv. U.P.

Piggott, F.T., Nationality, (1907) Clowes

Pollins, H., Economic History of the Jews in England, (1982) A.U.P.

Richardson, H.G., The English Jewry under Angevin Kings, (1960) Methuen

Roche, T.W.E., The Key in the Lock, (1969) Murray

Rose, E.J.B. et al., Colour and Citizenship, (1969) O.U.P.

Roth, C., History of the Jews in England, (1964) 3rd Ed. Clarendon

Smiles, S., Huguenots: their settlements, churches and industries in England and Ireland, (1880) Murray

Smith, T.E., Commonwealth Migration, (1981) Macmillan

Stacey, T., Immigration and Enoch Powell, (1970) Tom Stacey

Steel, D., No Entry, (1969) Hurst

Stent, R., A Bespattered Page? : the internment of His Majesty's 'most loyal enemy aliens', (1980) Deutsch

Stow, J., The Annals of England

Street, H., Howe, G., Bindman, G., Report on Antidiscrimination Legislation, (1967) Political and Economic Planning

Stringer, F.A., Practice of the High Court: in London and the District Registries under the Courts (Emergency Powers) Act 1914, Trading with the Enemy Acts 1914 and the Legal Proceedings against Enemies Act 1915, (1915) Sweet and Maxwell

Swinerton, E.N., Knepper, W.G., Lackyey, G.L., Ugandan Asians in Great Britain, (1975) Croom Helm

Tannahill, J., European Volunteer Workers in Britain, (1958) Manchester U.P.

Thirsk, J., Cooper, J.P., eds., Seventeenth-Century Economic Documents, (1972) Clarendon

Thomas, B., Migration and Economic Growth, (1973) 2nd Ed. C.U.P.

Tilbe, D., The Ugandan Asian Crisis, (1972) (Brit. Council of Churches)

Tolstoy, N., Victims of Yalta, (1977) Hodder and Stoughton

Troup, Sir Edward, The Home Office, 2nd Ed., (1926) Putnam's

Wallace, T., U.K. Passport Holders in Kenya - the end of an era?, (1975) Runnymede Trust

Walvin, J., Black and White, (1973) Allen Lane

White, A. (ed.), The Destitute Alien in Great Britain, (1892) Swan Sonnenschein

Wilkins, W.H., The Alien Invasion, (1892) London

Williams, P., A Policy for Overseas Students, (1982) Overseas Students Trust

Wilson, C. et al., The Immigrant in English History, Economic Issues in Immigration, (1970) Inst. Ec. Affairs

Zubrzycki, J., Polish Immigrants in Britain, (1956) Nijhoff

Textbooks - General

Evans, J.M., Immigration Law, 2nd Ed., (1983) Sweet and Maxwell

Grant, L., Martin, I., Immigration Law and Practice, (1982) Cobden Trust

Gray, S. and Lowe, A., The Ins and Outs of Immigration and Nationality Law, (1983) Nat. Assoc. of C.A.Bs

Halsbury's Laws of England, 4th Ed., vol. 4, (1973) Butterworths

Macdonald, I.A., Immigration Law and Practice in the United Kingdom, (1983) Butterworths

Supperstone, M., Immigration: the Law and Practice, (1983) Oyez Longman

Articles and Pamphlets - General

Bertram, G.C.L., West Indian Immigration, (1958) Eugenics Society

Birmingham Community Development Project, People in Paper Chains, (1977)

Bonner, D., Marriage and Immigration, (1980) 130 New L.J. 696

Bottomley, A., Sinclair, G., control of Commonwealth Immigration, (1970) Runnymede Trust

Bottoms, A.E., Delinquency among Immigrants, Race, vol. VIII no.4 (1967)

Boyle, K., The Irish Immigrant in Britain, (1968) 19 N.I.L.Q. 418

Butterworth, E., The 1962 Smallpox Outbreak and the British Press, Race, vol. VII no.4 (1966)

Chitty, C.W., Aliens in England in the Sixteenth Century, Race, vol. VIII, (1966) p.129

Chitty, C.W., Aliens in England in the Seventeenth Century to 1660, Race, vol. XI, (1969) p.189

Cohen, S., From Aliens Act to Immigration Act, (1984) L.A.G. 13

Craies, W.F., Right of Aliens to enter British Territory, (1890) 6 L.Q.R. 27

Deakin, N., The Politics of the Commonwealth Immigrants Bill, (1968) 39 Political Quarterly, no.1

Dobson, R.B., The decline and expulsion of the medieval Jews of York, (1979) vol. 26 Trans. Jewish Hist. Soc. 34

Duffy, P.J., Article 3 of the Convention on Human Rights, (1983) 32 I.C.L.Q. 316

Dummett, M., Immigration: Where the debate goes wrong, (1978)

Dyche, J.A., The Jewish Immigrant, vol. LXXV, Contemporary Review, 379 (1899)

Edholm, F., Roberts, H., Sayer, J., Vietnamese Refugees in Britain, (1983) C.R.E.

Evans, A.C., Immigration Law Reform in France, (1983) 32 I.C.L.Q. 516

Evans, A.C., Political Status of Aliens, (1981) 30 I.C.L.Q. 20

Evans-Gordon, W., The Stranger Within Our Gates, vol. LXIX The Nineteenth Century, p.210 (February 1911)

Fox, D.W., Overseas Students and the Immigration Rules, (1982) 146 J.P. 52

Garrard, J.A., Parallels of Protest: English reaction to Jewish and Commonwealth Immigration, Race, vol. IX (1967) p.47

Hartley, T., Under one law? A criticism of the Immigration Bill, (1971) Bow Group

Haycraft, T.W., Alien Legislation and prerogative of the Crown, (1897) 13 L.Q.R. 165

Howard, M. et al, The Greatest Claim, (1970) Bow Group

Jenkins, R., address to Institute of Race Relations, Race, vol. VIII, (1966) p.215

Jones, S., Immigrants and Supplementary Benefit, (1982) LAG 44, 64

Kirk, R.E.G. and E.F., Returns of Aliens in London 1522-1625, vol. X, Huguenot Society

Leech, K., Migration and the British Population, 1959-62, Race, vol. VII no.4, (1966)

Macdonald, I.A., Police Raids and Searches for Immigrant Offenders, (1981) 131 New L.J. 768

M^cnair, A.D., Alien Enemy Litigants, (1915) 31 L.Q.R. 154, 34 L.Q.R. 134

M^cnair, A.D., British Nationality and Alien Status in Time of War, (1919) 35 L.Q.R. 213

Marshall, O.R., Legislation and Racial Equality, (1969) 22 Current Legal Problems 46

National Council for Civil Liberties, collection of files, Brynmor Jones Library, University of Hull

Newdick, C., Immigrants and the Decline of Habeas Corpus, (1982) Pub. L. 89

Ormrod, D., The Dutch in London 1550-1800, (1973) H.M.S.O.

Palmer, C., Rights without Remedies: The European Convention on Human Rights and U.K. Immigration Law, (1981) Runnymede Trust

Peach, C., West Indian Migration to Britain: the Economic Factors, Race, vol. VII, (1965) p.31

Pearl, D., Recognition of the Talaq [1984] C.L.J. 48, 249

Plender, R., Exodus of Asians, (1971) 19 Am. J.C.L. 287

Political and Economic Planning, Report on Racial Discrimination (1967)

Powell, J.E., text of speech delivered in Birmingham in 1968, Race, vol. X, (1968) p.94

Price, C., 'White' Restrictions on 'Coloured' Immigration, Race, vol. VII, (1965) p.217

Rex, J., Integration of Britain's Black Citizens, (1981) lecture, Univ. of Birmingham

Rothchild, D., Kenya's Minorities and the African Crisis over Citizenship, Race vol. IX, (1968) p.421

Routledge, R.A., Legal Status of the Jews in England 1190-1790, (1982) 3 Jo. Legal History 91

Sivanandan, A., Race and Resistance: the I.R.R. Story, (1974) Race Today Publications

Smith, G., Overseas Doctors in the National Health Service (1980)

Storey, H., Immigration Controls and the Welfare State, (1984) J.S.W.L. 14

Street, H., Howe, G., and Bindman, G., Street Report on Anti-Discrimination Legislation (1967), Political and Economic Planning

Taube, E., German Craftsmen in England during the Tudor Period, (1939) vol. 4 Economic History

Thornberry, C., The Stranger at the Gate, (1964) Fabian Society

Thornberry, C., Law, Opinion and the Immigrant, (1962) 25 M.L.R. 654

Vincenzi, C., Aliens and the Judicial Review of Immigration Law [1985] Pub.L. 93

Weisman, J., Restrictions on the Acquisition of Land by Aliens, (1980) 28 Am. J.C.L. 39

Winetrobe, B.K., M.Ps and Immigration Cases, (1982) 132 N.L.J. 152

Citizenship - Books

Bar-Yaacov, N., Dual Nationality, (1961)

Cable, J.L., Decisive Decisions of United States Citizenship, (1967) Michie

Cockburn, Sir Alexander, Nationality, (1869) London

Dummett, A., Nationality and Citizenship, (1976) Runnymede Trust

Dummett, A., Martin, I., British Nationality: The AGIN Guide to the New Law, (1982) National Council for Civil Liberties

Fransman, L., British Nationality Law and the 1981 Act, (1982) Fourmat

Jones, J.M., British Nationality Law, (1956) Clarendon

Justice, British Nationality (1980)

Macdonald, I.A., Blake, N., The New Nationality Law, (1982) Butterworths

Odges, W.B., Nationality and Naturalisation, (1916) London

Page, W., Letters of Denization and Acts of Naturalisation, (1893) Huguenot Society

Parry, C., Nationality and Citizenship Law, (1957) Stevens

Stanbrook, I., British Nationality: the New Law, (1982) Clement

Weis, P., Nationality and Statelessness in International Law, (1979) 2nd Ed., Sijthoff & Noordhoff

Citizenship - Articles

Bates, T.St.J.N., Judicial Review and Nationality Law, (1982) Pub. L. 179

Blake, C., British Nationality Act 1981, 45 M.L.R. 179

Bonner, D., Clear and Enduring Scheme of Citizenship? (1982) J.S.W.L. 260

Dixon, The British Nationality Act 1981, (1983) Jo. Law and Soc. 161

Evans, A.C., Nationality Law in Pre-union Scotland, (1983) Juridical Review 36

Ginsburgs, G., 1980 Nationality Law of China, (1982) 30 A.J.C.L. 459

Khan, A.N., British Nationality Act 1981, (1982) 126 So. J. 403, 421, 440, 459

Osakwe, C., Recent Soviet Citizenship Legislation, (1980) 28 A.J.C.L. 625

Poddnick, A., Note - teachers must be U.S. citizens, (1979) 54 Tu. L.R. 225

Ross, J.M., English Nationality Law, (1972) Grotius Society Papers

Ross, J.M., Naturalisation of Jews in England, (1975) 24 Trans. Jewish Hist. Soc.

Williams, G.L., Allegiance and Protection, (1948) 10 C.L.J. 54

White, R.M., Hampson, F.J., British Nationality Law - Proposed Changes, (1981) 30 I.C.L.Q. 247 and (1982) Pub. L. 6

White, R.M., Evans, A.C., Hampson, F.J., Unsanguine observations on the British Nationality Bill (1981) 131 New L.J. 328

Williams, J.F., Denaturalisation, (1927) 8 B.Y.B.I.L. 45

Passports

Diplock, K., Passports and Protection in International Law, (1946) 32 Grotius Soc. 42

Ehrlich, T., Passports, (1966) 19 Stan.L.Rev. 129

Hurwitz, Judicial Control over Passport Policy, (1971) 20 Clev.St.L.Rev. 271

Justice, Going Abroad, (1974)

Laursen, T.E., Constitutional Protection of Travel, 81 Col.L.Rev. 902 (1981)

Notes - 61 Yale L.J. 170, 41 Geo L.J. 63, 7 India J.I.L. 526

Turack, D.C., The Passport in International Law (1972) Heath

Williams, D., British Passports and the Right to Travel, (1974) 23 I.C.L.Q. 642

Williams, D., Without Let or Hindrance, (1973) New L.J. 605

Refugees

Bernard, W.S., (1976) Int.Migration 267 (immigrants, refugees)

Burns, J.S., History of the Foreign Protestant Refugees, (1846) Longman

Edholm, F., Roberts, H., Sayer, J., Vietnamese Refugees in Britain, (1983) C.R.E.

Elliott, M.R., Pawns of Yalta (1982) Univ. of Illinois

Fawcett, A.C., Immigration and Refugee Reform, (1982) 22 Virg. J.I.L. 805

Gilbert, G.S., Right of Asylum: a change of direction, (1983) I.C.L.Q. 633

International Bar Association, Comparative Immigration Law Seminar (1979)

Johnson, D.H.N., Refugees, Deportees and Illegal Migrants, 9 Sydney L.R. 11 (1980)

Kramer, J.M., (1977) N.Y.U.J.I.L.P. 203 (due process, aliens)

Kranz, F.E., Refugee as a Subject of International Law, (1966) 15 I.C.L.Q. 90

Maynard, P.D., Legal Competence of the U.N. High Commissioner, (1982) 31 I.C.L.Q. 415

Morgenstern, F., Right of Asylum, (1949) 26 B.Y.B.I.L. 327

Mutharika, A.P., Regulation of Statelessness under International and National Law, (1977) Oceana

Pauw, R., Refugee Act 1980 (U.S.) 21 Harv. I.L.J. 742 (1980)

Porter, B., The Refugee Question in mid-Victorian politics, (1979) C.U.P.

Sherman, A.L., Island Refugee: Britain and refugees from the Third Reich, (1973) Elek

Sibley, N.W., Elias, A., The Aliens Act and the Right of Asylum, (1906) Clowes

Simpson, J.H., The Refugee Problem, (1939) O.U.P.

Vincent-Daviss, D., Research Guide to the Literature - Refugees, 14 N.Y.U.J.I.L.P. 487 (1982)

Wasserstein, B., Britain and the Jews of Europe 1939-1945, (1976) Clarendon

Weis, P., International Protection of Refugees, (1954) 48 A.J.I.L. 193

Weis, P., Draft U.N. Convention on Territorial Asylum, (1979) 56 B.Y.B.I.L. 151

Removal

Burgess, D., Bail or Temporary Release, 129 New L.J. 235 (1979)

Dickinson, I., Due Process of Deportation, 127 New L.J. 867 (1977)

Evans, A.C., Expulsion under the 1971 Immigration Act, (1983) 46 M.L.R. 433

Goodhart, A.L., Extradition and Deportation, (1963) 79 L.Q.R. 41

Home Office, A Review of the Law and Practice of Extradition in the United Kingdom (1982)

Home Office, Extradition, Green Paper (1985) Cmnd. 9421

Hepple, B.A., Aliens and Administrative Justice: the Dutschke case, (1971) 34 M.L.R. 501

O'Higgins, P., Disguised Extradition: the Soblen case, (1964) 27 M.L.R. 521

Reid, C.T., Improper Extradition, (1984) S.L.T. 21

Thornberry, C., Dr. Soblen and the Alien Law, (1963) 12
    I.C.L.Q. 414

Australia - Books

Brain, P.J. et al, Population, Immigration and the Australian
    Economy, (1979) Croom Helm

Campbell, P.C., Chinese Coolie Emigration, (1923) King & Son

Choi, C.Y., Chinese Migration and Settlement in Australia,
    (1975) Sydney U.P.

Churches, S., Justice and Executive Discretion in Australia,
    (1980) Pub.L. 397

Coper, M., The Commonwealth's Immigration Power, 50 Aust.
    L.Jo. 351 (1976)

Dallas, K.M., The Origins of "White Australia", vol. XXVII
    (no.1) Australian Quarterly, p.43 (1955)

Elkin, A.P., Rethinking the White Australia Policy, vol. XVII
    (no.3) Australian Quarterly, p.6 (1945)

Huttenback, R.A., Racism and Empire: White Settlers and
    Coloured Immigrants in the British Self-Governing
    colonies, (1976) Cornell U.P.

Kellaway, C., White Australia - How Political Reality became
    National Myth, vol. XXV (no.2) Australian Quarterly, p.7
    (1953)

London, H.I., Non-White Immigration and the 'White Australia'
    Policy, (1970) New York U.P.

Madgwick, R.B., Immigration into Eastern Australia, (1937)
    Sydney U.P.

Mansfield, B.C., The Origins of White Australia, vol. XXVI
    (no.4) Australian Quarterly, p.61 (1954)

Nairn, N.B., Survey of the history of the White Australia
    Policy, vol. XXVIII (no.3) Australian Quarterly, p.16
    (1956)

Palfreeman, A.C., The Administration of the White Australia
    Policy, (1967) Melbourne U.P.

Phillips, O.E., The Administration of Asian Immigration into
    Australia, vol. XXVIII (no.4) Australian Quarterly, p.29
    (1956)

Price, C.A., The Great White Walls are Built, (1974) A.N.U.P.

Price, C.A., White Restrictions on coloured Immigration, 7
    Race 217, (1966)

Willard, History of the White Australian Policy to 1920,
    (1967) Frank Cass

Yarwood, A.T., Asian Migration to Australia; the background to
    exclusion 1896-1923, (1964) Melbourne U.P.

Yarwood, A.T., the Dictation Test - Historical Survey, vol.
    XXX (no.2) Australian Quarterly, p.19 (1958)

Canada - Books

Andracki, S., Immigration of Orientals into Canada with
    Special Reference to Chinese, (1978) Arno Press

Black, W., Novel Features of the Immigration Act 1976, 56 Can.
    Bar. Rev. 561 (1978)

Carrothers, W.A., Emigration from the British Isles, (1929)
    King

Corbett, D.C., Canada's Immigration Policy, (1957) U. Toronto
    Press

Grey, J.H., New Immigration Law, 10 Ottawa L.R. 103 (1978)

Hart, A., Doing Business in Canada, (1977) 127 New L.J. 343,
    371

Hawkins, F., Canada and Immigration: Public Policy and Public
    Concern, (1972) Magill-Queen's U.P.

Hucker, J., Immigration, Natural Justice and the Bill of
    Rights, 13 Osgoode Hall L.J. 649 (1975)

'Immigration Appeals Board', study for the Law Reform
    Commission, (1976)

Lenoir, R.L., Citizenship as a Requirement for the Practice of
    Law, 13 Ottawa L.Rev. 527 (1981)

Richmond, A.H., Post-War Immigrants in Canada, (1967) U. of Toronto Press

Scott, J.V., Stonehouse, R.C., Canadian Encyclopedia Digest, vol.4, Title 27 (1980) Carswell

Timlin, M.F., Canada's Immigration Policy, 26 Canadian Jo. Economics and Political Science 517 (1960)

E.E.C. - Books

Castles, S., Kosack, G., Immigrant Workers and Class Structures in Western Europe, (1973) O.U.P.

Hartley, T.C., E.E.C. Immigration Law, (1978) North-Holland Publishing

Krane, R.E., International Labour Migration in Europe, (1979) Praeger

Sundberg-Weitman, B., Discrimination on Grounds of Nationality, (1977) North-Holland Publishing

Wyatt, D., Dashwood, A., Substantive Law of the E.E.C., (1980) Sweet and Maxwell

E.E.C. - Articles

Barav, A., Court recommendation to deport, (1981) 6 E.L.Rev. 139

Bennett, D., E.E.C. Nationals in the U.K., 128 New L.J. 43

Bentil, J.K. Equality of Educational Opportunity, (1977) 121 Sol.J. 327, 349

Evans, A.C., French Immigration Law, (1980) Pub.L. 132

Evans. A.C., Entry Formalities, (1981) 6 E.L.Rev. 3

Evans, A.C., European Citizenship, (1982) 45 M.L.R. 497

Evans, A.C., U.K. Courts and Removal under E.E.C. law, (1981) Pub.L. 497

Hartley, T.C., Internal Personal Scope of E.E.C. Immigration Provisions, (1978) 2 E.L.Rev. 191

Hartley, T.C., Impact of E.C. law on the Criminal Process, (1981) Crim.L.Rev. 75

Jacobs, F.G., Free Movement of Persons within the E.E.C., (1977) Current L. Problems 123

O'Keeffe, D., Practical Difficulties in the application of article 48, (1982) 19 C.M.L.R. 35

Paisley, S., European Community Law flows across the channel, (1982) 33 N.I.L.Q. 85

Plender, R., Deportation and E.E.C. law, (1976) Crim.L.Rev. 676 and (1983) L.Soc.Gaz. 37, 90

Pollard, S., Immigration and the E.E.C., (1981) L.A.G. 35

Reisner, R., National Regulation of Movement of Workers, (1964) 13 A.J.C.L. 360

Singer, L.H., the Public Policy exception, (1977) 29 Sta.L.Rev. 1283

Steiner, J., The Right to Welfare: Equality and Equity under Community Law, (1985) 10 E.L.Rev. 21

Wallace, R., Right of Establishment: Doctors, (1981) 131 N.L.J. 1259

Wooldridge, F., Free Movement of E.E.C. Nationals, (1977) E.L.Rev. 190

International

Bassiouni, M.C., International Extradition and World Public Order, (1974) Sijthoff

Booth, V.E.H., British Extradition Law and Procedure, 2 vols. (1980-81) Sijthoff

Goodwin-Gill, G.S., International Law and the Movement of Persons between States, (1978) Clarendon

Goodwin-Gill, G.S., The Rufugee in International Law, (1983)

Grahl-Madsen, A., Territorial Asylum, (1980) Oceana

Joseph, C., Nationality and Diplomatic Protection, (1969) Sijthoff

Lillich, R.B., The Human Rights of Aliens in Contemporary International Law, (1985) Manchester U.P.

Mutharika, A.P., The Regulation of Statelessness under International and National Law, 2 vols. (1980) Oceana

Nafziger, J.A.R., General Admission of Aliens under International Law, (1983) 77 Am. Jo. Int. Law 804

Plender, R., International Migration Law, (1972) Sijthoff

Shearer, I.A., Extradition in International Law, (1971) Manchester U.P.

Sinha, S.P., Asylum and International Law, (1971) Nijhoff

Stanbrook, I. and C., The Law and Practice of Extradition, (1980) Rose

Wijngaert, C.V., The Political Offence Exception to Extradition, (1980) Kluwer

New Zealand- Books

Fong, N.B., The Chinese in New Zealand, (1959) Hong Kong U.P.

Spoonley, P., Carwell-Cooke, K.A., Tolin, A.D., Immigrants and Immigration: a New Zealand Bibliography, (1980) Department of Labour

United States - Books

Abbott, E., Immigration: Select Documents and Case Records, (1924) Chicago U.P.

Auerbach, F.L., Immigration Laws of the United States, 3rd Ed. (Harper E.J.) 1975, Bobbs-Merrill Co.

Barth, G., Bitter Strength: a History of the Chinese in the United States 1850-1870, (1964) Harvard U.P.

Bennett, M.T., American Immigration Policies: a history, (1963) Public Affairs Press

Brye D.L., European Immigration and Ethnicity in the United States and Canada, a historical bibliography, (1983) Clio Press

Committee on the Judiciary, The Immigration and Naturalisation Systems of the United States, (1950) 81st Congress, Report no. 1515

Coolidge, M.R., Chinese Immigration, (1909) reprinted Arno Press, 1969

Curran, T.J., Xenophobia and Immigration 1820-1930, (1975) G.K. Hall (Boston)

Divine, R.A., American Immigration Policy 1924-1952, (1957) Yale U.P.

Garis, R.L. Immigration Restriction (1927) Macmillan

Gordon, C., Rosenfield H.N., Immigration Law and Procedure, (1959, 1973, rev. ed. 1982) Bender

Higham, J., Strangers in the Land - patterns of American Nativism 1860-1925, (1965) Atheneum

Hutchinson, E.P., Legislative History of American Immigration Policy 1798-1965, (1981) Univ. Pennsylvania

Ichihashi, Y., Japanese in the United States, (1969) Arno Press

Jones, M.A., American Immigration (1960) U. Chicago Press

Kansas, S., U.S. Immigration, Exclusion and Deportation and Citizenship (1948)

Konvitz, M.R., Civil Rights in Immigration (1953) Cornell U.P.

Lowenstein, E., The Alien and the Immigration Law: study of 1446 cases, (1958) Oceana

Mullaly, H.F., United States Refugee Policy 1789-1956, (1959) dissertation, N.York University

Post, L.F., Deportations Delirium of 1920, (1923) Chicago

Select Committee on Immigration and Naturalisation, Report, (1891) 51st Congress, Report no. 3472

Select Committee on alleged violation of the laws concerning contract labour, (1889) 50th Congress, Report no. 3792

Shepperson, W.S., British Emigration to North America, (1957) Blackwell

Stephenson, G.M., A History of American Immigration 1880-1924, (1926) Ginn & Co

Warne, F.J., The Immigrant Invasion, (1913) Dodd, Mead & Co.

Wasserman, J., Immigration Law and Practice (1973)

United States - Articles

Abrams, (1973) Public Interest 3 (analysis of Immigration and Nationality Act 1965)

Annual Surveys of American Law, passim, e.g. Miller (1977) p.205, Dixon (1978) p.679

Banoff, B.A., Pyle, C.H., To Surrender Political Offenders, 16 N.Y.U.J. Int. Law and Politics 169 (1984)

Dienstag, A.L., A comment on the denaturalisation of war criminals, 82 Col.R.Rev. 120 (1982)

Fawcett, A.C., Immigration and Refugee Reform, 22 Virg. J.I.L. 805 (1982)

Hahn, R.F., Power to Exclude Aliens, 82 Col.L.Rev. 957 (1982)

Hall, M.A., Lawful Domicile, 47 U.Chic L.R. 771 (1980)

Hofstetler, R., ed., Symposium on U.S. immigration policy, (1982) 45 Law and Contemporary Problems, no.2

Karst, K.L., Equal Citizenship under the 14th Amendment, 91 Harv. L.R. 1 (1977)

Levi, D.F., Equal Treatment of Aliens, 31 Stan. L.Rev. 1069 (1979)

M^cbride, D.R., Commentary on Haig v Agee, (1983) 13 Cal. W.I.L.Jo. 145

New York U.L.Rev. vol. 51 (1976), 'Good moral character' test, p.1021

                        52 (1977), Judicial Review of Visa Denials 1137

Rosberg, G.M., Aliens and the Right to Vote, 75 Mich. L.Rev. 1092 (1977)

Schander (1978) Int. Migration Rev. 117 (bibliography of law and practice in the U.S.)

Schuck, P.H., Transformation of Immigration Law, 84 Col.L.Rev. 1 (1984)

Shanks, B.F., Denaturalisation of War Criminals, 56 Tu.L.Rev.
    773 (1982)

Yale Law Journal, Note - State burdens on aliens, 89 Y.L.J.
    940 (1980)

INDEX

Accommodation 8

adjudications 360-61 <u>see also</u> I.A.T.

administrative direction (removal of illegal immigrants) 345-56

administrative instructions <u>see</u> Immigration Rules

adoption 117, 254-5

    in U.K. 21, 255

advisory services 167 <u>see also</u> U.K.I.A.S.

aliens

    historical treatment 51, 52, 53-4, 54-8, 64-7, 108, 141

        Napoleonic legislation 58-64

    inter-war years 73-5

    legislation 67-73

    1945-62 75-7

    <u>see also</u> Jews, Protestants, etc.

Aliens Act (1905) 22, 30, 67-72, 221, 242, 305, 316, 359

Aliens Act (1919) 73

Aliens Office 62-3

Aliens Order (1920) 73

Aliens Restriction Act (1914) 9, 72-3, 305

allegiance 104, 105, 107-8, 140

ambassadors 119, <u>see also</u> diplomats

America (pre-Independence) 57, 111, <u>see also</u> U.S.A.

American War of Independence 104, 108

amnesty (illegal immigrants) 18, 347

Ancient Greece 105, 106

appeals 359-63

    against deportation or removal 306, 315, 319-20, 322-5, 345-6

    against refusal of naturalisation 124-7

    asylum 217, 222-3, 362

    delays 363

    E.E.C. rules 210-11

    from overseas (entry clearance) 83, 165, 172, 348, 353

    historical (aliens) 62, 71

    no right of appeal 279, 362

arranged marriages 243, 248, 250, 252-3

arrest without warrant 347

artists and writers 281

'Asia Pacific Triangle' 12, 31, 76

asylum 178-9, 213-23

    appeals 217, 222-3, 362

    entry 216-17

    extradition 357

    history 60, 74

    refugee status 215, 220

au pairs 277, 281

Australia

    citizenship 112

Australia (cont)

    removals 16, 214-15, 304

    restricted entry 11-12, 30-31, 66, 113

B.C. (British Citizenship)

    acquisition of 115-28

        by birth in U.K. 115-18

        by birth outside U.K. 118-21

        by naturalisation 122-7

        by registration 121-2

    children 192

    deportation, exclusion from 326

    deprivation of 133-5

        nullity 134

        renunciation 135

    ex-U.K.C.s 127-8

    Falkland Islands 127

    Gibraltar 127

    potential citizens 120-21

    resumption of 135

    see also citizenship, U.K.C.s etc

B.D.T.C. (British Dependent Territory Citizenship) 31, 114, 117, 129, 136

    registration 121

B.N.(O.) (British National (Overseas)) 114, 130-31, 136

    registration 121

B.O.C. (British Overseas Citizenship) 31, 114, 129-30, 136

    registration 121

    see also U.K.P.H.s

B.P.P. (British Protected Person) 113, 114, 132

    registration 121

B.S. (British Subject) 114

    registration 121

Bail Act (1976) 321

Bill of Rights, lack of 13, 15, 20, 139, 356

binding over, requirement to leave U.K. 358

bi-partisan approach 22-5, 200, 384

birth

    in U.K. 115-17

    outside U.K. 118-21

        first generation 118-19

        second generation 119-21

'boat people' see Vietnamese

British Brothers League 68

British Citizenship see B.C.

British Council 286-8

British Dependent Territory Citizenship see B.D.T.C.

British National (Overseas) see B.N.(O.)

British Nationality Act (1948) 13, 22, 76, 86, 112-15, 131-2

British Nationality Act (1981) 13, 23, 24, 31, 113-15, 192, 193, 249, 253

British Nationality (Falkland Islands) Act (1983) 127

British Overseas Citizenship see B.O.C.

British Protected Persons see B.P.P.

British Subject see B.S.

British Subject without citizenship 113, 131-2

British Union of Fascists 68

Brunei 132

Budd, Zola 137

businessmen, entry of 282-3

C.R.E. (Commission for Racial Equality) 87-9, 139, 383 see also race relations

Calvin's case 198

Canada 22, 136

    appeals 16

    citizenship 112-13, 125, 139

    discrimination 12

candour, duty of 349-52

Caribbean see West Indies

Carta Mercatoria 51

Catholics 53, 109

census 33, 34

change of circumstance 176-7

children

    citizenship 115-21, 192

children (contd)

    daughters 257-8

    deportation 314-15

    entry clearance 255

    financial contributions to 256

    immigration rights 192

    joining relative other than parent 257

    legal custody 256

    limiting entry 79, 81

    over 18 257-8

    parent, definition 254

        adoptive 254-5

        sole responsibility 256

Chinese Passengers Act 66

citizenship 12, 105-7, 109-12

    historical 9, 50-52, 107-9, 380

    role of 55-8, 104-5

    see also B.S., denization, U.K.C.s

civil liberties 18, 125-6

    awareness 87, 377

    rights at stake 3-4, 140, 143

cohabitation 244, 245

Commission for Racial Equality see C.R.E.

Common Travel Area 192-3

Commonwealth citizen 132, 136, 380

    deportation 306, 327

419

Commonwealth citizen (contd)

    right to enter U.K. 74, 76, 113, 193, 377

    U.K.C.s 112-13

Commonwealth Immigrants Act (1962) 11, 12, 17, 61, 77-80, 164, 193, 195, 306

Commonwealth Immigrants Act (1968) 12, 17, 26, 80-83, 197, 346

Commonwealth Immigrants Advisory Council 26

compassionate circumstances, asylum 215

computers, machine readable passports 141, 307 309, 355, 381

conviction, deportation after 316-18

correspondence courses 287

country of destination after deportation 322-3

court recommendations 316-28

Criminal Justice Act (1982) 321

criminal record 178

Crown discretion see discretion

crown service 119, 122 see also public service

cultural identity 105-6

    safeguarding 8

D.H.S.S. 15-16

'dangerous' aliens 305

Data Protection Act (1984) 27, 381

death of spouse 208

Declaration of Fidelity 57, 111

defence 104, 105, 110

delays

   appeals 363

   asylum 218

   citizenship 137

   entry clearance 27, 165, 168, 170-2

denization 51-4, 56, 109, 110, 124

Department of Employment see Employment,
   Department of

dependants 30, 78, 191, 195-6

   B.O.C. 129

   children 254-8

   definition of 30

   E.E.C. 204

   elderly 81-2

   husbands and fiances 246-54

   others 258-62

   register of 37, 175

   wives and fiancees 243-6

deportation 73-4, 78, 208

   breach of conditions or overstaying 307-9

   conducive to public good 309-13, 358

   court recommendations 316-28

   exceptions 326-8

   state's right 303

deportation order 179

    confirmation 325

    duration 325-6

    procedure 322

    revocation 325-6

detention

    illegal immigrants 355-6

    whilst deportation is considered 320-21

Diplomatic Privileges Act (1964) 326

diplomats 24

    immunity 326-7

discretion

    Crown 61

    Home Secretary 18, 124-7

    Secretary of State 17

        acquisition of citizenship 115-17, 119, 122, 123, 129, 133, 138-9

        appeals 360

    deportation 309, 311, 316, 319, 322, 325

    entry 177

    historical background 62, 71-2, 111

    students 287

discrimination 20, 138-9, 206, 210, 219

    against non-citizens 106

    E.E.C. decision 207

    racial 12, 80, 88, 251-2

discrimination (contd)

see also sex discrimination

distant relatives 84

divorce 208, 245

Dominions' citizenship 112

dual nationality 9, 107, 117, 133, 140, 253,
    326

Dutch Protestants 53, 220

E.c.o. see entry clearance officer

E.E.C. 104, 119, 143, 282, 378

　　family and dependants 204-5

　　freedom of movement 143, 201-4, 277

　　impact of 201-13

　　nationals 114

　　Passport Union 104, 213, 378

　　prohibited illnesses 178

　　public service 212

　　removal 208-11

　　stay 205-8

E.E.C. Protected Persons 201

East Africa 80, 82, 195-6

East African Asians (U.K.P.H.s) 221, 251-2, 377

　　citizenship 113

　　entry vouchers 14

　　responsibility for 24, 130, 197

economy 106, 277

education see students

Eire see Irish

emergency legislation 75

emigration 33-4, 65, 74

employers, applications by 278

Employment, Department of 15, 84, 277-8, 279-80

employment protection 276

employment voucher see work permit

entertainers 281

entitlement to remain in E.E.C. 203

entry clearance 196, 249

    to E.E.C. 204

    possible reforms 174-5

    procedure 87

    visitors 291

entry clearance certificate 83, 164, 165, 166-79

    delay 27, 165, 168, 170, 171-2

    documentation 166-7

    interview 165, 167-8, 250

    letter of consent 166

    proof 168-70

    visa 166

entry clearance officers 16, 84, 170, 250, 257

    appeals 170, 172, 174-5

    assessments 166, 262

entry clearance officers (contd)

   decisions 361-2

   guidance 383

   interviews 166-70

   shortage of 165, 174

   training 170

entry vouchers see quota system, vouchers,
   work permits

European Commission of Human Rights 197, 218,
   248, 316, 324

European Convention on Human Rights 20, 24, 200,
   248, 324, 378

European Court of Human Rights 29, 246, 251, 378

European Court of Justice 201, 206, 209, 212-13

European Economic Community see E.E.C.

European Volunteer Workers 75

evidence 255

exclusion on ethnic basis 30 see also Australia,
   U.S.A. etc

Expropriated Properties Act (1982) 198

extradition 24, 310, 356-8

   political character, interpretation 357

   treaties 61, 356

Falkland Islands 127, 130, 136

false representations 176

families

    deportations 313-16

        children 314-15

        definition 313

        order 315

        wives 313-14

    separation of 173

    units 242

fees for citizenship, increases in 138

fiancees 245 _see also_ wives and fiancees

fiances and husbands _see_ husbands and fiances

Flemish 51

foreign labour 4-5

Foreign Office 14, 15, 214

France, colonial history 7

Fugitive Offenders Act (1967) 357

General Medical Council 281

Germany 7

Gibraltar 24, 127, 136, 377

'good character' 15, 106, 124-7

'grandfather clause' 83, 111-12 _see also_
    patriality

guidance 14, 383 _see also_ Immigration Rules

Habeas corpus 354

    deportation 21, 321

    historical 62, 73

    illegal entry 18-19, 347-51, 353

Hanseatic League 52

Hindu Marriages Act (1955) 244

historical controls

    pre-15th Century 50-52

    15th Century 52

    16th Century 53-4

    17th and 18th Century 54-8

    Napoleonic era see Napoleonic legislation

    1836-1905 64-7

    1905 to present 67-89

Home Affairs Committee Report 81, 172-4, 198-200

Home Office 14, 16, 74, 75, 279

    Immigration Department 15

    statistics 33

    see also discretion

Home Office Intelligence Unit 176

Hong Kong 24, 127, 130, 221, 378

Huguenots 53, 55, 220

humanitarianism 5

husbands and fiances 29, 34, 36, 173, 246-54,
    378

    arranged marriage 248, 250-52

husbands and fiances (contd)

    entry clearance 249

    genuine marriage 247-8, 249

    marriage breakdown 251

    'primary purpose' test 251, 252, 378

    probationary period 247, 249

I.A.T. see Immigration Appeal Tribunal

identity cards 203, 378, 381

illegal entries

    asylum 216-17

    definition 345

    removal 345-56

immigrants

    current position 35-7

    disabilities of 380-82

    encouragement of 110

    motives of 6

    rights 377-9

    see also dependants, entry clearance,
       statistics etc etc

immigration

    advantages of 4-6

    controls, legal characteristics 12-22

    hostility, causes of 6-12

428

immigration (contd)

    policy 22-29

       options 29-32, 378-9

    within colonies 65-7

Immigration Act (1971) 83-4, 277

    appeals 16, 17, 165, 360

    citizenship 127-8

    deportation 304, 327

    historical background 49

    patriality 31, 192

    reliance on Rules 13, 253, 279

Immigration Appeals Act (1969) 16, 82, 165, 359

Immigration Appeal Tribunal (I.A.T.) 83, 360, 362

    children 254-8

    'compassionate grounds' 178

    deportation 309-11, 325

    entry clearance 176

    other dependants 258-62

    students 285-6, 289

Immigration Board 72

immigration officers 72, 176-8, 291

Immigration Rules 382-4

    asylum 214

    businessmen 282-3

Immigration Rules (contd)

citizenship 192

deportation 304, 308

E.E.C. 204, 208, 209, 212

entry clearance 165, 179, 242, 246

historical framework 49, 73

status 13-14, 21, 83, 259-60, 279-80

students 283

technicality 20

Immigration Service Intelligence and Investigation Unit 354

imperialism 11

trade 54

India 196, 198, 199

U.K.P.H.s 15, 129, 200

international controls 32, 104

international pressure 82

interviews 165, 167-8, 250

Iranians 222

Irish 76

Common Travel Area 192-3

excluded from deportation 327

historical treatment 64

Nationality Act (1981) 114, 132

voting rights 380

ius soli 107, 112, 117-18, 136, 192

Jesuits 54

'Jew Bill' (1753) 11, 57, 111

Jews

    E. European/Russian 64, 67, 220-21

    historical treatment 26, 50-51, 55, 72,
        305, 376

        banishment 32

        Oath and Sacrament 10, 57, 109, 111

    pre-war refugees 5-6, 74-5, 124, 354, 384

Joint Council for the Welfare of Immigrants 27

judicial review 143, 211, 280, 306, 351-4, 362

Kenya see East Africa

Labour, Ministry of 73, 78 see also Employ-
    ment, Department of

language 8

    euphemistic 28-9

    tests 123

'last refuge' (asylum) 219-20

leave to enter, refusal 345

    reasons 176-9

leave to remain, exceptional (asylum) 215-16

legal representation 317-18, 323

literacy tests 9, 12

London Transport 79

M.P.s 361

    asylum 217, 222

    deportation 306, 320, 325

    removal 347

Magna Carta 51, 59, 141, 304

marriage

    to alien 111

    arranged 243, 248, 250, 252

    breakdown 251

    divorce 208, 245

    nullity 245

    prohibited forms 245

    to U.K.C. husband 112

    see also husbands, wives

material fact, disclosure see candour duty of

media 29

    pressure 219

medical grounds

    for entry refusal 8, 71, 79, 171, 177-8, 262

    for removal 209

medical treatment in U.K. 177

Members of Parliament see M.P.s

Mental Health Act (1983) 358-9

Mental Health Review Tribunal 359

Monday Club 28

Moser, Sir Claus 33-4

Mountbatten, Lord 79

N.H.S. see National Health Service

Napoleonic legislation 58-64, 376

   basis for later legislation 72, 73

   national security 9

   passports 141

   removals 304, 305

National Commission for Commonwealth Immigrants 26, 79

National Front 68

National Health Service 281

   charges 380

national insurance cards 382

nationalism 110-12

Nationality Act (1844) 123

naturalisation 56, 57, 109, 110, 112-17

   of foreign Protestants 111

      by marriage 123

Naturalisation Act (1870) 108, 133, 380

Navigation Acts 52, 54, 56, 106, 110

New Zealand 66, 113

non-judicial decrees (talaqs) 245

nullity, marriage 245

Oath and Sacrament 10, 56, 57, 109, 111

offences, deportation after certain 318

    balancing factors 318-19

Office of Population and Censuses and Surveys
    33

Official Secrets Act (1911) 310

Ombudsman 126, 139, 143

open-door policy 29-30

Osborne, Sir Cyril 80

Overseas Students Trust 22

overstaying 346, 354-5

Parents/grandparents 258-61

    degree of dependence 259-61

    isolation 261

    as visitors 292

Passport Union (E.E.C.) 104, 213, 378

passports 59, 63, 140-44

    computer readable 141, 307, 309, 355, 381

    refusal or withdrawal 142-3

    secret codes 15

    U.K. practice 142-3

patriality 31, 280

    citizenship 112-14, 127, 192

    controversy 83, 111

    deportation 326

persecution, fear of (asylum) 218-19

Police and Criminal Evidence Act (1984) 382

Polish refugees 75, 216, 221

Polish Resettlement Act (1947) 75

political cases, deportation 310-11

polygamy 244

ports of entry, authorised 59, 73, 164

    controls 69, 175-9

Powell, Enoch 28

primary immigrants 82, 191

'primary purpose' 246, 251, 252, 378

prisoners, repatriation of 359

privacy, lack of (entry clearance) 168, 171,
    246

probationary period, marriage 247, 249

proof, burden of 249

propaganda 5

Protection of Terrorism (Temporary Provisions)
    Act (1984) 193

Protestant refugees 5, 53, 55, 110, 220, 376

'public good' 134, 177, 193, 305, 309-13

    conducive to 59

    deportation 320, 358

    security and political cases 310-11

    'undesirables' 311-12

public service 10

    definition 212

    see also Crown Service

publicity 221, 306, 358

Quakers 57, 111

quota system (U.K.P.H.s) 7, 15, 31, 81, 199

    annual 175, 278

    East Africa 81, 198

    India 15

    see also vouchers, work permits

Race relations 29, 88

    damage to 168, 199, 248, 252, 258, 381

    importance of 85, 376, 377

    legislation 25

    training in 176

Race Relations Act (1965) 19-20, 26, 80

Race Relations Act (1968) 19-20, 80, 82

Race Relations Act (1976) 19-20, 80, 87, 288,
    382

racial

    harmony 22

    hatred, incitement to 11, 85

    purity 11-12

    superiority 11

    see also discrimination

Recognition of Divorces and Legal Separations
    Act (1971) 245

re-entry

    permits 194

    right of 211

refoulement 219-20

refugee status 215

    benefits of 220

    see also asylum

refugee travel document 220

Refugee unit 178-9

refugees 5, 24, 53, 64-5, 213-23, 327

    see also Hong Kong, Jews, Protestants
        etc

refusal of leave to enter see leave to enter,
    refusal of

register of dependants see dependants,
    register of

registration 112

    after 10 years 192

    of birth abroad 120

    British connected 121-2, 128

religion 105-6 see also refugees etc

removal of immigrants

    administrative direction 345-56

    appeals 359-63

    binding over 358

    deportation 305-28

removal of immigrants (contd)

    extradition 356-8

    powers of 62

    repatriation of prisoners 359

    under Mental Health Act 358-9

repatriation of prisoners 359

Representation of the People Act (1949) 380

residence in U.K. 120, 193

    permits 201, 203, 205-8

restricted returnability 178

resumption of British Citizenship 123, 129

returning residents 27, 193-5

right of entry 114, 127

    asylum 216-17

    Commonwealth citizens 74, 76, 113, 193, 377

    E.E.C. nationals 203

rights, immigrants' 377-9

Roman law 106

Royal Proclamation 305

Rules see Immigration Rules

Scarman Report 21

secondary immigrants see dependants

secrecy 15, 323-4

Secretary of State, discretion see discretion

Securicor 355

security cases, deportation 310-11

    appeal against 323-5

Select Committee on Race Relations and Immi-
    gration 27, 33, 84

self-employed 281, 282-3

sex discrimination 138

    dependants 204, 258

    E.E.C. rulings 249, 251-2, 316

    marriage 123, 251

    U.K.P.H.s 196, 200

Sex Discrimination Act (1975) 80, 196, 200, 252,
    288

Sidney Street siege 72

slavery, abolition of 66

Smethwick 79

'social advantages' (E.E.C.) 206, 213

social identity 105

social security see state benefits

sovereignty 1, 2-3

special vouchers 195-6

Sri Lanka 132, 219, 222

state benefits

    as checks 141

    deportation 313, 318

    E.E.C. 202, 206

    hostility to 8-9

state benefits (contd)

    prohibition (students) 289

    reimbursement 242

statelessness 108, 121, 129, 135, 137, 166

statistics 32-7, 173-4

    acceptances for settlement 35

    deportations 307, 310, 316

    entry clearance appointments 173

    illegal immigrants 346

    unreliability 89, 199, 247

    refugees 221

    visitors 290

Status of Aliens Act (1914) 135

students 22, 33, 34-5, 279, 283-90

    conditions of entry 284-5

    courses 286-8

    entry clearance 285-6

    fees 284

    maintenance 288

    stay 289

    see also training

Suspect Index 15, 355

Talaqs 245

Tamils see Sri Lanka

tape recording interviews (entry clearance)
168, 170

temporary entry

business 282-3

employment 276-82

students 283-90

visitors 290-93

trade, protection of 110 see also economy

training

definition 207

entry without permit 281

fees for 207-8

see also students

transmigrants (port of call) 65, 70

Treaty of Rome 10, 24, 201 see also E.E.C.

U.K.C. (United Kingdom and Colonies)

citizen of 80, 112-14, 127-8, 195

see also B.C. (British Citizen)

U.K.I.A.S. (United Kingdom Immigrants Advisory
Service) 167, 170, 217, 291

U.K.P.H.s (United Kingdom Passport Holders) 195-201

responsibilities towards 24, 82, 86

quota/voucher scheme 15, 31, 129

as visitors 292

see also East Africa, India

U.N. Conventions 24, 178, 214, 327

U.N. High Commissioner for Refugees 216, 219, 220

U.S.A. 9

    appeals 16, 360

    citizenship 106

    entry 1-3, 24, 30, 70

    exclusion 303, 353-4

    racial harmony 23

    see also America

Uganda 82

    Asians (U.K.P.H.s) 24, 130, 197, 221, 377

    see also East Africa

'undesirables' 177, 346

United Kingdom and Colonies see U.K.C.

United Kingdom Immigrants Advisory Service see U.K.I.A.S.

United Kingdom Passport Holders see U.K.P.H.s

United Nations see U.N.

United States of America see U.S.A.

unmarried mothers 259

Victorian age 64-7

Vietnamese 24, 214, 220-21, 377

virginity tests 14, 15, 88, 171, 246

visas 74, 164, 166, 222

    requirements 278-9

visitors 290-93

voluntary departure 315, 319-20

vouchers

    special (U.K.P.H.s) 195-6

    <u>see also</u> quotas, work permits

Wages 278

waiting-time, statistics <u>173</u> <u>see also</u> delays

wardship 19

warrants 347

welfare benefits <u>see</u> state benefits

West Indies 35-6, 76

wives and fiancees 243-6

    deportation 313-14

    entry clearance 243-6

    validity of marriage 244

    <u>see also</u> sex discrimination

work permits 7, 31, 73, 75, 164, 276-82

    categories 78-9, 195, 278

    renewal or change 279

    <u>see also</u> quota system

working holidays 280-1

writers and artists 281

X-ray tests 14, 15, 171

Note: Tables of figures are underlined